W9-CHP-517

Open Source Web Development with LAMP

Open Source Web Development with LAMP

Using Linux, Apache, MySQL, Perl, and PHP

James Lee

Brent Ware

Addison-Wesley

Boston • San Francisco • New York • Toronto • Montreal
London • Munich • Paris • Madrid
Capetown • Sydney • Tokyo • Singapore • Mexico City

Many of the designations used by manufacturers and sellers to distinguish their products are claimed as trademarks. Where those designations appear in this book, and Addison-Wesley was aware of a trademark claim, the designations have been printed with initial capital letters or in all capitals.

The authors and publisher have taken care in the preparation of this book, but make no expressed or implied warranty of any kind and assume no responsibility for errors or omissions. No liability is assumed for incidental or consequential damages in connection with or arising out of the use of the information or programs contained herein.

Netscape Communicator browser window ©1999–2002 Netscape Communications Corporation. Screen captures used with permission.

The publisher offers discounts on this book when ordered in quantity for bulk purchases and special sales. For more information, please contact:
    U.S. Corporate and Government Sales
    (800) 382-3419
    corpsales@pearsontechgroup.com

For sales outside of the U.S., please contact:
    International Sales
    (317) 581-3793
    international@pearsontechgroup.com

Visit Addison-Wesley on the Web: *www.awprofessional.com*

Library of Congress Cataloging-in-Publication Data

Lee, James B.
    Open source web development with LAMP: using Linux, Apache, MySQL, Perl, and PHP / James B. Lee, Brent Ware.
       p. cm.
    Includes bibliographical references and index.
    ISBN 0-201-77061-X (alk. paper)
      1. Computer software—Development.   I. Ware, Brent. II. Title.

QA76.76.D47 L435 2003
005.1—dc21   2002026195

ISBN 0-201-77061-X
Text printed on recycled paper

1 2 3 4 5 6 7 8 9 10—MA—0605040302
First printing, December 2002

To my wife Kelli and our three children Ryan, Christian, and Madeline.
–J.L.

To my pup Hanchau. Sorry I missed so many W-A-L-Ks.
–B.W.

Contents

Foreword xvii

Preface xix

Acknowledgments xxiii

About the Authors xxv

Introduction **xxvii**

I.1 The Best of All Possible Worlds . . . xxviii

I.2 Open Source Software xxviii

I.3 Summary xxxiii

I.4 Resources xxxiv

PART I STRUCTURAL 1

1 The Web Explained 3

1.1 How It Works 3

  1.1.1 Serving Up Static Data 5

  1.1.2 Serving Up Dynamic Data 6

  1.1.3 Serving Up Content with Embedded HTML 7

1.2 What We Don't Talk About 8

1.3 Security 9

1.4 Summary 10

1.5 Resources 10

2 Linux—The Choice of a GNU Generation 11

2.1 Introduction 11

  2.1.1 Linux Distributions 11

2.1.2 Download and Install   14

2.1.3 Decisions, Decisions   15

2.1.4 Linux Partition Sizes   16

2.1.5 Accounts   18

2.1.6 Security   20

2.2 Basic Unix   20

2.2.1 Shell   22

2.2.2 Owner, Groups, Permissions, Ownership   22

2.2.3 Processes   23

2.2.4 PATH and Environment   24

2.2.5 Commands   25

2.2.6 Basic Filesystem Essentials   28

2.2.7 Useful Programs   30

2.3 Summary   31

2.4 Resources   31

3 Apache Web Server   33

3.1 Introduction   33

3.1.1 Apache Explained   34

3.2 Starting, Stopping, and Restarting Apache   36

3.3 Configuration   39

3.3.1 Modifying the Default Configuration   39

3.4 Securing Apache   41

3.4.1 Set User and Group   41

3.4.2 Remove Online Manuals   41

3.4.3 Consider Allowing Access to Local Documentation   42

3.4.4 Don't Allow public_html Web Sites (Unless You
      Want To)   42

3.4.5 .htaccess   43

3.4.6 Remove server-status and server-info   43

3.5 Create the Web Site   46

3.5.1 Downloading the Examples   46

3.5.2 Creating Them Yourself   48

3.6 Apache Log Files   50

3.6.1 Access Control with .htaccess   50

3.7 Summary 55

3.8 Resources 55

4 Perl 57

4.1 Introduction 57

4.2 Perl Documentation 58

4.3 Perl Syntax Rules 59
   4.3.1 A First Perl Program—hello, world 59
   4.3.2 Another Example 60
   4.3.3 Declaring Variables with use strict; 61
   4.3.4 Variables 63
   4.3.5 Operators 71
   4.3.6 Flow-Control Constructs 77
   4.3.7 Regular Expressions 81
   4.3.8 Functions 87
   4.3.9 File I/O 93
   4.3.10 Additional Perl Constructs 99
   4.3.11 Making Operating System Calls 103

4.4 A Quick Introduction to Object-Oriented Programming 104

4.5 What We Didn't Talk About 106

4.6 Summary 107

4.7 Resources 107

5 MySQL 109

5.1 Introduction 109

5.2 Tutorial 109
   5.2.1 The SHOW DATABASES and CREATE DATABASE
        Commands 111
   5.2.2 The USE Command 111
   5.2.3 The CREATE TABLE and SHOW TABLES Commands 112
   5.2.4 The DESCRIBE Command 114
   5.2.5 The INSERT Command 114
   5.2.6 The SELECT Command 115
   5.2.7 The UPDATE Command 117
   5.2.8 The DELETE Command 118

5.2.9 Some Administrative Details   119
5.2.10 Summary   121

5.3 Database Independent Interface   122

5.4 Table Joins   127

5.5 Loading and Dumping a Database   129

5.6 Summary   130

5.7 Resources   130

PART II   STATIC   131

6   Website META Language   133

6.1   Introduction   133
6.1.1 A Note about Apache and This Chapter   134
6.1.2 WML Programs   134

6.2   Installation   135

6.3   The Basics   135
6.3.1 Building the HTML Files   135
6.3.2 WML Phases   136
6.3.3 The <protect> Tag   138

6.4   Creating a Template   138
6.4.1 Varying the Template Files   140
6.4.2 The use Statement   143

6.5   Other Helpful Includes   147
6.5.1 wml::std::page   147
6.5.2 wml::std::toc   149
6.5.3 wml::des::navbar   151
6.5.4 wml::fmt::xtable   156
6.5.5 wml::des::all   161

6.6   Diversion   162

6.7   A Better Template   165

6.8   Configuring WML with .wmlrc   167
6.8.1 Defining Variables   168
6.8.2 Include Directories   170

6.9   Macros—Creating Custom Tags   170

6.10 Programming Code—eperl 174

6.11 Project 179
    6.11.1 Defining New Tags 179
    6.11.2 Varying the Title 180
    6.11.3 The Bread Crumb Trail 180
    6.11.4 The Left Rail 181
    6.11.5 The Right Rail—Yes or No? 181
    6.11.6 Include PAGE_BODY 182
    6.11.7 A Page without a Right Rail 182
    6.11.8 A Page with a Right Rail 182
    6.11.9 The RIGHTRAIL Section 183

6.12 Summary 184

PART III DYNAMIC 185

7 The Common Gateway Interface 187

7.1 Introduction 187
    7.1.1 CGI Explained 188

7.2 Apache Configuration 190

7.3 A First CGI Program 191

7.4 What Can Go Wrong? 196

7.5 CGI.pm Introduced 197

7.6 CGI.pm HTML Shortcuts 200
    7.6.1 Using HTML Shortcuts 200
    7.6.2 Named Parameters versus Ordered Arguments 202

7.7 Information Received by the CGI Program 202
    7.7.1 Request Information 202
    7.7.2 Path Information 205
    7.7.3 Processing Posted Form Data 206

7.8 Form Widget Methods 216

7.9 CGI Security Considerations 218
    7.9.1 Avoid Shipped and Downloaded
        CGI Programs 218
    7.9.2 Never Assume Anything 219
    7.9.3 Always Check Data, Including the Length 219

7.9.4 Never Trust Hidden Fields   220
7.9.5 Don't Trust Filenames   221
7.9.6 Don't Trust Referer Headers   221
7.9.7 Don't Trust Cookies or JavaScript Preprocessing   221

7.10 A Note about die()   222

7.11 Project—CGI/MySQL/DBI   223

7.12 Summary   230

7.13 Resources   230

8   mod_perl   231

8.1   Introduction   231
      8.1.1 How It's Faster   232

8.2   Configuration   233

8.3   Turning CGIs into mod_perl Programs   235
      8.3.1 Apache::Registry   235
      8.3.2 A Speed Example or Two   237
      8.3.3 Apache::PerlRun   242

8.4   Pure mod_perl Programming   243
      8.4.1 An Important Note about mod_perl   246
      8.4.2 Handling Posted Form Data with mod_perl   246
      8.4.3 Apache::Request   249
      8.4.4 Getting the Path Information   251

8.5   Project: MySQL, DBI, and mod_perl   253

8.6   Other Stuff You Can Do   272

8.7   Summary   273

8.8   Resources   273

PART IV   EMBEDDED   275

9   Server Side Includes   277

9.1   Introduction   277
      9.1.1 How It Works   278
      9.1.2 Configuration   278
      9.1.3 Tutorial   279

9.2 Security Considerations 286

9.3 Summary 286

9.4 Resources 286

10 Embperl (HTML::Embperl) 287

10.1 Introduction 287

10.2 Installing Embperl 288

10.3 Apache Configuration 289

10.4 A Quick Example 291

10.5 Embperl Commands 292
10.5.1 [+ Perl Code +] 292
10.5.2 [- Perl Code -] 294
10.5.3 [! Perl Code !] 294
10.5.4 [# Some Text #] 295
10.5.5 [$ Command Arguments $] 295

10.6 Posted Data and %fdat 299

10.7 Other Embperl Variables—$row and $col 301

10.8 Embperl Project 304
10.8.1 The Problem 304
10.8.2 Creating a Consistent Look and Feel 305
10.8.3 Product Filter 319

10.9 What We Didn't Talk About 327
10.9.1 Persistent Database Connections 328
10.9.2 Session Handling with %udat and %mdat 328
10.9.3 Tons of Variables 328
10.9.4 XML and XSLT Support 329

10.10 Summary 329

10.11 Resources 329

11 Mason (HTML::Mason) 331

11.1 Introduction 331
11.1.1 Mason Compared with Embperl 332

11.2 Installation 333

11.3   Apache Configuration   334

11.4   A Quick Example   335

11.5   Inline Perl Sections   336
     11.5.1 The `<% ... %>` Tag   337
     11.5.2 % Lines   337
     11.5.3 The `<%perl>` ... `</%perl>` Tag   342

11.6   Handling Posted Data with `%ARGS` and `<%args>`   343
     11.6.1 The `<%args>` ... `</%args>` Tag   344

11.7   Mason Components   348
     11.7.1 Components and `<%args>`   350
     11.7.2 The `<%init>` ... `</%init>` Section   353
     11.7.3 The `<%once>` ... `</%once>` Section   354
     11.7.4 A Note about Mason Security   354

11.8   Mason Project   357

11.9   What We Didn't Talk About   372
     11.9.1 Tags for Initialization and Cleanup   372
     11.9.2 Session Handling   373
     11.9.3 Request API   373
     11.9.4 Component Class API   373
     11.9.5 Top-Level Components   374

11.10 Summary   375

11.11 Resources   375

12 PHP   **377**

12.1   Introduction   377

12.2   Embedding PHP into HTML   378

12.3   Configuration   379

12.4   A Couple of Quick Examples   379

12.5   Language Syntax   381
     12.5.1 Variables   382
     12.5.2 Data Types   383
     12.5.3 Web Variables   386
     12.5.4 Operators   390

12.5.5 Flow-Control Constructs   391

12.5.6 Writing PHP Functions   399

12.6 Built-In PHP Functions   405

12.6.1 Important Functions   405

12.6.2 Array Functions   406

12.6.3 String Functions   410

12.6.4 Other Functions   411

12.7 PHP and MySQL   411

12.7.1 MySQL Functions, Part 1   411

12.7.2 MySQL Functions, Part 2   416

12.7.3 More PHP MySQL Functions   419

12.8 Project   420

12.8.1 Journal MySQL Database   420

12.8.2 Project Pages   422

12.9 Summary   431

12.10 Resources   431

Bibliography   433

Index   437

Foreword

When I was asked to review the manuscript of *Open Source Web Development with LAMP*, I was nervous about one thing. Certainly, I had experience with Linux, Apache, and Perl, and I knew I could bluff my way through the PHP stuff. But the MySQL chapter—warning bells! I've successfully avoided "real databases" throughout my career in the industry–entirely without intending to, I assure you. But somehow, despite nine years of World Wide Web development, I hadn't touched a line of SQL since my undergraduate database course.

Fortunately, I realized this put me in an ideal position to evaluate the book from the perspective of its intended audience: smart folks with a fair amount of web savvy, folks who are willing to pick up new things—with the benefit of two highly experienced guides. And that is what we have in James Lee and Brent Ware.

Certainly, the MySQL chapter succeeded in filling a gap in my professional education. More surprisingly, I learned many new things from each chapter, perhaps especially those that covered what I thought to be familiar ground. These authors had things to teach me about Linux configuration and Apache security and, of course, about Perl. I have come to realize that scarcely anyone knows all there is to know about the Perl programming language! Of course, that's one of the nicest things about Perl; as its inventor, Larry Wall, has often said, "There's more than one way to do it."

That remark applies to the whole of Open Source Web development as well. The techniques and tools introduced in this book overlap and complement each other; you need not master all of them to do tremendously productive work.

James Lee and Brent Ware have provided an excellent introduction to Linux, Apache, MySQL, Perl, PHP, and more. With the help of this book, you can get down to work immediately with any of them. I am sure you will find the book as useful as I have.

Thomas Boutell
President, Boutell.Com, Inc.
Author of *CGI Programming in C and Perl*

Preface

Is This Book for You?

This book's target audience is the person who wants to get an interactive database-based web site up and running without spending a whole bunch of money on a large stack of books and software. That person might be a technically competent Linux user who is not necessarily a Perl or a CGI whiz; a graphic designer, with a technical bent, who wants to build a web site without becoming a certified computer whiz; or an MCSE who has heard rumors that there might be another way to do things.

Up to now, these folks would have had to purchase four or five thick books and wade through them, picking out the knowledge needed to accomplish necessary tasks. It's likely they would accomplish this in a less than optimal way, picking up some things and missing others, revamping and redoing as they learn new things without being aware of the security considerations necessary to keep their site and computer safe. The goal of this book is to summarize much of the information about Open Source in one place and to do so in a manner that will get the prospective web developer up and running safely and efficiently, including pointers to other resources when it becomes necessary to have more knowledge than is provided here.

Our target audience, ideally, would have some familiarity with Unix, some sort of modern programming language (C, FORTRAN, Perl, Pascal, C++, Java—most anything will do), and HTML. The scope here, and the sheer constraints on its size, force us to limit explanations and assume some background knowledge; we touch on a lot of things, enough so that you ought to be able to ask the right questions on a search engine. If you don't have any Unix experience, or if you are not a seasoned programmer, this book can still be useful, with motivation and, perhaps, the purchase of a few other computer books.

What It Will Do

In this book, we introduce you to the pillars of LAMP—Linux, Apache, MySQL, and Perl and PHP, with mod_perl, Embperl, Mason, and WML tossed in for good measure. We are biting off a lot with this book, and this is what we intended to do. We want to cover as much ground as possible and present you with various approaches for programming a web site with Open Source products. The goal is to point out the part of each of these Open Source approaches that provides the most functionality.

Another goal is to make you aware of current techniques and standards: What is easily possible, what might be possible with more work, which tool is appropriate for which task. Just as important is how to discern the things you need from those you don't, or don't need just yet. Not least of all is how to do these things in as secure a fashion as possible. After all, you are opening up your box to the world with these techniques and should be wary of those with impure motives.

Based on experience, we believe that 80 percent of the utility of any complicated tool is the result of knowing 20 percent of the uses of that tool, whether that tool be software, hardware, mechanical, or electronic. Swiss Army knives are excellent and versatile tools, but most of the time, you just use the blade or the screwdriver.

The purpose of this book is to introduce you to that 20 percent—the blade and the screwdriver—that opens up the most functionality, and to make you aware of the remaining 80 percent so that you can use the other tools when appropriate.

And to teach you to not use the blade as a screwdriver.

Four Parts

The book is divided into four parts:

Part I, Structural: Linux, Apache, MySQL, Perl—the structural system foundations on which LAMP is built and the other programs run.

- Linux is the operating system this is all based on. We touch only lightly on Linux because it's a big subject and one that doesn't need to be dealt with much after it's installed.

- Apache is the webserver software that serves web pages up to clients and decides how requests for documents, forms, and so on will be processed. Chapter 1 talks about the basics of configuring and setting up a web site.

- MySQL is an SQL database program. It is "the world's most popular Open Source Database" (it says so on their web site).
- Perl is the programming language of choice for interacting with text files, shell scripts, and a million other things. (Python is similar to Perl in functionality; however, we chose Perl for our purposes because we know it better and like it.)

Part II, Static: WML is a set of programs that facilitates building and managing large-scale static web sites using HTML files.

Part III, Dynamic: CGI and mod_perl are the programs with which to build dynamic web sites.

- CGI is the tried-and-true way of generating dynamic content.
- mod_perl is a better, faster, and stronger way of generating dynamic content; mod_perl combines two pillars of Open Source: Apache and Perl.

Part IV, Embedded: SSI, Embperl, Mason, and PHP are embedding programs to use within HTML pages.

- Server Side Includes (SSI) is built into Apache. Its job is to preprocess HTML files, turning SSI directives into HTML text; it allows web programmers to embed executable code into HTML files.
- Embperl and Mason are Perl modules for building embedded web content.
- PHP is another way to embed executable code with HTML files. PHP does what Embperl and Mason do, just differently.

So why have so many choices? Read on, gentle reader, and you will discover that a myriad of choices is the Open Source way!

Does This Free Software Come with .docs?

Of course, with free software, there's free documentation—see `www.linuxdoc.org` and `httpd.apache.org/docs/`, to name two. The ultimate documentation, the source code, is available to anyone. (Thus the Open Source joke, "Use the source, Luke!") Because of the large community of developers and users, there are many newsgroups and discussion forums in which it is likely that someone else has had the same problem as you and has posted a solution. Search using Google (`www.google.com`) and its interface to the Usenet archive (`groups.google.com`).

If you've installed Linux from a distribution, much of the documentation is likely sitting on your hard drive. In an ideal world, you would just read it—that's what we did. Excellent resource though it is, it leaves something to be desired as a learning method. Much of it was written for reference, not instruction. Some of the documentation has not been updated along with the software. (Hey, these folks work for free. In any case, this is a problem to which closed-source software is not immune.)

The Old Bait and Switch

For all our talk of being self-contained, realistically, two books that you can't escape having handy are *Hacking Linux Exposed* and *Unix System Administration Handbook*—or, more generically, a book on security and another on system administration. These two are our favorites (hereafter known as *HLE* and *USAH*). Each of these subjects is much larger than can be covered here, and both are crucial and unavoidable (but also fun). Get them, read them, grok them.

Companion Web Site

In this book, you are shown examples of how to do all the things we discuss on an active web site (`www.opensourcewebbook.com/`) so that you can see the code and the results, and be pointed to additional resources. We're striving to be self-contained, but we like books, and often tell you which other ones you might want to look at. The entire web site can also be downloaded from `www.opensourcewebbook.com/sourcecode/`.

Acknowledgments

First, we would like to thank all the Open Source hackers who have spent many hours of their time creating the programs that we talk about in this book: Linus Torvalds and all Linux hackers, the Apache team, the MySQL team, Larry Wall and all Perl hackers, Ralf S. Engelschall for WML, Gerald Richter for `HTML::Embperl`, Jonathan Swartz for `HTML::Mason`, and the PHP team.

This book would not be what it is without the excellent input of our reviewers: Ralf S. Engelschall for WML, Gerald Richter for `HTML::Embperl`, Jonathan Swartz for `HTML::Mason`, Thomas Boutell, Richard Dice, Brian Hatch, Todd Haverkos, Lyn Millner, Gautam B. Singh, Daryl Wilding-McBride, Stefan Winz, and Sander van Zoest. A big thanks to Brian Hatch for being the outstanding Open Source hacker that he is. And a huge and enormous thanks to Daryl Lee for trying out all the examples in this book, and for his excellent comments.

A big thanks to all the folks at BDGI (`www.bdgi.com`) for the graphic design of `www.opensourcewebbook.com`, the bandwidth, and for putting up with James for so many months while he wrote this book: Ron Ballard, Mike Borchew, Gail Kimura, Deborah Sawyer, Tom VandeKerckhove, and Al Yalowitz—especially Al.

And thanks to the editors and fine folks at Addison-Wesley for keeping us in line and helping to create and produce a book we can be proud of: Alicia Carey, Mary O'Brien, Marilyn Rash, Jacquelyn Doucette, and all the other team members whose names we do not know.

Thanks to my wife Kelli and my children Ryan, Christian, and Madeline for putting up with my absence while I whisked my laptop off to the local coffee shop for late-night writing sessions. A big "Thank You" to Brent

Ware for coming on board this project and making this book ring with a voice so true—hey, I'm glad we are still friends! Thanks to Brian Hatch for the chance to work on *HLE* and to get my feet wet on book writing. Thanks to Daryl Lee, an uncle and a fellow geek (yes, geekness can run in families)—your comments greatly improved this book. And to Dave and Polly Pistole, Keith Lewis, and Frank Hunnicutt: thanks for everything, and you know what those things are.

James Lee

Thanks to James for asking me to coauthor this with him and for putting up with my occasional irascibility, and to Laura Newman for putting me up and putting up with me.

Brent Ware

About the Authors

James Lee (james@opensourcewebbook.com) is a hacker and Open Source advocate based in Illinois. He holds a master's degree from Northwestern University, where he can often be seen rooting for the Wildcats during football season. The founder of Onsight (www.onsight.com), he has worked as a programmer, trainer, manager, writer and Open Source advocate. He is the coauthor of the recently released *Hacking Linux Exposed, Second Edition* (McGraw-Hill/Osborne, 2002). He has also written a number of articles on Perl for the *Linux Journal*. Mr. Lee enjoys hacking Perl, developing software for the web, reading, traveling, and most of all playing with his kids who are too young to know why dad's favorite animals are penguins and camels.

Brent Ware (brent@opensourcewebbook.com) started out as an electrical engineer, then gave up a promising, well-paid, and boring career as an MSEE to go back to school and get a Ph.D in physics. After serving the requisite indentured grad student servitude in experimental high-energy physics searching for very small particles (University of Texas, BNL), he pursued the usual postdoc academic path, searching for very small ripples in space-time (Caltech, LIGO), followed by failing to find a tenure-track job, poverty, disillusionment, and worthless stock options in lieu of salary at a telecom dotcom in Seattle. He is now a scientist at Caltech/NASA's Jet Propulsion Laboratories in Pasadena.

In passing, he has been exposed to multiple operating systems on a variety of computers, the great majority of which are now museum pieces, and their software fodder for trivia questions on comp.os newsgroups. Linux seems to be a keeper, and he hopes it will stick around no matter what happens to Wintel. In any case, Brent took a vow to only use *nix and emacs and LaTeX and never burn any more neurons on transient, fly-by-night alternatives. He has been an unpaid sysadmin over the years on a variety of different platforms and contributed to *Hacking Linux Exposed*.

Introduction

It seems that now we've finally reached the era that has been promised for decades, since the advent of the mass-produced personal computer. Hardware is cheap and powerful. Bandwidth is available to almost everyone. Even our parents, in such disparate locales as rural Texas and suburban Los Angeles, have fast Internet connections using satellite and cable. Unless you're a serious gamer, the cheapest home computer will serve most every forseeable purpose.[1] Moore's Law has outrun feature creep, for now.

At the time this book was being written, a barebones GigaHertz (GHz) x86 box could be found for roughly $200—at Walmart, no less. That stripped-down machine has almost certainly gotten cheaper and faster in the interval between our writing and your reading. Or you can dumpster-dive one out of the trash of some failed dotcom for free, or cadge an old one from a friend who just upgraded.[2]

If you're willing to spend roughly the same amount for DSL or a cable modem (and soon enough, WiFi) as for your cable TV bill, you, or anyone, can have a constant Internet connection, send e-mail, and surf the Web. Hosting a web site is a bit more expensive and complicated, but not rocket science—you need a static Internet protocol (IP) address, a registered domain, and probably will have to give your Internet service provider (ISP) a bit more money. Cheap computing and reasonable bandwidth are available to most everyone. Primarily, it's only knowledge, or lack thereof, that keeps one from setting up a web site, home business, dotcom, or consulting firm. There's really no reason for a "digital divide" to exist, at least in the United States; any home that can afford a television and cable can afford a computer and a cable modem.

---

[1] Okay, we haven't reached computer nirvana yet—computers aren't as easy to use as they ought to be. Too much of the Web is a tradeoff of personal privacy versus ease of use. Our parents still have trouble installing their peripherals, and so do we, among other things.

[2] On the other hand, as someone famous once said, the computer you want costs $3,000—always has, always will.

I.1 THE BEST OF ALL POSSIBLE WORLDS . . .

Using free Open Source programs, a web site can be created for the truly amazing price of $0.00—zero, nada, zilch.[3] You can download Linux, Apache, MySQL and Perl/PHP to develop world-class, powerful, and useful web sites—thus the acronym, and the *LAMP* that will light our way. Of course, you could spend as much money as you like and get a web site running with commercial software, but we think there are good reasons, aside from initial and ongoing expenses, to use free Open Source solutions.

One common criticism of Open Source as a solution is that it's only free if your time isn't worth anything. This is true in one sense, but not in another. All software—free or commercial, Open Source or closed—takes time and effort to learn and to apply.

The following are several reasons this book should be a valuable resource as you turn to Open Source software:

- It distills the essential knowledge needed to create a good, secure, standards-compliant, Open Source web site in one place.
- It provides alternatives to commercial solutions.
- It documents widely used Open Source programs.
- It shares the fun we've had using Open Source software.

I.2 OPEN SOURCE SOFTWARE

First, what is Open Source? What does that mean? Open Source means that, unlike most of the software you might buy shrink-wrapped down at Joe Bob's Computer Hut, you have access to the raw source code—the human-readable C, C++, Perl, etc.—files that get compiled down into the binary that is executed by the computer. This executable binary—.exe—is all you get from closed-source proprietary sources. Should you so desire, you can view the source files to see why that darn error message keeps popping up, or how to make that widget default to a different directory, or how to add a cool new function. Once you start looking at the source, you've started down the path of becoming an Open Source programmer. That's the beauty of Open Source.

---

[3]Well, no cash outlay and a bunch of mental elbow grease, anyway; and, of course, there are obvious issues to take up with your ISP should your web site become popular.

You can make changes and submit them for others to look at. You can design a new widget to emulate a feature or a program that you liked on a different system, or to do something entirely new because you, using the available Open Source software, can look at the code that drives Linux™, or Apache™, or the Gimp™, or Open Office™, or Mozilla™. You can write code to use it, to improve it, to hook to it, and/or to make it do almost anything else. Then changes can be shared with others as they did with you; with Open Source it's not only OK to copy, to improve, to use, and to return the source code to the community of users, but it is expected.

You may never do this; you may use Linux and Apache and Perl and never look at a line of code, never change a default in a configuration file. But, you could if you wanted to—you don't have to live with what someone else decided is best.

The philosophy of Open Source software, among other things, is that many hands and eyes make for good software, unlike too many cooks spoiling the broth. Bugs are more likely to be caught, and more important, fixed, if everyone has access to the source. As in cryptography, closed systems cannot be proved to be free of flaws or errors. While it's no guarantee that no bugs exist, open systems can be examined for flaws; closed systems can only be tested against known bugs (security through obscurity). It's the unknown unknowns that can bite you.[4]

As anyone who's ever participated in design or code review knows, only by getting other people to look at your system or code have you any hope of finding the bugs—everyone has blind spots. The more eyes that look at the source, the better. With Open Source, it isn't just a few people in a suburb east of Seattle who eyeball the code, but hundreds if not thousands of people all over the world. When, not if, a bug is discovered, anyone can fix it without depending on a software company to do a cost analysis of whether to issue a new free service pack or to include the update in the next dot revision and charge $99.95 for it.

Another tenet of the Open Source philosophy is giving back to the community. Most Open Source software falls under some form of a license. The various Open Source licenses are listed at `www.opensource.org`. Among

---

[4] *Unknown unknowns* are the problems that you don't even know about. When you start something new, you know that some things are going to be a problem and can anticipate other things that could be a problem. But then there are the "unknown unknowns"—the problems you aren't even aware of until they jump up and bite you, usually with customers standing in the room during a demo. One of the best engineers we ever knew, Duane Sanner, called them "unk-unks."

others, the GPL (www.gnu.org/copyleft/gpl.html), LGPL (www.gnu.org/copyleft/lesser.html), or one of the BSD licenses (www.opensource.org/licenses/bsd-license.html).[5] Most of these require that, if you redistribute the code, any Open Source software changes be committed back to the community; some are stricter than others. This isn't to say that you can't make money using your Open Source code, but simply that it's only good manners if you take advantage of all the work others have freely given you to build on that you freely return your changes and improvements to the community. Of course, if you keep it for just personal use, you can make any changes you want to any Open Source code. If you want to redistribute your changes, however, the revisions should be Open Source. This is mandatory with the GPL, and good manners with most others.

I.2.1 It's All Based on Open Source

Many of the programs on which the Internet was built are Open Source: Sendmail, Apache, BIND. Before anyone espoused Open Source as a concept, the programmers who built the Internet wrote cool software to do useful stuff—e-mail, TCP/IP, the Web—and shared the source code freely with others to maintain, to improve, and to impress their peers with the coolness of their hacks.

We mean *hack* in the original sense of the word, exemplified by the HAKMEM (www.tuxedo.org/~esr/jargon/html/entry/HAKMEM.html), that hacking is what good programmers do when solving problems on their own systems, and cracking is what people with less-than-pure motives do to other people's computers without regard for the consequences to anyone other than themselves. This is an important distinction, which has unfortunately been blurred by sensationalism and ignorance, but one that we'll maintain in this book.

I.2.2 There's a Disclaimer

Of course, no rose is without its thorns, and the Open Source model is not without its drawbacks. There may or may not be support for the software you wish to use. The only documentation might be the source. Your platform or hardware may or may not be supported. This gets better every day, but it means you have to do research. That said, not every device is

---

[5]For a comparison of the various licenses, see zooko.com/license_quick_ref.html.

supported by Apple or Microsoft either, so you still have to do research. *Caveat emptor.*

Some Open Source companies provide technical support for a fee, but with many programs and distributions, it's up to the administrator (you) to check for updates; be aware of security bugs by following Bugtraq (www.securityfocus.com), or the program's web site, or Slashdot (www.slashdot.org); and upgrading when necessary. Then again, some people might consider being vigilant about maintaining their computer a good thing, no matter what the operating system.

At the basic level, you are your own sysadmin and webmaster—you are responsible for watching logs, maintenance, dealing with problems. You may have to roll your own software; configure it for your system, which may not be the same as the default; and actually have to RTFM.[6] The documentation that you get may be out of date or inaccurate; but, then, all these drawbacks are also inherent in closed-source software—you can't just turn your computer on and ignore security updates, patches, and upgrades. The nicely formatted and printed documentation is often wrong and/or out of date. Generally, the patches and upgrades come at a price, either dollars or time.

You may not be able to run all of the applications that you can use on your Windows or Mac system, although we've found that there are translators, emulators, or equivalents for most things.[7] For us, this has not been a limitation in Linux, even though sometimes it is a timesink. It is not a limitation that closed-source systems are immune to however. One of this book's authors spent hours while writing this trying to convince one Mac program to read in data from another, and more hours installing an FTP server on a Windows NT box so that he could copy large amounts of data without transferring it to an intermediate medium—no FTP server installed by default!? And, there's no native secure copy at all.

It's also the norm in Linux to install and to upgrade software without having to reboot, and for systems to be inherently stable—no blue screen

---

[6]If you don't know what RTFM means, then RTFM (www.tuxedo.org/~esr/jargon/html/entry/RTFM.html). Use this site to figure out what RTFM means. There's lots of other great stuff in the Jargon files. This is a great place to go to learn computer history a little bit at a time.

[7]We have a special fondness for VMware (www.vmware.com) and Mac-on-Linux (www.maconlinux.org); we were much fonder of the former when they had a personal use price of $75 instead of $400, and OS X has largely obviated the need for the latter. The WINE project (www.winehq.com) is another attempt to be able to run Windows programs on Linux, but it isn't there yet even though the price is right.

of death, no bombs, no control-alt-delete three-fingered Vulcan mind grips. Linux uptimes typically run in months, and the limiting factor is quite possibly your connection to the wall (in California, due to rolling blackouts; in Illinois, due to three kids playing around the server). Not to say you won't ever have to reboot or that your machine won't lock up, but, in our experience, it's much rarer.[8] Mostly, we have to reboot our machines only when we feel like trying out a new kernel.

You may also have to deal with some bias. If you have to answer to an IT manager, or your nontechnical spouse, you may have some explaining to do if you want to run Linux and everyone else is running Windows. But that isn't a bad thing. You should have good reasons for going Open Source, or at least reasons.

I.2.3 It's Not Just for Linux

Although the focus here is on Linux and how LAMP programs interact with Linux, much of this is directly applicable to many operating systems, especially Unix variants (*nix). For the most part, the configurations are independent of the platform, and this software runs on many platforms. If you run Solaris on Sun, or YDL on PPC, or OS X on a Mac, or any version of BSD, many of the things we talk about here are generally applicable to your system. The information here should be useful not only to the Linux user but also for most *nix users. In fact, this book was written on Apple PowerBook G4 laptops using BSD Unix-based OS X, an Apple G4 running LinuxPPC, and several different x86s running Red Hat 7.

This book was written entirely with Open Source software: emacs, vi, LaTeX, CVS, Ghostview, xdvi, ps2pdf, xpdf, and dvipdf on Linux and OS X. Frankly we couldn't imagine writing something of this length and complexity in Word. Shudder!

The HTML files and programs located at www.opensourcewebbook.com were developed concurrently on an x86 laptop running Red Hat 7.2 and a dual Pentium 450MHz server running Red Hat 7.2 using vi, SSH, and all the technologies we discuss in this book. That's another beauty of Open Source—given most any *nix system, one can use CVS, SSH, emacs, vi, and LaTeX to work on a huge document anywhere.

---

[8]Windows 2000 and XP have much better track records in this regard than previous versions, although we still find them less stable than Linux or OS X.

I.3 SUMMARY

Open Source is a viable alternative to commercial closed-source software, and both can be used for the purpose of setting up a web site. Although various software packages have different qualities, Open Source has both the advantage and drawback of putting the user in charge. This means more responsibility.[9] By accepting less responsibility, however, you're at the mercy of manufacturers when things you install don't work, when you discover a bug, when you find out that software won't do what you want it to do, when you discover that the nicely printed manual describes only the pulldown menus, and/or when you can't locate information on how to setup an important option. You may even find that the manufacturer has changed the licensing policy and from now on you have to pay a yearly fee to keep using the software, or that the manufacturer has altered all your web pages to make links to its own (see `www.slashdot.org/article.pl?sid=01/06/07/1252227`, which describes the Microsoft "smart tags"). Heck, with Linux, you can keep Windows or Mac on your system and run it in a window in the background with a low priority. The best of both worlds!

So, believing in controlling our own destinies, and that the Open Source solution is superior for some applications and at least equivalent for many others, we've chosen to spend our time with LAMP. Even Apple has seen some light at the end of the tunnel and released a new operating system based on BSD; the underpinnings of the system, Darwin, are Open Source, and Open Source programs can be ported to it.

I.4 RESOURCES

Books

[Hatch+ 02] Hatch, Brian, James Lee, and George Kurtz. *Hacking Linux Exposed: Linux Security Secrets Solutions, Second Edition.* Get this book!

[Himanen+ 01] Himanen, Pekka, Manuel Castells, and Linus Torvalds. *The Hacker Ethic.* An intellectual treatment of hacking and hackers.

---

[9]We won't say more time, because anyone who's spent time rebooting a Wintel box because of repeated crashes or simply because you upgraded a program or installed a Windows Security Update knows the advantage of being able to kill and restart the program rather than reboot the whole machine.

[Nemeth+ 02] Nemeth, Evi, Garth Snyder, Trent R. Hein, and Adam Boggs. *Unix System Administration Handbook.* This is the Bible for Unix sysadmins.

[Raymond+ 97] Raymond, Eric S., and Bob Young. *The Cathedral and the Bazaar: Musings on Linux and Open Source.* An interesting read about the nature of Open Source, based on Eric Raymond's experience with the development of fetchmail.

[Schneier 00] Schneier, Bruce. *Secrets and Lies: Digital Security in a Networked World.* Not a book on how to be secure, but on how to think about security, and just how difficult it is to be truly secure. A must-read for just about anyone in this networked world.

[Torvalds+ 01] Torvalds, Linus, and David Diamond. *Just for Fun: The Story of an Accidental Revolutionary.* The biography of the creator of Linux that's a short, easy, and fun read.

Web Sites

Apache: www.apache.org—the official Apache web page

Bugtraq: www.securityfocus.com—use to keep track of security vulnerabilities

Hacker information: www.tuxedo.org/~esr/jargon/html/entry/HAKMEM.html— what hacking is all about. See also www.tuxedo.org/~esr/jargon/html/entry/hack.html—the real definition of hacker

Linux: www.linux.org—information on Linux

Linux security: www.linuxdoc.org/HOWTO/Security-HOWTO.html—a must-read for securing your Linux box

Mozilla: www.mozilla.org—the Mozilla browser is an Open Source web browser

MySQL: www.mysql.com—the official MySQL web page

Open Source Development Network: www.osdn.com—a network of Open Source web sites including Slashdot, Freshmeat, Sourceforge.net

Open Source: www.opensource.org—interesting information and history relating to Open Source software

Perl: www.perl.com—all things Perl begin here

Python: www.python.org

PHP: www.php.net—PHP central

Sendmail: www.sendmail.org—sendmail is the ubiquitous Open Source program that routes the majority of e-mail around the Internet

Slashdot: www.slashdot.org—worth looking at daily

Source Forge: www.sourceforge.net—Open Source software code for many projects is available here

Part I
Structural

1

The Web Explained

The World Wide Web may seem like magic, until you understand how it works. In this chapter, we offer a brief introduction of what happens when you click a link, enter a URL into the location box, or otherwise request a web page. This description is necessary to understand how the different components of the Web fit together and how the tools presented in this book fit into the Web's framework.

1.1 HOW IT WORKS

To give you a clear picture of how the parts discussed in this book interrelate, Figure 1.1 shows a pictorial overview of the Web. The Web is usually accessed through a browser, the most well known of which are Netscape/Mozilla and Internet Explorer. There are many alternative browsers, including Galeon, Konquerer, OmniWeb, and Opera, and also text-based options such as Lynx, links, and w3g.

When you click a link or type a URL into the location box (for instance, `www.example.com`), the browser makes a socket connection (also known as a network connection) to the server `www.example.com`. The name `www.example.com` maps to an Internet address, which is a number in the form 1.2.3.4—an IP, or dotted quad. The browser connects to `www.example.com` using port 80, the port that the server operating system opens for such HTTP requests. This port is standardized. Other ports are used for other Internet connections: 22 for SSH, 23 for Telnet, and so on. (SSH and Telnet are addressed in Chapter 2.) It should be made clear that IP port numbers are not related to the physical ports of the machine (COM1 and COM2, USB, Firewire, parallel printer port, etc.).

3

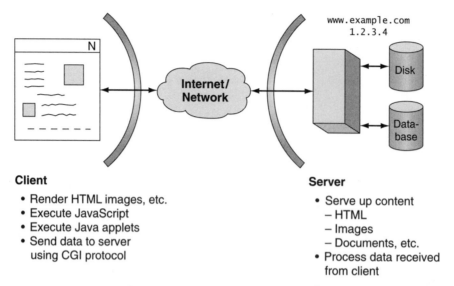

Client
- Render HTML images, etc.
- Execute JavaScript
- Execute Java applets
- Send data to server
  using CGI protocol

Server
- Serve up content
  - HTML
  - Images
  - Documents, etc.
- Process data received
  from client

Figure 1.1   How the Web works

Based on what the client requests, the server serves up, or delivers, information to the client. The type of data the server serves up includes plain text (this includes HTML), images, Java applets, various types of documents, PDFs, etc. This content that the server delivers can be generated by the server in one of several ways: static, dynamic, or embedded (each of these is discussed later).

The client's job is to receive from the server a stream of text, images, Java applets, documents, and so on and render, or appropriately display, them. The client also executes any JavaScript code and Java applets that are served up.[1] The client can send form data to the server using the Common Gateway Interface (CGI) protocol (see Chapter 7). The server can then process this data in whatever way it chooses. There are two sides to the processing that goes on: the client side and the server side. These two terms mean pretty much exactly what they seem to mean. The cool thing about this, as with many other things Web, is that once protocols are established,

---

[1] JavaScript should not be confused with Java; they are two different things. JavaScript, originally called LiveScript, is a language created by Netscape (www.netscape.com) that executes within the browser to do clever things like pop up new windows, image rollovers, and other nifty client-side things. Java is a platform-independent programming language created by Sun Microsystems (www.sun.com) that is often used to create applets that are downloaded and executed within the browser.

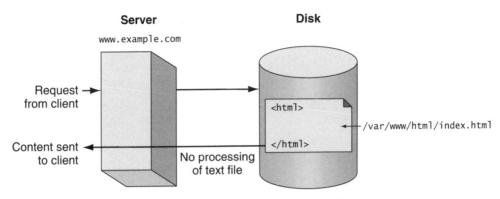

Figure 1.2 Serving up static data

what happens on the client side or the server side is independent. If the client wants to block pop-up ads, there isn't much the server can do about it. If someone develops a new server-side application or improves an old one, the client doesn't care, as long as protocols are adhered to.

1.1.1 Serving Up Static Data

The simplest thing for the server to do is to serve up *static data,* or data that is the same for every client and changes only when an HTML programmer changes the source file. The server accomplishes this by locating an HTML (or image or PDF or ...) file on the local hard drive and sending that content back to the client unchanged. This requires no server programming—the Apache web server does all the work.

This is illustrated in Figure 1.2. Let's say the user enters the URL www.example.com/. The server www.example.com is contacted, and a request is made that causes the server to locate a file (/var/www/html/index.html) on its local drive. The file is located and sent back, as is, to the client.[2]

We discuss static content when we talk about how to set up and use the Apache web server (see Chapter 3). We also discuss how to easily create and manage a large (or small, for that matter) static Web site using the Website META Language (WML)—see Chapter 6.

---

[2]Actually, the server prepends some information, called the *header,* to the content and sends the header followed by the contents of index.html. More on this in Chapter 3.

1.1.2 Serving Up Dynamic Data

A more complex way of generating HTML is to execute a server-side program that dynamically generates the HTML that is sent to the browser. There are many flavors of server-side programming, including tried-and-true CGI (Chapter 7) and the more flexible and powerful mod_perl (Chapter 8). The program generally does some sort of server-side processing, such as reading from a database or executing some other server-side program.

Dynamic web pages should not be confused with dynamic HTML, a term usually used when discussing web pages that exhibit dynamic behavior such as pop-up windows, image rollovers, dynamic clickable menus, and similar super-duper fancy eye candy. Dynamic HTML is often implemented with JavaScript and the Document Object Model (DOM).

Dynamic content is illustrated in Figure 1.3. If the user enters the URL `www.example.com/cgi-bin/a.cgi`, the server (`www.example.com`) receives a request to execute a program named `a.cgi` (the server knows it is an executable program because of the `cgi-bin` in the URL). The server locates the file on its local drive, perhaps at `/var/www/cgi-bin/a.cgi`, and executes the program. This program's job is to produce HTML (along with doing some useful task for which it was created, such as reading from a database, sending e-mail, or writing to a log file) that will be sent back to the client.

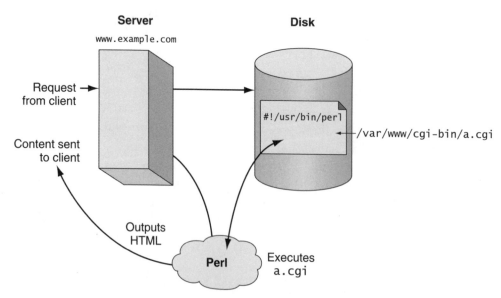

Figure 1.3   Serving up dynamic data

1.1.3 Serving Up Content with Embedded HTML

Another, more flexible way to create dynamic web pages is to use embedded HTML, or executable code embedded within an HTML file. This is a good approach when those working on the web site are from disparate backgrounds. For instance, if a person who knows HTML but is not a programmer builds the template for the web page, a programmer can come behind them and add executable code directly into the HTML file to make the page come alive. Not static, not quite dynamic, embedded web pages provide a measure of flexibility.

This enables a Web designer—perhaps an artist or a graphic designer rather than the stereotypical artistically challenged nerd (like us)—to create a web site that is usable and eye-pleasing instead of average and plain.[3] Then, after the artist has created the look and feel, the programmers can come in and add executable code right into the HTML to change the static content into dynamic content, livening a good-looking but otherwise static site. Of course, one of the target audiences of this book is the graphic designers and artists who design web page look and feel, potentially cutting out the necessity for nerds entirely. Not vice versa, though, because it's far easier to learn programming than to do graphical design.

Figure 1.4 shows how this type of processing works. Let's say the user enters the URL www.example.com/a.html. The web server grabs the HTML file, perhaps /var/www/html/a.html, and preprocesses it in some way, generating HTML by executing the code within the original HTML file; the result is then sent to the client.

We examine four approaches to embedded programming:

- SSI (Server Side Includes; see Chapter 9)—a simple solution that is built into Apache, using a syntax that is unique to SSI

- Embperl (see Chapter 10)—a Perl module that enables an HTML file to have Perl code embedded within it

- Mason (see Chapter 11)—another Perl module that, like Embperl, enables an HTML file to have Perl code embedded within it

- PHP (see Chapter 12)—a language unto itself, Perl-like in its syntax and providing a rich collection of built-in functions to perform various tasks

---

[3]An example of the former is this book's web site—www.opensourcewebbook.com—designed by the excellent artistic folks at BDGI (www.bdgi.com). An example of the latter can be found at www.ifokr.org.

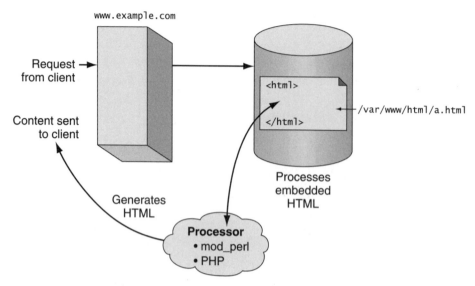

Figure 1.4　Serving up embedded data

SSI, being simple, is limited in what it can do. We discuss it only because you may come across SSI pages that need maintenance. Embperl, Mason, and PHP are rich in features. With these languages, the HTML page has access to posted form data, can connect to databases, can read and write files, and can perform any task that you can do in an arbitrary program. This enables you to make HTML files programs that can be bent to your will, creating web sites that not only are things of beauty, serving up live, dynamic data, but also can become applications, performing many tasks.

1.2　WHAT WE DON'T TALK ABOUT

There is a long list of Web technologies that we do not discuss in this book. This is mainly because this book is already loaded with good information, and some of the popular technologies are not strictly Open Source. Here we mention some of the omitted technologies—things that are important to know—but you need to look elsewhere for discussions about them.

XML Extensible Markup Language—the future of the Web, according to many in the industry. XML will one day replace HTML as the language used to create web pages.[4] XML is also widely used to represent and transmit data on the network.

Java An object-oriented programming language used to create applets (programs executed within the browser) and stand-alone applications. Java has an extensive API that provides methods to create GUI applications, socket programs, and more. Included under the Java umbrella is JSP, or JavaServer Pages. Java isn't discussed in this book because it isn't part of LAMP, and it's really closer to C++ at heart, a programming language.

JavaScript A Java-like language that manipulates the client browser. JavaScript is used to pop up new browser windows (have you ever visited a web site that opens a new window with one of those pesky advertisements? Eeeeuuuuwwww! This is done with JavaScript), perform image rollovers, implement layers, and do other nifty things that happen on the client. Because this is a book about Web server programming, we don't talk about this topic, but many good books on it are available.

1.3 SECURITY

Security is absolutely crucial. There are a lot of folks on the Internet who want to crack into your computer. It is in your best interest and everyone else's that you do all you can to deny them this bizarre satisfaction. Cracking is a time-honored culture (perhaps "honored" is not the right word); it should be more of a time-honored tradition to make it difficult. However, this is not a book on securing your computer; it is a book on Open Source web development. We discuss security issues when appropriate, and highly recommend (for obvious reasons) *Hacking Linux Exposed* (`www.hackinglinuxexposed.com` [Hatch+ 02]) as a good reference. Also, check out the Linux Security HOWTO at `www.linuxdoc.org/HOWTO/Security-HOWTO.html`; this is a must-read for securing your Linux box.

Security is a process, not a step.[5] Every time you write a program, install software, or change a password, security should be foremost in your mind.

---

[4]Although we want to note that HTML is not going anywhere for a while.

[5]See *Secrets and Lies: Digital Security in a Networked World* [Schneier 00]. A must-read, not for what it says about how to secure your computer, but how to think about security in general. It points out many of the fallacies common in most half-baked security measures taken today, and just how difficult it is to be secure.

1.4 SUMMARY

In this chapter, we've given you the basic definitions of how things on the Web talk to each other, and the differences between the various types of client-server relationship. Based on these relationships, we've structured the topics in this book around the concepts of static, embedded, and dynamic applications, and have placed each of the web applications into one of these categories. There is also another category of structural components, things that aren't really web programming languages, but the components upon which these applications are built: Linux, Apache, MySQL, Perl. The next section of the book starts out building this structure.

1.5 RESOURCES

Books

[Hatch+ 02] Hatch, Brian, James Lee, and George Kurtz. *Hacking Linux Exposed: Linux Security Secrets and Solutions, Second Edition.* Blatant plug: Get this book!

[Schneier 00] Schneier, Bruce. *Secrets and Lies: Digital Security in the Networked World.* Not a book on how to be secure, but on how to think about security, and just how difficult it is to be truly secure. A must-read for just about anyone in this networked world.

Web Sites

Linux Security: `www.linuxdoc.org/HOWTO/Security-HOWTO.html`—A must-read for securing your Linux box.

Mozilla: `www.Mozilla.org`—The Mozilla browser is on Open Source web browser.

2

Linux—The Choice of a GNU Generation

2.1 INTRODUCTION

Linux is an Open Source version of Unix developed by Linus Torvalds to port Unix to the Intel x86 processor [Torvalds+ 01]. This made Unix available on the most ubiquitous computer hardware that has ever existed, and therefore available to almost everyone. Linux has since been ported to almost every processor and function one could imagine, including game-boxes, personal digital assistants (PDAs), personal digital video recorders, and IBM mainframes, expanding the original concept of Unix for x86 to Unix for everything. Linux isn't the only version of Unix available to most people (also notable are the various BSD variants, also Open Source), but it's by far the most popular.

In this chapter, we discuss how to get Linux, how to install it, and some of the basic commands. Here we are caught in a familiar bind: If you are familiar with Linux, this will be too simplistic, and if you are not, it will not be nearly enough. If you are in the former category, you can skim or skip this chapter; if the latter, we try to point you in the right direction.

2.1.1 Linux Distributions

Although Linux is free and Open Source, and you can download individual packages and compile them all yourself, that's rather masochistic. Most people get Linux as a packaged distribution from a vendor, either by paying for a CD or downloading it. The distribution route is fast and easy and resolves many hardware and software dependency issues (though not all of them). Paying for a CD both gives the prospective user the documentation and usually some degree of technical support, and supports the companies that propagate and improve Linux.

Many individuals, organizations, and companies make Linux distributions for different purposes and with different philosophies. The following is a quick list of the main ones, in no particular order (see `www.distrowatch.com` to keep up with them):

Debian Debian GNU/Linux is developed and maintained entirely by volunteers. The Advanced Package Tool (`apt`) is very powerful and highly esteemed—many people think this is the best updater around. It is one of the easiest distributions to keep up to date. The `apt-get` mechanism handles package dependencies neatly.

Red Hat This is probably the most popular Linux distribution in the United States. Red Hat has worked with a number of vendors to provide Red Hat Linux preinstalled on PCs. Red Hat is feature and application rich, and easy for new Linux users to learn. Red Hat created the Red Hat Package Manager (RPM) system, a system similar to `apt` to keep software up to date, which is used by many distributions. The Red Hat `up2date` mechanism provides a package dependency resolution similar to `apt-get`. For what it's worth, `apt-get` has been ported to Red Hat, and you can update your distribution in that manner. Red Hat boasts a number of high-profile Open Source software employees.

Slackware One of the first Linux distributions, Slackware is still used by many hard-core Linux users. It contains user-friendly interfaces similar to other Linux distributions, but it generally goes for "power over pretty."

SuSE The most popular distribution in Europe, especially Germany, SuSE has become more popular in the United States as well. It uses a variant of the RPM package format and includes a sophisticated system configuration tool called YaST (Yet another Setup Tool) to make administration easier. SuSE supports many types of hardware and many configurations not available in other distributions, and includes several security scripts and tools that can be run to inform you of problems.

Mandrake Mandrake took the Red Hat distribution, added an easy-to-use installer, and changed the default desktop from Gnome to KDE, thus arriving at one of the more popular distributions. It has a reputation for being easy to use, easy to install, and cutting-edge.

A Disclaimer: We don't work for any of the companies we mention here, nor do we own any of their stock, at least not enough to get rich by recommending them. We mention these companies because we like their stuff, have used it, and have had good experiences with it. Patronize them or not, as *you* choose.

There's also Immunix, a distribution based on Red Hat, which is hardened for security. The NSA also makes a secure version of Linux (see www.nsa.gov/selinux/).

Because we have to choose *something*, Red Hat Linux version 7 (the latest distribution as of this writing[1]) will be our base. Aside from the usual holy wars about Linux distributions (and you can always roll your own from the source) or Linux versus BSD, we've found that Red Hat is the one you're most likely to be able to walk into a store in the United States and buy. Although this is not an endorsement,[2] Red Hat does a good job of keeping up to date with bug fixes and security issues and making its distribution relatively painless. Many resources are available for Red Hat, and one of our favorites, the *Unix System Administration Handbook, Third Edition* [Nemeth+ 01], now includes Red Hat Linux explicitly, which is very nice since Red Hat, like all the other distributions of Linux, does things slightly different from other Unices.[3]

The directory structure referenced here is based on Red Hat. The Red Hat structure differs slightly from the Filesystem Hierarchy Standard, aka Linux Filesystem Standard (www.pathname.com/fhs/). All the configurations and directory structures we discuss in this book are based on the standard Red Hat RPMs.

However, you can use any other Linux distribution or package manager if you prefer, including ./configure; make; make install. If you've already installed a non–Red Hat Linux, you should be able to translate these instructions to another distribution with little difficulty.

---

[1] You'll grow weary of that phrase soon.

[2] Unpaid, it should be noted. Call us, RH—our people will talk with your people.

[3] Unix is Unix is Unix, and once you know one, you pretty much know them all, but even aside from SysV versus BSD, all Unices do things slightly differently. Think Ford versus GM for Red Hat versus Debian, and GM versus Toyota for SysV versus BSD. You can jump in and drive any of them, though you might have to look around to find the dimmer switch.

2.1.2 Download and Install

The easiest way to get this free software is to pony up a sawbuck or two for a shrink-wrapped CD with instructions—this might seem an oxymoron, but it's a capitalistic society. Or get it from `www.cheapbytes.com` for a very minimal cost. Because most of this is Open Source software, you don't have to buy any of it—you can download it for free. But free might not be cheap, depending on how you value your time.

Failing that, you can download the software from Red Hat (or whatever distribution you choose) or a mirror under your existing non-Linux software and burn a CD or do a network install. Having a CD around is nice for reinstalling, fixing problems, having a backup, and other necessary tasks.

One issue to consider if you aren't purchasing a distribution with a CD, printed instructions, and so forth, is that the computer won't have a network connection or browser or printer while you are doing the installation, so you have to be prepared and have access to the instructions, documentation, etc., beforehand—it's not always feasible to stop in the middle because you don't know the answer to a question. Once you start installing Linux, you can't click on the browser (on that machine—if you have another, no problem) and look up the answer—the browser won't be installed yet.

We're going assume you have a CD in hand, because otherwise the options branch too much for us to cover all the complications, and if you aren't installing from a CD, you aren't going to take our advice anyway—you know what you are doing.

Once you have the software in hand, you can run the installer (whether Red Hat or not, most are fairly painless these days), following either the instructions you printed or the book you got with your distribution.

Having learned from experience, we highly recommend keeping an old-fashioned paper logbook of your setup, starting with how your disk is partitioned. If you have to tweak some odd configuration, you'll be very happy two years from now when you're installing your new system on your 5GHz Pentium 9 if you've written it down and very frustrated if you haven't—especially when you're trying to recover your system after that hard disk that you got for $50 from Joe Bob's Computer Hut dies. The utility of keeping it on paper should be obvious, as is the canard about computers making for a paperless society. Back up your important data, and keep track of changes made to system configuration files somewhere other than on your system.

It's also a really good idea to make a copy of any configuration file before you change it, renaming it with the date, and placing it out of the install path. Extensions—.orig, .bak, etc.—are not recommended because many install scripts use those to save the files they're about to overwrite. Consider keeping a directory in your home path with the latest version of working configuration files, in addition to backups and paper copies, or better yet, on another computer entirely. You could also use something more technical for this purpose, such as CVS.

2.1.3 Decisions, Decisions

Before you start the installation, you must make some important decisions about your installation. Do you want to have a dual Windows/Linux boot or run strictly Linux? If you dual boot, do you want to put both operating systems on one disk, or do you want to install another hard drive for Linux? Is this going to be a workstation in addition to being a server, or strictly a command line interface (CLI) accessed server?

One advantage of dual booting is that you get to keep all the Windows software you already paid for, because of the nonmonopolistic practices that make it easy for you to buy a computer without a Microsoft operating system preinstalled (sarcasm alert!).[4] With dual booting, you can even run Windows under an emulator in Linux.

But if this machine is to be a full-time webserver, not a user machine, you may want to keep things simple and go with Linux as your only operating system. This does make installation much simpler.

N If you decide to go strictly with Linux, you can't go back to Windows without reformatting your hard disk and reinstalling Windows.

As always, before you start any major system task like this, *back up!* Back your system up—you can lose everything when you start playing with fundamental things like disk partitions. At the very least, copy your important files to another computer, a CD-ROM, a tape, or an external disk. Therefore, there are several installation options.

---

[4]A large portion of the cost of any PC is due to the Microsoft operating system, which it is required to have (the so-called Microsoft tax—try buying a computer in the United States without *any* operating system).

Single disk, Linux boot Simple enough—just insert the installation disk and follow the instructions.

Single disk, dual boot In a dual boot system, Windows must reside on its own partition—not least because Windows and Linux use incompatible filesystems. The Red Hat installer comes with a disk utility, called `fips`, that allows you to shrink the existing Windows partition of your disk without destroying the existing data, though the disk must be defragmented before you do this (see `www.igd.fhg.de/~aschaefe/fips/`).

This program works for older versions of Windows that are based on the FAT filesystem: Windows 95, 98, 2000, and ME.

Unfortunately, newer versions of Windows (NT, XP) are based on the proprietary NTFS filesystem, which breaks `fips`. It is unlikely that someone will reverse engineer this system and implement something similar to `fips` for NTFS, because the Digital Millennium Copyright Act (DMCA) makes reverse engineering a proprietary closed system a felony![5] A couple of programs purport to do the same thing as `fips`, but they aren't as well tested. Red Hat doesn't include them on the install disk—draw your own conclusions. You pays your money, you takes your chances. It's your data.

A program called Partition Magic does alter NTFS partitions, but it costs between $50 and $75, so you are left with the choice of ponying up for the software or just getting a cheap 10GB or 20GB disk and installing Linux on that. The cost is roughly the same, plus or minus an Andy Jackson. We recommend the latter, if your computer supports an extra hard drive. Same cost, much simpler, more flexible.

Multiple disks, dual boot If you decide to go with the two-disk method, Linux installation is simple enough. When you boot from the installation disk, it asks which disk you want to install on, `hda` or `hdb` (or something similar). Your Windows software will be on the former, so pick the latter and install Linux on that.

2.1.4 Linux Partition Sizes

You should create several partitions for Linux (see Table 2.1). You could use a single partition, but your life as a sysadmin and webmaster will be easier if you create several. The advantage to having several partitions is

---

[5]Search Slashdot, `http://slashdot.org`, for DMCA. Write your congressperson.

Table 2.1 Recommended Linux Partition Sizes.

Partition	Size	Description
/boot	32MB	Where the boot files live.
/	512MB	The / partition is the base of the OS.
/home	1GB	User files live here (not /usr!). Add more space if you have a bunch of MP3s, less if this is a webserver and not a user machine.
/usr	5GB	All the programs and documentation live here.
/var	2.25GB	This is where all your web source will be and where all the logs accumulate. This needs to be big.
/tmp	256MB	This is where temporary files are stored.
/web	Optional	An optional place to put web source.
/root	Optional	The root user space.
swap		Up to two times the amount of physical memory you are ever likely to have—be generous, because you don't want to have to reformat if you add more memory later. Red Hat limits this to a max of 2GB. Since there is about 750MB left, use that. Make it bigger if you have more space, up to the limit.

that it provides a degree of protection against filling up a disk, or accidently overwriting data, or should you need to reinstall the system, losing user data. It also makes for simpler upgrades because the system software will be installed into its own partition and will leave /home alone.

Red Hat uses software called Disk Druid to partition the disk during installation. You can have the Red Hat installer automatically partition the disk if you wish.

Assuming you have a 10GB disk, we recommend making these partitions. If you have a larger disk, you could add extra partitions for such things as /web[6] and /root, and add more space in /home and /usr.

---

[6]If you do this, translate /var/www/ throughout this book to /web.

After you've backed up and partitioned, the next thing to do is insert the Linux installation CD and reboot from it. Follow the directions included with your distribution, and install everything.[7] You probably have no need for Samba, cluster software, multiple language support, etc., but you can turn this stuff off and remove it later after reading HLE. It's possible to install Linux using a very small amount of disk space (a few megabytes), but this requires some know-how, and if you really have gigabytes of disk space, it's not worth doing—it isn't Linux that'll be using it up, it's your MP3s. You do need to install the development packages so that you will have a compiler environment because some of the software that will be installed later will have to be compiled. If this is to be a user machine in addition to a webserver, install one or more of the graphical user interfaces (GUIs), KDE or Gnome.

In the best of all possible worlds, the webserver itself would be separate from the machine on which code is developed and tested, and the webserver would run only the necessary daemons to be a secure server, and all the X Windows and Gnome/KDE GUI and development code would be necessary only on the development machine.

For most of us, however, the server and development box will be one and the same, meaning that you should install everything you want on this one machine.

2.1.5 Accounts

The installer will ask you to create at least one account, the `root` account. The `root` account, or superuser, is the godlike figure of the system. Just like the real Supreme Being, as countless explanatory tales from *Paradise Lost* onward tell, it's easy to use your rootly powers for destructive purposes, and it requires care to use your superpowers only for good—that is, you can screw up your system royally if you `rm -rf *` under the # prompt.

At this time, it would be convenient to create at least one other user account for yourself and an account for any other user of the system. Other

---

[7]We debated awhile the utility of installing *everything*. You don't need it, and some of it is a security risk. But a list would be very long and would change with every release, and it's difficult to determine all the interrelated dependencies. So install everything, read the USAH, and uninstall unused programs as you learn more.

By convention, most Unix `root` accounts use the hash character (#—also known as the pound sign) in the shell prompt to make it immediately clear that this is a root shell. When Red Hat is installed, `root` has a system prompt that resembles the following (assuming you are in `root`'s home directory):

```
[root@localhost root]#
```

We use the following convention in this book: If you see the hash as the system prompt, the command that is shown is to be executed by `root`. So, when you see this:

```
#
```

it means you are logged in as `root`, and you should be careful. Don't do things as `root` that aren't necessary.

users can be added later. As a general practice, you should not log in as `root` but as a user; then `su` to a `root` account.

The Red Hat installer creates several other users for specific purposes: Apache will be owned by the `apache` user, Squid under `squid`, etc. This is part of a strategy to keep powerful daemons that run on low ports walled away from the `root` account. Ports numbered under 1024 are owned by `root`, and by accessing one of these ports, a cracker could compromise your system. Apache runs on port 80 and thus must have this sort of access, but it can be walled off from an actual `root` account by running under its own user, which has certain powers but isn't `root`.

When a non-`root` user is created in Red Hat, a default system prompt is given that resembles the following (assuming the user `jrl` is in their home directory):

```
[jrl@localhost jrl]$
```

The important distinction is that the normal, non-`root` user has as their system prompt the dollar sign ($), not the hash. By convention in this book, when you see examples of Unix commands executed and the prompt is the dollar sign, the command is to be executed by a non-`root` account. Don't be `root` for these commands!

2.1.6 Security

Red Hat now allows you to pick the services turned on during installation; in fact, it actively requires that you turn things on. Woo-hoo! This is a major security improvement and much better than in the old days (two years ago), when everything was turned on by default, and the secure user had to know to go through and turn things off.

Leave everything off except secure services that you know you will use, such as secure shell (SSH). Do not turn on FTP, Telnet, Apache (`httpd`), or any of the other services. Not to worry—when and if they are needed, they can be started later in a secure fashion. Red Hat also allows you to pick a firewall level of security during installation, with the default of medium. Choose this for now.

Once you get started or even before, read *Hacking Linux Exposed* [Hatch+ 00]. Build a firewall and implement a log-watching program and a tripwire. Investing $80 in a firewalled router (such as an SMC Barricade) is a cheap first (but not last) step toward security.

Be paranoid. They are out to get you.

2.2 BASIC UNIX

This section should provide a basic overview of Unix for someone who doesn't know anything about it. If you do, you can skip to the next chapter. If you don't, this will only be a snippet of knowledge, and you need to get a real Unix book to put by your bedside, alongside the USAH (which covers this ground most excellently), HLE, and *Unix Power Tools* [Powers+ 02] (hereafter called UPT). The goal here is not to explain every nuance of Unix but to make the first-time user aware and knowledgeable enough to ask the right questions. We hope that sometimes simply a mention is enough to get you to ask the right questions.

First, Linux is primarily used through a *command line interface*. You open a terminal shell and enter text commands on the command line—see Figure 2.1 for an example of the `ls` and `date` commands entered into a shell. You probably installed one or more of the Linux desktop graphical interfaces, Gnome or KDE. When your Linux system boots, it will probably

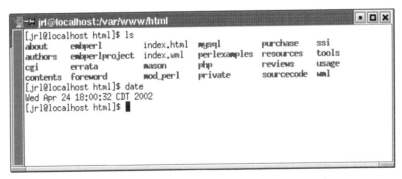

Figure 2.1   The shell command line interface

come up with a login to this graphical interface.[8] After logging in to the GUI as a normal user, you can open a terminal shell (look in the menus), work from there, and log in as root from there.

Once you open a terminal shell, you can get information on any of the commands by using the Unix man (short for manual) system. The command man man gives you information on how man works. Each of these pages gives information on the valid options for the command. Some provide examples and pointers to other, similar commands. If you don't know the name of the command, you can do man -k *commandname*. This often gets you much more information than you want, so you can pipe it through a pager such as less or more: man -k *commandname* | less.

Most Linux distributions come with some sort of desktop to give you that Apple/Windows feel, and these work fine—even better than Apple/Windows in some respects, because OS X and XP have yet to come up with anything equivalent to the multiple virtual desktops that are standard in Gnome and KDE. But since much of the work that has to be done in web site development and administration has to be done as root, it's still better to do most things in a shell through the command line. You can move files and folders (in Unix, folders are really directories) via a graphical window interface, but you typically don't want to do this as root. It's better to learn how to drive a stick—you have more control.

---

[8]Unless you have told the system to bring you up into text-shell (runlevel 3 instead of runlevel 5, found in /etc/inittab). You can always boot into nongraphical mode by editing LILO or GRUB to add either the failsafe or single command to the kernel parameters.

2.2.1 Shell

You have many choices for your shell interface. This is a *Good Thing*, because we all have different preferences. Many, if not most, people go with bash as their shell interpreter (largely because bash is the default shell when Red Hat is installed). Others prefer tcsh, a variation on the original csh. There are also zsh and ksh. You can pick and choose. If you are new to this, go with the default on your system until you know enough to have a preference.

The preferences for your shell are found in .tcshrc or .bashrc or .zshrc, and so on (use ls -a to see the normally hidden files that start with a "."). Even if you haven't created a local .tcshrc, a systemwide resource file provides global defaults. Most Unix folks pick a shell, develop an extensive customized dotfile (as these things are called—there are also dotfiles for X Windows, Gnome, KDE, SSH, and combing your hair), and just move it around from system to system. There is also a dotfile generator, which you can use to create dotfiles for many different programs until you get the hang of it (www.blackie.dk/dotfile/).

You can change the shell with the chsh command, which asks for a password.

2.2.2 Owner, Groups, Permissions, Ownership

Everything in Unix is a file, and each of the files has associated with it an *owner* and a *group*. If you do an ls -l in a directory, you might see something like Table 2.2, though it won't have column titles like those shown here.

The long listing shows that J. Random Luser (jrl) owns three files (junk.txt, foo.html, and bar.cgi) and one directory (bin) in this directory. The permissions of junk.txt are such that the owner of the file (jrl) and the group associated with the file (jrl) can read and write the file, and the rest of the world can read it. The file foo.html is a bit more private, and only jrl can alter it, though staff members may view its contents. The world cannot see it at all. The file bar.cgi appears to be an executable, and J. Random Luser can change it, staff can view it, and both staff and he can execute it.

Table 2.2 Sample Directory Listing

Permissions		Owner	Group	Size	Date	Time	Name
-rw-rw-r--	1	jrl	jrl	27	Jan 8	13:11	junk.txt
-rw-r-----	1	jrl	staff	1160	Jan 10	15:31	foo.html
-rwxr-x---	1	jrl	staff	1160	Jan 9	09:31	bar.cgi
drwxrwxr-x	9	jrl	jrl	4096	Jan 8	15:42	bin/

The ownership of a file can be changed using the chown command, and the permissions changed via chmod. A typical thing to do would be chmod a+x bar.cgi, which would change the permissions to allow all to execute it. Similarly, one could change the permissions via chmod go-r junk.txt to allow only the owner to read the file.

Old-school Unix types like to use the octal numeric mode to change file permissions, thus leading to such commands as chmod 666 foo.bar. The value 666 is an octal number representing the three permission groups: user/group/world. If the value of one of the groups is 6, the permissions are "read on, write on, execute off," represented as rw-. Therefore, 666 represents rw-rw-rw-. The value 751 would be rwxr-x--x. Other file attributes, such as the sticky bit, can be changed with these commands; use man chmod to see all the possibilities.

2.2.3 Processes

Every object in Unix is a file; everything that runs is a *process*. Some run once and quit; others run constantly in the background as *daemons*. Each process has an owner and a process ID (PID). The owner is important because that's who controls the process—J. Random Luser can't kill rootly processes, though root can kill JRL's processes. There are also subtler issues with process ownership—processes that run under root ownership are vulnerable to being cracked and allowing the cracker to gain root access (which is very bad).

Useful commands associated with processes are `ps`, which shows the processes running, and `top`, which gives an overview of the processes running. End `top` with q. There are many useful options for these programs— as usual `man` *function* is a good place to start. Another useful command is `man-k` *best guess at a useful function.*

Unix is not perfect, of course, and sometimes a process gets out of hand and must be terminated. The appropriate command for this is either `kill` or `killall`.[9] The `kill` command takes as its argument a PID gotten from `ps` or `top`, and `killall` works on a command name. Typical usage is `kill 396` or `kill -9 396` if 396 is the PID to be terminated. A `killall foo` kills all processes named `foo`. The -9 or -KILL signals indicate the severity of the action you wish to take: -1 is a gentle request, whereas -9 is termination with extreme prejudice. Do a `man 7 signal` for more details on signals.

2.2.4 PATH and Environment

When a Unix command, such as `ls`, is executed, how does Unix know where to find the `ls` program? An *environment* variable is set, called the PATH, which defines where things are looked for first. Execute the command `printenv` from a terminal shell. You'll see many environment variables, one of which is the PATH, and in that variable you should see something like `/usr/local/bin:/usr/bin:/bin:/usr/bin/X11`.[10] This says that Unix first looks in `/usr/local/bin`, then in `/usr/bin`, then in `/bin`, then in `/usr/bin/X11` for any program or command you want to execute, if you don't specify the direct path. It executes the first one it finds, so two programs of the same name could exist in different directories, and Unix would always execute the first one found in the order of the path unless explicitly told to go the other. You can alter the PATH, but the installer probably gave you an excellent beginning one, so leave it alone until you are sure you have a reason to change it.

Environment variables tell many different programs where to look to find things. For instance, what is the default editor (the variable EDITOR will tell you), where is the mail spool (MAIL), what is the default shell (SHELL), and so on? For an example of a few environment variables displayed in a shell, see Figure 2.2.

---

[9]Use with caution on Solaris.

[10]You could simply do a `printenv PATH`, but that's much less interesting.

```
jrl@localhost:/var/www/html
[jrl@localhost html]$ echo $USER
jrl
[jrl@localhost html]$ echo $PATH
/bin:/usr/bin:/usr/X11R6/bin:/usr/local/bin
[jrl@localhost html]$ echo $MAIL
/var/spool/mail/jrl
[jrl@localhost html]$
```

Figure 2.2   Environment variables

2.2.5 Commands

Next we provide a short introduction to commands we use in this book, and
we leave you to man to find out more about them. Raising your awareness
is all we can achieve here. Also, be aware that any problem you've had,
any trick you seek to accomplish has probably been tried by someone else.
USAH, UPT, and/or Google can ease your efforts.

man The first command to know is man, your friend and helper, the manual
command—that is, show the manual for this command, the options, and
typical usage. Use it. The command man man is a good place to start. Most
man pages have usage examples and further links at the bottom. You can
use man -k foo when you don't know exactly what you are looking for.

cd Change directory. It operates either on a fixed path (cd /usr/share/
misc) or on a relative path (cd bin would take you to the bin directory below your current working directory, if that directory exists). The
following are a few standard shortcuts:

- ~ is your home directory. The command cd ~/bin means go to
  /home/jrl/bin.

- . is the current directory. The command cd ./bin means go the
  directory bin below this one. The command ./configure means
  execute the configure file in the current working directory. Because
  the current directory is probably not in the PATH, if you typed
  configure at the shell prompt, Unix would first search through all the
  directories in the defined PATH, not find configure, or find a different
  one and execute that instead—the Wrong Thing. Some people put .
  in their PATH, but this is a Bad Thing for many reasons.

- .. is the directory above this one. The command cd .. means go to the next directory up. Similarly, ../.. means go two directories up.

mkdir Make a new directory. If you should decide to delete a directory, you have to use rm -rf, but this is powerful and dangerous, so be sure you know what you are doing.

pwd Print working directory (where am I?). There are many ways to have this information show up in your prompt and/or the top of your terminal shell. Do a Google search for your particular shell to find out how to do this.

ls List the files in the current directory. The options ls -l, ls -a, and ls -F are very useful.

mv Move this file. The command mv junk junk2 moves the existing file junk to junk2. There is no rename command, only mv. A useful option is mv -i for *interactive,* which prompts before overwriting another file.

rm Remove. Definitely read the man page before using this.

cp Copy.

ln Create a link (alias or shortcut in the Apple/Windows world) to another file. There are hard and soft links—read the man page.

popd Pop to another directory, remembering where you came from, so that you can pop back.

pushd Push the current directory on the stack so that you can pop back to it.

df Disk free. How much disk space is being used?

du Disk usage. How big are the files in this directory?

grep Find a string within a file. The command grep -i string *.tex finds all the occurrences of string regardless of case (-i) in any or all of the files ending with .tex (* is a *wildcard*) in the current directory. The grep command has amazing power, and it is well worth spending some time learning regular expressions to use it.[11]

locate Find all files on the computer with names matching the given string. There is also a similar command, find. The locate command

---

[11]We discuss the basics of Perl regular expressions in Chapter 4, and much of that information applies to grep.

works via a database that is created only at specific times (via the `cron` daemon, usually at night), so it may not find files that have been added since the last time the database was updated, but is very fast. The `find` command does a real-time search (which might be very slow) and has a more complicated syntax.

more Page through a file without using an editor. It also can be used to view multiple pages—for example, `locate config | more` generates pages and pages of output that normally scroll past, but when `pipe`d (the | character is a `pipe`) through `more`, the output shows up one terminal screen at a time. A similar command is `less`.

uname Basic system description. Try `uname -a`.

ifconfig, netstat What is the network doing?

chkconfig A Red Hat program that controls which daemons in `/etc/init.d` run at what point in the start-up (and shutdown) process.

which, where These commands are useful for figuring out where commands live, what a command might be aliased to, and which commands are executed first. Try it with any of the commands listed previously.

who Who's logged in to the system?

There are a few commands that we have *aliased* with various options in our `.bashrc` permanently, and you might find them useful also. For example:

```
alias ls='ls -F --color=auto'
```

This modifies the default nature of `ls` by adding some helpful information to the typical list, by using markers (`-F`) and colors in the directory listings (if you have a color xterm, links, directories, devices, etc., will all have different colors). In `bash`, all command-line arguments to the command are passed along automatically to the alias. If you simply type `ls`, you get `ls -F --color`. But if you type `ls -a -B foo*.*bar*`, the qualifiers and wildcards are passed into the alias for the plain `ls` to use as usual, in addition to the `-F --color` switches already defined.

Here are a few other useful aliases for `ls`:

```
alias ll='ls -l --color=auto'
alias l.='ls -d .[a-zA-Z0-9]* --color=auto'
```

The first alias shortens the directory in long format (show file permissions, owner, size, date, etc.) to `ll`. The second displays all files, including hidden files that begin with the period character, shows directories as entries (instead of contents) and uses color markup.

Other useful Unix staples include `sed` and `awk`, which allow one to do such useful things as replace all the occurrences of a string within many files with another string. They are much more powerful than this, but that's a start.

2.2.6 Basic Filesystem Essentials

For a complete explanation of where things go and why they go there, see www.pathname.com/fhs/. Here we give a brief list of directories that you'll probably visit and what they are. The various versions of Unix each do things slightly differently, so there are no hard-and-fast rules. By the way, looking in all these directories to see what's there is an excellent learning exercise.

/home User directories. Your directory will be under /home/your_name_goes_here.

/root The home directory of root.

/usr/bin The main executables are here. This should be in your path.

/bin Boot-level executables are here, and this should be in your path.

/usr/sbin The main superuser commands. This should be in the root path but not in a user path.

/sbin Basic boot-level superuser commands. Ditto.

/usr/lib Contains dynamic libraries and static files for the executables in /usr/bin and /usr/sbin.

/lib Contains libraries for the executables in /bin and /sbin.

/usr/src Kernel source.

/usr/local, /opt This is where optional (*local*) software is installed.

/usr/X11R6 X Windows commands and libraries.

/tmp Temporary files are stored here. In most Unices, `cron` runs a daemon that eventually deletes anything here, and some systems delete these files every time the system is rebooted.

/var/tmp/ Another place for temporary files, which will not be deleted automatically.

/var The "variable" directory. Everything here changes often.

/var/spool Mail, printer, and other spools. Mail that is sent to J. Random Luser comes to `/var/spool/mail/jrl` until J. Random transfers the mail to another directory.

/var/log Log files. These files keep track of what's gone on your system. Do a `tail -50 /var/log/maillog` to see an example, or do a `less /var/log/boot.log`. Logwatch and other tripwire security programs watch these files to see what's going on—so should you. What is written here is determined by `/etc/syslog.conf`.

/var/www Web files (this is where the action is for us in this book).

/boot Basic Linux boot files. The Linux kernel lives here. The kernel is the basic executable that runs everything else in Linux. Generally, the kernel is very stable, and the average non–power user never has to deal with it (unless you want to get into the fun business of compiling your own kernels).

/etc Systemwide configuration files. For example, Apache configuration files are under `/etc/httpd/conf/` and sendmail is under `/etc/mail/`. Studying `/etc` is an excellent start to a sysadmin education.[12]

/etc/X11 X Windows configuration files.

/etc/init.d A link to `/etc/rc.d/init.d`, and the place where the startup configuration files live. For instance, this is where you can execute `/etc/init.d/httpd status`.

/mnt Mount points for removable media (CD-ROMs, floppies). Do a `man mount`.

/dev The Unix device directory, which you will probably not have to deal with until you have some advanced problem, such as your mouse not working.

/proc The Unix process directory, which acts as an interface to the internal data structures of the kernel. Some of these are readable directories, and you can do such things as `cat /proc/uptime`. Try it and see what happens.

---

[12]One of the best sysadmin/programmers (Brian Hatch) we know learned Unix with `vi /etc/*` and learned to program in C with `man gcc`.

2.2.7 Useful Programs

Here is a list of Linux programs that we find extremely useful. A good place to find these sorts of things is `freshmeat.net`. For RPM-based distributions, another good site is `rpmfind.net`. Some of these programs are included with Red Hat and some are not.

log watch, swatch These programs watch log files, can send e-mails documenting daily occurrences, and can alert based on unusual behavior.

bk2site Turns a list of bookmarks into a set of web pages that can be browsed.

gkrellm A system monitor that keeps track of CPU, memory, the network, what's playing on your CD player, etc.

etherape, ntop Network traffic monitors.

linuxconf, webmin Configuration programs for newbie system administrators. They don't relieve the sysadmin from the responsibility of knowing what's going on, but they help. Be careful—you can overwrite important system configuration files with these programs. If you use these to alter system files, save the original elsewhere before you fire them up. Using them is also good practice for figuring out what configuration files control what and how changes affect the system. Eventually, the budding sysadmin needs to be able to configure the system by editing text files, but these are a fairly painless way to start.

CUPS A printer administration tool.

nessus A system security tool that scans your system (or someone else's) to look for security holes. **SAINT** and **SARA** are similar.

AIDE, tripwire Watch system configuration files to see if a cracker is altering them.

Privoxy Gets rid of banner ads in your browser, and controls cookies.

If you need to change your configuration after installation (and you will), Red Hat includes GUI configuration programs that save the budding system administrator from having to edit text files by hand. Among these are the following:

neat Network

sndconfig Sound card

Xconfigurator X Windows

usbview USB

mouseconfig Mouse

kbdconfig Keyboard

printtool Printer

linuxconfig System

2.3 SUMMARY

In this chapter, we've given the Linux newbie a short, intense lesson in how to get, install, and use the basics of Linux. The main purpose is to give guidance on setting up a Linux box as a webserver and to touch on the decisions that have to be made when installing a Linux operating system. We hope it wasn't too painful.

2.4 RESOURCES

Books

[Hatch+ 02] Hatch, Brian, James Lee, and George Kurtz. *Hacking Linux Exposed.* We think this is the best book on Linux security.

[McCarty 02] McCarty, Bill. *Learning Red Hat Linux.* Covers installing, configuring, and using Red Hat 7.2.

[Nemeth+ 01] Nemeth, Evi, Garth Snyder, Scott Seebass, and Trent R. Hein. *Unix System Administration Handbook.* The Bible. There is now a version of this book by a subset of the same authors specifically for Linux. We've just got our copy and haven't had a chance to look through it, but based on their previous work, we're sure it's good.

[Powers+ 02] Powers, Shelley, Jerry Peek, Tim O'Reilly, Mike Loukides, and Laurie Petrycki. *Unix Power Tools.* All the tricks.

[Siever+ 00] Siever, Ellen (Ed.), with Jessica P. Hekman, Stephen Figgins, and Stephen Spainhour. *Linux in a Nutshell: A Desktop Quick Reference, Third Edition.* A good reference for all things Linux.

[Torvalds+ 01] Torvalds, Linus, and David Diamond. *Just for Fun: The Story of an Accidental Revolutionary.*

[Welsh+ 99] Welsh, Matt, Matthias Kalle Dalheimer, Lar Kaufman, and Matthew Welsh. *Running Linux, Third Edition.* A guide to installing, configuring, and using Linux.

Web Sites

Debian: `www.debian.org/`—A popular and easy-to-maintain distribution.

Mandrake: `www.linux-mandrake.com/`—A variant of Red Hat that is very popular these days.

Red Hat: `www.redhat.com/`—Where to find Red Hat Linux.

Slackware: `www.slackware.com/`—Slackware is one of the oldest and most hard-core distributions.

SuSE: `www.suse.com/`—The most popular Linux distribution in Europe.

TurboLinux: `www.turbolinux.com/`—TurboLinux distribution.

3

Apache Web Server

3.1 INTRODUCTION

The web pages you see when you surf the Web (quit slacking, you!) are served up via the HyperText Transfer Protocol (HTTP) by an httpd daemon—the "d" at the end means *daemon,* programs that are always running in the background.[1]

Currently, Apache is the webserver of choice, and not just for Open Source bigots. As of this writing, Apache has more than 60 percent of the active site webserver market (see www.netcraft.com/survey/). Because it is so widely used, it is widely tested, and when a bug is discovered or a new Web feature is implemented, bug fixes and updates are almost instantaneous. Apache has a BSD-type Open Source license, making it attractive for both commercial and noncommercial applications. Its modular architecture makes it feasible to tailor Apache to the environment you want to serve. Examples of major sites using Apache are Amazon and Yahoo—people who know how to handle Web traffic.

Apache originated, as did many things Web,[2] as an indirect offshoot of the National Center for Supercomputing Applications (NCSA) at the University of Illinois Urbana-Champaign (UIUC).[3]

---

[1]In some distributions, the daemon is called apache instead of httpd.

[2]Tim Berners-Lee invented the World Wide Web at CERN, the European high-energy physics (HEP) laboratory. One of us is a high-energy physicist, and WWW was invented so that large HEP collaborations consisting of hundreds of scientists at dozens of locations could communicate results, data, software, and papers. The Open Source applications most of us use today, Netscape and Mozilla and Apache, originated from NCSA in one way or another.

[3]The NCSA webserver was widely used, but eventually NCSA stopped supporting it. Many people began creating patches to add functionality and fix bugs (it was Open Source, after all). Eventually, developers decided to make it a full-blown non-NCSA project called Apache because it was based on "a patchy" bit of code. There's also a good story from these origins about Mosaic, Netscape, failed dotcoms, and monopolistic rulings about software companies. But not here, not now ...

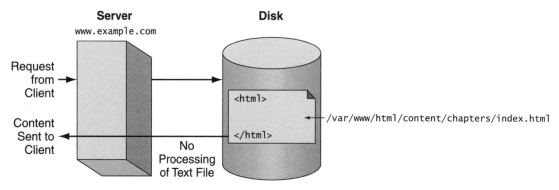

Figure 3.1 Apache explained

In this chapter, we configure Apache, set up the necessary directories for a basic Web site, and add a few simple HTML files. We assume that you already know some basic HTML; if not, see the list of suggested books at the end of this chapter. HTML is easy to learn.

3.1.1 Apache Explained

Figure 3.1 depicts what happens when a user requests a web page from the Apache webserver.

The webserver recognizes an HTTP request by the URL of the thing requested or by the filename extension. For instance, If the URL `www.example.com/content/chapter1/` were loaded into a browser, the webserver contacted (`www.example.com`) would receive a request that might look like this:[4]

```
GET /content/chapter1/ HTTP/1.0
```

The server determines that the thing requested is underneath the *document root,* a directory where the HTML files reside. For the examples in this book, that is `/var/www/html`. The text `/content/chapter1/` directs Apache to navigate to those directories underneath the document root and grab the HTML file named `index.html` (by default, the server looks for the file with this name, but this is configurable, as are most things related to Apache).

The result is that the server grabs the file `/var/www/html/content/chapter1/index.html`, which is simply a text file. It then takes the content

---

[4]This example demonstrates the simpler HTTP protocol version 1.0. It is more likely that the version used will be 1.1, but 1.0 still works, and because it is simpler, we use it here.

of this file and prepends an important piece of information called the *header*. The header tells the client how to interpret the information that is to follow. For an HTML file, the header tells the client that what follows is text, which is to be interpreted as HTML code. The header is separated from the content that follows by a blank line. Of course, webservers can dish up more than HTML these days: music, streaming video, PDF, etc.

It's an instructive exercise to view the header, blank line, and body that the server serves up, and this can be achieved without using a browser. This can be done in a shell window. (That's good to know if you are someplace that doesn't have a browser but does have a shell. This used to be more common, but now you are likely to find things the other way around.) This example connects to a server and asks for `index.html` in the directory `/content/chapter1/`:

```
$ telnet www.not_a_real_web_server.com 80
Trying 1.299.299.1
Connected to www.not_a_real_web_server.com (1.299.299.1)
Escape character is '^]'.
GET /content/chapter1/ HTTP/1.0

HTTP/1.1 200 OK
Date: Thu, 17 Jan 2002 19:57:05 GMT
Server: Acme Web Server Version 0.001b
Connection: close
Content-Type: text/html

<html>
<head>
....
```

When the server accepts the connection, it tells the client (us) so. Then we make the HTTP request:

```
GET /content/chapter1/ HTTP/1.0
```

followed by a blank line. The webserver prints out some header stuff, including the content type `text/html`, followed by a blank line, followed by the contents of the HTML file. Had a browser, instead of a Telnet session, made the same request, the browser would have taken the information in the header and then the body and rendered it appropriately. That's what browsers are programmed to do.

That's it! Not so magical once the details are known.

3.2 STARTING, STOPPING, AND RESTARTING APACHE

If you installed Linux as suggested in Chapter 2, Apache should be running when you start your machine. To check, load this URL in your browser:

http://localhost/

You should see the Apache welcome page, as shown in Figure 3.2. If not, Apache may not be running. Not a major crisis—in fact, it's a good thing if daemons such as Apache don't run unless you explicitly start them. If Apache has been running since you booted and plugged in the TCP/IP connection, other services are probably running, and you should configure

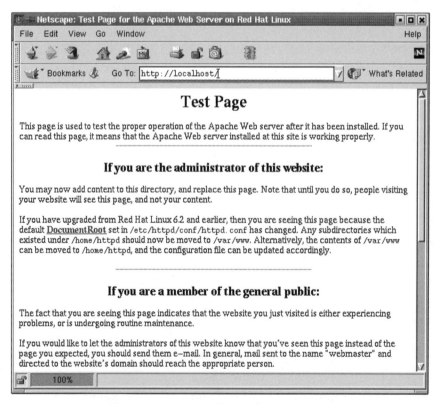

Figure 3.2   Apache welcome page

them as you wish, firewall them, or turn them off (see [Hatch+ 02]). To check whether Apache is running, try the following:

```
# ps ax | grep httpd
```

Although the program is called Apache, the daemon's name is `httpd` on Red Hat, `apache` on some others. You should see something like this:

```
1922 ?          S      0:00 /usr/sbin/httpd
1927 ?          S      0:00 /usr/sbin/httpd
1928 ?          S      0:00 /usr/sbin/httpd
1929 ?          S      0:00 /usr/sbin/httpd
1930 ?          S      0:00 /usr/sbin/httpd
1932 ?          S      0:00 /usr/sbin/httpd
1933 ?          S      0:00 /usr/sbin/httpd
1935 ?          S      0:00 /usr/sbin/httpd
1937 ?          S      0:00 /usr/sbin/httpd
```

Several copies of the server are running, so Apache can process more than one request at a time.

If you don't see a number of `httpd` PIDs, start the server as follows:

```
# /etc/init.d/httpd start
```

In addition to using the `ps` command, you can check the status of your server by executing the following command:

```
# /etc/init.d/httpd status
```

The output of this command should resemble this:[5]

```
httpd (pid 1937 1935 1933 1932 1930
          1929 1928 1927 1922) is running...
```

If you didn't get this sort of result, or you got an error message, review the logs in `/var/log/httpd` for error messages, specifically `error_log`, and read the `man` page (`man httpd`, *not* `man apache`). Unfortunately, the number of possible errors is great, and we can't possibly cover all of them—the logs are key to narrowing down the problem.

If `httpd` is running, and you didn't see the welcome page when you loaded `http://localhost/`, you have a problem.

---

[5]Reformatted to fit the page. We often have to do this, so don't sweat small differences like this.

First, try restarting it. There are several ways to do this—the easiest is to use the provided start-up script:

```
# /etc/init.d/httpd stop
# /etc/init.d/httpd start
```

Also good to know is this:

```
# /etc/init.d/httpd help
```

The option `help` is not a defined option, but if you pass an invalid option to /etc/init.d/httpd, it will tell you all the valid ones.

You can also do this—it sends the USR1 signal to all occurrences of httpd, making the daemon reload the configuration file:

```
# /etc/init.d/httpd graceful
```

or:

```
# killall -USR1 httpd
```

Killall may not be installed on your system. If it isn't, consider finding it and installing it; it's invaluable. It saves the step of finding the process ID and passing that to the `kill` command. The parameter USR1 (man `kill` and man `signal`) is the graceful way to reload a process—it allows the process and its children to exit after serving existing requests before starting again. If all else fails, there's always `kill -9`.

N   The gentlest way to restart apache is to use the **graceful** option to the start-up script. Therefore, hereafter when we need to restart the server (usually to reread the configuration file), we will execute the following command:

```
# /etc/init.d/httpd graceful
```

If all this doesn't work, you may need to adopt sterner measures. See the Apache documents at httpd.apache.org/docs/. The Linux Documentation Project at www.linuxdoc.org/ is another excellent place to waste a few hours. Another excellent way to figure out how to fix errors, or to find a support group to commiserate with, is to paste the error (enclosed in quotes) into Google or Google's group interface.

Once you have Apache running, make sure it starts at boot. Execute chkconfig:

```
# chkconfig --list httpd
httpd   0:off  1:off  2:off  3:on   4:on   5:on   6:off
```

If you do not see output indicating that 3, 4, and 5 are on, turn them on:

```
# chkconfig httpd on
# chkconfig --list httpd
httpd   0:off  1:off  2:off  3:on   4:on   5:on   6:off
```

Next time you reboot the machine (`shutdown -r now` as `root` or with `sudo`), check that `httpd` starts with `ps` or `/etc/init.d/httpd status`.

3.3 CONFIGURATION

Apache was designed to be modular, so you can run as lean, or as bloated, a webserver as you like. We discuss the basic configuration and some minor tweaks; all the directives are described at `httpd.apache.org/docs/mod/directives.html`, but during your Linux installation, the documents were placed in `/var/www/html/manual/mod/directives.html`. You can reach them via the link on the default web page (for the time being, anyway, because we will be moving these documents later): `http://localhost/manual/mod/directives.html`.

3.3.1 Modifying the Default Configuration

Apache's configuration file is `/etc/httpd/conf/httpd.conf`. We'll start with the default configuration file from Apache version 1.3.24.[6] There are many comments in `httpd.conf`; read them! This is a great way to get a feel for how the Apache configuration file works. Most of it you'll leave unchanged, but the comments will familiarize you with the available capabilities.

First, change the following:

```
ServerAdmin root@webserver.example.com
```

to:

```
ServerAdmin webmaster@example.com
```

or whoever you want to get all the comments (and complaints) about your web site. You may want `joe_user@example.com` to be your e-mail address or, more preferably, a webmaster e-mail alias. It should be someone who

---

[6]Configuration files evolve over time, so don't worry too much if this stuff isn't exactly the same—it probably won't be. By the way, as of this writing, 1.3.24 was the latest Red Hat version, but 1.3.27 had already been released, and version 2.0 was in beta.

checks e-mail frequently, for some value of frequent proportional to how often people look at your web site.

Apache logs every hit to the webserver (see the section on log files later in this chapter). Some of the information that can be written to the log includes the following:

- The client (Web surfer) IP address
- The date
- The URI requested (all the stuff after `www.example.com/`)
- The referer[7]—the web page the client was at when they clicked the link to take them to our web page
- The user agent (the browser the client is using)

There are various predefined CustomLog options, logging more or less information. The default logged in `/var/log/httpd/` includes some of this information (the client IP address, the date, and a few others). Until your site is running smoothly (and maybe even after), you'll want more information, so use the format that includes the most information. Change the following:

```
CustomLog /var/log/httpd/logs/access_log common
```

to:

```
CustomLog /var/log/httpd/logs/access_log combined
```

Other options include

```
CustomLog /var/log/httpd/logs/access_log agent
CustomLog /var/log/httpd/logs/access_log referer
```

But the `combined` format includes this information, as you might expect from the name. Using combinations of these options, you can customize your logging experience.

---

[7]Yes, it's misspelled—it was misspelled in the original spec, and we continue to do so in honor of our forefathers. Or maybe because it's just too much work to change all the old documents.

3.4 SECURING APACHE

As we go through the book, we discuss security issues involved with giving people access to a low port on your machine, but we can't go into all the details—that would result in an almost 600-page book *Hacking Linux Exposed* [Hatch+ 02].

Most of the following configuration directives are optional; you can do as you wish for your setup, but you should be aware of the choices you're making. Remember, no decision is also a decision.

3.4.1 Set User and Group

Make sure the user and group are set to:

```
User apache
Group apache
```

The user and group could be `apache` or `bozo` or whatever. The important thing is that Apache doesn't run as `root`, which, if Apache were cracked, could allow someone to crack your box from the root Apache account (this is called *rooting your box* and is as bad as it gets). Red Hat defaults to `apache`. You could instead create a new user with `useradd`, with a locked account to run Apache, if you wish. For now, we recommend that you stay with the default.[8]

3.4.2 Remove Online Manuals

If you did the default Red Hat install (as suggested in Chapter 2), the Apache manuals were installed in the `html` directory `/var/www/html/manual/`, which can be accessed via `file:///var/www/html/manual/` or `http://localhost/manual/`, or `www.your_web_site.com/manual/`.

If you leave these on your machine, a cracker could gain information about your machine and installation (such as the server version) by simply hitting this directory. It's a good idea to move the manuals someplace out of the web path:

```
# mv /var/www/html/manual /usr/doc/apache-1.3.24/
```

---

[8]You might notice that if you do a `ps aux | grep httpd`, the first process listed is owned by `root`—this process binds the low port and spawns the `apache`-owned processes that actually handle the `httpd` requests.

Now you have the manual available to you (put the URL `file:///usr/doc/apache-1.3.24/` in your browser), but it will not be served by Apache to any would-be cracker.

3.4.3 Consider Allowing Access to Local Documentation

Red Hat defines the following by default:

```
Alias /doc/ /usr/share/doc/
<Location /doc>
  order deny,allow
  deny from all
  allow from localhost .localdomain
  Options Indexes FollowSymLinks
</Location>
```

This directive allows access to the local documentation in `/usr/share/doc`. Even though this directive allows access to these files only from `localhost` and `.localdomain`, we suggest you don't allow Apache to serve up these documents, so comment out this directive.

3.4.4 Don't Allow `public_html` Web Sites (Unless You Want To)

The `mod_user` module allows users to serve Web content without having access to the main web directory tree. For example, the user `jrl` could create a directory called `public_html` in his home directory, which would be available at the URL `http://servername/~jrl/`.

You may want to consider whether to allow users (if you have any) to create these `public_html` sites. Nothing is inherently wrong with allowing `public_html`, but it should be something you decide to allow rather than just letting it happen by default. Quite a few directives are involved in the configuration of this feature, but if you locate the line:

```
UserDir public_html
```

and modify it as follows:

```
UserDir disabled
```

this feature is turned off.

3.4.5 .htaccess

You can allow access control of individual directories with the following configuration module:

```
AccessFileName .htaccess
<Files ~ "^\.ht">
    Order allow,deny
    Deny from all
</Files>
```

The `AccessFileName` directive defines the name of the file Apache looks at to determine whether the client can view your web page or other parts of your site. The `Files` directive says that files beginning with `.ht` can't be seen by anyone even if they type the filename into their browser. `Order` and `Deny` determine how access is controlled. Sequence is important; the last command takes precedent. The rule here is to deny everything except that specifically allowed, a good rule of thumb. More on `.htaccess` later.

3.4.6 Remove server-status and server-info

The following directives allow clients to find out information about your machine and server. There's no reason to give crackers any more information than necessary. Comment this out for now:

```
#<Location /server-status>
#    SetHandler server-status
#    Order deny,allow
#    Deny from all
#    Allow from .your_domain.com
#</Location>
```

and this:

```
#<Location /server-info>
#    SetHandler server-info
#    Order deny,allow
#    Deny from all
#    Allow from .your_domain.com
#</Location>
```

If you decide to allow this information to be given out (perhaps for debugging from a remote site), change `.your_domain.com` to the specific sites you want to have access.

Disallow Symbolic Links

Allowing symbolic links from within your webserver document tree to other directories can cause content control problems. We suggest that you do not allow symbolic links unless you have to.[9] To disallow symbolic links, be sure that the `Options` directives do not include `FollowSymLinks`.

Do Not Allow Directory Indexes

If you add `Indexes` to the `Options` directive, clients can access directory listings if they type in a directory with no `index.html`—for example, `www.example.com/directory/`. This is generally a bad idea because it lets people look at the directory structure, perhaps to see files that you didn't want served up—`.htaccess` files, old versions, backups. Better to let them see only the files that you decided to serve up via the web page. Be sure `Indexes` is not part of your `Options` directive.

Don't Be a Proxy Server Unless You Want to Be

If you don't want to be a proxy server (if you don't know what this means, you don't want to be a proxy server), make sure the following sections are commented out:

```
#LoadModule proxy_module        modules/libproxy.so
```

and:

```
#AddModule mod_proxy.c
```

and:

```
#<IfModule mod_proxy.c>
#ProxyRequests On
#
#<Directory proxy:*>
#     Order deny,allow
#     Deny from all
#     Allow from .your_domain.com
#</Directory>

#
# Enable/disable the handling of HTTP/1.1 "Via:" headers.
```

---

[9]Symbolic links are good for making links to large files instead of having multiple copies, but bad because J. Random Luser could make a link to a sensitive file—for instance, `/etc/passwd`. Disk space is cheap. Make copies.

```
# ("Full" adds the server version; "Block" removes
# all outgoing Via: headers)
# Set to one of: Off | On | Full | Block
#
#ProxyVia On

#
# To enable the cache as well, edit and uncomment
# the following lines:
# (no caching without CacheRoot)
#
#CacheRoot "/var/cache/httpd"
#CacheSize 5
#CacheGcInterval 4
#CacheMaxExpire 24
#CacheLastModifiedFactor 0.1
#CacheDefaultExpire 1
#NoCache a_domain.com another_domain.edu joes.garage_sale.com

#</IfModule>
```

Disable CGI Programs

We will talk more about CGI later, but for now, disable any CGI scripts that were shipped with Apache, as follows:

```
# chmod -x /var/www/cgi-bin/*
```

Better yet, remove them:

```
# rm -rf /var/www/cgi-bin/*
```

And don't download CGI scripts from the Web. Whether they are malicious or simply badly written, CGI scripts are an excellent way to get your system cracked. In Chapter 7, you'll learn to write your own scripts and how to avoid common problems with them, so that even if you do use a script from someplace such as the Comprehensive Perl Archive Network (CPAN) at www.cpan.org, you can vet it for security.

Reload the Configuration File

Now that we are finished securing Apache, let's reload the configuration file as follows:

```
# /etc/init.d/httpd graceful
```

3.5 CREATE THE WEB SITE

The best way to learn is by doing, so you'll build an example web site on your machine as we go along. After you're done, you'll have installed and configured the sections you're interested in, and you can use this as a model for your own system, then delete it when you're confident you understand what's going on. This way, you can practice cgi-bin, mod_perl, PHP, dynamic web content, etc., in the privacy of your own home before you unleash your server on the World (Wide Web).

There are two approaches you can take to experiment with the examples in this book: Either download the entire web site, including all of the examples, or you can create the examples yourself using your favorite editor.[10]

3.5.1 Downloading the Examples

If you follow the lazy approach to programming, you understand the importance of copy-paste. If you choose to download all the examples, go to www.opensourcewebbook.com/sourcecode/. Follow the instructions on how to obtain a username/password. You will need the password to download the source and view all the examples. Once you are ready, click the link for source.tar.gz and enter the username/password. Save the tarball in a convenient place, say in /tmp.

Now, as root, execute the following commands:

```
# mv /var/www /var/www.old
# mkdir /var/www
# chown jrl /var/www
# cd /var/www
# tar xzvf /tmp/source.tar.gz
# find . -exec chown jrl { }\;
```

First, the web site that came with Red Hat is moved to /var/www.old. Then, a new directory is made for the downloaded source, and this new directory is modified to be owned by jrl (select a user that you created

---

[10]Microsoft Word and its ilk are not suitable for much of the editing you will do in this book. These graphical editors use a nonstandard character set and insert characters that break configuration files, which need to be plain ASCII. They are also the source of most of the screwed-up text you see on web pages and newsgroups. Use something else—emacs, vi.

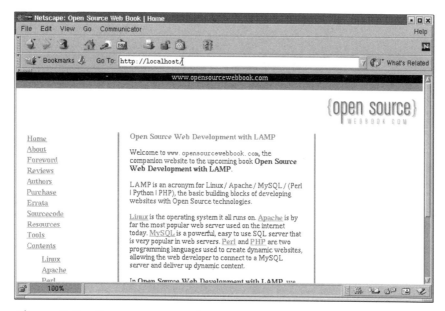

Figure 3.3   Screen capture from `www.opensourcewebbook.com`

on your machine in place of our favorite user, `jrl`). Then, the source is untarred in the new directory. And finally, all files in the new directory are changed to be owned by `jrl` (again, select an appropriate user on your machine).

Now, you are ready to rock with the new web site. To see whether everything worked, point your browser to `http://localhost/`. It should resemble `www.opensourcewebbook.com/`, which is shown in Figure 3.3.

Recall that when the location `http://www.localhost/` is loaded in the browser, the server will locate a file named `index.html` in the document root (remember, that is the directory under which all the HTML files are found; in this case, `/var/www/html`). This default name, `index.html`, is configurable in the Apache configuration file (see the `DirectoryIndex` directive in `httpd.conf`). Therefore, the file requested is `/var/www/html/index.html`, and if you look at that file's contents, you will see the HTML that builds Figure 3.3.

Look in the directory `/var/www`. You will see several files and many directories—that is the source for all the examples in this book, and you will study them all in short order.

3.5.2 Creating Them Yourself

If you choose not to download all the examples as we have just shown (are you sure about that?) and would rather create each example as it is discussed, you can either type them all in or download them from the web site one at a time. The source for all the programs in this book is available from www.opensourcewebbook.com/contents. When it is time to experiment, you can download the example from there, save it into the appropriate directory, and experiment with it at that time.

If you are going this route, let's start with a simple example. First, create an HTML file in /var/www/html/index.html. Place the following text in index.html:

```
<!DOCTYPE HTML PUBLIC "-//W3C//DTD HTML 4.0 Transitional//EN"
 "http://www.w3.org/TR/REC-html40/loose.dtd">
<html>
<head>
</head>
<body>
hello, world
</body>
</html>
```

Set the permissions so that you can write to the file and the rest of the world can read it; if the file and directory are not world readable, others won't have permission to view the page in their browser. It's a good idea to view your web pages from a different machine (and using different browsers) to catch this sort of error.

```
$ chmod a+r /var/www/html/index.html
```

The first two lines of our example, starting with <!DOCTYPE and continuing to .dtd">, contain the *doctype,* which is required for the page to pass strict HTML muster. This page does. However, having a doctype in all our examples seems a bit cluttered (all browsers will render the page without it), so we drop it in the rest of our examples. An excellent place to vet HTML code can be found at www.validator.w3.org.

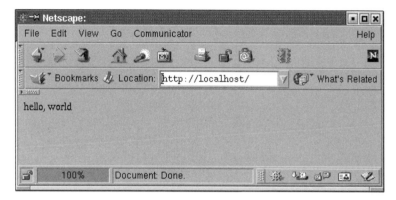

Figure 3.4 Hello, world

Reload your browser (Shift-Reload in Netscape and Mozilla to clear the cache and reload from scratch) with `http://localhost/`. You should see Figure 3.4.

Now, we will do something that is more complicated. For this, go to `www.opensourcewebbook.com/`. As we saw, this page is shown in Figure 3.3. View the document source for this file by selecting View Page Source (or something similar) from one of the menus in your browser (some browsers allow you to do the same using the right mouse button). Copy all the source that you see to `/var/www/html/index.html`. Reloading `http://localhost/` should display a page similar to Figure 3.3. However, you will notice that the logo is broken—the image file for that logo does not (yet) exist on your machine. To copy this logo, go to `www.opensourcewebbook.com`, hover the mouse over the logo in the top right corner of the page, and, using the right mouse button, save the image to `/var/www/icons/logo.gif` (be sure the image file is world readable). Reloading `http://localhost/` now shows the image displayed on the page.

Creating web pages is as simple as creating directories and `.html` files. Creating *good* web pages is another matter—for that, you need a good eye for design in addition to simple geek skills such as writing markup language. For instance, `www.opensourcewebbook.com` was designed by a graphic artist,[11] not a geek.[12]

---

[11] Created by the fine folks at BDGI (`www.bdgi.com`).

[12] To see an example of a page that a geek would design, see `www.bware.org`.

3.6 APACHE LOG FILES

Apache keeps detailed logs of accesses to your web site, errors, and more. The Apache logs are located at `/var/log/httpd/access_log` and `/var/log/httpd/error_log`. These locations are configurable in `httpd.conf`.

It's a good idea to have a log monitor program running, such as `swatch` or `logwatch`, to keep an eye on these files for security violations and problems (see `www.logwatch.org`). It's also a good idea to rotate them regularly via `logrotate`, because they'll get big otherwise.

Of course, the most important use of the logs is to look at them when there is a problem to figure out what went wrong.

An `access_log` entry might look like this:

```
192.168.1.12 - - [21/May/2001:14:10:05 -0600]
                "GET / HTTP/1.0" 200 43
"http://www.onsight.com/" "Mozilla/4.77 [en]
        (X11; U; Linux 2.4.2-2 i686; Nav)"
```

Earlier in the chapter, we discussed how to select the information that is displayed in the Apache log file (we suggested the `combined` output). This log selection displays the previous information. Most of these entries should be clear: the IP address of the requestor, the date and time of the request, the browser used (though clever programs such as Opera let you tell the server anything you want, and you can define this to be anything you want if you change the headers and recompile Mozilla), the language (`[en]`), and some system details of the requestor. `"GET / HTTP/1.0" 200 43` means an HTTP request, no errors (`200`), and 43 bytes were sent. (A list of errors can be found at `www.ietf.org/rfc/rfc2616.txt`.)

3.6.1 Access Control with `.htaccess`

Earlier we discussed how to enable `.htaccess` files in your configuration. Now we'll show you how they're used. This is useful for restricting access to certain portions of your web site, either by allowing access only from specific IP addresses or domains or by password control. In `httpd.conf`, look for the line `Directory /var/www/html` (or whatever the default directory is). There you will see:

```
AllowOverride    None
```

Change this to:

```
AllowOverride    AuthConfig
```

This change tells the server to change its behavior from allowing anyone to connect to allowing only those clients whose attributes match those in an authorization file to connect to the files in that directory.

Make sure the .htaccess filename definition is uncommented. You could change the name of the .htaccess file via this directive:

```
AccessFileName .htaccess
```

We mentioned this directive before, but it deserves mentioning again. Since we use the file .htaccess to control access, make sure the htaccess directive is uncommented (see Section 3.4.5)—it denies serving any file whose name begins with .ht, meaning that clients can't look at your .htaccess file to figure out what that file is and who you allow to look at this directory. Now restart the server:

```
# /etc/init.d/httpd graceful
```

To see how .htaccess works, create a directory for some private information:

```
$ cd /var/www/html
$ mkdir private
$ chmod a+rx private
$ cd private
```

And create a simple index.html file (remember to make it readable with chmod a+r index.html):

```
<html>
<head>
<title>
My Private Directory
</title>
</head>
<body>
Congratulations!  You now have access to my private directory!
</body>
</html>
```

Now, create a password file. It's convenient and tempting to put it in the same directory and call it something like .htpasswd. **Don't.** Place it outside the document tree. If someone were to get access to this directory because of a server misconfiguration (hey, it happens—the configuration file is big and mistakes do happen), you wouldn't want them to have access to your password files (even though the passwords are encrypted), especially because many people tend to use the same passwords for many different purposes. This is a very bad idea, so not only do you as a sysadmin and webmaster want to advocate good habits, you want to defend against bad ones.

```
$ mkdir /var/www/misc
$ chmod a+rx /var/www/misc
$ cd /var/www/misc
```

Create a password file:

```
$ htpasswd -bc private.passwords neo anderson
Adding password for user neo
```

The option -b means we are supplying the password (anderson) on the command line, and -c means create the file. To add new users, leave off the -c.[13]

```
$ htpasswd -b private.passwords morpheus sleeps
```

Create the .htaccess file in the /private directory. This is not the password file but the file that points to the passwords.

```
$ cd /var/www/html/private
$ vi .htaccess
```

The file .htaccess has this in it:

```
AuthName "My Private Area"
AuthType Basic
AuthUserFile /var/www/misc/private.passwords
AuthGroupFile /dev/null

require valid-user
```

So when you point your browser to http://localhost/private/ or www.opensourcewebbook.com/private, you should see Figure 3.5. To get in, enter the username/password neo/anderson, as shown in Figure 3.6, and you should see Figure 3.7.

There's no encryption when you use passwords like this—the passwords go over the network in the clear (to be exact, the passwords are encoded,

---

[13] As always, man htpasswd is recommended before you do this stuff—if we told you to, you wouldn't do cd / ; rm -rf *, would you? Even if everybody else was doing it?

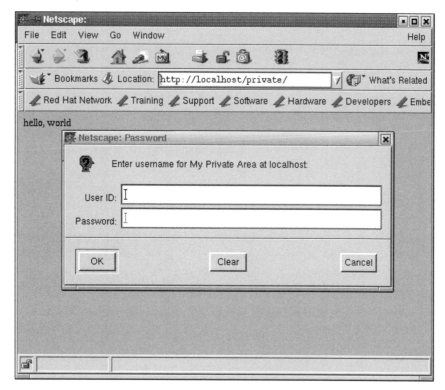

Figure 3.5 Login

then sent in the clear, but the encoded passwords are easily decoded if a cracker knows how to decode them, and they *do* know how to decode them), which as you might imagine, is not an optimal configuration. Be aware that doing so makes you vulnerable to password sniffing. If you do use this, don't use the same password as your Linux login, and be aware of your vulnerabilities. You can monitor access to these directories with your log monitoring program if you desire. You can use HTTPS to have secure communications for this kind of thing, but that is (for now) beyond our scope.

You can also do simple IP verification by putting the following in your `.htaccess` file:

```
Order deny,allow
Deny from all
Allow from 192.168.1.100
Allow from 10.0.1.0
Allow from 127.0.0.1
```

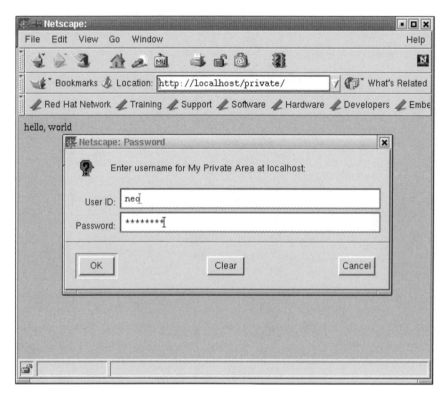

Figure 3.6   Username, password

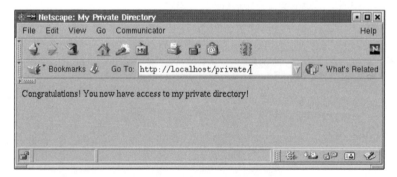

Figure 3.7   Access granted

In the preceding example, the first two IP addresses are special local networks. Although most IP addresses are assigned by ICANN and distributed by DNS, the 192.168 and 10.0 IP subnets are not unique and are used for internal networks behind a firewall. The third IP address, `127.0.0.1`, is a special IP address, that of `localhost`. Everyone's computer assigns this IP to itself, in addition to any external IP address. If you point your web browser to `localhost` or `127.0.0.1`, it will serve up the default page of the local Apache host. Your `localhost` is not the same as the fellow in the next cubicle, though.

You can combine passwords and IP verification for additional security.

3.7 SUMMARY

These are the basics of using the Apache Web server. Apache is a versatile, highly configurable program, capable of doing everything from serving up pictures of your dog to running the largest Web businesses in existence, so as you might imagine, we haven't covered everything here. But it's a start and (we hope) 80 percent of the way there.

3.8 RESOURCES

Books

[Aulds 00] Aulds, Charles. *Linux Apache Web Server Administration (Linux Library).*

[Engelschall 01] Engelschall, Ralf S. *Apache Desktop Reference.*

[Hatch+ 02] Hatch, Brian, James Lee, and George Kurtz. *Hacking Linux Exposed, Second Edition.*

[Laurie+ 02] Laurie, Ben, Peter Laurie, and Robert Denn (editors). *Apache: The Definitive Guide.*

[Stein 97] Stein, Lincoln D. *How to Set Up and Maintain a Web Site, Second Edition.*

[Wainwright 02] Peter, Wainwright. *Professional Apache.*

HTML Books

[Musciano+ 02] Musciano, Chuck, and Bill Kennedy. *HTML and XHTML: The Definitive Guide, Fourth Edition.*

[Niederst 02] Niederst, Jennifer. *HTML Pocket Reference, Second Edition.*

[Raggett+ 97] Raggett, Dave, et al. *Raggett on HTML 4, Second Edition.*

Web Sites

Apache: `http://www.apache.org/`

Apache downloads: `httpd.apache.org/dist/httpd/`

Apache information: `httpd.apache.org/ABOUT_APACHE.html`

Apache webserver: `httpd.apache.org/`

Apache webserver documents: `httpd.apache.org/docs/`

HTML W3C home page: `www.w3.org/MarkUp/`

Netcraft survey: `www.netcraft.com/survey/`

This book: `www.opensourcewebbook.com/`

4
Perl

4.1 INTRODUCTION

The fourth letter in the LAMP acronym stands for Perl (along with the other Ps). Although you don't *have* to understand any Perl to build a web site, it helps (Python and PHP work too). In many examples that follow throughout this book, we use the basics of Perl extensively.

The purpose of this chapter is to familiarize the Perl novice with the basics. If you already know a C-like language, much of this will be familiar. If not, this chapter should introduce you to the concepts we use throughout the rest of the book. If you already know Perl, good for you! But this will be a rehash—feel free to move on.

Perl has become a popular all-purpose programming language because of its power and ease of use. Once you have mastered the language rules, you can do a lot with a little. One of the mottoes of Perl is *Perl Makes Easy Tasks Easy and Hard Tasks Possible.* Another is *There's More Than One Way To Do It*—TMTOWTDI, pronounced "Tim-Toe-Di."

Perl originated as a text processing language.[1] Larry Wall, the creator, needed a language to manage and manipulate a database of text files. He designed Perl to be a language with built-in text processing by incorporating regular expressions and providing a number of text processing functions. There are and have been many other text processing languages: REXX, awk, sed, etc. But Perl has struck a chord, and not only with Open Source developers—it has been ported to all major operating systems and many minor ones. It has been (lovingly) referred to as the duct tape that holds the Internet together. One of the happy results of the spread of Perl is

---

[1]There are histories of Perl at www.perl.org/press/history.html and history.perl.org.

its portability; if created properly, Perl scripts will run on many operating systems with only minor changes, if any.

The name Perl is an uncapitalized acronym for Practical Extraction and Report Language, or Pathologically Eclectic Rubbish Lister— TMTOWTDI.

As it evolved, Perl grew (some would say mutated) from a text processing language into a powerful, multipurpose object-oriented programming language used to solve all kinds of real-world problems: system administration, network programming, database management, and CGI programming.

Perl's syntax is C-like.[2] Its operators, constructs, and lexical conventions are similar to those of C. However, some of the language rules, especially regular expressions, can be a bit overwhelming at first. It's common for eyes to cross a bit when looking at one of the ubiquitous strings of punctuation representing a regular expression: `/^(?:To:)\s*(\S*)$/`—not comic strip expletives, but the coin of the Perl realm. However, by concentrating on the basic rules, you can quickly learn to use the language to solve real problems—this is the beauty of the language. Of course, then you are suckered in and have become yet another Perl acolyte.

We give only a basic overview here; the Camel Book [Wall+ 00] is the bible for Perl. Perl is the big, fat, top-of-the-line Swiss Army knife. We don't talk about all the nifty gadgets, only the major functionality. We can't teach you programming in this short chapter, so this is a high-level introduction. Again, we assume you know the basics of programming: variables, flow constructs (`if` statements, `while` loops), functions, reading from and writing to files, and so on.

4.2 PERL DOCUMENTATION

A wealth of information is available for Perl both on your Linux machine and online. There are several `man` pages:

```
$ man perl
$ man perlop
$ man perlsyn
```

---

[2]Collectively, the trinity of C, C++, and Java are referred to as *C-like* languages.

A program called `perldoc`:

```
$ perldoc perldoc
$ perldoc -f print
```

And a Web site: `www.perldoc.com/`. There are also newsgroups, CPAN at `www.perl.com` and big, fat Perl books, should these not suffice.

4.3 PERL SYNTAX RULES

First, the basic Perl syntax rules. Hang in there; although there are a plethora of `hello, world`'s here, the somewhat unnerving friendliness and patience engendered by repeating this mantra will serve you well later when things get more involved.

4.3.1 A First Perl Program—`hello, world`

As always, the best way to learn is by doing. For example, here is the ever popular `print hello, world` program:

```
#! /usr/bin/perl -w
# file: hello.pl

print "hello, world!\n";
```

The first line is a shell directive (also known as the *hash/bang* or *shebang*). This line informs the shell that this script uses `/usr/bin/perl`. Your distribution might have it in a different place, `/usr/local/bin/perl`, for example.[3] The -w switch causes Perl to print warnings to the standard error (`stderr`) output.[4] The -w switch is recommended when you are developing Perl scripts, because it is possible to write programs that are syntactically correct but logically incorrect because of typos or just bad programming.

The next line, which begins with #, is a comment. Comments extend from the first # to the end of line. The print statement:

```
print "hello, world!\n";
```

---

[3]Remember that `which`, `where`, `find`, and `locate` are your friends!

[4]The terms `stdout`, `stdin`, and `stderr` are Unix file descriptors that, by default, point to the terminal (tty) you ran the program from but can be piped to a file or `/dev/null`. You can also `cat` the output to a file with the ">" redirection.

executes the built-in `print()` function, which writes text to standard output (`stdout`). The "\n" is the newline character and prints a carriage return to standard output.

Put the preceding text in a `hello.pl` text file and make it executable.

```
$ chmod a+x hello.pl
```

To execute it, type

```
$ ./hello.pl
```

The "./" tells the shell to execute the file in this directory (".") and not look for it in your PATH. If all goes as expected, you'll see this wonderfully reassuring message:

```
hello, world!
```

You may notice a few other things about the language from this example.

- Perl is free format—whitespace can be scattered about to make code more readable, as much or as little as you like.
- All statements must end in a semicolon (";") except the first line, which is not really a Perl statement but a shell escape to execute Perl.
- Variables do not have to be declared but can be.
- The Perl scripts are stored as text files. When executed (`$ ./hello.pl`), the source text file is first compiled into *byte code,* an intermediate form, not text and not binary. Perl then interprets the byte code, executing it. Therefore, each time a Perl script is executed, it is compiled and then interpreted (this is not the place to go into the compiled versus interpreted languages). This leads to the question, Is there a Perl compiler that compiles the Perl script into binary form? The answer is, Yes, but ... The Perl compiler is still in beta test, and it doesn't always work very well. Feel free to try it—`perlcc`.
- Built-in functions, such as `print()` can be invoked with or without parentheses. In the preceding, we are invoking `print()` without parentheses, but we could if we wanted to or needed to.

4.3.2 Another Example

This program adds two numbers:

```
#! /usr/bin/perl -w
# file: simpleadd.pl
```

```
$a = 5;
$b = 6;
$c = $a + $b;

print "\$c is now: $c\n";
```

$a, $b, and $c are examples of scalar variables (more on these later). Note that unlike other C-like languages, in Perl you don't have to explicitly declare them as variables (but you could if you wanted to, and we will in the next section)—we simply use them, and voilà! They are created for us.

Put this into the file simpleadd.pl and execute it as earlier:

```
$ ./simpleadd.pl
$c is now 11
```

Because in this example we want the dollar sign to be printed for pedantic purposes, the output starts with $c. The dollar sign is *escaped* in the string (escaped means "preceded by the backslash character so that the print statement knows to print the character literally instead of using it in its regular Perl use"):

```
print "\$c is now: $c\n";
```

We'll talk more about this soon.

4.3.3 Declaring Variables with use strict;

Perl, as a scripting language, has looser rules than other "real" programming languages like C and Java. One such quality is the ability to create variables by simply using them, much as in shell programming. Still, it is considered good style to declare them. Doing so can preclude the silly typo problems that everyone is likely to incur from time to time:

```
$food = ´pizza´;
print "I am hungry for $foo!\n";
```

The variable $food is assigned, but $foo will be printed. Perl allows this without a syntax error because neither variable has to be declared.

The output of the program will be "I am hungry for !" because $foo is undeclared and has no value. Perl will warn about this sort of thing if the -w flag is used, as it should be.

Another alternative to this situation is to force declaration of all variables before use, just as in the more strict, prescriptive compiled languages. For example:

```
use strict;
```

With this, variables must be declared before use, and this is done with the my() function as follows:

```
my $a;
my $b;
```

Variables can be declared and initialized at the same time:

```
my $a = 5;
my $b = 6;
```

More than one variable can be declared at the same time (the parentheses are required):

```
my($a, $b, $c);
```

If we do a use strict; and declare the variables, the earlier food example becomes:

```
use strict;

my $food = 'pizza';
print "I am hungry for $foo!\n";
```

Since $foo is not declared with my(), the use of $foo returns a syntax error, forcing the correction of the typo before the program can execute.

We recommend use strict;—it catches many common errors, requires a more disciplined programming mind-set, and is in general just good practice—so the examples from this point on use it. However, TMTOWTDI.

The previous simple example becomes:

```
#! /usr/bin/perl -w
# file: simpleadd.pl

use strict;

my $a = 5;
my $b = 6;
my $c = $a + $b;

print "\$c is now: $c\n";
```

4.3.4 Variables

Perl has several types of variables. We discuss the major ones.[5]

Scalar Variables

A scalar variable is a variable that holds a single value.

- It can hold the value of a number (integer or floating) or a string (from zero characters to enough characters to consume your virtual memory).[6]
- The value can change over time, and it can change type (for example, it can change from an integer to a float to a string and back to an integer)
- Numeric literals are in the following format:
  - Integers:
    * Decimal: 10   −2884   2_248_188   The underscore can be used to chunk numbers for ease of reading, but don't use the usual comma format, as in 2,248,188, because that means something completely different.
    * Octal: 037   04214
    * Hexadecimal: 0x25   0xaB80
  - Floats:
    * Standard: 7.1   .8   9.
    * Scientific: 3.4E−34   −8.023e43

- String literals can be created with either single quotes or double quotes:
  - Single quotes: ´hello, world´
  - Double quotes (needed to evaluate variables and special characters): "hello, world\n", "\$c is now $c\n"

---

[5]Perl has several minor data types, including *loop labels*, *directory handles*, and *formats;* see the Camel Book [Wall+ 00] for details.

[6]It can also hold the value of a reference, but that's beyond the scope of this book.

One must take care with quotes and scalar variables in Perl.

First, there is a difference between a tick (´) and a backtick (`), and a double quote ("). Mostly, we use ticks and double quotes—the backtick has a special purpose in Perl, which we will talk about later. To show how these affect scalar variables within quotes, you should assume that $name has a value:

```
$name = ´Larry Wall´;
```

Because scalar variables are replaced with their values within double-quoted strings, the string "Hello $name!" has the value Hello, Larry Wall! If the $ is escaped with the backslash, "Hello \$name!", the value is Hello $name!. Single quotes do not replace the variable with its value, so ´Hello $name!´ has the value Hello $name!.

Array Variables

An array is an ordered collection of scalars. Array names begin with the @ character:

```
@data = (´Joe´, 39, "Test data", 49.3);
```

Like scalars, they can be declared with my(), as in:

```
my @data = (´Joe´, 39, "Test data", 49.3);
```

The data in this array includes strings, an integer, and a floating point number. Unlike many languages, Perl allows the scalars in an array to have different types (they are all really the same data type: scalars). This example shows printing an array variable:

```
#! /usr/bin/perl -w
# file: array1.pl

use strict;

my @data = (´Joe´, 39, "Test data", 49.3);

print "Within double quotes: @data\n";
print "Outside any quotes: ", @data, "\n";
print ´Within single quotes: @data´, "\n";
```

This is what prints:

```
$ ./array1.pl
Within double quotes: Joe 39 Test data 49.3
```

```
Outside any quotes: Joe39Test data49.3
Within single quotes: @data
```

Placing the array within the double quotes inserts spaces between the array elements, while placing it outside does not, and placing it within single quotes prints the array name itself, not the elements thereof.

As in C, Perl arrays start at element 0. For @data, the elements are:

```
0: ´Joe´
1: 39
2: ´Test data´
3: 49.3
```

To access an individual array element, use the $array_name[index] syntax:

```
#! /usr/bin/perl -w
# file: array2.pl

use strict;

my @data = (´Joe´, 39, ´Test data´, 49.3);

print "element 0: $data[0]\n";
print "element 1: $data[1]\n";
print "element 2: $data[2]\n";
print "element 3: $data[3]\n";
```

That code produces:

```
$ ./array2.pl
element 0: Joe
element 1: 39
element 2: Test data
element 3: 49.3
```

A useful array-related variable is $#array_name, the last index of the array. For example:

```
#! /usr/bin/perl -w
# file: array3.pl

use strict;

my @data = (´Joe´, 39, ´Test data´, 49.3);
print "last index: $#data\n";
```

That code produces:

```
$ ./array3.pl
last index: 3
```

Array Functions

Perl has a variety of functions that implement commonly performed array functions, saving you from having to write your own.

push() and pop() The push() and pop() functions modify the right side of an array. The push() function adds elements to the right, and pop() removes the rightmost element:

```
#! /usr/bin/perl -w
# file: pushpop.pl

use strict;

my @a = (2, 4, 6, 8);
print "before: @a\n";

push(@a, 10, 12);
print "after push: @a\n";

my $element = pop(@a);
print "after pop: @a\n";
print "element popped: $element\n";
```

That code changes the array in the following fashion:

```
before: 2 4 6 8
after push: 2 4 6 8 10 12
after pop: 2 4 6 8 10
element popped: 12
```

unshift() and shift() These functions are similar to push() and pop() except that they operate on the left side of the array.

```
#! /usr/bin/perl -w
# file: unshiftshift.pl

use strict;

my @a = (2, 4, 6, 8);
print "before: @a\n";
```

```
unshift(@a, 10, 12);
print "after unshift: @a\n";

my $element = shift(@a);
print "after shift: @a\n";
print "element shifted: $element\n";
```

That code alters the array:

```
$ ./unshiftshift.pl
before: 2 4 6 8
after unshift: 10 12 2 4 6 8
after shift: 12 2 4 6 8
element shifted: 10
```

sort()* and *reverse() These functions are *nondestructive*—they don't change the arrays or lists that are being sorted. The sort() function sorts lists (as you might have guessed), and the reverse() function reverses lists (as you might have guessed):

```
#! /usr/bin/perl -w
# file: sortreverse.pl

use strict;

my @a = ('hello', 'world', 'good', 'riddance');
print "before: @a\n";

my @b = sort(@a);
print "sorted: @b\n";

@b = reverse(@a);
print "reversed: @b\n";
```

```
$ ./sortreverse.pl
before: hello world good riddance
sorted: good hello riddance world
reversed: riddance good world hello
```

Hash Variables

Hashes (also known as *associative arrays*) are arrays that are indexed not by a number but by a string. In other words, instead of accessing an array by its position with an element like **0** or **1**, we can access a hash with an index like **name** or **age.** For instance, data indexed as an array:

```
index      value
-----      -----
0          Joe
1          39
2          555-1212
3          123 Main. St.
4          Chicago
5          IL
6          60601
```

could instead be indexed as a hash:

```
key        value
-----      -----
name       Joe
age        39
phone      555-1212
address    123 Main. St.
city       Chicago
state      IL
zip        60601
```

By indexing with a string, instead of a number, we can access the data structure by a more meaningful (at least to us humans) bit of information.

A hash variable is defined to be a collection of zero or more key/value pairs (a hash can be empty, with zero pairs). The keys must be unique strings; the values can be any scalar. A hash variable name begins with the percent sign: %person.

To create a hash, assign to it a list, which is treated as a collection of key/value pairs:

```
%person = (
    'name', 'Joe',
    'age', 39,
    'phone', '555-1212',
    'address', '123 Main St.',
    'city', 'Chicago',
    'state', 'IL',
    'zip', '60601'
);
```

Or you can use the => operator to make the code more readable:

```
%person = (
    name    => 'Joe',
    age     => 39,
    phone   => '555-1212',
    address => '123 Main St.',
    city    => 'Chicago',
    state   => 'IL',
    zip     => '60601'
);
```

If the key contains no space characters, like the example above, it does not need to be quoted if the => operator is used.

Accessing a value in a hash is similar to accessing values in an array, indexed with the key string in curly braces, instead of a number within square brackets: $person{name}. The key does not need to be quoted within the curly braces (unless the key contains a whitespace character). For example:

```
#! /usr/bin/perl -w
# file: hash1.pl

use strict;

my %person = (
    name    => 'Joe',
    age     => 39,
    phone   => '555-1212',
    address => '123 Main St.',
    city    => 'Chicago',
    state   => 'IL',
    zip     => '60601'
);

print "$person{name} lives in $person{state}\n";
print "$person{name} is $person{age} years old\n";
```

That code produces:

```
$ ./hash1.pl
Joe lives in IL
Joe is 39 years old
```

A hash can be declared with the my() operator just like scalars and arrays, and they must be declared if we do a use strict;.

Hash Functions

The most common way to process a hash is by looping though the keys. The keys are obtained by executing the built-in keys() function. For example:

```
#! /usr/bin/perl -w
# file: hash2.pl

use strict;

my %person = (
    name    => 'Joe',
    age     => 39,
    phone   => '555-1212',
    address => '123 Main St.',
    city    => 'Chicago',
    state   => 'IL',
    zip     => '60601'
);

my @k = keys(%person);

print "The keys are: @k\n";
```

That code produces:

```
$ ./hash2.pl
The keys are: state zip address city phone age name
```

What's this? The keys() function returns the keys in an apparently random order. They are not in the order created, nor the reverse, nor sorted in any obvious way, but according to how the key hashes. In Perl, the keys are returned in the order in which they are stored in memory. The keys can be sorted by using the (surprise!) sort() function. For example:

```
#! /usr/bin/perl -w
# file:  hash3.pl

use strict;

my %person = (
    name    => 'Joe',
    age     => 39,
    phone   => '555-1212',
    address => '123 Main St.',
    city    => 'Chicago',
    state   => 'IL',
    zip     => '60601'
);
```

```
my @k = keys(%person);
my @sk = sort(@k);
# or: @sk = sort(keys(%person));

print "The sorted keys are: @sk\n";
```

That code produces:

```
$ ./hash3.pl
The sorted keys are: address age city name phone state zip
```

4.3.5 Operators

Perl operator precedence, the order in which math things are executed, is C-like. It's also junior high school algebra-like—the usual stuff. For exact rules, see one of the recommended books or man perlop. We discuss each operator but not in precedence order.

Arithmetic

Perl arithmetic is quite C-like, as you might expect.

+	addition
-	subtraction
*	multiplication
/	division
%	modulus
**	exponentiation[7]

For example:

```
#! /usr/bin/perl -w
# file: operators.pl

use strict;

my $i = 10;
my $j = 4;

print '$i + $j = ', $i + $j, "\n";
print '$i * $j = ', $i * $j, "\n";
print '$i / $j = ', $i / $j, "\n";
print '$i % $j = ', $i % $j, "\n";
print '$i ** $j = ', $i ** $j, "\n";
```

---

[7]Strictly speaking, ** is FORTRAN-like, not C-like, though that's C's loss.

gives the results:

```
$ ./operators.pl
$i + $j = 14
$i * $j = 40
$i / $j = 2.5
$i % $j = 2
$i ** $j = 10000
```

One difference from C-like arithmetic is that when Perl divides integers, the result is automatically typed as floating point—not the usual C integer division, which truncates the result to an integer. That's much more sensible, as with Perl providing an exponentiation operator. To emulate integer division, use the built-in `int()` function:

```
$integer_value = int($a / $b);
```

String

As befits its origins, Perl has powerful built-in string processing. Perl has two useful string operators:

```
.    string concatenation
x    string replication
```

For example:

```
#!/usr/bin/perl -w
# file: string.pl

use strict;

my $a = 'hello';
my $b = 'world';
my $msg = $a . ' '. $b;

print "\$msg : $msg\n";

$a = 'hi';
$b = $a x 2;
my $c = $a x 5;

print "\$b : $b\n";
print "\$c : $c\n";
```

Executing that code gives:

```
$ ./string.pl
$msg : hello world
$b : hihi
$c : hihihihihi
```

True and False

There are three false values in Perl:

```
´´      empty string
´0´     the string of the single character 0
0       the number 0
```

Every other value is true. So in Perl, the following are all true values:

```
1
10
´hi´
```

Numerical Comparison

Perl has the usual numerical comparison operators, with one addition, the *compare operator*, <=>. All of these, with the exception of the compare operator, evaluate to either true (1) or false (empty string—not zero!). The following are the operators:

```
<       less than
<=      less than or equal to
>       greater than
>=      greater than or equal to
==      equal to
!=      not equal to
<=>     compare
```

Here are some examples:

```
if ($i < 10) {
    print "\$i is less than 10\n";
}

if ($j >= 20) {
    print "\$j is greater than or equal to 20\n";
}
```

A common mistake (not just in Perl) is to use the assignment operator (=) when comparing numbers instead of the equivalence operator (==). The former actually changes one of the values—the statement $a = $b changes $a to be the same as $b, while the latter returns a logical true or false but changes neither $a nor $b. Remember that the two operations are different and have different effects.

The compare operator, <=>, evaluates to either 1, 0, or -1. The expression:

```
$a <=> $b
```

evaluates to:

```
1     if $a > $b
0     if $a == $b
-1    if $a < $b
```

String Comparison

Since Perl scalars are either numbers or strings, and we already know how to compare numbers, we need a way to compare strings—string comparison operators. These are similar to the numeric operators in that, with the exception of cmp, they evaluate to either true or false:

```
lt    less than
le    less than or equal to
gt    greater than
ge    greater than or equal to
eq    equivalent to
ne    not equal to
cmp   compare
```

String comparison is an ASCII-betic (similar to but not the same as alphabetic) comparison based on the ASCII values (man ascii) of the characters.

```
if ($name gt 'Joe') {
    print "$name comes after Joe alphabetically\n";
}

if ($language ne 'Perl') {
    print "Your solution is a 2 step process. Step 1, install Perl.\n";
}
```

The string comparison operator, cmp, evaluates to either 1, 0, or -1. The expression:

```
$a cmp $b
```

evaluates to:

```
1     if $a gt $b
0     if $a eq $b
-1    if $a lt $b
```

Increment and Decrement

Perl has the following autoincrement and autodecrement operators:

```
++    autoincrement
--    autodecrement
```

These operators provide a simple way to add 1 to a variable (with ++) or subtract 1 from a variable (--). The location of the operator is important. If placed on the left side of the variable, it increments before the variable is used (preincrement); on the right side, it increments after the variable is used (postincrement). For example:

```
#! /usr/bin/perl -w
# file: increment.pl

use strict;

my $i = 10;
my $j = ++$i;
print "\$i = $i, \$j = $j\n";

$i = 10;
$j = $i++;
print "\$i = $i, \$j = $j\n";
```

Executing that code gives:

```
$ ./increment.pl
$i = 11, $j = 11
$i = 11, $j = 10
```

To illustrate pre- and postincrements, consider the statement:

```
$j = ++$i;
```

$j is assigned the result of ++$i. This preincrement (since the ++ is on the left side of $i) causes the variable $i to be incremented first to 11; then the value of $i is assigned to $j. The result is that both $i and $j have the value 11.

Conversely, consider this statement:

```
$j = $i++;
```

In the postincrement, the ++ is on the right side of $i. $i is incremented after its value is taken. First, $j is assigned the current value of $i, 10; then $i is incremented to 11.

The decrement operator (--) works in a similar manner: If the -- is on the left side, it is a predecrement, subtracting 1 first, if it is on the right side, it is a postdecrement, subtracting 1 last.

Logical

Perl's logical operators are similar to C and C++, with the addition of three very readable ones:

&&	logical and
||	logical or
!	logical not
and	logical and
or	logical or
not	logical not

You can use either or both, depending on your tastes. There is a difference in precedence. The operators and, or, and not have extremely low precedence—they are at the bottom of the precedence table. See man perlop for all the details.

Here are a couple of examples of their use:

```
if ($i >= 0 && $i <= 100) {
    print "\$i is between 0 and 100\n";
}

if ($answer eq ´y´ or $answer eq ´Y´) {
    print "\$answer" equals ´y´ or ´Y´\n";
}
```

The low precedence of and, or, and not can work in our favor, allowing us to drop parentheses in some cases (we'll see this later when we discuss short-circuited logic operators), but it can cause us problems as well. Here are some gotchas:

```
$a = $b && $c;      # like: $a = ($b && $c);     good!
$a = $b and $c;     # like: ($a = $b) and $c;    oops!
$a = $b || $c;      # like: $a = ($b || $c);     good!
$a = $b or $c;      # like: ($a = $b) or $c;     oops!
```

4.3.6 Flow-Control Constructs

Flow-control constructs are the familiar `if`, `else`, `while`, etc. Do this if this *condition* is met, do that if not—flow control. An important thing about these constructs in Perl, unlike C, is that the curly braces, {}, are *required*. Omitting them is a syntax error.

Conditional Constructs

The `if` statement is the most common conditional construct. The syntax for it is:

```
if (condition) {
    statements
} else {
    statements
}
```

If the *condition* in parentheses evaluates as true, the first set of statements is executed; otherwise, the second set of statements is executed. The `else` part is optional. The condition can be any statement that evaluates to true or false, such as `$a < $b`, or far more complicated things.

Nested `if` statements have this syntax:

```
if (condition1) {
    statements
} elsif (condition2) {
    statements
} else {
    statements
}
```

Here is an example of the `if` statement:

```
if ($answer eq ´yes´) {
    print "The answer is yes\n";
} else {
    print "The answer is NOT yes\n";
}
```

Looping Constructs

The `while` Loop   A common looping construct, it has the syntax:

```
while (condition) {
    statements
}
```

The *condition* is tested, and if true, the *statements* are executed; then
the *condition* is tested, and if true, the *statements* are executed; then the
condition is tested... You get the picture. The loop terminates when the
condition is false. For example:

```
$i = 1;
while ($i <= 5) {
    print "the value is: $i\n";
    $i++;
}
```

Executing that code produces:

```
the value is 1
the value is 2
the value is 3
the value is 4
the value is 5
```

One might process an array variable (keep in mind that $#names is the
last index of the array @names):

```
#! /usr/bin/perl -w
# file: whilearray.pl

use strict;

my @names = ('Joe', 'Charlie', 'Sue', 'Mary');
my $i = 0;
while ($i <= $#names) {
    print "Element $i is $names[$i]\n";
    $i++;
}
```

That code produces:

```
$ ./whilearray.pl
Element 0 is Joe
Element 1 is Charlie
Element 2 is Sue
Element 3 is Mary
```

Or one might process a hash sorted by its keys:

```
#! /usr/bin/perl -w
# file: whilehash.pl

use strict;
```

```perl
my %capitals = (
    Illinois   => 'Springfield',
    California => 'Sacramento',
    Texas      => 'Austin',
    Wisconsin  => 'Madison',
    Michigan   => 'Lansing'
);

my @sk = sort(keys(%capitals));

my $i = 0;
while ($i <= $#sk) {
    print "$sk[$i]:  \t$capitals{$sk[$i]}\n";
    $i++;
}
```

The \t is the tab character. That code produces:

```
$ ./whilehash.pl
California:    Sacramento
Illinois:     Springfield
Michigan:     Lansing
Texas:        Austin
Wisconsin:    Madison
```

The for Loop This loop has the syntax:

```perl
for (init_expression; condition; step_expression) {
    statements
}
```

The *init_expression* is executed first and only once. Then the *condition* is tested to be true or false. If true, the *statements* are executed, then the *step_expression* is executed, and then the *condition* is tested. The loop stops when the *condition* evaluates as false.

Our earlier `while` loop example could have been written to process @names as:

```perl
for ($i = 0; $i <= $#names; $i++) {
    print "Element $i is $names[$i]\n";
}
```

That gives the same result, and the %capitals example could be written using the for as:

```perl
for ($i = 0; $i <= $#sk; $i++) {
    print "$sk[$i]:  \t$capitals{$sk[$i]}\n";
}
```

There's more than one way to do it.

The foreach Loop Perl has a nifty loop used to process lists and arrays called the foreach loop. It has this syntax:

```
foreach scalar_variable (list) {
    statements
}
```

The *statements* are executed *for each* item in the list (hence the name), meaning we don't have to know how long the list is or check to see whether the end has been reached. For example:

```
#! /usr/bin/perl -w
# file: foreach1.pl

use strict;

my @a = (2, 4, 6, 8);
foreach my $i (@a) {
    print $i, ´ ** ´, $i, ´ = ´, $i ** $i, "\n";
}
```

That code produces:

```
$ ./foreach1.pl
2 ** 2 = 4
4 ** 4 = 256
6 ** 6 = 46656
8 ** 8 = 16777216
```

Did you see the way $i was declared with my() within the foreach construct?

This example shows the control variable being modified. Note that when the control variable is modified, the array element itself is modified:

```
#!/usr/bin/perl -w
# file: foreach2.pl

use strict;

my @a = (2, 4, 6, 8);
foreach my $i (@a) {
    $i = $i * 2;
}
print "@a\n";
```

This code produces:

```
$ ./foreach 2.pl
4 8 12 16
```

As strange as this may sound, the keywords `for` and `foreach` are inter-changeable. We can use `for` in place of `foreach` (which is not uncommon) and `foreach` in place of `for` (which is rare). So don't be surprised if you see code that resembles `for (@a) { ... }`.

Other Constructs

There are more control flow constructs in Perl, including `unless` and `until`, which we will discuss later.

4.3.7 Regular Expressions

Regular expressions (*regexes*) are a powerful, strange, beautiful, and complex part of Perl. These can match a string against a general pattern, perform string substitution, and extract text from a string. This sounds simple, but within this simple notion, a world of complexity lies. Much of Perl's power and usefulness derives from the use of regular expressions. So much more can be done with this than we can describe here—the Camel Book [Wall+ 00] expends many pages on this, but we will try to explain the useful basics in just a few.

To match a string, use the following syntax:

```
$string_variable =~ /pat/
```

That is `=~` (equal-tilde), not `= ~` (equal-space-tilde).

This returns true if the variable `$string_variable` matches the pattern `pat`, false if it does not. For a string to match a pattern, only a portion of the string needs to match, not the entire string. For example:

```
if ($name =~ /John/) {
    print "\$name matches `John´\n";
}
```

If the variable `$name` matches the pattern `"John"`, the `if` condition is true and the result is printed. In order for `$name` to match the regex `"John"`, only a portion of the string needs to match. For instance, all the following values for $name would match the regex `John`:

```
John
```

```
John Lennon
```

```
Andrew Johnson
```

Patterns

When we create regexes, we abstract patterns to be compared with the text. Let's examine the rules of patterns.

Characters

Most characters match themselves:

a	matches a
b	matches b
ab	matches a immediately followed by b
abc	matches a immediately followed by b immediately followed by c

Some characters have a special meaning:

.	matches any character except newline (\n)
^	matches the beginning of the string
$	matches the end of the string

Thus:

a.b	match a followed by any character but \n followed by b
	a1b
	azb
	a+b

^abc	match a string that begins with `abc`
	abcdefg
	abc123

abc$	match a string that ends with abc
	123abc
	I learned my abc

Character Classes

Square brackets, [], create a character class, which matches any single character in that class. A dash (-) can be used to specify a range:

```
[abcd]        one of either a or b or c or d
[a-d]         the same
[0-9]         one digit character
[a-zA-Z]      one alpha character, upper or lowercase
```

If the caret character ($\char`\^$) is the first character in the class, any single character that is *not* in the class listed will be matched:

```
[^abcd]       any character except a or b or c or d
[^a-d]        the same
[^0-9]        one nondigit character
[^a-zA-Z]     one nonalpha
```

As an example of the previous concepts, let's say we want to match a phone number in the following format: 800 867 5309. This is a regex to match any number of this format:

```
/[0-9][0-9][0-9] [0-9][0-9][0-9] [0-9][0-9][0-9][0-9]/
```

This is read as one digit followed by one digit, followed by one digit, followed by one space (the spacebar), followed by one digit, followed by ... **This is one place where whitespace does count!**

Some character classes occur frequently and are given predefined character classes:

```
\d       digit character [0-9]
\D       nondigit character
\w       word character [a-zA-Z0-9_]
\W       nonword character
\s       space character [ \r\n\t\f]
\S       nonspace
```

The phone-number-matching regex could be rewritten:

```
/\d\d\d\s\d\d\d\s\d\d\d\d/
```

That is, three digits followed by one space character, followed by three digits, followed by one space character, followed by four digits.

Quantifiers

Quantifiers express quantity. How many of an element are there? How does one match multiple instances? It's awkward to use the multiple instances of

[0-9] or \d\d\d as we did earlier. Quantifiers allow us to clean up this sort of thing. These are the Perl quantifiers:

*	0 or more
+	1 or more
?	0 or 1
{m}	exactly m
{m,}	m or more
{m,n}	m through n, inclusive

Quantifiers operate on the element immediately to the *left* of the quantifier (parentheses can be used to apply precedence):

xy*z	match x followed by 0 or more y followed by z
(xy)*z	match 0 or more xy followed by z

For example:

xy*z   match x followed by 0 or more y followed by z
           xz
           xyz
           xyyz
           xyyyz
           . . .

xy+z   match x followed by 1 or more y followed by z
           xyz
           xyyz
           xyyyz
           . . .

xy?z   match x followed by 0 or 1 y followed by z
           xz
           xyz

xy3z   match x followed by exacty 3 y followed by z
           xyyyz

xyz2y   match x followed by y followed by exacty 2 z followed by y
           xyzzy

xy3,z   match x followed by 3 or more y followed by z
           xyyyz
           xyyyyz
           xyyyyyz
           . . . . .

xy3,5z   match x followed by 3 to 5 y followed by z
           xyyyz
           xyyyyz
           xyyyyyz

So the phone-number-matching regex can be rewritten yet again:

/\d{3}\s\d{3}\s\d{4}/

And even as this:

/(\d{3}\s){2}\d{4}/

One could argue that the previous code is approaching being unreadable.[8] Ain't Perl fun?

Memory

Perl has a mechanism that allows it to remember patterns previously matched. Expressions that have been matched by a regex within a set of parentheses are stored in the special variables $1, $2, $3, and so on.[9]

When one set of parentheses is used, the text within it is stored in $1:

```
#!/usr/bin/perl -w
# file: memory1.pl

use strict;

my $name = 'John Doe';

if ($name =~/^(..)/) {
    print "^(..) : $1\n";
}

if ($name =~/^(\w+)/) {
    print "^(\\w+)   :   $1\n";
}

if ($name =~/(\w+)$/) {
    print "(\\w+)\$   :   $1\n";
}
```

Executing that code produces:

```
$ ./memory1.pl
^(..) : Jo
^(\w+) : John
(\w+)$ : Doe
```

---

[8]On the old-school theory of "It was hard to write, it should be hard to read."

[9]This memory function can also help with matching recurring text by using the related variables \1, \2, and \3—see the Camel Book [Wall+ 00] for details.

If more than one set of parentheses is used, the first set will remember its characters in $1, the second set in $2, the third set in $3, and so on.

For instance, you could have a file full of records with three fields, containing an account number, name, and phone number, and write a regex that would go through the record and print each field separately:

```
#!/usr/bin/perl -w
# file: memory2.pl

use strict;

# create a record, 3 fields, colon-separated
my $record = '32451:John Doe:847 555 1212';

# see if the record contains:
#   beginning of the string
#   followed by 0 or more of any character but \n
#     (remembered into $1)
#   followed by a colon (':')
#   followed by 0 or more of any character but \n
#     (remembered into $2)
#   followed by a colon (':')
#   followed by 0 or more of any character but \n
#     (remembered into $3)
#   followed by the end of the string
if ($record =~/^(.*):(.*):(.*)$/) {
    print "The record is:\n";
    print " account number: $1\n";
    print " name:           $2\n";
    print " phone number:   $3\n";
}
```

Executing that code produces:

```
$ ./memory2.pl
The record is:
    account number: 32451
    name:           John Doe
    phone number:   847 555 1212
```

This record is only one entry long for this example, but we could have processed more than one entry. One could also imagine creating a regex that matched "John Doe," his phone number, or his account number.

Regular expressions are incredibly useful—now you can write a script that goes through your old e-mail files, picking out phone numbers. To make it robust, you'd have to figure out how to disregard parentheses, dashes, and dots, but that isn't hard to do. Or you could write a script to scan your Apache logs for a certain IP address.

You can also apply these same principles to the Unix commands `grep`, `sed`, and `awk` and their variants, which also use regular expressions with minor differences. This knowledge adds a great deal of utility to system administration and just general user coolness.

4.3.8 Functions

User-defined functions are created as follows:

```
sub function_name {
    # body
}
```

In Perl, the terms *function* and *subroutine* are used interchangeably. Some programmers like to call them functions, other prefer subroutine.[10] We like the term function. TMTOWTDI. To invoke the function, do this:

```
function_name()
```

For example:

```
#! /usr/bin/perl -w
# file: function1.pl

sub say_hello {
    print "hello, world!\n";
}

say_hello();
```

Executing that program produces:

```
$ ./function1.pl
hello, world!
```

By convention, functions are defined above the point where first called but can be defined after it.

---

[10]Some say a function is a subroutine that returns a value, but this is not a firm definition.

```
#! /usr/bin/perl -w
# file: function2.pl

say_hello();

sub say_hello {
    print "hello, world\n";
}
```

Usually, we prefer to define functions before they are used, especially because it allows us to use the lazy way of calling functions by dropping the parentheses: say_hello;. However, the lazy way of invoking functions is not suggested by most Perl programmers, so most of us would suggest using the parentheses. So, before or after—no difference. Still, we put them before. TMTOWTDI.

Return Values

All Perl functions return the last value evaluated by the function. The following example shows two functions returning values differently. The function test1() returns a scalar value, and the function test2() returns a list:

```
#!/usr/bin/perl -w
# file: return1.pl

sub test1 {
    $a = 10;
    $b = 11;

    # return the sum
    $a + $b;
}

sub test2 {
    @a = ('testing', 'one', 'two', 'three');

    # return the sort of @a
    sort(@a);
}

$c = test1();
print "\$c = $c\n";

@b = test2();
print "\@b = @b\n";
```

Executing that code produces:

```
$ ./return1.pl
$c = 21
@b = one testing three two
```

Perl also has the `return` operator, which can be used to escape grace-fully from the middle of a block or simply for readability, which is a Good Thing.

```
#!/usr/bin/perl -w
# file: return2.pl

sub pick_a_restaurant {
    if ($cash > 150.00) {
        return 'Chez Paul';
    } elsif ($cash > 50.00) {
        return "Pete Miller's Steak House";
    } elsif ($cash > 10.00) {
        return "Pancakes 'R' Us";
    } else {
        return 'Fast Food Delight';
    }
}

# we are a little light today...
$cash = 10.00;

print 'You should eat at: ', pick_a_restaurant(), "\n";
```

Executing that code produces:

```
$ ./return2.pl
You should eat at: Fast Food Delight
```

The variable `$cash` used within `pick_a_restaurant()` is global because all variables in a function are, by default, global. Using global variables is something one should not do without intent, so we need to learn how to use local variables.

Local Variables

To create local variables in a function, use `my()`:

```
#! /usr/bin/perl -w
# file: function3.pl

use strict;
```

```
sub print_my_i {
    my $i = 10;
    print "in print_my_i(): $i\n";
}

my $i = 20;

print "outside print_my_i(): $i\n";
print_my_i();
print "outside print_my_i(): $i\n";
```

Using use strict; requires that the variables within the function be declared and makes them local—another good reason to do a use strict;.

Executing that code produces the following result. The $i within print_my_i() is lexically scoped with the function and does not change the value of the global $i.

```
$ ./function3.pl
outside print_my_i(): 20
in print_my_i(): 10
outside print_my_i(): 20
```

Function Arguments

Arguments are passed into functions through the special array @_:

```
#! /usr/bin/perl -w
# file: printargs1.pl

use strict;

sub print_args {
    my $i = 0;

    # loop through @_ and print each element
    # and yes, that is $#_, the last index of @_
    while ($i <= $#_) {
        print "arg $i: $_[$i]\n";
        $i++;
    }
}

# some variables to pass in
my $num = 10;
my $name = 'Joe';

print_args($num, $name, 3.14159, 'hello, world!');
```

Executing that code produces:

```
$ ./printargs.pl
arg 0: 10
arg 1: Joe
arg 2: 3.14159
arg 3: hello, world!
```

Arguments are often copied into my variables like this:

```
#! /usr/bin/perl -w
# printargs2.pl

use strict;

sub print_args_2 {

    # copy the arguments into $a, $b and $c
    my($a, $b, $c) = @_;

    # print the arguments
    print "\$a is: $a\n";
    print "\$b is: $b\n";
    print "\$c is: $c\n";
}

my $num = 10;
my $name = 'Joe';

print_args_2($num, $name, 3.14159);
```

Executing that code produces:

```
$ ./printargs2.pl
$a is: 10
$b is: Joe
$c is: 3.14159
```

Next, we show an example of a program with two functions. The first, munge_phone(), checks a phone number to see whether it is in this format: 847 555 1212; if so, extracts the three-digit parts and returns the string in the format (847) 555-1212. If the phone number does not match the required format, the function prints a statement to that effect and exits gracefully.

The second function, matches_class(), takes two arguments: The first is the string to be matched, and the second, the character class to match it against. If the string contains one or more characters of the class, it indicates a match, and if not, indicates no match. In both cases, it returns the string it tried to match.

```perl
#!/usr/bin/perl -w
# file: function4.pl

use strict;

sub munge_phone {
    my($phone) = @_;

    # check to see that the phone number is
    # in the form 847 555 1212
    if ($phone =~ /(\d{3})\s(\d{3})\s(\d{4})/) {
        return "($1) $2-$3";
    } else {
        return 'Phone improperly formed';
    }
}

sub matches_class {
    my($str, $char_class) = @_;

    if ($str =~ /^[$char_class]+$/) {
        print "[$str] matches /[$char_class]/\n";
    } else {
        print "[$str] does not match /[$char_class]/\n";
    }
}

# let's try a properly formed phone number
my $p1 = 'phone number: 847 555 1212';
my $p2 = munge_phone($p1);
print "before: $p1    after: $p2\n";

# now let's try an improperly formed phone number
my $p3 = '847 555-1212';
my $p4 = munge_phone($p2);
print "before: $p3    after: $p4\n";

# let's check some strings against a class
my $s1 = 'A string of only alphas and space';
my $s2 = 'A string with 1 digit';
my $c = 'a-zA-Z ';
matches_class($s1, $c);
matches_class($s2, $c);
```

When that program is executed, this is the result:

```
$ ./function4.pl
before: phone number: 847 555 1212    after: (847) 555-1212
before: 847 555-1212    after: Phone improperly formed
[A string of only alphas and space] matches /[a-zA-Z ]/
[A string with 1 digit] does not match /[a-zA-Z ]/
```

4.3.9 File I/O

Since the Web is interactive, Perl scripts which don't interact with the outside world will be of limited use. The scripts have to be able to accept input and write output. This is where file input/output comes in, or File I/O.

Standard Output

We have already been sending text to standard output (probably right on the terminal on the monitor you're looking at now) using the print() function:

```
print "hello, world\n";
```

Standard Input

You can imagine how it might be useful to be able to read data from the outside world. This can be done using standard input, <STDIN>, which is typically the keyboard, though it can be redirected to be a file or something else.

To read input into a scalar variable, up to and including the newline character \n, you need only to add $line = <STDIN>;.

More usefully, this example reads the next line of data into $line, including the newline character:

```
#! /usr/bin/perl -w
# file: stdin1.pl

use strict;

print "Enter your name: ";

my $name = <STDIN>;

print "Hello $name!\n";
```

Executing that program produces:

```
$ ./stdin1.pl
Enter your name: J. Random Luser
Hello J. Random Luser
!
```

The exclamation point (!) appeared on the next line after the name. That is because <STDIN> reads up to and including the newline character, so $name contains the text "J. Random Luser\n." To remove the newline character, chomp() it:

```
$name = <STDIN>;
chomp($name);
```

Or:

```
chomp($name = <STDIN>);
```

For example:

```
#! /usr/bin/perl -w
# file: stdin2.pl

use strict;

my $name;

print "Enter your name: ";

chomp($name = <STDIN>);

print "Hello $name!\n";
```

Executing that code produces:

```
$ ./stdin2.pl
Enter your name: J. Random Luser
Hello J. Random Luser!
```

You can also read the input into an array variable:

```
@all_lines = <STDIN>;
```

That reads all remaining lines of standard input into the array @all_lines. Each line of input (including the newline character) is now an element of @all_lines. This behavior, reading until the end of file in one statement, is so important that it has a special term: a STDIN *slurp*.

```
#! /usr/bin/perl -w
# stdin3.pl

use strict;
```

```
print "Enter your text: \n";

my @all_lines = <STDIN>;

my $i = 0;
while ($i <= $#all_lines) {
    print "line $i: $all_lines[$i]";
    $i++;
}
```

That code produces:

```
$ ./stdin3.pl
Enter your text:
hello
world
good bye
^D
line 0: hello
line 1: world
line 2: good bye
```

The ^D character (Ctrl + D) is the end-of-file character for standard input. Also, each line of text contains the newline character, so when we print each line of text in line 6 of the program, we do not need to include the newline character. The text can be read, and the newlines removed on each line, by passing the array variable as the argument to chomp():

```
@all_lines = <STDIN>;
chomp(@all_lines);
```

Or:

```
chomp(@all_lines = <STDIN>);
```

Perl programmers often *slurp* and chomp() but otherwise have good manners.

Reading from a File

To read from (or write to) a file, you must first open the file. To open a file, use the open() function:

```
# this opens 'test.txt' in read mode
open FH, '<test.txt';
```

FH is a filehandle variable. By convention, all filehandles are named with uppercase letters. The less-than symbol (<) indicates that the file is to be opened in read mode. Read mode happens to be the default, so if the less-than symbol is not used, the file will still be opened in read mode. Some consider it good programming practice to explicitly open in read mode (it is more secure; we talk about this in Chapter 7), so we do that in this book, but if you choose to drop the less-than symbol, it will work just the same.

The open() function returns true if successful, false if it fails. If open() returns false, we should handle this as a serious error, and in Perl, when serious errors occur, we die() (serious business, this programming stuff). The following code will die() if the file fails to open:[11]

```
if (! open (FH, `<test.txt`)) {
    die "Can't open test.txt: $!";
}
```

The die() function takes its argument, prints it to standard error output, cleans up, and exits with a nonzero exit status. The funny-looking variable $! contains the error status of why the open failed. Although that code works, it is more Perl-like to write it thus:

```
open(FH, `<test.txt`) or die "Can't open test.txt: $!";
```

We will discuss the logic of the or operator in a bit, when we talk about short-circuited evaluation. If you can't wait for that discussion, then this logic means that if the file test.txt can't be opened, the program will die().

```
#! /usr/bin/perl -w
# file: file1.pl

use strict;

my $line;

open (FH, `<test.txt`) or die "Can't open test.txt: $!";
while ($line = <FH>) {
    print "Line is: $line";
}

close (FH);
```

---

[11]Death, when programming Perl, is not inherently bad, except when programming CGIs. CGI programs need to die in a more acceptable fashion—we talk about this in Chapter 7.

At the end of the program, close the file: `close()`. Boy, this Perl stuff is complicated. It is considered good style to close a file once you are finished with it.

So if `test.txt` contains:

```
goodbye
cruel
world
Perl is cool
```

and you operate on it with `file1.pl`, you get:

```
$ ./file1.pl
Line is: goodbye
Line is: cruel
Line is: world
Line is: Perl is cool
```

A complete file can also be read into an array variable:

```
@all_lines = <FH>;
```

The preceding line of code reads the entire contents of the file into the array `@all_lines`. Each line of the file is stored as an individual array element, newlines included. This is called a *file slurp*.

```
#! /usr/bin/perl -w
# file2.pl

use strict;

open (FH, `<test.txt´) or die "Can't open test.txt: $!";

my @all_lines = <FH>;

my $i = 0;
while ($i <= $#all_lines) {
    print "Line is: $all_lines[$i]";
    $i++;
}
close (FH);
```

Executing that code produces:

```
$ ./file2.pl
Line is: goodbye
Line is: cruel
Line is: world
Line is: Perl is cool
```

The newlines can be removed with `chomp()`:

```
chomp(@all_lines = <FH>);
```

Writing to a File

To open a file in write mode, use the `open()` function:

```
open FH, '>output.txt' or die "Can't open output.txt: $!";
```

The > tells Perl that the file is to be opened in write mode. This will overwrite the file if it exists, so be careful! To write into the file, execute `print()` with an additional argument: the filehandle variable:

```
print FH "hello, world\n";
```

Yes, that's right—there is no comma after `FH`. Here is an example:

```
#! /usr/bin/perl -w
# file3.pl

use strict;

my $line;

open (FH, '>output.txt') or die "Can't open output.txt: $!";

while ($line = <STDIN>) {
    print FH "You entered: $line";
}

close (FH);
```

This program loops through standard input, writing the line entered to the file `output.txt` prepended with the text `"You entered: "`. If the program is executed like this:

```
$ ./file3.pl
hello
world
good bye
^D
```

the resulting contents of `output.txt` would be:

```
You entered: hello
You entered: world
You entered: good bye
```

4.3.10 Additional Perl Constructs

Perl allows you to write code that reads a lot like English. It also allows you to write code that's completely unreadable, but that's another issue.[12]

The unless Statement

The unless is like the if, except the logic is reversed. The basic syntax is:

```
unless (condition) {
    statements
}
```

The condition is tested, and if it is false, the statements are executed.

Thus, this if statement:

```
if (not $done) {
    print "keep working!\n";
}
```

can be written as:

```
unless ($done) {
    print "keep working!\n";
}
```

The until Loop

The until loop is like the while loop, except the logic is reversed. The basic syntax is:

```
until (condition) {
    statements
}
```

The condition is tested, and if it is false, the statements are executed. Then the condition is tested, and if it is false...

Thus, this while loop:

```
while (not $done) {
    keep_working();
}
```

---

[12]The Perl Journal (www.tpj.com/) conducts the annual Obfuscated Perl Coding Contest—an enlightening, if somewhat frightening, experience.

can be rewritten as:

```
until ($done) {
    keep_working();
}
```

Expression Modifiers

Expression modifiers Perl has—also known as the backward (Yoda) form (TMTOWTDI). For instance, the if statement:

```
if (condition) {
    statements
}
```

can be written backward as:

```
    statements if condition;
```

The following if statement:

```
if ($hungry) {
    eat();
}
```

can be rewritten as:

```
eat() if $hungry;
```

And this statement:

```
if ($error_condition) {
    die "we have an error...";
}
```

can be written as:

```
die "we have an error..." if $error_condition;
```

The unless can be written in backward form as well:

```
unless ($happy) {
    complain();
}
```

rewritten can be as:

```
complain() unless $happy;
```

The `while` and `until` loops work this way as well:

```
while ($tired) {
    sleep();
}
```

can be written as:

```
sleep() while $tired;
```

This `until` loop:

```
until ($done) {
    cook_the_burgers();
}
```

can be written as:

```
cook_the_burgers() until $done;
```

Expression modifiers can be used only when the body of the construct is a simple statement. In other words, the body cannot be an `if` or a `while` or any other multistatement body. For instance, this is illegal in Perl (but possible in reality):

```
print "rebooting..." if $os ne ´Linux´ until $end_of_time;
```

Short-Circuited Logic Operators

The logic operators `&&`, `and`, `||`, and `or` are *short-circuited*—if the entire result of the operator can be established at any point, the rest of the expression is not evaluated, because it doesn't need to be. With the logical `and` operator, if the first operand is false, we know that the result of the operand is false (because "false and false" is false and "false and true" is false). Therefore, in *expression1* `&&` *expression2*, if *expression1* is false, *expression2* is not evaluated because of this short-circuited nature. If *expression1* is true, *expression2* must be evaluated to determine the result of the `&&` operator. Thus, the `&&` is logically equivalent to the `if` statement. This code:

```
expression1 && expression2
```

is equivalent to this:

```
if (expression1) {
    expression2
}
```

Therefore, this `if` statement:

```
# set this variable to true (1) if we want to print
# debug output, 0 if not
$debug = 1;

...

if ($debug) {
    print_debug_output();
}
```

can be written as:

```
$debug && print_debug_output();
```

or:

```
$debug and print_debug_output();
```

The short-circuitedness of the logical `and` can be used as an `if`, but some might question whether that is a Good Thing.

The short-circuited nature of the logical `or`, on the other hand, is widely thought to be a Good Thing. The logical `or` is similar to the logical `and`, but negated. If the first operand is true, the result of the `or` operator is true (because "true or false" is true and "true or true" is true). So in this case:

```
expression1 || expression2
```

if *expression1* is true, *expression2* is not evaluated, because *expression1* short-circuits it. If *expression1* is false, *expression2* must be evaluated to determine the result of the `||` operator. Thus, the `||` is logically equivalent to the `unless` statement. This code:

```
expression1 || expression2
```

is equivalent to:

```
unless (expression1) {
    expression2
}
```

So this `unless` statement:

```
unless (open (FH, '<myfile.txt')) {
    die "can't open myfile.txt: $!";
}
```

can be written as:

```
open (FH, '<myfile.txt') or die "can't open myfile.txt: $!";
```

Be careful about the difference of precedence between **&&** and **and**, as well as the difference between **||** and **or**:

```
$c = $a && $b;    # good, like $c = ($a && $b);
$c = $a and $b;   # not so good, like ($c = $a) and $b;
```

4.3.11 Making Operating System Calls

Perl includes some convenient functions and operators to perform system calls. We look at only two of these, so see the Camel Book [Wall+ 00] for more.

The system() Function

The system() function takes its argument and executes it as if it were a system command typed into the shell. The output of the command is sent to standard output for the program.

This code:

```
system '/bin/ls';
```

executes the /bin/ls system command, showing the files in the current directory in sorted order, much as if you had entered that command to the shell. The output of the system() function, here a listing of all files in the current directory, is sent to STDOUT just as if you executed from the shell.

The system() function can be called by giving it a list of arguments. This invocation is more secure than having only one argument, because system() is written so that it does not interpret the shell metacharacters (such as * and ;) as anything special. For instance, let's say we have this code:

```
system "/bin/ls $user_supplied_input";
```

Imagine if $user_supplied_input had the value ; rm -rf /. This would be like executing:

```
system "/bin/ls ; rm -rf /";
```

This can cause a problem. If we instead use system as a list, like this:

```
system "/bin/ls", $user_supplied_input;
```

then the metacharacter ; is not treated as anything special—in other words, ls tries to list the file named simply ;. Then it tries to list the files rm, -rf and /.

Use a list of arguments to system() if appropriate.

Backquotes

Backquotes, ``, are similar to the system() function, except the standard output of the command is brought into the program. For instance:

```
$my_working_directory = `/bin/pwd`;
```

Now $my_working_directory contains a value that resembles "/home/jrl\n".

N The output ends in the newline character (just as it does when executed from the shell). Using chomp()—chomp($my_working_directory = `/bin/pwd`), you can remove it.

When using system() and backquotes, be sure to use full pathnames (for example, /bin/ls) instead of relying on the user's PATH variable (for example, ls). Who knows what the user's PATH is set to? If you want them to execute the official ls, say it explicitly.

4.4 A QUICK INTRODUCTION TO OBJECT-ORIENTED PROGRAMMING

There is no way to avoid it—we have to talk about object-oriented programming (OOP) using Perl. Object-oriented programming is not a big deal though; it is just a way to give an object (a thing) actions (behaviors, also known as *methods*). Let's say we have an object named $car. We can drive the car by executing that object's drive() method, using the nifty arrow notation: $car->drive(). Easy, eh? Well, of course it is not so easy, so we suggest that if you want an excellent discussion of all things OOP in Perl, see *Objected-Oriented Perl* [Conway 99].

Most of the time, when we do OOP in Perl, we will use objects that others have defined. In Chapter 7, when we learn how to do CGI programming with Perl, we will use a *module,* or object class definition, named `CGI.pm`. We will use this module with a pragma named (believe it or not) `use`, as in:

```
use CGI;
```

A Perl *pragma* is a message to the compiler to behave in a way that is not the default—in the `use` pragma, we are telling the compiler to use a specific Perl module that it does not normally include, telling Perl to locate the module file `CGI.pm` and do some OOP magic, making all the methods, or object functions, available to us. For instance, in the `CGI` module, a method named `header()` is defined, and because we told Perl we want to use the `CGI` module, we can call this method.

Once we have `use`d a module, we can then usually create an object of that type by executing `new`, which is a method that is defined to construct the object:

```
$obj = new CGI;
```

Once an object is created, methods can be invoked by using the arrow notation:

```
$obj->header();
$obj->pre();
$obj->b();
```

This syntax means "execute the `header()` (or `pre()` or `b()`) method using the object named `$obj`, which is an object of class `CGI`."

Hundreds of modules are available for Perl. You can find them all for free at the Comprehensive Perl Archive Network (CPAN)—`www.cpan.org/`. We suggest that you check out what is there. You might find that the problem you are trying to solve, or will need to solve in the future, has a module written for it that could make your life easier.

Installing a module is a snap. First, find the module you want at `www.cpan.org`. Let's say we want the module `Nifty`. We find the latest version of `Nifty`, let's say version 1.03. We download the tarball from CPAN

As with most things Perl, there is *a Better Way* to install modules—use the CPAN module. In this book, we demonstrate installing Perl modules the explicit way, as just shown, in case you are unable to get CPAN to install the module you need. If you are interested, check out `perldoc CPAN`. Here is a quick example of installing the preceding module:

```
# perl -MCPAN -e shell
cpan> install Nifty
```

That's it! Easy as pie.

named `Nifty-1.03.tar.gz` and save it somewhere convenient, let's say `/tmp`. Then, all we do is this:

```
# cd /tmp
# tar xzvf Nifty-1.03.tar.gz
# cd Nifty-1.03
# perl Makefile.PL
# make
# make test
# make install
```

Now, `Nifty.pm` is installed. To use it, we add this to our Perl scripts:

```
use Nifty;
```

That is all you need to know to be able to use the modules in this book. If you are interested in the workings of objects or are going to be creating your own classes, read *Object-Oriented Perl* [Conway 99]—you will be happy you did.

4.5 WHAT WE DIDN'T TALK ABOUT

As has been said *ad nauseam,* much of the complex functionality of Perl is beyond the scope of this book; the Camel Book is fat and thick, and we couldn't possibly do it justice here. As you continue your webmaster and Linux experience, you will want to learn more about Perl or a similar scripting language—you'll certainly be exposed to it peripherally in scripts, installation packages, and more. Among the topics we didn't cover, the following might be of interest:

- Special variables, especially `$_`
- Reading input with `<>`

- Assignable lists
- Slices
- String functions such as `index()`, `rindex()`, `substr()`, and `length()`
- References and complex data types

4.6 SUMMARY

Perl is a useful and easy-to-use tool for many purposes, not just on Linux systems, not just for administration, and not just for CGI script programming. We haven't discussed the myriad uses of Perl in this quick-and-dirty introduction, but perhaps some inklings went through your mind as you read. We talk about uses for Perl throughout the book, and you can find many scripts at CPAN to get started.

N *A Word of Warning* We've said it before, and we'll say it again: If you run scripts, even from a trusted source, without scanning them to see what they'll do, you're on your own. Don't run them as `root`. Be paranoid.

4.7 RESOURCES

Books

[Christiansen+ 98] Christiansen, Tom, and Nathan Torkington. *Perl Cookbook.* Recipes to do all types of tasks in Perl.

[Conway 99] Conway, Damien. *Object-Oriented Perl.* A complete introduction to the object-oriented features of Perl. A must-read for those wanting to learn how to use Perl for object-oriented programming.

[Friedl 02] Friedl, Jeffrey E. F. *Mastering Regular Expressions.* An excellent book covering a complex topic—a must have for those of us creating complex regexes.

[Hall+ 98] Hall, Joseph N., and Randal Schwartz. *Effective Perl Programming: Writing Better Programs with Perl.* A very good book discussing many advanced features of Perl, including references and modules.

[Schilli 98] Schilli, Michael. *Perl Power: A JumpStart Guide to Programming with Perl 5.* A good introduction to the language.

[Schwartz+ 01] Schwartz, Randal L., and Tom Phoenix. *Learning Perl, Third Edition.* An excellent introduction to Perl.

[Stein 01] Stein, Lincoln D. *Network Programming with Perl.* If you want to use Perl to write network programs, get this book. An excellent treatment of networking with Perl.

[Wall+ 00] Wall, Larry, Tom Christiansen, and Jon Orwant. *Programming Perl, Third Edition.* The bible, Larry Wall version. Read it, study it, grok it.

Tutorials

Perl in 20 pages: `www.best.com/~quong/perlin20/`

Tom's object-oriented tutorial for Perl: `http://language.perl.com/all_about/perltoot.html`

University of Missouri Tutorial: `www.cclabs.missouri.edu/things/instruction/perl/perlcourse.html`

Web Sites

Comprehensive Perl Archive Network (CPAN): `www.cpan.org/`

Latest Perl source: `www.perl.com/CPAN/src/stable.tar.gz`

Perl advocacy: `www.perl.org`

Perldoc.com: `www.perldoc.com/`

Perl home page: `www.perl.com/`

The Perl Journal: `www.tpj.com/`

Perl mongers: `www.pm.org/`

Perl news: `www.use.perl.org/`

The Perl Review: `www.theperlreview.com`

5
MySQL

5.1 INTRODUCTION

Many of the applications that a Web developer wants to use can be made easier by the use of a standardized database to store, organize, and access information. MySQL is an Open Source (GPL) Standard Query Language (SQL) database that is fast, reliable, easy to use, and suitable for applications of any size. SQL is the ANSI-standard database query language used by most databases (though all have their nonstandard extensions).

MySQL can easily be integrated into Perl programs by using the Perl DBI (DataBase Independent interface) module. DBI is an Application Program Interface (API) that allows Perl to connect to and query a number of SQL databases (among them MySQL, mSQL, PostgreSQL, Oracle, Sybase, and Informix).

If you installed Linux as suggested in Chapter 2, MySQL and DBI are already installed.

5.2 TUTORIAL

Following the Swiss Army knife theory (20 percent of the functions give you 80 percent of the utility), a few SQL commands go a long way to facilitate learning MySQL/Perl/DBI.

To illustrate these, we create a simple database containing information about some (fictional) people. Eventually, we'll show how to enter this information from a form on the Web (see Chapter 7), but for now we interface with SQL directly.

First, try to make a connection to our MySQL server as the root MySQL user:

```
$ mysql -u root
```

N The MySQL root user is different from the Linux root user. The MySQL root user is used to administer the MySQL server only.

If you see the following output:

```
ERROR 2002: Can't connect to local MySQL server through socket
'/var/lib/mysql/mysql.sock'(2)
```

it likely means the MySQL server is not running. If your system is set up securely, it shouldn't be running, because you had no reason, before now, for it to be running. Use chkconfig as root to make sure it starts the next time the machine boots, and then start it by hand as follows:

```
# chkconfig mysqld on
# /etc/init.d/mysqld start
```

Now you should be able to connect (*not* logged in as the Linux root user):

```
$ mysql -u root
```

If not, see the MySQL log file at /var/log/mysqld.log. If so, you'll see a welcome message and the MySQL prompt:

```
Welcome to the MySQL monitor. Commands end with ; or \g.
Your MySQL connection id is 3 to server version: 3.23.36

Type 'help;' or '\h' for help. Type '\c' to clear the buffer

mysql>
```

As suggested, enter help; at the prompt. A list of MySQL commands (not to be confused with SQL commands) will be displayed. These allow you to work with the MySQL server. For grins, enter status; to see the status of the server.

To illustrate these commands, we will create a database called people that contains information about people and their ages.

5.2.1 The SHOW DATABASES and CREATE DATABASE Commands

First, we need to create the new database. Check the current databases to make sure a database of that name doesn't already exist; then create the new one, and verify the existence of the new database:

```
mysql> SHOW DATABASES;
+----------+
| Database |
+----------+
| mysql    |
| test     |
+----------+
2 rows in set (0.00 sec)

mysql> CREATE DATABASE people;
Query OK, 1 row affected (0.00 sec)

mysql> SHOW DATABASES;
+----------+
| Database |
+----------+
| mysql    |
| people   |
| test     |
+----------+
3 rows in set (0.00 sec)
```

SQL commands and subcommands (in the previous example, CREATE is a command; DATABASE is its subcommand) are case-insensitive. The name of the database (and table and field) are case sensitive. It's a matter of style whether one uses uppercase or lowercase, but traditionally the SQL commands are distinguished by uppercase.

One way to think of a *database* is as a container for related *tables.* A table is a collection of *rows,* each row holding data for one *record,* each record containing chunks of information called *fields.*

5.2.2 The USE Command

Before anything can be done with the newly created database, MySQL has to connect to it. That's done with the USE command:

```
mysql> USE people;
```

5.2.3 The CREATE TABLE and SHOW TABLES Commands

Each table within the database must be defined and created. This is done with the CREATE TABLE command.

Create a table named age_information to contain an individual's first name, last name, and age. MySQL needs to know what kind of data can be stored in these fields. In this case, the first name and the last name are character strings of up to 20 characters each, and the age is an integer:

```
mysql> CREATE TABLE age_information (
    -> lastname    CHAR(20),
    -> firstname   CHAR(20),
    -> age         INT
    -> );
Query OK, 0 rows affected (0.00 sec)
```

It appears that the table was created properly (it says OK after all), but this can be checked by executing the SHOW TABLES command. If an error is made, the table can be removed with DROP TABLE.

When a database in MySQL is created, a directory is created with the same name as the database (people, in this example):

```
# ls -l /var/lib/mysql
total 3
drwx------    2 mysql     mysql        1024 Dec 12 15:28 mysql
srwxrwxrwx    1 mysql     mysql           0 Dec 13 07:19 mysql.sock
drwx------    2 mysql     mysql        1024 Dec 13 07:24 people
drwx------    2 mysql     mysql        1024 Dec 12 15:28 test
```

Within that directory, each table is implemented with three files:

```
# ls -l /var/lib/mysql/people
total 10
-rw-rw----    1 mysql     mysql        8618 Dec 13 07:24 age_information.frm
-rw-rw----    1 mysql     mysql           0 Dec 13 07:24 age_information.MYD
-rw-rw----    1 mysql     mysql        1024 Dec 13 07:24 age_information.MYI

mysql> SHOW TABLES;
+------------------+
| Tables_in_people |
+------------------+
| age_information  |
+------------------+
1 row in set (0.00 sec)
```

This example shows two MySQL datatypes: character strings and integers. Other MySQL data types include several types of integers (for a complete discussion of MySQL's data types, see `www.mysql.com/documentation/mysql/bychapter/manual_Reference.html#Column_types`):

`TINYINT`	-128 to 127 (signed) or 0 to 255 (unsigned)
`SMALLINT`	-32768 to 32767 (signed) or 0 to 65535 (unsigned)
`MEDIUMINT`	-8388608 to 8388607 (signed) or 0 to 16777215 (unsigned)
`INTEGER` (same as `INT`)	-2147483648 to 2147483647 (signed) or 0 to 4294967295 (unsigned)
`BIGINT`	-9223372036854775808 to 9223372036854775807 (signed) or 0 to 18446744073709551615 (unsigned)

and floating points:

`FLOAT`

`DOUBLE`

`REAL` (same as `DOUBLE`)

`DECIMAL`

`NUMERIC` (same as `DECIMAL`)

There are several data types to represent a date:

`DATE`	YYYY-MM-DD
`DATETIME`	YYYY-MM-DD HH:MM:SS
`TIMESTAMP`	YYYYMMDDHHMMSS or YYMMDDHHMMSS or YYYYMMDD or YYMMDD
`TIME`	HH:MM:SS
`YEAR`	YYYY or YY

The table `age_information` used the `CHAR` character data type. The following are the other character data types. Several have `BLOB` in their name—a `BLOB` is a Binary Large OBject that can hold a variable amount of data. The types with `TEXT` in their name are just like their corresponding `BLOB`s except when matching is involved: The BLOBs are case-sensitive, and the TEXTs are case-insensitive.

VARCHAR	variable-length string up to 255 characters
TINYBLOB TINYTEXT	maximum length 255 characters
BLOB TEXT	maximum length 65535 characters
MEDIUMBLOB MEDIUMTEXT	maximum length 16777215 characters
LONGBLOB LONGTEXT	maximum length 4294967295 characters

5.2.4 The DESCRIBE Command

The DESCRIBE command gives information about the fields in a table. The fields created earlier—lastname, firstname, and age—appear to have been created correctly.

```
mysql> DESCRIBE age_information;
+-----------+----------+------+-----+---------+-------+
| Field     | Type     | Null | Key | Default | Extra |
+-----------+----------+------+-----+---------+-------+
| lastname  | char(20) | YES  |     | NULL    |       |
| firstname | char(20) | YES  |     | NULL    |       |
| age       | int(11)  | YES  |     | NULL    |       |
+-----------+----------+------+-----+---------+-------+
3 rows in set (0.00 sec)
```

The command SHOW COLUMNS FROM age_information; gives the same information as DESCRIBE age_information; but DESCRIBE involves less typing. (If you're really trying to save keystrokes, you could abbreviate DESCRIBE as DESC.)

5.2.5 The INSERT Command

For the table to be useful, we need to add information to it. We do so with the INSERT command:

```
mysql> INSERT INTO age_information
    ->        (lastname, firstname, age)
    ->        VALUES ('Wall', 'Larry', 46);
Query OK, 1 row affected (0.00 sec)
```

The syntax of the command is INSERT INTO, followed by the table in which to insert, a list within parentheses of the fields into which information is to be inserted, and the qualifier VALUES followed by the list of values in parentheses in the same order as the respective fields.[1]

5.2.6 The SELECT Command

SELECT selects records from the database. When this command is executed from the command line, MySQL prints all the records that match the query. The simplest use of SELECT is shown in this example:

```
mysql> SELECT * FROM age_information;
+----------+-----------+------+
| lastname | firstname | age  |
+----------+-----------+------+
| Wall     | Larry     |   46 |
+----------+-----------+------+
1 row in set (0.00 sec)
```

The * means "show values for all fields in the table"; FROM specifies the table from which to extract the information.

The previous output shows that the record for Larry Wall was added successfully. To experiment with the SELECT command, we need to add a few more records, just to make things interesting:

```
mysql> INSERT INTO age_information
    ->         (lastname, firstname, age)
    ->         VALUES ('Torvalds', 'Linus', 31);
Query OK, 1 row affected (0.00 sec)

mysql> INSERT INTO age_information
    ->         (lastname, firstname, age)
    ->         VALUES ('Raymond', 'Eric', 40);
Query OK, 1 row affected (0.00 sec)

mysql> SELECT * FROM age_information;
+----------+-----------+------+
| lastname | firstname | age  |
+----------+-----------+------+
| Wall     | Larry     |   46 |
| Torvalds | Linus     |   31 |
| Raymond  | Eric      |   40 |
+----------+-----------+------+
3 rows in set (0.00 sec)
```

---

[1]We did extensive research to determine that none of the names used in this chapter belong to real people.

There are many ways to use the SELECT command—it's very flexible. First, sort the table based on lastname:

```
mysql> SELECT * FROM age_information
    ->          ORDER BY lastname;
+----------+-----------+------+
| lastname | firstname | age  |
+----------+-----------+------+
| Raymond  | Eric      |   40 |
| Torvalds | Linus     |   31 |
| Wall     | Larry     |   46 |
+----------+-----------+------+
3 rows in set (0.00 sec)
```

Now show only the lastname field, sorted by lastname:

```
mysql> SELECT lastname FROM age_information
    ->          ORDER BY lastname;
+----------+
| lastname |
+----------+
| Raymond  |
| Torvalds |
| Wall     |
+----------+
3 rows in set (0.00 sec)
```

Show the ages in descending order:

```
mysql> SELECT age FROM age_information ORDER BY age DESC;
+------+
| age  |
+------+
|   46 |
|   40 |
|   31 |
+------+
3 rows in set (0.00 sec)
```

Show all the last names for those who are older than 35:

```
mysql> SELECT lastname FROM age_information WHERE age > 35;
+----------+
| lastname |
+----------+
| Wall     |
| Raymond  |
+----------+
2 rows in set (0.00 sec)
```

Do the same, but sort by `lastname`:

```
mysql> SELECT lastname FROM age_information
    ->      WHERE age > 35 ORDER BY lastname;
+----------+
| lastname |
+----------+
| Raymond  |
| Wall     |
+----------+
2 rows in set (0.00 sec)
```

5.2.7 The UPDATE Command

Since the database is about people, information in it can change (people are unpredictable like that). For instance, although a person's birthday is static, their age changes. To change the value in an existing record, we can UPDATE the table. Let's say the fictional Larry Wall has turned 47:

```
mysql> SELECT * FROM age_information;
+----------+-----------+------+
| lastname | firstname | age  |
+----------+-----------+------+
| Wall     | Larry     |   46 |
| Torvalds | Linus     |   31 |
| Raymond  | Eric      |   40 |
+----------+-----------+------+
3 rows in set (0.00 sec)

mysql> UPDATE age_information SET age = 47
    ->      WHERE lastname = 'Wall';
Query OK, 1 row affected (0.00 sec)
Rows matched: 1  Changed: 1  Warnings: 0

mysql> SELECT * FROM age_information;
+----------+-----------+------+
| lastname | firstname | age  |
+----------+-----------+------+
| Wall     | Larry     |   47 |
| Torvalds | Linus     |   31 |
| Raymond  | Eric      |   40 |
+----------+-----------+------+
3 rows in set (0.00 sec)
```

Be sure to use that WHERE clause; otherwise, if we had only entered UPDATE `age_information SET age = 47`, all the records in the database would have been given the age of 47!

Although this might be good news for some people in these records (how often have the old-timers said "Oh, to be 47 years old again"—OK, probably not), it might be shocking news to others.

This method works, but it requires the database to know that Larry is 46, turning 47. Instead of keeping track of this, for Larry's next birthday we simply increment his age:

```
mysql> SELECT * FROM age_information;
+----------+-----------+------+
| lastname | firstname | age  |
+----------+-----------+------+
| Wall     | Larry     |   47 |
| Torvalds | Linus     |   31 |
| Raymond  | Eric      |   40 |
+----------+-----------+------+
3 rows in set (0.00 sec)

mysql> UPDATE age_information SET age = age + 1
    ->          WHERE lastname = 'Wall';

Query OK, 1 row affected (0.00 sec)
Rows matched: 1  Changed: 1  Warnings: 0

mysql> SELECT * FROM age_information;
+----------+-----------+------+
| lastname | firstname | age  |
+----------+-----------+------+
| Wall     | Larry     |   48 |
| Torvalds | Linus     |   31 |
| Raymond  | Eric      |   40 |
+----------+-----------+------+
3 rows in set (0.00 sec)
```

5.2.8 The DELETE Command

Sometimes we need to delete a record from the table (don't assume the worst—perhaps the person just asked to be removed from a mailing list, which was opt-in in the first place, of course). This is done with the DELETE command:

```
mysql> DELETE FROM age_information WHERE lastname = 'Raymond';
Query OK, 1 row affected (0.00 sec)
```

```
mysql> SELECT * FROM age_information;
+----------+-----------+------+
| lastname | firstname | age  |
+----------+-----------+------+
| Wall     | Larry     |   48 |
| Torvalds | Linus     |   31 |
+----------+-----------+------+
2 rows in set (0.00 sec)
```

Eric is in good company here, so put him back:

```
mysql> INSERT INTO age_information
    ->        (lastname, firstname, age)
    ->        VALUES ('Raymond', 'Eric', 40);

Query OK, 1 row affected (0.00 sec)

mysql> SELECT * FROM age_information;
+----------+-----------+------+
| lastname | firstname | age  |
+----------+-----------+------+
| Wall     | Larry     |   48 |
| Torvalds | Linus     |   31 |
| Raymond  | Eric      |   40 |
+----------+-----------+------+
3 rows in set (0.00 sec)
```

5.2.9 Some Administrative Details

All these examples have been executed as the root MySQL user, which, as you might imagine, is not optimal from a security standpoint. A better practice is to create a MySQL user who can create and update tables as needed.

First, as a security measure, change the MySQL root password when logging in to the server:

```
# mysqladmin password IAmGod
```

Now when mysql executes, a password must be provided using the -p switch. Here is what would happen if we forgot the -p:

```
$ mysql -u root
ERROR 1045: Access denied for user: 'root@localhost' (Using password: NO)
```

Try again using -p. When prompted for the password, enter the one given previously:

> Recall that the MySQL user is *not* the same as a Linux user. The `mysqladmin` command changes the password for the MySQL user only, not the Linux user. For security reasons, we suggest that the MySQL password never be the same as the password used to log in to the Linux machine. Also, the password `IAmGod`, which is clever, is a bad password for many reasons, including the fact that it is used as an example in this book. For a discussion on what makes a password good or bad, we suggest you read *Hacking Linux Exposed* [Hatch+ 02].

```
$ mysql -u root -p
Enter password:
Welcome to the MySQL monitor. Commands end with ; or \g.
Your MySQL connection id is 15 to server version: 3.23.36

Type 'help;' or '\h' for help. Type '\c' to clear the buffer
mysql>
```

Doing all the SQL queries in the `people` database as the MySQL `root` user is a Bad Idea (see HLE if you want proof of this). So let's create a new user. This involves modifying the database named `mysql`, which contains all the administrative information for the MySQL server, so first we use the `mysql` database and then grant privileges for a new user:

```
mysql> USE mysql;
Reading table information for completion of table and column names
You can turn off this feature to get a quicker startup with -A

Database changed
mysql> GRANT SELECT,INSERT,UPDATE,DELETE
    ->      ON people.*
    ->      TO apache@localhost
    ->      IDENTIFIED BY 'LampIsCool';
Query OK, 0 rows affected (0.00 sec)
```

The user `apache` (the same user that runs the webserver) is being granted the ability to do most everything within the database, including being able to delete entries in tables within the `people` database. However, `apache` cannot delete the `people` database, only entries within the tables in the database. The user `apache` can access the `people` database from `localhost` only (instead of being able to log in over the network from another machine).

The `IDENTIFIED BY` clause in the SQL command sets the `apache` user's password to `LampIsCool`. Setting the password is necessary only the first time permissions are granted for this user—later, when the apache user is given permissions in other databases, the password doesn't need to be reset.

To verify that these changes were made, log in as apache:

```
$ mysql -u apache -p
Enter password:
Welcome to the MySQL monitor. Commands end with ; or \g.
Your MySQL connection id is 27 to server version: 3.23.36

Type 'help;' or '\h' for help. Type '\c' to clear the buffer

mysql> USE people
Reading table information for completion of table and column names
You can turn off this feature to get a quicker startup with -A

Database changed
mysql> SHOW TABLES;
+------------------+
| Tables_in_people |
+------------------+
| age_information  |
+------------------+
1 row in set (0.00 sec)

mysql> SELECT * FROM age_information;
+----------+-----------+------+
| lastname | firstname | age  |
+----------+-----------+------+
| Wall     | Larry     |   48 |
| Torvalds | Linus     |   31 |
| Raymond  | Eric      |   40 |
+----------+-----------+------+
3 rows in set (0.00 sec)
```

5.2.10 Summary

As discussed, these commands are enough to do basic things with MySQL:

```
SHOW DATABASES
CREATE DATABASE
USE
CREATE TABLE
SHOW TABLES
DESCRIBE
INSERT
SELECT
UPDATE
DELETE
GRANT
```

5.3 DATABASE INDEPENDENT INTERFACE

Running MySQL commands from the shell is well and good the first 12 times it has to be done. After that, the typical lazy programmer starts thinking of ways to automate the process. Here, the answer is Perl and the DataBase Independent interface (DBI). DBI enables one to write programs to automate database maintenance and to write other scripts to interface with MySQL.

DBI is a Perl module that provides methods to manipulate SQL databases. With DBI, one can connect to a database within a Perl script and issue all kinds of queries, including SELECT, INSERT, and DELETE. For now, we create Perl scripts that can be run from the shell. Later, we'll use CGI, mod_perl, Embperl, Mason, and PHP to hook database independent interfaces into web programs.

First, a quick example. We put all these DBI examples in a directory that is under /var/www/ so that the examples are downloadable from www.opensourcewebbook.com/. In the real world, we do not suggest you create a directory under /var/www/ to create arbitrary Perl programs, but for our purposes, it just makes life easier when downloading all the examples. Create the directory and go there:

```
$ mkdir /var/www/bin
$ cd /var/www/bin
```

The first example demonstrates how to connect to a database. This code is stored in the file /var/www/bin/connect.pl and online at http://localhost/mysql/connect.pl or www.opensourcewebbook.com/mysql/connect.pl. The content of connect.pl is:

```
#!/usr/bin/perl -w
# connect.pl

# use the DBI module
use DBI;

# use strict, it is a Good Idea
use strict;

# connect to the database, assigning the result to $dbh
my $dbh = DBI->connect('DBI:mysql:people', 'apache', 'LampIsCool');
```

```
# die if we failed to connect
die "Can't connect: " . DBI->errstr() unless $dbh;

# all is well!
print "Success: connected!\n";

# disconnect from the MySQL server
$dbh->disconnect();
```

First, the use DBI method tells Perl to use the DBI module. This allows us to use all the methods in this class.

Calling the connect() method causes the Perl script to connect to the MySQL database using the Perl DBI class. The first argument to this method is the database to which you want to connect. In this example, the string DBI:mysql:people indicates that it should connect with the DBI module to the database people, which is housed on the local MySQL server. The second and third arguments to the connect() method are the username and password used to connect. Here user apache and the supersecret password are passed. If successful, connect() returns a *database handle* that is assigned to $dbh.

If one day we decide that we want to migrate to another database, such as Oracle, we merely need to change mysql to oracle, and the rest of the script stays exactly the same, assuming the script is not executing a query that is specific to that database server—certainly the case with the scripts in this book. Design for portability!

If connect() returns false, the script dies, printing the error string returned by the errstr() method. If the script doesn't die, it prints a message stating that all is well. This gives us a warm, fuzzy feeling (for maximum fuzzy feeling, perhaps we should have printed "hello, world").

The last thing done is to execute the disconnect() method, allowing the Perl script and database to properly shut down the connection. This is only polite, and if you don't call disconnect(), the script may generate an error message, and the MySQL server will not like you.

Executing this program from the shell produces:

```
$ ./connect.pl
Success: connected!
```

We've connected. But by itself, connecting isn't exceptionally useful, so let's see what records are in the `age_information` table. Create (or download) the script /var/www/bin/show_ages.pl. Online, it is at `http://localhost/mysql/show_ages.pl` or `www.opensourcewebbook.com/mysql/show_ages.pl`. Its contents are as follows:

```perl
#!/usr/bin/perl -w
# show_ages.pl

use DBI;

use strict;

# connect to the server, and if connect returns false,
# die() with the DBI error string
my $dbh = DBI->connect('DBI:mysql:people', 'apache', 'LampIsCool')
        or die "Can't connect: " . DBI->errstr();

# prepare the SQL, die() if the preparation fails
my $sth = $dbh->prepare('SELECT * FROM age_information')
        or die "Can't prepare SQL: " . $dbh->errstr();

# execute the SQL, die() if it fails
$sth->execute()
        or die "Can't execute SQL: " . $sth->errstr();

# loop through each record of our table,
# $sth->fetchrow() returns the next row,
# and we store the values in $ln, $fn and $age
my($ln, $fn, $age);
while (($ln, $fn, $age) = $sth->fetchrow()) {
    print "$fn $ln, $age\n";
}

# finish the statement handle, disconnect from the server
$sth->finish();
$dbh->disconnect();
```

Failure to connect is handled differently by this program. It executes `connect()` and uses the `or` to mimic an `unless`. If the `connect()` fails, the script `dies`.

The script then prepares the SQL query "SELECT * FROM age_information". The query is just like that we might have typed into the MySQL program in the earlier examples (except the command terminator ; is not required in the `prepare()` method). The `prepare()` method returns a *statement handle* object that can then be used to execute the SQL query by calling the `execute()` method. Note that with each of these calls, failure is handled with the `or die()` code.

The results of the SELECT query are handled with a `while` loop. The `fetchrow()` method returns a list of data for the next row of data that is returned by the query, which is then assigned to $ln (last name), $fn (first name), and $age. The information is then printed.

At the end, the `finish()` method is executed to properly clean up and because it is the right thing to do. Running this from the shell produces:

```
$ ./show_ages.pl
Larry Wall, 48
Linus Torvalds, 31
Eric Raymond, 40
```

How might we enter a new record into the table? This code is in the file /var/www/bin/insert.pl. The entire contents of this program can be found online at http://localhost/mysql/insert.pl or www.opensourcewebbook.com/mysql/insert.pl. Here is the good part:

```
# print a nice dashed line
print '-' x 40, "\n\n";

# now, prompt for and read in the data for the new record
print 'Enter last name: ';
chomp($ln = <STDIN>);
print 'Enter first name: ';
chomp($fn = <STDIN>);
print 'Enter age: ';
chomp($age = <STDIN>);

# prepare SQL for insert
$sth = $dbh->prepare('INSERT INTO age_information
                (
                        lastname,
                        firstname,
                        age
                )
        VALUES
                (
                        ?,
                        ?,
                        ?
                )')
        or die "Can't prepare SQL: " . $dbh->errstr();
```

```
# insert the record - note the arguments to execute()
$sth->execute($ln, $fn, $age)
        or die "Can't execute SQL: " . $sth->errstr();

# print another dashed line
print "\n", '-' x 40, "\n\n";
```

Before new data is inserted into the table, the script connects to the server and shows the current contents, just as in show_ages.pl.

Then the script asks the user to enter the last name, first name, and age of the person for the new record and chomp()s the newlines.

Be sure to use those question marks as placeholders. This prevents the need to escape quotes and other nasty characters, thus making the code more secure. Also, in this case, the last name is defined in the tables as 20 characters of text. If the user enters more than 20 characters, only the first 20 are used—hence, no overflow problem (although it wouldn't hurt to double-check the length of the input strings).

The next step is to prepare SQL for the INSERT query. Again, it looks much like what one would have typed in directly to SQL, with whitespace characters for readability, except that it has those three question marks. Those question marks are placeholders for the contents of the variables in the execute() method. The variables $ln, $fn, and $age are inserted into the query where the question marks are, in that order.

To check that the insert worked, the script displays the contents of the table after the INSERT is executed. Then the script cleans up after itself by finishing the statement handle and disconnecting from the MySQL server.

Executing that code produces:

```
$ ./insert.pl
Larry Wall, 48
Linus Torvalds, 31
Eric Raymond, 40
----------------------------------------
Enter last name: Ballard
Enter first name: Ron
Enter age: 31


----------------------------------------
```

```
Larry Wall, 48
Linus Torvalds, 31
Eric Raymond, 40
Ron Ballard, 31
```

5.4 TABLE JOINS

In the world of relational databases, data often has complex relationships and is spread across multiple tables. Sometimes it is necessary to grab information from one table based on information in another. This requires that the two tables be JOINed.

For an example, we create a new table in the people database called addresses that contains information about people's addresses (surprise!). First, it must be created as follows:

```
mysql> CREATE TABLE addresses (
    ->      lastname CHAR(20),
    ->      firstname CHAR(20),
    ->      address CHAR(40),
    ->      city CHAR(20),
    ->      state CHAR(2),
    ->      zip CHAR(10)
    -> );
```

The table needs some data:

```
mysql> INSERT INTO addresses
    ->      (lastname, firstname, address, city, state, zip)
    ->      VALUES ("Wall", "Larry", "Number 1 Perl Way",
    ->              "Cupertino", "CA", "95015-0189"
    -> );
mysql> INSERT INTO addresses
    ->      (lastname, firstname, address, city, state, zip)
    ->      VALUES ("Torvalds", "Linus", "123 Main St.",
    ->              "San Francisco", "CA", "94109-1234"
    -> );
mysql> INSERT INTO addresses
    ->      (lastname, firstname, address, city, state, zip)
    ->      VALUES ("Raymond", "Eric", "987 Oak St.",
    ->              "Chicago", "IL", "60601-4510"
    -> );
mysql> INSERT INTO addresses
    ->      (lastname, firstname, address, city, state, zip)
    ->      VALUES ("Kedzierski", "John", "3492 W. 75th St.",
    ->              "New York", "NY", "10010-1010"
    -> );
```

```
mysql> INSERT INTO addresses
    ->     (lastname, firstname, address, city, state, zip)
    ->     VALUES ("Ballard", "Ron", "4924 Chicago Ave.",
    ->             "Evanston", "IL", "60202-0440"
    -> );
```

To verify the tables were populated, do this:

```
mysql> SELECT * FROM age_information;
+------------+-----------+------+
| lastname   | firstname | age  |
+------------+-----------+------+
| Wall       | Larry     |   46 |
| Torvalds   | Linus     |   31 |
| Raymond    | Eric      |   40 |
| Kedzierski | John      |   23 |
| Ballard    | Ron       |   31 |
+------------+-----------+------+
5 rows in set (0.00 sec)
```

```
mysql> SELECT * FROM addresses;
+------------+-----------+------------------+---------------+-------+------------+
|lastname    |firstname  |address           |city           |state  |zip         |
+------------+-----------+------------------+---------------+-------+------------+
|Wall        |Larry      |# 1 Perl Way      |Cupertino      |CA     |95015-0189  |
|Torvalds    |Linus      |123 Main St.      |San Francisco  |CA     |94109-1234  |
|Raymond     |Eric       |987 Oak St.       |Chicago        |IL     |60601-4510  |
|Kedzierski  |John       |3492 W. 75th St.  |New York       |NY     |10010-1010  |
|Ballard     |Ron        |4924 Chicago Ave. |Evanston       |IL     |60202-0440  |
+------------+-----------+------------------+---------------+-------+------------+
5 rows in set (0.00 sec)
```

Now, on to the JOINs. Let's say we want to find out what city our under-40-year-old people live in. This requires looking up information in two tables: To find out who is under 40, we look in age_information, and to find out the city, we look in addresses. Therefore, we need to tell the SELECT command about both tables.

Because both tables are being used, we need to be specific about which table a particular field belongs to. In other words, instead of saying SELECT city, we need to say what table that field is in, so we say SELECT addresses. city. The addresses.city tells MySQL that the table is addresses and the field is city.

Moreover, we need to hook the two tables together somehow—we do so with the following command by making sure the lastname from the addresses row matches the `lastname` from the `age_information` row. Ditto for the `firstname`. So, our command is:

```
mysql> SELECT addresses.city
    ->     FROM addresses, age_information
    ->     WHERE age_information.age < 40 AND
    ->         addresses.lastname = age_information.lastname
    ->     AND addresses.firstname = age_information.firstname;
+---------------+
| city          |
+---------------+
| San Francisco |
| New York      |
| Evanston      |
+---------------+
3 rows in set (0.02 sec)
```

In English, we are saying, "give me the city for all the people with ages less than 40, where the last names and first names match in each row."

Let's grab the last names and zip codes for all those 40 and over, and order the data based on the last name:

```
mysql> SELECT addresses.lastname, addresses.zip
    ->     FROM addresses, age_information
    ->     WHERE age_information.age >= 40 AND
    ->         addresses.lastname = age_information.lastname AND
    ->         addresses.firstname = age_information.firstname
    ->     ORDER BY addresses.lastname;
+----------+------------+
| lastname | zip        |
+----------+------------+
| Raymond  | 60601-4510 |
| Wall     | 95015-0189 |
+----------+------------+
2 rows in set (0.02 sec)
```

As you can see, there are lots of different ways to query more than one table to get the exact information desired.

5.5 LOADING AND DUMPING A DATABASE

We can load a database or otherwise execute SQL commands from a file. We simply put the commands or database into a file—let's call it `mystuff.sql`—and load it in with this command:

```
$ mysql people < mystuff.sql
```

We can also dump out a database into a file with this command:

```
$ mysqldump people > entiredb.sql
```

For fun, try the `mysqldump` command with the `people` database (a gentle reminder: the password is `LampIsCool`):

```
$ mysqldump -uapache -p people
Enter password:
```

Notice that this outputs all the SQL needed to create the table and insert all the current records. For more information, see `man mysqldump`.

5.6 SUMMARY

MySQL is a powerful, sophisticated, and easy-to-use SQL database program. Using Perl and DBI, one can easily create programs to automate database management tasks. With this knowledge, the prospective web designer should be able to construct a database-based (for lack of a better term) web site that is portable, sophisticated, easy to manage, and professional appearing. We have examined only a small subset of all that MySQL provides (our 80/20 rule in effect).

5.7 RESOURCES

Books

[DuBois+ 99] DuBois, Paul, and Michael Widenius. *MySQL.* Covers MySQL for the newbie and the experienced user.

[Hatch+ 02] Hatch, Brian, James Lee, and George Kurtz. *Hacking Linux Exposed: Linux Security Secrets and Solutions, Second Edition.* Be sure to read the discussion on how to create good passwords.

[Yarger+ 99] Yarger, Randy Jay, George Reese, and Tim King. *MySQL and mSQL.* An excellent book that covers both MySQL and mSQL, two common databases on Linux systems.

Web Site

MySQL home page: `www.mysql.com/`

Part II
Static

6

Website META Language

6.1 INTRODUCTION

Website META Language (WML) is a programming language created by Ralf Engelschall to build HTML code—thus a *meta*language (see www.thewml.org). It provides a convenient way to create and maintain complex static web sites (as opposed to the dynamic web sites we'll create later with CGI, mod_perl, Embperl, Mason, etc.). It's especially useful for maintaining a consistent look and feel across the web site. As such, it's a step up from plain HTML for building a web site, but is easier to use and less complex than the dynamic web tools we'll study in later chapters.

If your site serves up a large number of static web pages, with WML you can change all the pages by changing one template and then executing a make-like command. Another advantage of using WML is that after compilation, there's no more server-side processing; in contrast, the dynamic languages we'll discuss later have to be executed on the server when they are called. In addition, with WML the client-side browser gains a speed advantage from being able to cache the static pages.

The distinction here is something like that of a compiled language versus an interpreted one, with WML being the former and Embperl, Mason, et al., being the latter.

As you go through this chapter, remember that in using WML, you should edit only the .wml files, *not* the .html files. The latter are the output of the former.

6.1.1 A Note about Apache and This Chapter

Our web site, `www.opensourcewebbook.com/`, serves up the WML examples in this chapter. The examples are stored in files named with the `.wml` extension. For you to read the WML sources properly, Apache must be configured to serve up these types of files as plain text, so, as `root`, we added the following line to `/etc/httpd/conf/httpd.conf`:

```
AddType text/plain .wml
```

You probably do not want to make your WML source files available for general perusal, just out of general paranoia. You can add the following `Files` directive to the bottom of the Apache configuration file (`/etc/httpd/conf/httpd.conf`) to deny access to these files. For all files that end in `.wml`, deny access from all clients.

```
<Files ~ "\.wml$">
    Order allow,deny
    Deny from all
</Files>
```

If you modified Apache's configuration file, be sure to restart `httpd`:

```
# /etc/init.d/httpd graceful
```

6.1.2 WML Programs

WML consists of a collection of programs used to build and maintain a web site. These programs are the following:

wml: Website META Language Control The control program for WML. It passes the `.wml` file through the nine phases of processing (discussed later). You seldom, if ever, need to run this manually.

wmk: Website META Language Make A high-level front end for `wml`. This program is usually used to invoke `wml` with command-line options.

wmd: Website META Language Documentation Browser Use it to browse the WML documentation.

wmu: Website META Language Upgrade Utility This is a nifty tool to automatically upgrade WML, if necessary, by fetching the file via

HTTP, extracting the tarball, and then building and installing the new version.

wmb: Website META Language Bug Reporting Tool Use this tool to send a bug report.

6.2 INSTALLATION

To install WML, get the latest version from `www.thewml.org/sw/wml/distrib`. As of this writing, the latest version was `wml-2.0.8.tar.gz`. Save the tarball in `/tmp`.

To build the software, unzip and untar the tarball in `/tmp`. Then, `cd` into the `wml` directory, run the provided `configure` program, and then make, test, and install in the usual manner. Only the last step need be done as `root`:

```
$ cd /tmp
$ tar xzvf wml-2.0.8.tar.gz
$ cd wml-2.0.8
$ ./configure
$ make
$ make test
$ su
# make install
```

Create a directory to work with WML:

```
$ mkdir /var/www/html/wml
$ chmod a+rx /var/www/html/wml
$ cd /var/www/html/wml
```

6.3 THE BASICS

First we discuss some basic ideas of WML—how the files are built and how WML processes them to make the resultant web page. This is important to our understanding of the capabilities and limitations of WML.

6.3.1 Building the HTML Files

WML source files are named with a `.wml` extension (e.g., `example.wml`). These files are not HTML but the WML code that is used to generate the HTML that the browser interprets. To create the HTML from the `wml` code, use the WML make program `wmk`.

```
$ wmk example.wml
wml -n -o example.html example.wml
```

This builds the HTML file `example.html`. The `-o example.html` option means that this is the output file to be generated.

To recursively build all the WML files in a directory and its subdirectories, use the `-a` option:

```
$ wmk -a .
```

This command builds all the files that end in `.wml`. If we don't want to build all the files, but only the files named `index.wml`, we can execute the following command:

```
$ find . -name index.wml -exec wmk {} \;
```

6.3.2 WML Phases

WML compilation is a nine-pass process. This is only a brief overview of the phases, but `wmd` describes the process completely.

Pass 1: Source reading and include file expansion Reads all files that are either `included` or `used`. The specified file is read from either the current directory or a directory indicated with the `-I` option to the `wml` command. The `-I` option can be set in the WML resource file `.wmlrc`. (We discuss resource file options later.) Also, the special strings `__FILE__` and `__LINE__` are expanded (more on this later, too). Either do a `man wml_p1_ipp(1)` or use the `wmd` browser for more information.

Pass 2: High-level macro construct expansion Processes the defined macros and expands them. We discuss this in detail later, but a simple example looks like this:

```
<define-tag myname>John Doe</define-tag>
My name is <myname>.
```

The result of this little example is the text "My name is John Doe." See `wml_p2_mp4h(1)`.

Pass 3: Programming construct expansion Executes the embedded Perl code (aka eperl[1]) in the file. (We discuss this later as well.) eperl code can be placed between the `<perl>` ... `</perl>`, the `<: ... :>`, or the

---

[1]Unfortunately called Embperl in some places. This is not the same as the Embperl we discuss in Chapter 10.

`<:= ... :>` tags. Here is a simple example:

```
#use wml::std::tags

<perl>
sub print_name {
    my($name) = @_;
    print "Hi, my name is $name!";
}
</perl>

The message is: <: print_name("John Doe") :>
```

This example generates "The message is: Hi, my name is John Doe!" See `wml_p3_eperl(1)`.

Pass 4: Low-level macro construct expansion Uses a low-level macro processor for low-level programming. We don't talk much about this phase, so if you want more information, see `wml_p4_gm4(1)`.

Pass 5: Diversion filter Allows us to create *locations* using syntax such as `#FOO#` or `<divert FOO> ... </divert>`, or `..NAME>>foo<<..`, and `<<FOO>>` or `<dump FOO>` to slurp them in later. We talk about this in detail in a later section, but here is a simple example:

```
..NAME>>John Doe<<..
My name is: <<NAME>>!
```

This example generates "My name is: John Doe!" See `wml_p5_divert(1)`.

Pass 6: Character and string substitution Substitutes characters and substrings within `{: ... :}` to support international and special characters. We don't talk about this (because in our experience it isn't used that much), so for details see `wml_p6_asubst(1)`.

Pass 7: Markup code fixup Repairs HTML code, a real help for programmers. Have you ever forgotten those double quotes for your attribute values? This pass adds them in. Have you ever forgotten your `HEIGHT` and `WIDTH` attributes in your `<img>` tag? Fear not, this pass adds them in. Often-forgotten attributes (`ALT` for images, `SUMMARY` for tables) are also added. Lazy programmers like us appreciate this phase. See `wml_p7_htmlfix(1)`.

Pass 8: Markup code stripping Removes unneeded characters. HTML files often contain extra whitespace characters that do nothing but add unneeded bytes, which someone has to wait to download. This pass strips those out, as well as other unneeded HTML characters. If you have a section of text that you do not want to be stripped, you can use the <nostrip> ... </nostrip> tags, and Pass 8 leaves them alone except for the <nostrip> tags themselves. See wml_p8_htmlfix(1).

Pass 9: Markup code splitting and output generation Allows splitting the output among more than one file, also known as a *slice*. This is handy if you need to generate one HTML file in English and another in German, for instance. This capability is useful but advanced for us, so for further information, see wml_p9_slice(1).

6.3.3 The <protect> Tag

Sometimes we don't want WML to process all of the code. An instance of this would be a listing of a shell script—WML would see the comments in the shell script and strip them out. These sections can be wrapped in <protect>...</protect> tags, and WML will not process them except for removing the <protect>...</protect> tag.

6.4 CREATING A TEMPLATE

With WML, it is straightforward to create and maintain an overall look-and-feel template for a web site. HTML code for specific sections of the page can be included on every page so that the header, footer, left and right rails, etc., look the same on every page:

```
#include 'header.wml'
#include "banner.wml"
```

WML makes an important distinction between single and double quotes. Single quotes mean that the file is loaded from the current working directory only, which can be used to force the loading of the local file. If double quotes are used, WML searches for the file in all the directories listed after the -I option (*include*). By default, the current working directory is searched first. Next, if the file is not found, directories are searched in the order specified by the -I option, and the first filename matched is used. In the previous example, if there is a banner.wml in the current working directory, it is the one used.

Let's start with a simple example that includes a header and a footer. Just for a change, the body of the file prints "hello, world!" The header file

/var/www/html/wml/head1.wml is simply basic HTML that is at the head of
an HTML page:

```
<html>
<head>
<title>WML hello1.wml</title>
</head>
<body bgcolor=#ffffff>
```

Similarly, the footer (/var/www/html/wml/foot1.wml) is:

```
</body>
</html>
```

Again, that is just simple HTML that gracefully ends the code started in
head1.wml.

The WML program is /var/www/wml/hello1.wml:

```
#include "head1.wml"

hello, world!

#include "foot1.wml"
```

When invoked, wmk calls wml, which during Pass 1 includes head1.wml;
then adds the body, "hello, world!" from hello1.wml; and finally includes
foot1.wml.

To build the HTML, execute the wmk command:

```
$ wmk hello1.wml
wml -n -o hello1.html hello1.wml
```

That generates /var/www/html/wml/hello1.html, the contents of which are:

```
<html>
<head>
<title>WML hello1.wml</title>
</head>
<body bgcolor="#ffffff">
hello, world!
</body>
</html>
```

Load this in the browser by going to either http://localhost/wml/
hello1.html or www.opensourcewebbook.com/wml/hello1.html. The result
can be seen in Figure 6.1.

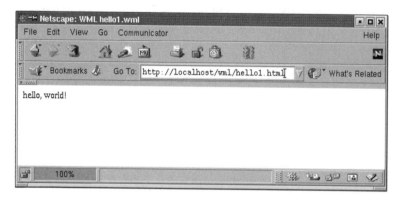

Figure 6.1 hello, world! Version 1 with WML

The two blank lines above and below the text "hello, world!" in `hello1.wml` did not end up in the resulting `hello1.html`, because one feature of WML is to remove any extraneous characters, such as whitespace.

Also, in `head1.wml` the background color `#ffffff` did not have double quotes around it, as it should in valid HTML, so WML is kind enough to put the proper quotes in the resulting `hello1.html`. This is a very nice feature of WML, though of course one shouldn't rely on it to fix everything.

6.4.1 Varying the Template Files

Although all this is static HTML, not every page will have the same title. WML allows you to pass parameters to the files:

```
#include "head.wml" title="Just Say Hello"
```

Then, in the WML file `head.wml`, the value passed is available as `$(title)` (these WML variables look just like those in a shell program). Those parentheses are important. It's `$(title)`, not `$title`.

The new header file using the passed parameter is `/var/www/html/wml/head2.wml`. Between the `<title>` tags the value of `$(title)` is evaluated. In this example, the background color is also passed into the file through `$(bgcolor)`.

```
<html>
<head>
<title>$(title)</title>
</head>
<body bgcolor=$(bgcolor:-"#ffffff")>
```

The background color is set with the syntax $(bgcolor:-"#ffffff")$. This shell-like syntax means "use the value of $(bgcolor)$ if it has a value, else use the default value #ffffff."[2]

Similarly, in the footer /var/www/html/wml/foot2.wml, the author can be supplied through the $(author)$ variable:

```
<hr>
Written by:          <b>$(author)</b>
</body>
</html>
```

The WML file that includes these two files is /var/www/html/wml/hello2. wml:

```
#include "head2.wml" title="WML hello2.wml"

hello, world!

<hr>

<pre>
    here      is    some

    preformatted     text
</pre>

#include "foot2.wml" author="Ron Ballard"
```

To build the HTML, use:

```
$ wmk hello2.wml
wml -n -o hello2.html hello2.wml
```

The result is written to /var/www/html/wml/hello2.html (via the -o hello2. html switch). In this case, hello2.wml does not pass the background color into head2.wml, so the default value #ffffff is used.

```
<html>
<head>
<title>WML hello2.wml</title>
</head>
<body bgcolor="#ffffff">
hello, world!
<hr>
```

---

[2]In WML, all the standard shell expansions are allowed—for a list, see www.gnu.org/manual/ bash-2.02/html_chapter/bashref_3.html#SEC29.

```
<pre>
    here    is    some

    preformatted   text
</pre>
<hr>
Written by: <b>Ron Ballard</b>
</body>
</html>
```

Here the title ends up between the `<title>` tags, the background color is in the `<body>` tag, and the author is in the footer area between the `<b>` ... `</b>` tags.

Again, the unnecessary whitespace disappears—newlines, extra spaces. Even the extra whitespace characters in this line:

```
Written by:            <b>$(author)</b>
```

But the important whitespace within the `<pre>` ... `</pre>` tags is maintained. Cool, huh?

To see this program in action, go to either `http://localhost/wml/hello2.html` or `www.opensourcewebbook.com/wml/hello2.html`. The result can be seen in Figure 6.2.

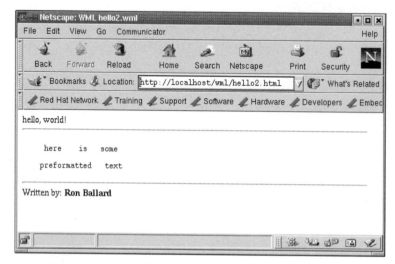

Figure 6.2   hello, world! Version 2 with WML

6.4.2 The use Statement

As the WML system gets more complicated, it's easy to imagine that a file could be `include`d more than once if the programmer were to lose track of things.

To preclude this situation, one can implement the `#use` directive instead of the `#include`. The statement:

```
#include "foo.wml"
```

is written with `#use` as:

```
#use wml::foo
```

Similarly, this statement:

```
#include "directory/file.wml" name="John Doe"
```

is written with `#use` as:

```
#use wml::directory::file name="John Doe"
```

Since `use` is more useful, we'll forget about `include` for everything else we do with WML.

Standard Includes

WML comes with many standard files for commonly used functions. They are usually `use`d like this:

```
#use wml::std::info
```

This specifies the file `info.wml` in the standard WML system include directory `/usr/local/lib/wml/include/std/`. This particular file includes definitions of information about the page. The information is made available by using the `<info>` tag. This standard include file allows us to include comments in the file, such as who wrote the file.

An example of `wml::std::info` is just around the corner.

File Information

Other information can be added to the HTML file, such as the filename (`__FILE__`) and the line number in the file (`__LINE__`). This information is useful for debugging but less so for security. Think carefully before advertising the name of the file to all the possible crackers out there.

Comments

Comments are begun with the pound sign (#), with the obvious exception of statements such as `#include` and `#use`. The end-of-line ends the comments, so each new line of the comment must begin with a new #. Lines that have a pound sign after only whitespace are comments, too. If the # occurs anywhere except at the beginning of the line or after whitespace, it is not treated as a comment. For example:

```
# here is a comment
# another comment

        # here is a comment preceded by only whitespace
this is not a # comment and will be compiled by WML
```

You can also add a marker to the file (__END__) that indicates that the WML code is finished. Any text that follows is thus a comment and not compiled as WML code.

To illustrate all these concepts, let's look at another variation of "hello, world!" The header file is /var/www/html/wml/head3.wml:

```
# use std/info.wml so we can use
# the <info> tag

#use wml::std::info

<html>
<head>

<info style=comment domainname="opensourcewebbook.com"
    copyright="2002 James Lee, Brent Ware
             http://www.opensourcewebbook.com/">

<title>$(title)</title>
</head>
<body bgcolor=$(bgcolor:-"#ffffff")>
<h3>Header Stuff</h3>
File: <b>__FILE__</b><br>
Line: <b>__LINE__</b>
```

This header uses `wml::std::info` so that we can use the `<info>` tag. The tag includes information about the file using the `comment` style (all the information is within an HTML comment). This file also prints the filename

(__FILE__) and line number (__LINE__). Similarly, we can use these in the footer in /var/www/html/wml/foot3.wml:

```
<hr>
<h3>Footer Stuff</h3>
Written by:          <b>$(author)</b>
<br>
File: <b>__FILE__</b><br>
Line: <b>__LINE__</b>
</body>
</html>
```

The only new thing here is the use of __FILE__ and __LINE__.

Here is the WML file that will use these two files, /var/www/html/wml/ hello3.wml:

```
#use head3.wml, setting the background color to #ffffcc

#use wml::head3 title="WML hello3.wml" bgcolor="#ffffcc"

# here is the body stuff

<h3>Body Stuff</h3>
hello, world!<br>
File: <b>__FILE__</b><br>
Line: <b>__LINE__</b>

# here is the footer

#use wml::foot3 author="Ron Ballard"

__END__

After the above marker, we can put any text in the file and it
would be treated as a comment.
```

Note the generous use of comments. Values are passed into head3.wml, including a value for the background color. The body HTML is written, including __FILE__ and __LINE__. Then the footer is used, including the author's name. Finally, after the __END__ marker, a section can be added for additional comments.

The following command generates the HTML:

```
$ wmk hello3.wml
wml -n -o hello3.html hello3.wml
```

which looks like this (hello3.html):

```
<html>
<head>
<!--
     Copyright (c) 2002 James Lee, Brent Ware
        http://www.opensourcewebbook.com/
     Author:   James Lee (james@opensourcewebbook.com)
     Modified: 2002-01-25 07:22:57.
     Generated from ``hello3.wml´´ via WML 2.0.8 (30-Oct-2001).
              by James Lee (james@opensourcewebbook.com)
              on 2002-01-25 07:22:59.

     DO NOT EDIT THIS FILE DIRECTLY! INSTEAD EDIT ``hello3.wml´´.

-->
<title>WML hello3.wml</title>
</head>
<body bgcolor="#ffffcc">
<h3>Header Stuff</h3>
File: <b>./head3.wml</b><br>
Line: <b>14</b>
<h3>Body Stuff</h3>
hello, world!<br>
File: <b>./hello3.wml</b><br>
Line: <b>14</b>
<hr>
<h3>Footer Stuff</h3>
Written by: <b>Ron Ballard</b><br>
File: <b>./foot3.wml</b><br>
Line: <b>5</b>
</body>
</html>
```

One useful reminder that we got for free with the <info> tag was the inclusion of this comment in the header:

```
DO NOT EDIT THIS FILE DIRECTLY! INSTEAD EDIT ``hello3.wml´´.
```

which should be perfectly obvious in its meaning. Any changes made to hello3.html will be overwritten the next time wmk is run. WML Rule Number 1 is "change only the .wml files."

To see what the HTML looks like, go to http://localhost/wml/hello3.html or www.opensourcewebbook.com/wml/hello3.html. The result can be seen in Figure 6.3.

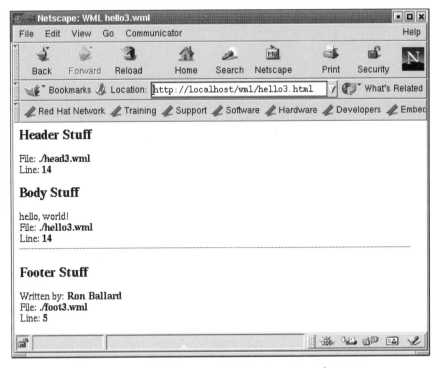

Figure 6.3   hello, world! Version 3 with WML

6.5 OTHER HELPFUL INCLUDES

WML comes with many standard include files that implement commonly used functions. Here we discuss a few of them, but there are more available than we can talk about. See the documents (wmd is your friend) for a complete list and more information.

6.5.1 `wml::std::page`

The `wml::std::page` include file produces a standard HTML page, complete with <html>, <head>, and <body> tags.

Here is a very simple example, found in /var/www/html/wml/page1.wml:

```
#use wml::std::page

<page>

hello, <b>world!</b>
```

This include file defines a new `<page>` tag. Using this tag at the top of our WML file, as in the previous example, generates all the HTML necessary to produce a basic page. The text after the `<page>` tage is placed between the `<body>` ... `</body>` tags, so the usual `hello, world` will be right where it's supposed to be, in the body of the document.

Build the HTML:

```
$ wmk page1.wml
wml -n -o page1.html page1.wml
```

That generates this HTML:

```
<html>
<head>
</head>
<body bgcolor="#ffffff" text="#000000" link="#333399" alink="#9999ff"
            vlink="#000066">
hello, <b>world!</b>
</body>
</html>
```

The `<page>` tag generates the `<body>` tag with default attributes.

You can probably guess what this will look like in the browser, but if you want to check it out, see `www.opensourcewebbook.com/wml/page1.html` or `http://localhost/wml/page1.html`. The `<page>` tag does not generate a title for the document in this example by default. There are two ways to generate it: either use the `<title>` ... `</title>` tag or provide attributes to the `<page>` tag. We use the latter approach.

This example sets the title as well as the background color in the `<page>` tag:

```
#use wml::std::page

<page title="Page 2 in WML" bgcolor="#ffffcc">

hello, <b>world!</b>
```

Build the HTML:

```
$ wmk page2.wml
wml -n -o page2.html page2.wml
```

That results in /var/www/html/wml/page2.html:

```
<html>
<head>
<title>Page 2 in WML</title>
</head>
<body bgcolor="#ffffcc" text="#000000" link="#333399" alink="#9999ff"
vlink="#000066">
hello, <b>world!</b>
</body>
</html>
```

Excellent—both the title and the background color have been set. Take a look by loading either `http://localhost/wml/page2.html` or `www.opensourcewebbook.com/wml/page2.html`.

6.5.2 `wml::std::toc`

HTML allows *named anchors,* and `wml::std::toc` provides an easy way to implement something similar. Named anchors allow one to use URLs to reference specific points in an HTML page so that clients can jump and link to the relevant part of the page. An example of the concept can be found at `www.opensourcewebbook.com/wml/toc.html`.

This page has a number of links at the top that, when clicked, jump to a section of the same document below (a named anchor). If you have a complex or often changing web page, keeping this sort of page working can be a nightmare, but `wml::std::toc` makes this easy.

This include file provides a new tag, `<toc>`, which builds a table of contents of all `<hN>` tags: `<h1>`, `<h2>`, etc. The level of `N` also controls the indentation of the table of contents.

Here is an example, found in `/var/www/html/wml/toc.wml`:

```
#use wml::std::page
#use wml::std::toc style=pre

<page title="toc example">

Table of Contents:

<toc>

<hr>

<h1>Chapter 1</h1>
<h2>Section 1</h2>
<h3>Subsection 1</h3>
<h2>Section 2</h2>
<h1>Chapter 2</h1>
<h2>Section 1</h2>
<h2>Section 2</h2>
```

Obviously, this page is devoid of content,[3] having only the <hN> tags.

The <page> tag builds all the good HTML tags that we need for our page. Our title is set to "toc example." (Still devoid of content.)

"Table of Contents" is the header for the table of contents. The <toc> tag builds the Table of Contents' content, pointing to all the <hN> tags below. When the <hN> tags are processed, WML automatically adds HTML named anchors (e.g., <a name="ToC1"> ... </a>) to which the links of the Table of Contents point.

To build the HTML, use this:

```
$ wmk toc.wml
wml -n -o toc.html toc.wml
```

The resulting code can be seen in /var/www/html/wml/toc.html, an example portion of which is shown here:

```
    .
    .
    .
Table of Contents:
<pre>
<a href="#ToC1"><strong>Chapter 1</strong></a>
    <a href="#ToC2"><strong>Section 1</strong></a>
        <a href="#ToC3"><strong>Subsection 1</strong></a>
    <a href="#ToC4"><strong>Section 2</strong></a>
<a href="#ToC5"><strong>Chapter 2</strong></a>
    <a href="#ToC6"><strong>Section 1</strong></a>
    <a href="#ToC7"><strong>Section 2</strong></a>
</pre>
<hr>
<h1><a name="ToC1">Chapter 1</a></h1>
<h2><a name="ToC2">Section 1</a></h2>
    .
    .
    .
```

To see the result in action, go to either http://localhost/wml/toc.html or www.opensourcewebbook.com/wml/toc.html. The result is shown in Figure 6.4.

There are several different ways to use this include file. Try this:

```
#use wml::std::toc style=ol type=A1ai
```

You can probably figure out what happened.

---

[3]Not unlike much of the Internet—content is harder than programming.

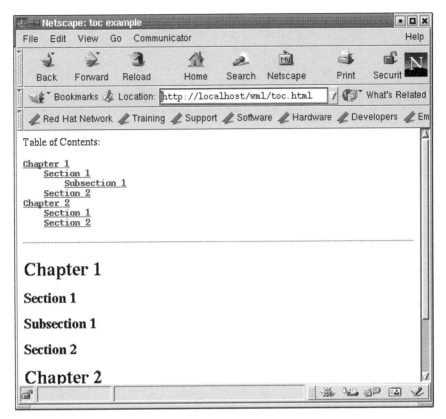

Figure 6.4 `wml::std::toc` in action

6.5.3 `wml::des::navbar`

Let's say you want to create a nifty navigation bar of the type often seen on web sites: When you roll over one of the links, the image becomes highlighted, hence the name "image rollover." A perfect example can be see at `www.hackinglinuxexposed.com/`, shown in Figure 6.5.

You can see the navigation bar along the left rail, showing links to the About page, the Contents page, and so on. When the mouse is moved over a link, the image changes to another image, one that is a different color, usually brighter, which basically says, "Hey, you are now over this link; click here and go somewhere important."

It happens that `www.hackinglinuxexposed.com/` is built with WML, so we can peek at a subset of the WML code that built that navigation.

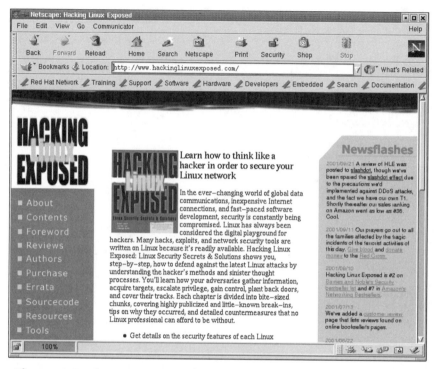

Figure 6.5 Screen capture from www.hackinglinuxexposed.com/

The code uses the include file `wml::des::navbar`. The `des` in the name stands for "design." In other words, this include file contains the definition for helpful tags in designing navigation bars. The example can be found in the file `/var/www/html/wml/navbar.wml`:

```
#use wml::des::navbar

#
# here is the navbar definition
#

<navbar:define name=navbar imgstar=":_on:_on" imgbase="/icons/"
            urlbase="/">
  <navbar:header>This is the Header<br></navbar:header>

  #   button epilog
  <navbar:epilog><br></navbar:epilog>

  #   the buttons
  <navbar:button id=about     url=about/     txt="About"
            img=nv_about*.gif>
```

```
<navbar:button id=contents  url=contents/  txt="Contents"
               img=nv_contents*.gif>
<navbar:button id=foreword  url=foreword/  txt="Foreword"
               img=nv_foreword*.gif>
<navbar:button id=reviews   url=reviews/   txt="Reviews"
               img=nv_reviews*.gif>
<navbar:button id=authors   url=authors/   txt="Authors"
               img=nv_authors*.gif>

#  bar footer
<navbar:footer>This is the Footer</navbar:footer>
</navbar:define>
```

In the navigation bar definition, there are several obvious attributes: `name` is the name of the navigation bar, `imgbase` is the base URI for the image locations, and `urlbase` is the starting point for the URLs for the buttons. The other attribute, `imgstar`, might not be so obvious. It is a string of three values, each separated by a colon. The first part is the suffix for the image displayed normally (no mouse over the item). The second is the suffix of the image to be displayed when a mouse hovers over the button. The third is the suffix of the image displayed when it is selected (being clicked by the mouse).[4]

For instance, if the image button is called `foo.gif`, the first part of `imgstar`, the empty string, is the suffix of the image, so the result is `foo.gif`. When the image is hovered over, `foo_on.gif` is displayed (because _on is the second part of `imgstar`). When the button is clicked, the client sees `foo_on.gif` (because _on is the third part of `imgstar`).

The next bit is `<navbar:header>`, which defines a header for the collection of buttons. Later comes `<navbar:footer>`, the footer text.

The tag `<navbar:prolog>`, which is not used in this example, enables the navigation bar to have HTML that comes before each button, while `<navbar:epilog>`, which is used, enables the navigation bar to have HTML that comes after each button.

Then each button is defined, given an `id`, `url`, and `txt`, which are displayed in the browser status bar they are hovered over, and `img`, which uses `imgstar` because it has the asterisk, or star character, in the names.

---

[4]All this is moot if the browser is Lynx or something similar, and you should design your web site so that there are reasonable defaults for those using such text-based browsers. Aside from crusty old-fashioned geeks like us who use Lynx, the visually impaired use text-based browsers as the input for word-to-speech programs. And some people just like to turn off JavaScript and images because they are on a slow connection.

The previous code set up the WML, and continuing on in `navbar.wml`, we reach the main part of the code, which renders the all-important message we wish to deliver:

```
#
# here is the main stuff
#

<html>
<head>
<title>navbar example</title>
<navbar:jsfuncs>
</head>
<body bgcolor="#ff0000" text="#ffffff">
hello, world
<hr>
<navbar:render name=navbar ≃ navbar>
<hr>
</body>
</html>
```

Within the HTML proper is `<navbar:jsfuncs>`, which generates the JavaScript functions (shown shortly). Finally, `<navbar:render>` generates the HTML to render the navigation bar. To build this code, use:

```
$ wmk navbar.wml
wml -n -o navbar.html navbar.wml
```

WML builds a plethora of stuff for us, including all the necessary JavaScript code in the header:

```
<script type="text/javascript" language="JavaScript">
<!-- Hiding the code
function nb_imgNormal(imgName) {
    if (document.images) {
        document[imgName].src = eval(imgName + '_n.src');
        self.status = '';
    }
}
function nb_imgSelect(imgName) {
    if (document.images) {
        document[imgName].src = eval(imgName + '_s.src');
        self.status = '';
    }
}
function nb_imgOver(imgName, nohints, descript) {
    if (document.images) {
        document[imgName].src = eval(imgName + '_o.src');
```

```
        if (! nohints) self.status = descript;
    }
}
// done hiding -->
</script>
```

And some JavaScript on the body:

```
<script type="text/javascript" language="JavaScript">
<!-- Hiding the code
if (document.images) {
    nb_img1_about_n = new Image();
    nb_img1_about_n.src = '/icons/nv_about.gif';
    nb_img1_about_o = new Image();
    nb_img1_about_o.src = '/icons/nv_about_on.gif';
    nb_img1_contents_n = new Image();
    nb_img1_contents_n.src = '/icons/nv_contents.gif';
    nb_img1_contents_o = new Image();
    nb_img1_contents_o.src = '/icons/nv_contents_on.gif';
    nb_img1_foreword_n = new Image();
    nb_img1_foreword_n.src = '/icons/nv_foreword.gif';
    nb_img1_foreword_o = new Image();
    nb_img1_foreword_o.src = '/icons/nv_foreword_on.gif';
    nb_img1_reviews_n = new Image();
    nb_img1_reviews_n.src = '/icons/nv_reviews.gif';
    nb_img1_reviews_o = new Image();
    nb_img1_reviews_o.src = '/icons/nv_reviews_on.gif';
    nb_img1_authors_n = new Image();
    nb_img1_authors_n.src = '/icons/nv_authors.gif';
    nb_img1_authors_o = new Image();
    nb_img1_authors_o.src = '/icons/nv_authors_on.gif';
}
// done hiding -->
</script>
```

And all the links. Here is an example of one:

```
<a href="/about/" onmouseover="nb_imgOver('nb_img1_about', 0, 'About');
return true" onmouseout="nb_imgNormal('nb_img1_about'); return true"
onfocus="nb_imgOver('nb_img1_about', 0, 'About'); return true"
onblur="nb_imgNormal('nb_img1_about'); return true">
<img name="nb_img1_about" src="/icons/nv_about.gif" alt="About" border="0">
</a><br>
```

WML is building all that JavaScript. Nice for us, because we don't have to worry about it. And look at all the HTML for the links and images (we cleaned it up a bit so you can read it—it really comes out all on one line).

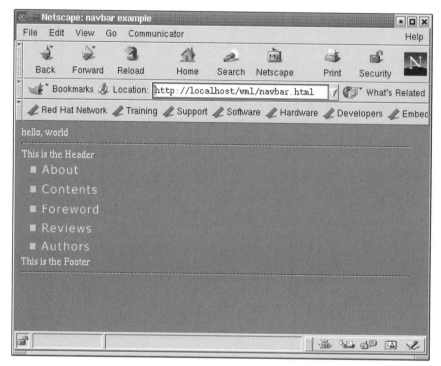

Figure 6.6 The `wml::des::navbar` in action

To see the result of this code, go to `http://localhost/wml/navbar.html` or `www.opensourcewebbook.com/wml/navbar.html`. The result is shown in Figure 6.6.

6.5.4 `wml::fmt::xtable`

If you've written HTML, you know how tedious it is to create tables using the `<table>` ... `</table>` tags. If you haven't, take our word for it. All the `<tr>` and `</tr>` tags must be included in the proper order, not to mention the `<th>`, `</th>`, `<td>`, and `</td>` tags. When you make a mistake in your table tags, finding the place where you failed to open or close a cell can be a nightmare. WML provides a nice solution in `wml::fmt::xtable`.

The include file `wml::fmt::xtable` defines `<xtable>` ... `</xtable>` tags to ameliorate these headaches. Other tags for table headers, table data, and more can also be defined.

Let's start with a simple example, which can be found in `/var/www/html/wml/xtable1.wml` or online at `http://localhost/wml/xtable1.wml` or www.opensourcewebbook.com/wml/xtable1.wml. The contents of this file are as follows:

```
#use wml::fmt::xtable
<xtable>
  ((1,1))
  first - header
  (1,2)
  second - data
  ((2,1))
  third - header
  (2,2)
  fourth - data
</xtable>
```

To build the file, use:

```
$ wmk xtable1.wml
wml -n -o xtable1.html xtable1.wml
```

This build results in this output:

```
<!-- WARNING: The following table was produced by freetable. -->
<!-- Unless you know what you are doing, you should not edit
     it here, -->
<!-- but edit sources and then run freetable to rebuild this
     table -->
<table summary="">
<tr>
    <th>first - header</th>
    <td>second - data</td>
</tr>
<tr>
    <th>third - header</th>
    <td>fourth - data</td>
</tr>
</table>
```

The observant reader will see a comment within the generated tables that starts with WARNING. This should be heeded.[5] It tells the reader that the table was generated with freetable. <xtable> .. </xtable> is a wrapper around freetable.

---

[5]Remember that you should never modify the HTML files—they will simply be overwritten the next time wmk is run, so any changes in the HTML will be transitory.

The starting tag is `<xtable>`. This begins the table, because it causes WML to output the `<table>` tag. In the example, the `<xtable>` tag generates:

```
<table summary="">
...
</table>
```

The `summary` attribute is added automatically.

Any attributes that are provided to `<xtable>` are passed along to `<table>`. For instance:

```
<xtable border="1">
```

creates:

```
<table border="1" summary="">
```

Within the `<xtable>` ... `</xtable>` tags, each table cell is defined. The table headers, `<th>` elements, are defined as:

```
((ROW, COL))
header text
```

Note the use of double parentheses on `((ROW, COL))`. The text for the element is on the next line after the double-parentheses pair, as in the example:

```
((1,1))
first - header
```

creates `<th>first - header</th>` for the upper left cell.

The table data elements, `<td>`, are defined as:

```
(ROW, COL)
data text
```

Now notice the use of single parentheses. Again, the text to be put in that cell is provided on the next line. Thus in our example:

```
(1,2)
second - data
```

creates `<td>second - data</td>` for the upper right cell.

In HTML tables, cells can be formatted with different attributes—the elements can be aligned right or left, or centered. The same thing can be done with WML. For example:

```
(1,2) align=right
second - data
```

That generates `<td align="right">second - data</td>`.

WML also makes it easy to assign an attribute to multiple cells at once. At the top of the `<xtable>` definition, the following could be placed to provide an attribute for every cell in the first row:

```
(1,*) valign=top
```

The text `(1,*)` tells WML to apply the attribute to all columns in the first row. The "*" is a wildcard meaning all elements. For all these columns in the specified row, `valign="top"` is set.

Similarly, `(*,1) align=left` does the same thing for rows. In the first column of every row, WML applies the attribute `align="left"`.

One can get even more complicated; the formulation `(*,2|3) align=right` means that for every row, the second and third columns get the attribute `align="right"`.

An example that illustrates all these concepts can be found in `/var/www/html/wml/xtable2.wml`. This example creates two tables. The first table creates a border (by using `border="1"`). Every element in the first row, `(1,*)`, is given the attribute `valign="top"`. The first column in all rows, `(*,1)`, is granted `align="left"`. For all rows, the second and third columns, `(*,2|3)`, are `align="right"`. A table of three rows and three columns is created.

The second table is given a little spacing and padding with `cellpadding="5"` and `cellspacing="5"`. Then all columns in all rows `((*,*))` have `valign="top"`. We then define a table with three rows and two columns. Here is the example:

```
#use wml::std::page
#use wml::fmt::xtable

# get the standard page html
<page>

<h3>Table with a border</h3>

<xtable border="1">
  (1,*) valign=top
  (*,1) align=left
  (*,2|3) align=right
  ((1,1))
```

```
   Heading 1
   ((1,2))
   Heading 2
   ((1,3))
   Heading 3
   (2,1)
   one for the money
   (2,2)
   two for the show
   (2,3)
   three to get ready
   (3,1)
   four score and seven years
   (3,2)
   five easy pieces
   (3,3)
   six million dollar man
</xtable>

<hr>

<h3>Table without a border and with a little space</h3>

<xtable cellpadding="5" cellspacing="5">
  (*,*) valign=top
  (1,1)
  Chapter 1:
  (1,2)
  Introduction
  (2,1)
  Chapter 2:
  (2,2)
  Linux - The Choice of a GNU Generation
  (3,1)
  Chapter 3:
  (3,2)
  Apache
</xtable>
```

The HTML is generated from the wml in the usual manner:

```
$ wmk xtable2.wml
wml -n -o xtable2.html xtable2.wml
```

The file /var/www/html/wml/xtable2.html contains the resulting HTML. The tables are built as follows:

```
<h3>Table with a border</h3>
<!-- WARNING: The following table was produced by freetable. -->
<!-- Unless you know what you are doing, you should not edit it here, -->
<!-- but edit sources and then run freetable to rebuild this table -->
<table border="1" summary="">
```

```
<tr>
  <th valign="top" align="left">Heading 1</th>
  <th valign="top" align="right">Heading 2</th>
  <th valign="top" align="right">Heading 3</th>
</tr>
<tr>
  <td align="left">one for the money</td>
  <td align="right">two for the show</td>
  <td align="right">three to get ready</td>
</tr>
<tr>
  <td align="left">four score and seven years</td>
  <td align="right">five easy pieces</td>
  <td align="right">six million dollar man</td>
</tr>
</table>
```

and:

```
<h3>Table without a border and with a little space</h3>
<!-- WARNING: The following table was produced by freetable. -->
<!-- Unless you know what you are doing, you should not edit it here, -->
<!-- but edit sources and then run freetable to rebuild this table -->
<table cellpadding="5" cellspacing="5" summary="">
  <tr>
    <td valign="top">Chapter 1: </td>
    <td valign="top">Introduction</td>
  </tr>
  <tr>
    <td valign="top">Chapter 2: </td>
    <td valign="top">Linux - The Choice of a GNU Generation</td>
  </tr>
  <tr>
    <td valign="top">Chapter 3: </td>
    <td valign="top">Apache</td>
  </tr>
</table>
```

To see the result, go to www.opensourcewebbook.com/wml/xtable2.html or http://localhost/wml/xtable2.html. The result can be seen in Figure 6.7.

6.5.5 wml::des::all

This include file includes all the Web design category includes. These are as follows:

- wml::des::gfont—graphical font tag
- wml::des::imgbg—background images

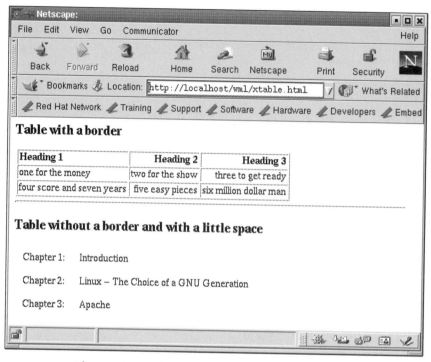

Figure 6.7   The `wml::fmt::xtable` in action

- `wml::des::imgdot`—one pt. dot images
- `wml::des::lowsrc`—low source attribute for image tags
- `wml::des::navbar`—navigation bar (discussed earlier)
- `wml::des::preload`—preload page contents
- `wml::des::rollover`—rollover-style image button
- `wml::des::space`—layout space
- `wml::des::typography`—typography

Although these are worthwhile, we'll not go into them here. For details about them, use the `wmd` browser.

6.6 DIVERSION

In the process of making the HTML files, WML implements a *text diversion filter*. That bit of jargon means that a section of text can be created in one place in a file, or in a completely separate file, and then included somewhere else within the HTML. This is most helpful with templates, because a template is an HTML file that usually defines the outer HTML (the top, sides, and bottom), and the inner HTML (the page contents) is in a separate file.

This is one syntax to create a diversion:

```
..DIVERSION>>This is the diversion text<<..
```

The marker ..DIVERSION>> begins the text. The name DIVERSION is all uppercase by convention. The diversion does not have to be named DIVERSION; it can be named anything you want as long as the name begins with an alpha and is followed by zero or more alphas, digits, or underscores, upper- or lowercase. The text in the diversion continues until the end-of-diversion marker <<.. is found.

To use the diversion later (or even before its definition) use this:

```
<<DIVERSION>>
```

This causes the text in the definition to be included at this point.

An example can be found in /var/www/html/wml/diversion.wml:

```
..NAME>>John Doe<<..

Hello <<NAME>>!
<br>
Here is my message:  <<MSG>>

..MSG>>
WML is cool!
<<..
```

The example starts with a diversion definition for NAME, "John Doe." The next line uses the diversion <<NAME>> in the text:

```
Hello <<NAME>>!
```

This line becomes this, after WML is finished processing:

```
Hello John Doe!
```

The definition of NAME comes before its use. That's fine. The next line, however, uses a diversion not yet defined:

```
Here is my message:  <<MSG>>
```

The diversion for MSG is defined *after* it is used. That's kosher—because WML is a multipass process, the definition can be before or after. This definition:

```
..MSG>>
WML is cool!
<<..
```

spans multiple lines. That's fine too—you are free to add whitespace as needed or desired.

To build the HTML, make the WML in the usual fashion:

```
$ wmk diversion.wml
wml -n -o diversion.html diversion.wml
```

The resulting HTML file is:

```
Hello John Doe!
<br>
Here is my message:
WML is cool!
```

If you want to see this example, check out `http://localhost/wml/diversion.html` or `www.opensourcewebbook.com/wml/diversion.html`.

There are other diversion syntaxes as well. One such syntax is:

```
# create the diversion to use later
{#NAME#:
John Doe
:##}

# use the diversion
My name is: {#NAME#}!
```

This is another syntax, which requires the use of `wml::std::tags`:

```
#use wml::std::tags

<divert NAME>John Doe</divert>

My name is: <dump NAME>!
```

We most often use the `..NAME>>` ... `<<..` syntax, but on occasion we use the `<divert NAME>` ... `</divert>` syntax—TMTOWTDI (in WML as well as in Perl and most things LAMP).

6.7 A BETTER TEMPLATE

In order to have a header and footer HTML in the previous examples, we used two separate files. It is preferable to maintain one template file—it's simpler and easier to maintain, and there are fewer opportunities to induce bugs. Both the header and footer HTML can be folded into one file with the following syntax:

```
# put all the HTML for the top of the page here

<<PAGE_BODY>>

# put all the HTML for the bottom of the page here

..PAGE_BODY>>

# the syntax above means to take all the next stuff and stuff it
# into the <<PAGE_BODY>> section
```

The diversion PAGE_BODY (again, the name PAGE_BODY is arbitrary; it could have been named just about anything) is included between the HTML for the top of the page and the HTML for the bottom of the page. Then, the last noncomment line of the file is ..PAGE_BODY>>, which means everything that follows is the definition of the PAGE_BODY diversion that is to be included above.

What follows? In this file, nothing, but this file will be used by another WML file, so the contents of that file are what follows. This is possible because that file, the one that uses this file, has an implicit <<.. terminating the PAGE_BODY definition.

Here is a real, albeit simple, example. This template file is stored in /var/www/html/wml/template1.wml:

```
#
# define the head of the template
#
<html>
<head>
<title>Our Template</title>
</head>
<body bgcolor="#ffffff">
<h1>Welcome to www.opensourcewebbook.com!</h1>

#
# here we end the head, and add the body with
# <<PAGE_BODY>>, then start the footer
#
```

```
<<PAGE_BODY>>

<hr>
Copyright 2002, <a href="/">www.opensourcewebbook.com</a>.
<br>
Comments are appreciated.  Please send them to our
<a href="mailto:webmaster@opensourcewebbook.com">webmaster</a>.

#
# the following is added to say "whatever follows is to be
# dumped into where we say <<PAGE_BODY>>", which is above,
# so all the following text is slurped into the PAGE_BODY
# section, and the following text comes from the file that
# uses or includes this one
#
..PAGE_BODY>>
```

The file that uses this template is /var/www/html/wml/better1.wml:

```
#use "template1.wml"

foo
bar
baz
blah
```

The file `better1.wml` uses the template file. That file defines the HTML in the head and the foot of the document. Then, the rest of the page body, which is the stuff in this file after the `use`, is included between the header and the footer stuff with <<PAGE_BODY>>. To build this, execute:

```
$ wmk better1.wml
wml -n -o better1.html better1.wml
```

The resulting HTML file is in `better1.html`:

```
<html>
<head>
<title>Our Template</title>
</head>
<body bgcolor="#ffffff">
<h1>Welcome to www.opensourcewebbook.com!</h1>
foo
bar
baz
blah
<hr>
Copyright 2002, <a href="/">www.opensourcewebbook.com</a>.
<br>
Comments are appreciated. Please send to our
<a href="mailto:webmaster@opensourcewebbook.com">webmaster</a>.
```

The contents of `better1.wml` are inserted into the body of the document, and the extra blank lines are removed.

You can view this example by going to `http://localhost/wml/better1.html` or `www.opensourcewebbook.com/wml/better1.html`. The result can be seen in Figure 6.8.

Figure 6.8 Our first template

6.8 CONFIGURING WML WITH `.wmlrc`

Like many other things Unix, WML has an *rc* file, another of those invisible configuration files such as `.bashrc` and `.tcshrc` that can be seen with `ls -a`. Unsurprisingly enough, it's called `.wmlrc`.[6]

If this file is placed into a directory, the commands and preferences within are applied to that directory and all its subdirectories. This file is a useful way to declare WML variables, specify include directories, etc.

---

[6]The name `rc` comes from runcom.

6.8.1 Defining Variables

Variables can be defined in `.wmlrc` in one of two ways. First:

```
-DVARIABLE=value
```

The value can then be used by the syntax `$(VARIABLE)`.

As an example, parts of the www.opensourcewebbook.com web site were developed with WML. As we wrote this book, the title was in flux. This title is used on many of the HTML pages, so instead of hard-coding a title that would probably have to be changed in a great many places, we created a variable that holds the title's value. In the `.wmlrc` file in the root directory of the HTML tree, we put:

```
-DBOOK_TITLE="Open Source Web Development with LAMP"
```

So, one of the web pages may say this:

```
Go buy <b>$(BOOK_TITLE)</b>!
```

That gets expanded into:

```
Go buy <b>Open Source Web Development with LAMP</b>!
```

Then, when we changed the name (which we did frequently, for WML testing only, you understand), we simply changed the definition in `.wmlrc` and ran `wmk` recursively, and the entire web site got the same book title. Sweet! At least for the WML portions of the site.

We also defined another helpful variable, the URL for the book's web site:

```
-DOSWB="http://www.opensourcewebbook.com/"
```

This is the other way to define variables:

```
-DVARIABLE~value
```

This creates the variable named `$(VARIABLE)`, and its value changes depending on the directory in which the `.wml` resides. For instance, let's say we add the following variable assignment to the `.wmlrc` file in the HTML document tree root:

```
-DIMG~images
```

This defines $(IMG) as the images subdirectory of the HTML root directory. If this WML code is added to a .wml file in the same directory:

```
<img src="$(IMG)/pic.png">
```

when the WML file is made with wmk, this is the resulting HTML:

```
<img src="images/pic.png" alt="">
```

This means "Grab the file pic.png in the images subdirectory of this directory (the HTML document root)." Now, let's say there is a subdirectory of the HTML root. Within a .wml file within that directory we add this:

```
<img src="$(IMG)/pic.png">
```

This generates:

```
<img src="../images/pic.png" alt="">
```

This means "Grab the file pic.png in the images directory that is a subdirectory of our parent directory (our parent is the HTML root)." Notice that the relative link is created automagically—hence the beauty of this type of variable.

Now, if we had a subdirectory of a subdirectory of the HTML root, the same WML code produces this:

```
<img src="../../images/pic.png" alt="">
```

The great thing about this magic is that the link that is generated is relative to the directory in which the .wml file is found. So, if the file is moved to another directory, simply rerun wmk, and the links will work.

In the book's web site, we added the following to the .wmlrc file in the HTML root directory:

```
-DROOT~.
```

This means that $(ROOT) has the value of ".", or the current directory (the HTML root). Therefore, whenever $(ROOT) is used throughout our web site, the magic relative links are created.

6.8.2 Include Directories

When we were designing and developing the web site for this book, we wanted to maintain a consistent look and feel, an image in the graphic design business. Most of the pages of the web site would follow this layout. The layout consists of a heading at the top, a list of links on the left rail, and content in the middle. To top it off, some pages have content along the right rail (usually links to examples), and some do not.

To implement this look and feel, we created a WML template, `oswb.wml`. That template is in a directory named `/var/www/wml-lib/`—*not* within the Apache HTML root so that a would-be cracker would not find the template in a directory served up by Apache. All the WML files find this file by simply saying:

```
#use wml::oswb
```

WML knows to look for `oswb.wml` in the proper directory because we put `-I /var/www/wml-lib/` in the `.wmlrc` file. The `.wmlrc` has:

```
-I.
-I/var/www/wml-lib
```

This means "For the files I use, first look in the current directory, then look in `/var/www/wml-lib`, then look in the default WML library location." For this example, that is `/usr/local/lib/wml/include/`.

We've talked about several different things to put in the `.wmlrc` file. Here are the complete contents of the `.wmlrc` file found in the directory `/var/www/html/`:

```
-DOSWB="http://www.opensourcewebbook.com/"
-DROOT~.
-DBOOK_TITLE="Open Source Web Development with LAMP"
-I.
-I/var/www/wml-lib
```

6.9 MACROS—CREATING CUSTOM TAGS

The WML macro processor enables us to define custom tags that implement WML macros. Creating custom tags saves typing and enables us to change a lot of HTML by simply changing the definition. To define a new tag, we use the `<define-tag>` macro.

There are two types of tags in HTML: those that have closing tags, such as `<b> ... </b>`, and those that do not, such as `<img>`.

For HTML tags that require closing tags, a new tag is defined as:

```
<define-tag red whitespace=delete endtag=required>
<font color="#FF0000">%body</font>
</define-tag>
```

This defines a tag named `<red>` .. `</red>`. The end tag is indeed required because we say `endtag=required`. The `whitespace=delete` tag tells WML not to preserve superfluous whitespace characters. The stuff between `<define-tag>` .. `</define-tag>` is the text that this tag will be translated into—in this case, `<font color="#FF0000">%body</font>`. `%body` is replaced by whatever is between the `<red>` .. `</red>` tags. Therefore, this tag:[7]

```
<red>Hello, world!</red>
```

becomes:

```
<font color="#FF0000">Hello, world!</font>
```

If we wanted a tag to make not only red text but bold red text, we would change the definition to this:

```
<define-tag red whitespace=delete endtag=required>
<font color="#FF0000"><b>%body</b></font>
</define-tag>
```

Now, `<red>Hello, world!</red>` produces this:

```
<font color="#FF0000"><b>Hello, world!</b></font>
```

Similarly, for a tag that has no closing tag, an example would be a tag `<lamp>`, which outputs the title of this book, *Open Source Web Development with LAMP:*

```
<define-tag lamp whitespace=delete>
Open Source Web Development with LAMP
</define-tag>
```

There are two ways to use unclosed tags:

```
<tag>
```

or:

```
<tag/>
```

---

[7]Hmm, looks a bit like XML.

The first one is HTML-style, and the second is XML-style (note the closing
/>).

Now, `You are reading <lamp>`! produces:

```
You are reading Open Source Web Development with LAMP!
```

Consider another example. We have a style for the web site links that
we want to apply to all the links on the page. It could be:

```
<a href="a.html"><font color="#999966"><b>go to a.html</b></font></a>
```

To create the tag to make this easy, the definition is:

```
<define-tag link whitespace=delete>
<preserve href>
<preserve text>
<set-var %attributes>
<a href="<get-var href>"><font color="#999966"><b><get-var text></b>
        </font></a>
<restore href>
<restore text>
</define-tag>
```

Here a tag named `<link>` is defined. Again, WML will remove superfluous whitespace characters. The attributes to the tag (here `href` and
`text`) are passed into the tag through the variable `%attributes`, so the line
`<set-var %attributes>` indicates that the current definition should be used.
However, in WML, tag attributes are kept in a stacklike data structure, so
before the attributes in the tag can be used, the current values must be
preserved with `<preserve href>` and `<preserve text>`. This means taking
the current values of these two variables, if there are any, and saving them
for later use, clearing their values for this particular tag. Then, after using the values in `%attributes` with `<get-var href>` and `<get-var text>`, the
previous values of the variables can be restored with `<restore href>` and
`<restore text>`.

Then the HTML to which this tag gets converted is defined—the
`<a href> .. </a>` tag. To use the `<link>` tag, input either the HTML-style:

```
<link href="http://www.perl.com/"
    text="Perl is cool">
```

or the XML-style:

```
<link href="http://www.thewml.org/sw/wml/"
    text="WML Home Page"/>
```

All this is put together into an example stored in /var/www/html/wml/define.wml:

```
<define-tag red whitespace=delete endtag=required>
<font color="#FF0000">%body</font>
</define-tag>
<define-tag lamp whitespace=delete>
Open Source Web Development with LAMP
</define-tag>
<define-tag link whitespace=delete>
<preserve href>
<preserve text>
<set-var %attributes>
<a href="<get-var href>"><font color="#999966"><b><get-var
text></b></font></a>
<restore href>
<restore text>
</define-tag>

<html>
<body bgcolor="#ffffff">
<red>Hello, world!</red>
<hr>
You are reading <lamp>!
<hr>
<link href="http://www.perl.com/"
     text="Perl is cool">
<hr>
<link href="http://www.thewml.org/sw/wml/"
     text="WML Home Page"/>
</body>
</html>
```

Use this to generate the HTML:

```
$ wmk define.wml
wml -n -o define.html define.wml
```

This is the resulting HTML, in /var/www/html/wml/define.html:

```
<html>
<body bgcolor="#ffffff">
<font color="#FF0000">Hello, world!</font>
<hr>
You are reading Open Source Web Development with LAMP!
<hr>
<a href="http://www.perl.com/"><font color="#999966">
             <b>Perl is cool</b></font></a>
<hr>
<a href="http://www.thewml.org/sw/wml/"><font color="#999966">
             <b>WML Home Page</b></font></a>
</body>
</html>
```

To see this, load in either `http://localhost/wml/define.html` or `www.opensourcewebbook.com/wml/define.html`. The result can be seen in Figure 6.9. For more information on defining tags, see `man wml_p2_mp4h`.

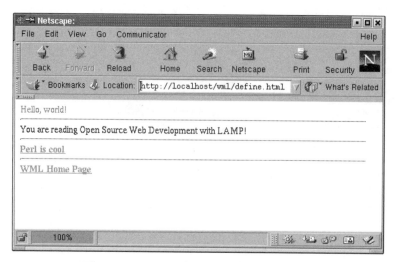

Figure 6.9 Defining your own tags

6.10 PROGRAMMING CODE—eperl

A nice feature of WML is that executable Perl code can be embedded (embedded Perl code in WML= eperl!= `HTML::Embperl`)[8] within the HTML document, allowing the performance of arbitrary computations to be output in HTML.

Perl code can be inserted into the document using the `<: ... :>` syntax. For a simple example, check out `/var/www/html/wml/eperl1.wml`:

```
<:
    print "Hello, world!";
:>
```

---

[8]Covered in Chapter 10.

To build the HTML use:

```
$ wmk eperl1.wml
wml -n -o eperl1.html eperl1.wml
```

The resulting HTML is in `/var/www/html/wml/eperl1.html`:

```
Hello, world!
```

We are sure you can guess what this looks like, but to prove that you are right, check out `www.opensourcewebbook.com/wml/eperl1.html` or `http://localhost/wml/eperl1.html`. This example illustrates that all the stuff printed within the eperl block is output by `wmk`.

Some people (not us) would argue that having to `print()` text in the eperl block to have it displayed is a pain—why not just have what is in the block displayed? To address this, WML allows the following syntax, which is an implied print:

```
<:=
    "Hello, world!";
:>
```

We prefer not to use this syntax—we want to tell WML when we want our text to be outputted, but you may disagree. That's fine—TMTOWTDI to the rescue.

Eperl allows arbitrary computations. This example creates a Perl hash variable and processes it, generating links to web sites. It can be found in `/var/www/html/wml/eperl2.wml`:

```
<:
    %websites = (
        Google   => 'http://www.google.com/',
        OSWB     => 'http://www.opensourcewebbook.com/',
        HLE      => 'http://www.hackinglinuxexposed.com/',
        BLVPNs   => 'http://www.buildinglinuxvpns.net/'
    );

    foreach $site (sort keys %websites) {
        print "<a href=\"$websites{$site}\">$site</a><br>\n";
    }
:>
```

This code assigns a hash variable, `%websites`, information about four web sites. Then the hash is sorted by its keys, and the HTML is printed.

The HTML is generated with:

```
$ wmk eperl2.wml
wml -n -o eperl2.html eperl2.wml
```

The resulting HTML is in /var/www/html/wml/eperl2.html:

```
<a href="http://www.buildinglinuxvpns.net/">BLVPNs</a><br>
<a href="http://www.google.com/">Google</a><br>
<a href="http://www.hackinglinuxexposed.com/">HLE</a><br>
<a href="http://www.opensourcewebbook.com/">OSWB</a><br>
```

There are now four links that connect to four important web sites. To follow these links, go to www.opensourcewebbook.com/wml/eperl2.html or http://localhost/wml/eperl2.html.

This can be quite useful in templates—for instance, to generate a bread crumb trail (a list of links that show where you are in the web site and that link to other pages on the web site—for an example, see the part of www.opensourcewebbook.com/contents/wml/ that begins "Page Path"). This can be done by creating a template that accepts a variable called $(page) that is defined in this form:

```
URI1:Text1:URI2:Text2:URI3:Text3:Other text
```

For instance, using this value:

```
/book1/:Book 1:/book1/chapter3/:Chapter 3:Section 2
```

the first pair, /book1/ and Book 1, ends up as a link that looks like this:

```
<a href="/book1/">Book 1</a>
```

The second pair, /book1/chapter3/ and Chapter 3, ends up as a link that looks like this:

```
<a href="/book1/chapter3">Chapter 3</a>
```

The last element of $(page), Section 2, is not part of a pair, so it is printed simply as plain text.

Moreover, this example demonstrates the use of $(ROOT), which was defined in the .wmlrc file as -DROOT~..

Recall that this means that the directory that contains the .wmlrc file, here /var/www/html/, will be the root of the HTML document tree. Then, any WML file that uses this variable will have the link magically created so that it is relative to the directory that contains the .wml file. For instance, if the file is in the directory /contents/, this:

```
<a href="$(ROOT)/sourcecode/">
```

becomes this:

```
<a href="../sourcecode/">
```

If the file is in the directory /contents/wml/, the result becomes:

```
<a href="../../sourcecode/">
```

Look at the template in /var/www/html/wml/breadcrumb.wml:

```
<html>
<head>
<title>Bread Crumb Example</title>
</head>
<body bgcolor="#ffffff">
<:
    # grab the page information passed in
    my $page_string = "$(page)";

    # if the page info is not blank, process it
    if ($page_string ne "") {

        # first, print some red text
        print "<font color=\"#FF0000\"><b>Page Path - </b></font>";

        # split the line on the colon in case we are passing more
        # than one piece of information as in:
        #   href1:text1:href2:text2:final text
        # loop through, building the link
        my @page = split(/:/, $page_string);
        while (@page > 1) {
            my $href = "$(ROOT)" . shift(@page);
            my $text = shift(@page);
            print "<a href=\"$href\"><font color=\"#999966\">
                        <b>$text</b></font></a> - ";
        }
        print "$page[0]";
    } else {
        print "No bread crumbs!\n";
    }

:>
</body>
</html>
```

The first thing done in this eperl block is to take the WML variable $(page) and convert it to a Perl variable with $page_string = "$(page)". The double quotes are mandatory—if they aren't used, Perl will not interpret the contents correctly.

The code then checks to ensure that the string is not empty. If not, it is processed. If it is an empty string, the code simply prints "No bread crumbs." This won't be necessary for a real template, but it will give us a warm fuzzy feeling while testing the code.

Processing the page string starts by printing some HTML to display the red text Page Path -. Then the string is split on the colon, and while there is still more than one element in the list of stuff, the template outputs the HTML to build the link. Finally, the last text is printed, which is the text with no partner, here stored in $page[0].

The code that uses this template is /var/www/html/wml/eperl3.wml (this should all be on one line, but it wrapped here so that it would fit on the page):

```
#use wml::breadcrumb page="/contents/:Contents:/contents/wml/
                    :WML:Bread Crumbs"
```

It's exceptionally simple—just a use statement. The variable page is assigned a string that has five pieces separated by colons. Therefore, we should end up with two links and some text at the end.

Use this to build the HTML:

```
$ wmk eperl3.wml
wml -n -o eperl3.html eperl3.wml
```

The resulting code is in /var/www/html/wml/eperl3.html. It should be noted that the line beginning with <font color= and ending prior to </body> is all one line and is broken for clarity:

```
<html>
<head>
<title>Bread Crumb Example</title>
</head>
<body bgcolor="#ffffff">
<font color="#FF0000"><b>Page Path - </b></font>
  <a href="../contents/"><font color="#999966">
          <b>Contents</b></font></a> -
  <a href="../contents/wml/"><font color="#999966">
          <b>WML</b></font></a> -
</body>
</html>
```

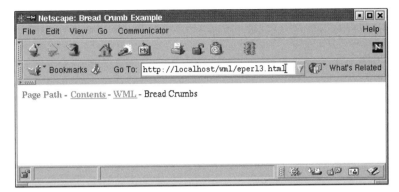

Figure 6.10 Bread crumbs

The result can be seen in Figure 6.10. To see for yourself, go to `www.opensourcewebbook.com/wml/eperl3.html` or `http://localhost/wml/eperl3.html`.

One important thing to note—check out these link `href`s:

```
href="../contents/"
href="../contents/wml/"
```

They are relative links based on the variable `$(ROOT)`.

6.11 PROJECT

The project is to create a template for `www.opensourcewebbook.com`, where we put together all the pieces that we have discussed. The complete source can be found on this book's web site. Snippets are discussed later in this section.

The first source file to examine is the template file, `oswb.wml`. This file can be found online at either `http://localhost/wml/oswb.wml` or `www.opensourcewebbook.com/wml/oswb.wml`. The first thing to notice is that the template uses `wml::std::info`. Some nifty information is included in the header using the `<info>` tag.

6.11.1 Defining New Tags

At the top of the template, two tags, `link` and `red`, are defined:

```
<define-tag link whitespace=delete>
<preserve href>
<preserve text>
```

```
<set-var %attributes>
<a href="<get-var href>"><font color="#999966">
        <b><get-var text></b></font></a>
<restore href>
<restore text>
</define-tag>

<define-tag red whitespace=delete endtag=required>
<font color="#FF0000"><b>%body</b></font>
</define-tag>
```

This makes creating links and marking red text lead-pipe simple.

6.11.2 Varying the Title

The title tag is defined as:

```
<title>Open Source Web Book | $(title)</title>
```

When this template is used, we can say something like this:

```
#use wml::oswb title="Errata"
```

6.11.3 The Bread Crumb Trail

Here is the eperl code to generate the bread crumb trail. As we saw earlier, this is generated by giving the variable $(page) a value.

```
<:
    # grab the page information passed in
    my $page_string = "$(page)";

    # if the page info is not blank, process it
    if ($page_string ne "") {

        # first, print some red text
        print "<font color=\"#FF0000\"><b>Page Path - </b></font>";

        # split the line on the colon in case we are passing more
        # than one piece of information as in:
        #   href1:text1:href2:text2:final text
        # loop through, building the link
        my @page = split(/:/, $page_string);
        while (@page > 1) {
            my $href = "$(ROOT)" . shift(@page);
            my $text = shift(@page);
            print "<a href=\"$href\"><font color=\"#999966\">
                        <b>$text</b></font></a> - ";
        }
```

```
    print "$page[0]";
  }

:>
```

6.11.4 The Left Rail

Several links make up the left rail of the page:

```
<tr><td><link href="$(ROOT)/" text="Home"></td></tr>
<tr><td><link href="$(ROOT)/about/" text="About"></td></tr>
<tr><td><link href="$(ROOT)/foreword/" text="Foreword"></td></tr>
...
```

$(ROOT) is used here to make all the links relative to the desired directory /var/www/html.

6.11.5 The Right Rail—Yes or No?

Two eperl sections in the template check the value of $(rightrail), which determines whether there will be a right rail on the page. Some pages have a right rail that usually includes links to examples, but some do not. The first eperl block that checks this variable prints the width of a <td> tag. If the right rail is present, its width is 333; otherwise, its width is 550:

```
<:
   my $rr = "$(rightrail)";
   if ($rr eq "no") {
       print "<td width=\"550\" valign=\"top\">\n";
   } else {
       print "<td width=\"333\" valign=\"top\">\n";
   }
:>
```

The next block checks to see whether the page has a right rail; if it does, it builds the HTML for the <td> tags:

```
<:
   my $rr = "$(rightrail)";
   if ($rr ne "no") {
       print "<td width=\"20\"> </td>\n";
       print "<td width=\"2\" bgcolor=\"#999966\"> </td>\n";
       print "<td width=\"15\"> </td>\n";
       print "<td width=\"180\" valign=\"top\"><<RIGHTRAIL>> 
                     </td>\n";
   }
:>
```

In the last `<td>` tag, there is a `<<RIGHTRAIL>>`. This is a diversion that will be defined later, in a page that has a right rail, such as /var/www/html/contents/wml/index.html.

6.11.6 Include PAGE_BODY

Somewhere in the middle of the file is the text `<<PAGE_BODY>>`. At this point all the things in this diversion are included. The last line of the template is `..PAGE_BODY>>`, which says that all that follows (the stuff in the file that is using this template) is the text that is inserted into `<<PAGE_BODY>>`.

6.11.7 A Page without a Right Rail

First, a page that does not have a right rail: /var/www/html/wml/errata/index.wml. The first line of this page is:

```
#use wml::oswb title="Errata" page="Errata" rightrail="no"
```

This sets the title and page path (with no links, because there is only one thing in the string) and says "no" to the right rail. The rest of the file is the HTML that will be included in the template when it uses the diversion `<<PAGE_BODY>>`.

Try this yourself. First, build the HTML:

```
$ wmk index.wml
wml -n -o index.html index.wml
```

Then go to either http://localhost/errata/ or www.opensourcewebbook.com/errata/. The result can be seen in Figure 6.11. No right rail, as asked for.

6.11.8 A Page with a Right Rail

Now, a page with a right rail. One can be found in /var/www/html/contents/wml/index.wml. The first line is:

```
#use wml::oswb title="Content | WML" page="/contents/:Contents:WML"
```

This page has set the title and the bread crumb trail and has not assigned the `rightrail` variable, which means we will have a right rail (we could have also assigned it anything other than "no" to achieve this).

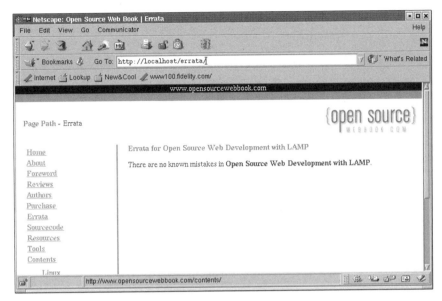

Figure 6.11 Errata

The stuff following this line is the HTML that will be in the middle of the page.

6.11.9 The RIGHTRAIL Section

We then see the line `<divert RIGHTRAIL>`, which begins the HTML that will be displayed in the right rail of the page.[9] It is a bunch of links to the examples in this chapter. The definition of this diversion continues until `</divert>` at the end of this file.

Try this yourself. First, build the HTML:

```
$ wmk index.wml
wml -n -o index.html index.wml
```

Then go to `http://localhost/contents/wml/` or `www.opensourcewebbook.com/contents/wml/` (the first if you built it yourself, the latter if you are being lazy). The result can be seen in Figure 6.12.

---

[9]We could have used the syntax ..RIGHTRAIL>> ... <<.. if we had wanted to.

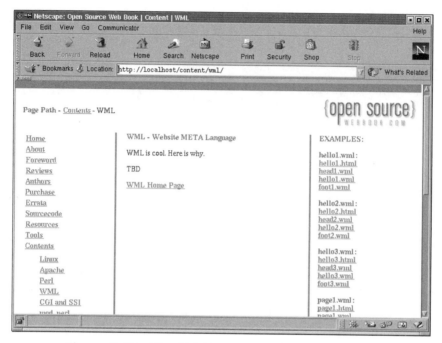

Figure 6.12   The WML page—right rail example

6.12 SUMMARY

WML provides an excellent and powerful way to create static web pages. The pages can be quite complicated, but the make capacity of WML enables much of the complexity to be put into variables, templates, and custom tags that can be reused. WML also incorporates all the power of Perl. WML is like a compiled language, as opposed to the interpreted Web languages Mason and Embperl, which we cover later.

Part III
Dynamic

7

The Common Gateway Interface

7.1 INTRODUCTION

Thus far we have dealt only with static web pages, which are simply HTML text files that don't change except when the file is edited by hand or generated by WML. In this chapter, we learn about *dynamic* web pages, which contain content that is created when requested. Now all the Perl that you learned in Chapter 4 and the MySQL that you learned in Chapter 5 will come in handy.

In this chapter, we discuss the basic way to create dynamic web pages: the Common Gateway Interface (CGI), a standard for communication between a client and the server. CGI scripts can be written in almost any language; we like Perl. Perl is well suited to the types of text processing common for many tasks, such as search engines and forms interfaces. Other benefits of Perl include portability, ease of programming, and overall computational power and performance. And to top it off, the Perl module CGI.pm is a useful way to make Perl CGI script writing quick and easy.

CGI scripts can do simple things that require no input from the client, such as displaying the current time or a random banner when a web page is accessed. Or they can do more complicated tasks involving posted form data from the client, such as entering a credit card number, searching a database and returning the information, and filling out a form. In Chapter 8, you'll find that mod_perl is equally suitable for this purpose, and in many cases, mod_perl is faster, so why learn about CGI scripts at all?

First, the basics of how data is passed from browser to server and from server to browser are the same using either CGI or mod_perl. CGI scripting is easy. There are a wealth of examples to draw from. Apache is probably

Many web sites have Perl CGI programs available for free download. There are too many to mention here, and we wouldn't anyway because it has been our experience that many of the CGI programs available for download—both free and payware packages—are poorly written at best and serious security risks at worst. Therefore, allow us to go on record as saying that although scripts available online can be useful for learning, we suggest that you avoid using them without careful examination. But you wouldn't use a program that you downloaded from Joe Schmoe's web site without looking it over, would you? *Caveat emptor.*

already configured for CGI.[1] mod-perl often requires you to restart the server when a program changes, but CGI changes do not. The rest of the world uses CGI. And you already know Perl. So the main reason to use CGI is that it's common, and at some point in your webmaster career, you'll need to understand how CGI works because you or one of your clients will want to use an existing script. And most everything you learn here will be applicable for mod-perl in some way or another.

7.1.1 CGI Explained

Figure 7.1 depicts what happens during the request and execution of a CGI program. The webserver recognizes a CGI request by the location of the thing requested (or by the filename extension). For instance, if you load the URL `www.example.com/cgi-bin/a.cgi` into the browser, the webserver contacted, `www.example.com`, receives a request such as the following:

```
GET /cgi-bin/a.cgi HTTP/1.0
```

The server notices that the directory that contains the thing requested is `cgi-bin`. It is configured to take the object requested, here `a.cgi`, which is a program located on the server, and execute it as a stand-alone program. The program generates standard output (in Perl, we would use `print()`). This output is in an important format: a header, a blank line, and the body.

---

[1]It is if you installed Linux as we suggested in Chapter 2.

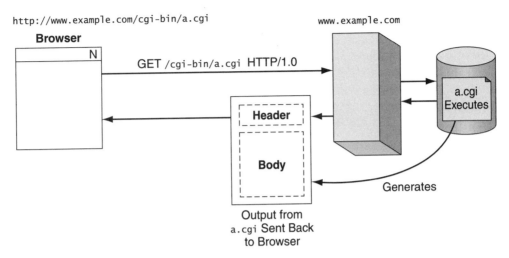

Figure 7.1   CGI explained

The header is a very important piece of information that is sent back to the browser because it tells the browser how to render the data that follows. The primary piece of information that is sent in the header is the `Content-type`. If the header contains `Content-type: text/plain`, the browser displays the data that follows as plain text. If the header contains `Content-type: text/html`, the browser treats the data that follows as HTML and renders it appropriately. And this is what is really important: Programs must output the header, then a blank line, and then the content to be displayed. The blank line is essential—it tells the browser that the header is complete and the body is about to begin.

It is easy to see the header, blank line, and body output from a CGI program by using a shell and telnetting to a server. The following code is an example of connecting to a CGI program named `test.cgi`, which simply prints the content type, the blank line, and some important text:

```
$ telnet www.not_a_real_web_server.com 80
Trying 1.299.299.1
Connected to www.not_a_real_web_server.com (1.299.299.1)
Escape character is '^]'.
GET /cgi-bin/test.cgi HTTP/1.0

HTTP/1.1 200 OK
Date: Thu, 17 Jan 2002 19:57:05 GMT
Server: Acme Web Server Version 0.001b
```

```
Connection: close
Content-Type: text/plain

There's more than one way to do it.
Connection closed by foreign host.
```

When the server accepts the connection, it tells the client so. Then we see the HTTP request:

```
GET /cgi-bin/test.cgi HTTP/1.0
```

followed by a blank line. The webserver prints some header stuff, including the content type that the program prints, followed by a blank line that the program prints, followed by an important philosophical assertion in the next-to-last line. Then, had we used a browser intead of a telnet session, it would have taken the information in the header and the body and rendered it appropriately based on the content type in the header.

Again, that blank line that separates the header and the body is *important.* If it is not present, a server error will result.

7.2 APACHE CONFIGURATION

Apache should be correctly configured if Linux was installed as suggested in Chapter 2. Nonetheless, two directives in /etc/httpd/conf/httpd.conf should be checked before you start using CGI. The ScriptAlias directive should be set to the proper directory:

```
ScriptAlias /cgi-bin/ "/var/www/cgi-bin/"
```

The cgi-bin directory should have the proper options:

```
<Directory "/var/www/cgi-bin">
  AllowOverride None
  Options None
  Order allow,deny
  Allow from all
</Directory>
```

The AllowOverride directive tells the server how to handle HTTP authentication with .htaccess files. When the directive is set to None, .htaccess files are ignored.

If you changed anything in `httpd.conf`, restart the server:

```
# /etc/init.d/httpd graceful
```

7.3 A FIRST CGI PROGRAM

CGI using Perl is straightforward. If you can write a Perl program to print "hello, world!" you're halfway there. So, to be consistent with previous first examples (and because we haven't chanted the mantra in a while), let's start with "hello, world!". Change to the proper directory that contains the server's CGI programs:

```
$ cd /var/www/cgi-bin
```

Create the file `hello.cgi`, which contains the following text:[2]

```
#!/usr/bin/perl
# hello.cgi

print "Content-type: text/plain\n";
print "\n";
print "hello, world!";
```

The program must be executable by all users:[3]

```
$ chmod a+rx hello.cgi
```

Point your browser to one of these URLs, depending on whether you are following the bouncing ball or not: `http://localhost/cgi-bin/hello.cgi` or `www.opensourcewebbook.com/cgi-bin/hello.cgi`. In either of these, you should end up seeing something very similar to Figure 7.2.

The first line of this "hello, world!" CGI script is the usual shell directive telling the shell to run Perl. Because this is a Perl script, the second line is a comment, prefaced with # just as in regular Perl scripts. The rest of this CGI program is simply a series of `print()` function calls.

---

[2]The file extension is a matter of style (or lack thereof); we use `.cgi` for the CGI programs in this book. Another logical option might be the `.pl` extension, because the program is Perl, but we'll maintain a somewhat artificial distinction between plain-Jane Perl scripts and CGI web scripts.

[3]Hereafter, we will assume that you will make all the following CGI programs executable by all users.

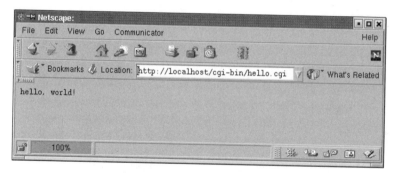

Figure 7.2   hello, world!

Recall from the previous discussion that the CGI program must print the content type followed by a blank line, and the first two `print()` functions do that. The first prints information that will be passed to the browser in the *header*. It tells the browser that the following information is to be interpreted as `text/plain`, or, as you might say out loud (until you've been doing it for a while and become a nerd), plain text. The next statement, `print "\n";` is the all-important, gotta-have-it, don't-forget-it-or-you-will-get-a-server-error print-the-newline character—\n—which is equivalent to printing a blank line. This blank line terminates the header so that the browser knows that the header is finished and anything following is to be displayed in the browser. The next line is of course where the action is, displaying your cheerful and by now almost mantralike greeting to any observer.

In general, CGI programs aren't used to print plain text but to create HTML for the client browser. As an example, create a new program named `hello2.cgi`:

```
#!/usr/bin/perl
# hello2.cgi

print "Content-type: text/plain\n";
print "\n";
print "<b>hello</b>, <i>world</i>!";
```

This HTML made "hello" **bold** and "world" *italicized*. Load this code into the browser via one of these URLs—`http://localhost/cgi-bin/hello2.cgi` or `www.opensourcewebbook.com/cgi-bin/hello2.cgi`—and you should see Figure 7.3.

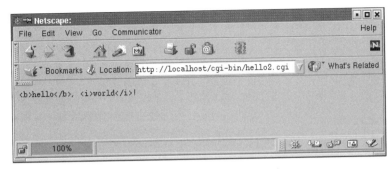

Figure 7.3   hello, world! take 2

Oops. Something's wrong with this picture! Oh, it's because we set the MIME[4] type to `text/plain`. It should be `text/html`. This change is made in `hello3.cgi`:

```
#!/usr/bin/perl
# hello3.cgi

print "Content-type: text/html\n";
print "\n";
print "<b>hello</b>, <i>world</i>!";
```

Go to one of these URLs—`http://localhost/cgi-bin/hello3.cgi` or `www.opensourcewebbook.com/cgi-bin/hello3.cgi`—and you should see what's shown in Figure 7.4.

Usually, we want CGI programs to do more than simply print "hello, world".[5] So let's see an example that displays the date, time, and hostname on a web page:

```
#!/usr/bin/perl
# info.cgi

use strict;
my($host, $date);

# get the info from the system
chomp($host = `/bin/hostname`);
chomp($date = `/bin/date`);
```

---

[4]Multipurpose Internet Mail Extensions. MIME tells the browser (or e-mail program and so on) what kind of content (`Content-type`) this is, and the application decides how to handle it based on that.

[5]Though perhaps by this time, you have become mesmerized by its Zenlike simplicity and cheeriness.

```
# Pass info about the following text in the header
print "Content-type: text/html\n";
print "\n";

# Print the information in HTML on the web page
print "<html>\n";
print "<head>\n";
print "<title>System Information</title>\n";
print "</head>\n";
print "<body bgcolor=\"#520063\" text=\"#ffffff\">\n";
print "<h1>Hello from $host!</h1>\n";
print "The current time is now: $date\n";
print "</body>\n";
print "</html>\n";
```

If you point your browser to either `http://localhost/cgi-bin/info.cgi` or `www.opensourcewebbook.com/cgi-bin/info.cgi`, you will see something very similar to Figure 7.5. The hostname and time will likely be different.

Figure 7.4   hello, world! take 3

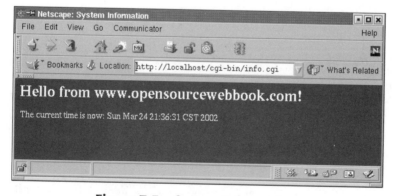

Figure 7.5   System information

The first thing that happens in this script is the execution of two system commands, /bin/hostname and /bin/date, the results of which are placed into appropriately named variables. Note that the commands are enclosed within *backticks* that execute the command and capture the standard output, and are chomped to get rid of the returned newline.

As discussed before, the content type is sent with the print() function, and the header is ended by the newline, which generates a blank line. Last, the HTML to generate the web page is generated via print() functions, including the hostname and date stored in $host and $date, respectively.

There is one big problem with this program: It's hard to read with all those print statements—and this with only a few lines of text. Imagine if your program printed a whole bunch of HTML. Having that many print() statements would make it difficult to read, not to mention debug. There is, of course, another way (TMTOWTDI, remember?)—instead of multiline prints, use a here document:

```
#!/usr/bin/perl
# info2.cgi

use strict;

my($host, $date);

chomp($host = `/bin/hostname`);
chomp($date = `/bin/date`);

print <<EOHTML;
Content-type: text/html

<html>
<head>
<title>System Information</title>
</head>
<body bgcolor="#520063" text="#ffffff">
<h1>Hello from $host!</h1>
The current time is now: $date
</body>
</html>
EOHTML
```

That generates the same web page as shown in Figure 7.5.

In the second program, the here document begins with the syntax <<EOHTML. You don't have to use the particular string EOHTML—the text after

"<<" can be virtually any string of characters, including no characters. EOHTML stands for the End Of HTML. We could have used EOS—End Of Stuff, for instance. The here document, and hence the text that is to be printed, continues until the marker, EOHTML, is on a line by itself—that means it starts in the first column, and nothing else follows it. This last bit is important. It can't be in the second column, and nothing can follow it, not even whitespace.

Another advantage of the here format, besides the text being more readable, is that the double quotes no longer need be escaped, as shown in the <body> tag.

7.4 WHAT CAN GO WRONG?

Many of the errors that can occur with CGI programs produce a page displayed in the browser as shown in Figure 7.6. Pretty helpful, huh?

There could be many causes of this condition. The following are some common things to check.

- The script is syntactically incorrect (try `perl -c script.cgi`).
- The first line is not `#!/usr/bin/perl`.

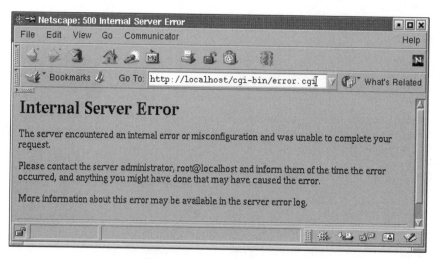

Figure 7.6 Server error

- There are incorrect file permissions (try `chmod a+rx script.cgi` or `ls-l`).

- There are incorrect directory permissions (be sure the `cgi-bin` directory has 755 permissions).

You can also run the program from the command line:

```
$ ./error.cgi
syntax error at ./error.cgi line 6, near ") chomp"
Execution of ./error.cgi aborted due to compilation errors.
```

A clue! The script has a syntax error near line 6.

When all else fails, check the error log file `/var/log/httpd/error_log`. You might see a line that looks like this:

```
syntax error at /var/www/cgi-bin/error.cgi line 6, near ") chomp"
Execution of /var/www/cgi-bin/error.cgi aborted due to compilation
errors. [Fri Mar 25 10:23:17 2002] [error] [client 127.0.0.1] Premature
end of script headers: /var/www/cgi-bin/error.cgi
```

Aha! Another clue pointing to line 6!

7.5 CGI.pm INTRODUCED

So far, this has been pretty thin gruel. To do more complicated things in an easier fashion, we introduce the Perl/CGI programmer's friend: CGI.pm.

CGI.pm is a Perl module written by Lincoln Stein. Our discussion of CGI.pm is just an introduction. Much more documentation is available. We recommend that you check out Lincoln Stein's *Official Guide to Programming with CGI.pm* [Stein 98]. You can also check out the CGI.pm documentation with `perldoc CGI`.

To use CGI.pm, tell Perl that you want to use it with the `use` pragma:

```
use CGI;
```

After Perl executes this statement, your program has access to all the methods that CGI.pm provides. The module can be further refined by specifying a more convenient programming style, called the `standard` style:

```
use CGI ':standard';
```

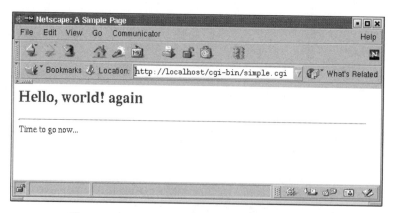

Figure 7.7   A simple page with CGI.pm

Here's an example of some simple HTML that creates Figure 7.7:

```perl
#!/usr/bin/perl
# simple.cgi

use CGI ':standard';

print
    header(),
    start_html(-title   => 'A Simple Page',
               -bgcolor => '#ffffff',
               -text    => '#520063'),
    h1('Hello, world! again'),
    hr(),
    'Time to go now...',
    end_html();
```

The fourth line indicates that we want to use the CGI.pm module, passing the string `':standard'` into the `use` pragma. This ensures that we will use only functions that are appropriate for the widest range of browsers, up to HTML version 3. To use all the HTML there is, we could `use CGI ':all';`. These are the two most widely used options.

The use of `':standard'` also enables us to call CGI.pm methods such as `hr()` directly without an object. If we did not use `':standard'` mode, we would have to create a CGI object and execute the methods with it, as in this code:

```perl
$q = new CGI;

print
```

```
$q->header(),
   .
   .
   .
$q->hr(),
   .
   .
   .
```

As you can see, using `':standard'` mode is much nicer—it looks cleaner and we avoid the difficult-to-type `$q->`. Also, using `':standard'` ensures you of the widest possible audience because the HTML generated will support most major browsers.

The rest of the program is all part of the same `print()` function call. We could have printed each piece separately, but the convention is to combine the multiple `prints` into a single `print()` function.

These are the other methods used in this program.

- `header()` generates the header `"Content-type: text/html\n\n"`; CGI.pm adds the extra newline automatically.
- `start_html()`] generates the HTML for the start of the web page: `<HTML><HEAD>...`; within this, note the use of the following:
  - `title => 'A Simple Page'` sets the title within the title tags: `<TITLE>A Simple Page</TITLE>`.
  - `bgcolor => '#ffffff'` sets the background color within the body tags, used with `-text`, described next.
  - `text => '#520063'` sets the color of the text within the body tags. Used with the previous `-bgcolor`, this produces `<BODY BGCOLOR="#ffffff" TEXT="#520063">`.
- `h1()` generates an `<H1>` tag, and the argument is placed within the tags; in this example, the HTML produced is `<H1>Hello, world! again</H1>`.
- `hr()` generates `<HR>`.
- `end_html()` generates `</BODY></HTML>`.

This program can be run from the command line to see the output (enter `ctrl-D` after the `offline mode` prompt):

```
$ ./simple.cgi
(offline mode: enter name=value pairs on standard input)
^D
Content-Type: text/html

<!DOCTYPE HTML PUBLIC "-//IETF//DTD HTML//EN">
```

```
<HTML><HEAD><TITLE>A Simple Page</TITLE>
</HEAD><BODY TEXT="#520063" BGCOLOR="#ffffff"><H1>Hello, world!
                    again</H1>
<HR>Time to go now...</BODY></HTML>
```

7.6 CGI.pm HTML SHORTCUTS

In addition to the methods discussed previously, CGI.pm has functions for most of the commonly used HTML tags, including headings (h1(), h2(), h3(), etc.), paragraph breaks (p()), lists (li(), dl(), ul(), dd(), etc.), and text-formatting commands (i(), em(), blockquote()). See the CGI.pm documentation for details of all the shortcuts available.

7.6.1 Using HTML Shortcuts

Using these shortcuts is as straightforward as the previous example. Printing a heading:

```
<H1>Welcome to www.opensourcewebbook.com</H1>
```

becomes:

```
$server_name = `/bin/hostname`;
print h1("Welcome to $server_name")
```

An HTML paragraph, <P>, is formatted as print p(); (no arguments), while

```
print p(´This is a new paragraph´);
```

is equivalent to this:

```
<P>This is a new paragraph</P>
```

A list of arguments gets concatenated. This CGI.pm code:

```
$name = ´John Doe´;
print p(´hello ´, $name, ´, how are you?´);
```

results in this:

```
<P>hello John Doe, how are you?</P>
```

Like HTML commands, the shortcuts can be nested inside one another:

```
<P>Here is some <B>bold</B> text</P>
```

The previous statement can be programmed in CGI.pm as

```
print p('Here is some ', b('bold'), ' text');
```

We can use one example to show many of these methods. The following program uses these shortcuts and others as well as a Perl built-in function ($localtime()$) and a CGI.pm method ($server\_name()$). In the end, with all this fancy Perl programming, this program creates the same web page created in the earlier example (see Figure 7.5) but in a much more flexible way:

```
#! /usr/bin/perl
# info3.cgi

use strict;

use CGI ':standard';

my $host = server_name();
my $date = localtime();

print
    header(),
    start_html(-title   => 'System Information',
               -bgcolor => '#520063',
               -text    => '#ffffff'),
    h1("Hello from $host!"),
    "The current time is now: $date",
    end_html();
```

After CGI.pm is used, the program gets the local time and the hostname, as in the earlier example. The $server\_name()$ function, provided by CGI.pm, returns the name of the webserver. The $localtime()$ function is a Perl built-in function that determines the local time on the machine; when assigned to a scalar, here $date, it returns the time in a nice, readable format. After these dynamic values are obtained, the HTML is printed, using the just-obtained values of $host and $date.

7.6.2 Named Parameters versus Ordered Arguments

When we executed `start_html()`, we used *named parameters*—for example, `-title` and `-bgcolor`. CGI.pm provides this way of invoking functions so that we can pass a lot of data into them in a readable, maintainable way. But there is another way of calling CGI.pm functions, which is based on the order of arguments.

For instance, we could invoke `start_html()` as:

```
print start_html(-title => ´My Title´);
```

or by order, as in:

```
print start_html(´My Title´);
```

CGI.pm is written so that if named parameters are not used, it knows the order of the arguments. We know that the first argument to `start_html()` is the title. This invites the question, What is the second argument? This difficult-to-remember detail is obtainable by quickly skimming the documents (`perldoc CGI`).

7.7 INFORMATION RECEIVED BY THE CGI PROGRAM

A CGI program receives three types of information from the server:

- Client request information
- Path information
- Posted data

We look at each of these in turn.

7.7.1 Request Information

The webserver makes available to the CGI script information about the current request called *session information*. This information can be retrieved with several provided methods.

Client information consists of the following:

- `remote_host()`—the name of the client machine
- `user_name()`—the name of the user if authenticated

- `user_agent()`—the browser that the user is surfing with
- `referer()`—the referer (remember, this is misspelled)
- `path_info()`—the path information
- `query_string()`—the query string

The first four items are straightforward. The two functions `path_info()` and `query_string()` are a bit more involved, and they are discussed in detail in Sections 7.7.2 and 7.7.3. Server information consists of:

- `server_name()`—the hostname of the webserver
- `server_software()`—the name of the webserver software
- `virtual_host()`—the name of the virtual host
- `server_port()`—the port that the server is using (usually 80)
- `script_name()`—the name of the script

Most of this client/server information is available in the CGI programs through the environment inherited by the script and stored in %ENV. For instance, if we want the query string, we can look in $ENV{QUERY_STRING}. If we want the server name, we can look at $ENV{SERVER_NAME}. Most programmers prefer the CGI.pm functions listed earlier, but TMTOWTDI.

We can show the use of many of these methods in a single example:

```
#! /usr/bin/perl
# info4.cgi

use CGI ':standard';

print
    header(),
    start_html('More System Information'),
    h1('Client Information'),
    'Here is some information about the client:',
    ul(
        li('The remote host: ', remote_host()),
        li('The user agent: ', user_agent()),
        li('The referer: ', referer())
    ),
```

```
h1('Server Information'),
'Here is some information about the server:',
ul(
   li('The server name: ', server_name()),
   li('The server software: ', server_software()),
   li('The server port: ', server_port()),
   li('The script name: ', script_name())
),
end_html();
```

The result of this program can be seen in Figure 7.8.

The example uses two methods to generate HTML lists, ul() and li(). The ul() method generates <UL> ... </UL> and the li() method generates <LI> ... </LI>. The methods nest, so the result of the CGI.pm method is the same as:

```
<UL><LI>The remote host: www.opensourcewebbook.com</LI>
    <LI>The user...</LI></UL>
```

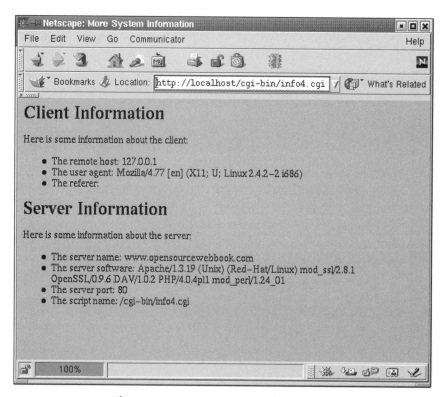

Figure 7.8   More CGI information

7.7.2 Path Information

The *path information* is text that is passed into the CGI program if it exists in the URL after the CGI program name and before the question mark (we talk about the question mark next, when we discuss processing posted form data). This data can be used for a variety of reasons: as information about a path, data that causes the CGI program to perform in a specific manner, or just about anything that you need.

For instance, let's say we are writing a messaging system allowing the user to post to and read from message boards. There are a number of boards and in each board a number of messages. We could pass the board that the user is browsing and the message they are reading in through the path information, as in this URL:

```
http://www.example.com/cgi-bin/messageboard/webprogramming/19312
```

In this example, the name of the program is messageboard (yes, it could be named messageboard.cgi, but this is a matter of preference), the board the user is browsing is webprogramming, and the message is number 19312 (perhaps a message about this book?).

So the path information can be just about any information that you choose to pass in to the CGI program. The path information can be obtained either from %ENV, the hash that contains the CGI program's environment:

```
$env_path = $ENV{PATH_INFO} || ´ ´;
```

or by using the CGI method path_info():

```
$method_path = path_info() || ´ ´;
```

Here's an example of a CGI program that displays the path information using both %ENV and path_info(). Place this code in the file /var/www/cgi-bin/path_info.cgi:

```
#! /usr/bin/perl
# path_info.cgi

use strict;
use CGI ´:standard´;

# get the path from %ENV, then from the
```

```
# CGI method path_info()
my $env_path    = $ENV{PATH_INFO} || '';
my $method_path = path_info()     || '';

print
    header,
    start_html(-title => 'Path Information',
               -bgcolor => '#ffffff'),
    'From %ENV: ',
    b($env_path),
    br(),
    'From path_info(): ',
    b($method_path),
    end_html();
```

As an example, load one of these URLs in your browser: `http://localhost/cgi-bin/path_info.cgi/foo/bar` or `www.opensourcewebbook.com/cgi-bin/path_info.cgi/foo/bar`. Notice that the text "/foo/bar" that follows the CGI program name is the path information. Proof of this can be seen in Figure 7.9.

Figure 7.9   CGI path information

7.7.3 Processing Posted Form Data

Were you wondering when we were going to talk about the mysterious *query string?* That time has come.

The third class of information that the CGI script receives is posted form data (if any). An example is data that comes from an HTML form that has as its action the CGI program in question. Here is a form example stored in `/var/www/html/cgi/nameage.html`:

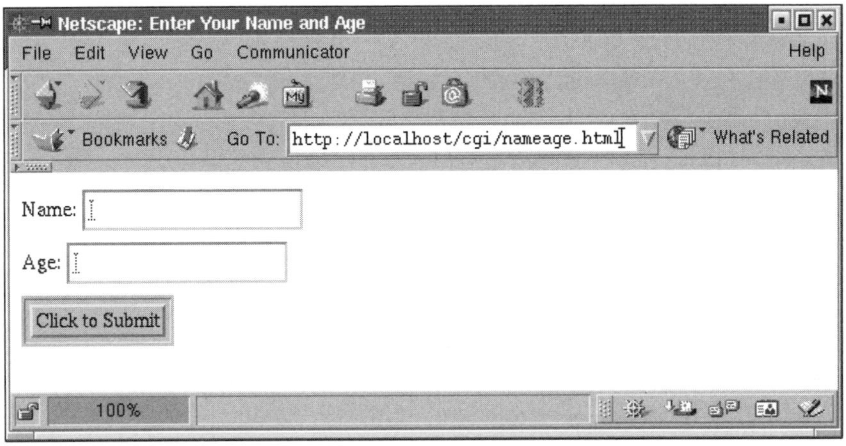

Figure 7.10 Enter name and age

```
<html>
<head>
<title>Enter Your Name and Age</title>
</head>
<body bgcolor="#ffffff">
<form action="/cgi-bin/nameage.cgi" method="get">
Name: <input type="text" name="yourname">
<br>
Age: <input type="text" name="age">
<br>
<input type="submit" value="Click to Submit">
</form>
</body>
</html>
```

This program results in a web page like that shown in Figure 7.10.

When the user clicks the Click to Submit button, the program given as the `action`—in this case `/cgi-bin/nameage.cgi`, which corresponds to the executable program `/var/www/cgi-bin/nameage.cgi`—is executed. Posted data is sent to the program—here the posted data is the name of the fields (`yourname` and `age`) and the values entered into those fields.

Notice that when the data is sent to the program, the URL resembles this:

```
http://localhost/cgi-bin/nameage.cgi?yourname=J.+Random+Luser&age=55
```

The program's name is followed by a question mark (?). The question mark is then followed by this funny looking text:

```
yourname=J.+Random+Luser&age=55
```

This data is called *URL encoded data* and is passed into the CGI program through the *query string*. It is the data from the form that is encoded into a format that can be sent to the webserver through the URL.

> If we wanted to look at this data in the program, we could get the query string information by executing `query_string()`. But usually we don't grab the data directly. Instead, we let CGI.pm take care of things for us.

The query string format is a collection of form widget name/value pairs separated by the equal sign (=), each pair separated from the next by an ampersand (&). So in the example, there are two name/value pairs:

```
yourname=J.+Random+Luser
age=55
```

The text that is posted may contain text that is not legal in a URL (such as a space). This text is encoded before being sent to the server. Spaces are replaced with the plus sign (+), as shown in the example, and other disallowed characters are replaced with a percent character followed by the hexadecimal representation of that character's ASCII value. For instance, the exclamation point character (!) is replaced with %21.

The URL contains the posted data following the "?" because the form was created with `method="GET"`. The GET method passes the data through the URL in the query string. The alternative is to use `method="POST"`. This method passes the data to the CGI program through its standard input instead of through the URL. Either way, CGI.pm handles the data passed in. These are the contents of `nameage.cgi`:

```perl
#!/usr/bin/perl
# nameage.cgi

use strict;
use CGI ':standard';

my $name    = param('yourname') || 'John Doe';
my $age     = param('age')      || 0;
my @params  = param();
```

```
print
    header(),
    start_html('Your Name and Age'),
    "Hello $name, you are $age years old.",
    hr(),
    'The parameters entered are: ',
    b("@params"),
    end_html();
```

The most important method shown in this example is the param() method. This method works either with or without an argument. If param() is called with an argument:

```
$name = param('yourname') || 'John Doe';
```

it returns the value posted for that form widget. Note that the name of the form text widget for the name is "yourname". Passed with that name is the value that the user enters. Executing param('yourname') returns the value entered by the user into the form, or the empty string if the user does not enter any text into that widget. Recall from Chapter 4 that the "logical or" operator used in this statement, ||, is really shorthand for this logic:

```
if (param('yourname') ne '') {
    $name = param('yourname');
} else {
    $name = 'John Doe';
}
```

This makes sure that $name is valid no matter what the user enters, defaulting to "John Doe" if the user doesn't enter a value.

If param() is called with no arguments:

```
@params = param();
```

it returns a list of all the widget names in the form—'yourname', 'age'. If the user entered the name J. Random Luser and the age 55 into the form, the result of nameage.cgi would look like Figure 7.11.

Let's examine a more complicated example showing many more form widgets. The example in /var/www/html/cgi/widgets.html can be found on-line at http://localhost/cgi/widgets.html.txt or www.opensourcewebbook. com/cgi/widgets.html.txt. It creates the form shown in Figure 7.12.

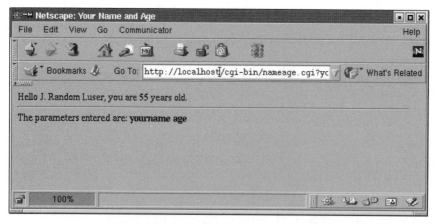

Figure 7.11 Name and age results

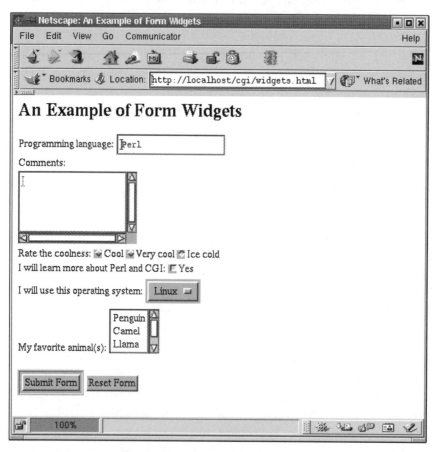

Figure 7.12 Widget examples

After the beginning HTML, we see the creation of the form:

```
<form action="/cgi-bin/widgets.cgi" method="post">
```

This means that when this form is submitted, all the data in the form are sent to the program `widgets.cgi`. Then a bunch of widgets are created.

A text widget, or a one-line box in which the user can enter text:

```
Programming language: <input type="text" name="language" value="Perl">
```

A text widget, or a multiline area in which the user can enter lines of text:

```
Comments:
<br>
<textarea name="comments" cols="20" rows="5"></textarea>
```

A radio button group allowing the user to select one-of-many choices:

```
Rate the coolness:
<input type="radio" name="coolness" value="cool"> cool
<input type="radio" name="coolness" value="very cool"> very cool
<input type="radio" name="coolness" value="ice cold" checked> ice cold
```

A check box, or an on-or-off selection:

```
I will learn more about Perl and CGI:
<input type="checkbox" name="learnmore" value="yes" checked> Yes
```

Two menus are defined with the `<select>` tag.

```
I will use this operating system:
<select name="operating_system" size="1">
    <option>Linux</option>
    <option>Solaris</option>
    <option>HPUX</option>
</select>
<br>
My favorite animal(s):
<select name="animal" size="3" multiple>
    <option>Penguin</option>
    <option>Camel</option>
    <option>Llama</option>
    <option>Panther</option>
</select>
```

The first is a menu button that is clicked, and then the item desired is selected. This is a menu button because the size is set to 1, so only one item is shown in the GUI until the widget is clicked. The other `<select>` widget is a scrolling list box—since the size is 3, three selections are shown in the box, and the others are viewable by scrolling (hmmm, scrolling list box...that's a good name for this widget). Note that the attribute `multiple` is indicated, which means the user can select more than one option by control-clicking the additional items. The fact that more than one item can be selected becomes important when the values selected are grabbed.

The submit and reset buttons are created:

```
<input type="submit" value="Submit Form">
<input type="reset" value="Reset Form">
```

If the submit button is clicked, the data is sent to the program `widgets.cgi`. If the reset button is clicked, the form is reset to its original values.

The associated CGI script to process the posted data is in the file `/var/www/cgi-bin/widgets.cgi`. You can find this file at `http://localhost/cgi/widgets.cgi` or `www.opensourcewebbook.com/cgi/widgets.cgi`.

First we see something important:

```
#! /usr/bin/perl
# widgets.cgi

use strict;
use CGI ':standard';
```

It is a Perl script. Yes! Also, we are using the CGI.pm module in the standard mode, as we have done before.

Then we see the code to grab the posted data:

```
# get the posted form data
my $language        = param('language')          ||'Perl';
my $comments        = param('comments')          ||' ';
my $coolness        = param('coolness')          ||'Ice Cold';
my $learnmore       = param('learnmore')         ||'no';
my $operating_system = param('operating_system') ||'Linux';

# use an array here since we can choose more than one animal
my @animal          = param('animal');
```

Note how each variable that is being assigned posted data has an appropriate default value. Also, because more than one animal can be selected (remember, the `<select>` widget had the `multiple` attribute set, so the user can select more than one animal), the `param()` function is assigned to an array—CGI.pm returns all the items selected as a list, here assigned to `@animal`.

Then we see the code to print the content:

```
print
    header(),
    start_html(-title   => 'Process Widgets',
               -bgcolor => '#ffffff'),
    h1('Process widgets'),
    'You entered the following information into the form:',
    br(),
    'Language: ',
    b($language),
    br(),
    'Comments:',
    br(),
    b($comments),
    br(),
    'Coolness level: ',
    b($coolness),
    br(),
    'You want to learn more about Perl and CGI: ',
    b($learnmore),
    br(),
    'Your operating system of choice is: ',
    b($operating_system),
    br(),
    'Your favorite animal(s) is/are: ',
    b("@animal"),
    end_html;
```

This looks like the code we have seen before. A sample result is shown in Figure 7.13.

This works well enough, but there is a drawback. There are two files to maintain: `widgets.html` and `widgets.cgi`. Wouldn't it be nice to simply have one file that we need to maintain? This is possible if we write the CGI program more generally to have two distinct functions.

- If no data is posted, build the form.
- If data is posted, process the data.

This can be done by modifying `widgets.cgi` with an `if` statement, as shown in `/var/www/cgi-bin/widgets2.cgi`. You can view it in its entirety at `http://localhost/cgi/widgets2.cgi` or `www.opensourcewebbook.com/cgi/`

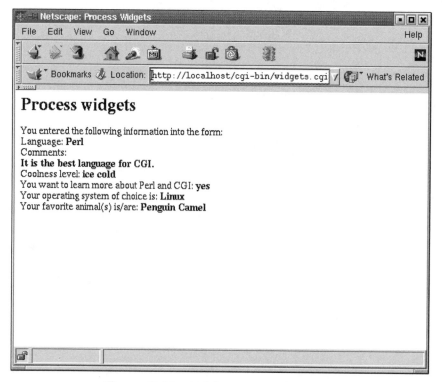

Figure 7.13 Widget example result

`widgets2.cgi`. A quick look at the overall program shows that it is one big `if ... else`:

```
if (param) {

    # we have posted parameters, so process them

} else {

    # no posted data, so build the form

}
```

The `if` portion of `widgets2.cgi` resembles the previous example, `widgets.cgi`:

```
if (param) {

    # we are here if there was any data posted, so process it
    # get the posted form data
```

```
my $language        = param('language')          || 'Perl';
my $comments        = param('comments')          || ' ';
my $coolness        = param('coolness')          || 'Ice Cold';
my $learnmore       = param('learnmore')         || 'no';
my $operating_system = param('operating_system') || 'Linux';

# use an array here since we can choose more than one animal
my @animal          = param('animal');

print
    header(),
    start_html(-title   => 'Process Widgets',
               -bgcolor => '#ffffff'),
    h1('Process widgets'),
    'You entered the following information into the form:',
    br(),
    'Language: ',
    b($language),
    br(),
    'Comments:',
    br(),
    b($comments),
    br(),
    'Coolness level: ',
    b($coolness),
    br(),
    'You want to learn more about Perl and CGI: ',
    b($learnmore),
    br(),
    'Your operating system of choice is: ',
    b($operating_system),
    br(),
    'Your favorite animal(s) is/are: ',
    b("@animal"),
    end_html;
```

The else part, executed if no parameters are posted, is one big here
document (after the header() is printed). The nice thing about the here
document is that the HTML printed is more or less exactly the same as
we saw in widgets.html (we won't show all of it):

```
} else {
    # if we are here, then we need to build the form
    # so print the header, then the html

    print
        header(),
        <<EOHTML;
<html>
<head>
<title>An Example of Form Widgets</title>
```

```
</head>
<body bgcolor="#ffffff">
<h1>An Example of Form Widgets</h1>
<form action="/cgi-bin/widgets2.cgi" method="post">
Programming language: <input type="text" name="language" value="Perl">
<br>
.
.
.
</form>
</body>
</html>
EOHTML
}
```

You can try it out at this book's web site or on your own server by going to `http://localhost/cgi-bin/widgets2.cgi` or `www.opensourcewebbook.com/cgi-bin/widgets2.cgi`.

7.8 FORM WIDGET METHODS

The `here` document, though handy, may not be the best way to build every HTML page. CGI.pm provides several other methods to create widgets, including:

- `start_form()`—start tag for the form
- `textfield()`—tag for a text widget
- `textarea()`—tag for a text area
- `radio_group()`—tags for a radio button group
- `checkbox()`—tag for a check box
- `popup_menu()`—tag for a pop-up menu
- `scrolling_list()`—tags for a scrolling list box
- `submit()`—tag for a submit button
- `reset()`—tag for a reset button
- `end_form()`—</FORM>

The following example, `/var/www/cgi-bin/widgets3.cgi`, uses these methods and produces the same form shown in Figure 7.12. You can find its code at `http://localhost/cgi/widgets3.cgi` or `www.opensourcewebbook.com/cgi/widgets3.cgi`. To prove it works, load one of the URLs.

The `if` part is just like `widgets2.cgi`, so we won't show it here. The `else` part is of interest here:

```
} else {
    # if we are here, then we need to build the form
    # so print the header, then the html

    print
        header(),
        start_html(-title   => 'An Example of Form Widgets',
                   -bgcolor => '#ffffff'),
        h1('An Example of Form Widgets'),
        start_form(),
        'Programming language: ',
        textfield(-name => 'language', -value => 'Perl'),
        br(),
        'Comments:',
        br(),
        textarea(-name => 'comments',
                 -cols => 20,
                 -rows => 5),
        br(),
        'Rate the coolness: ',
        radio_group(-name    => 'coolness',
                    -values  => ['cool', 'very cool', 'ice cold'],
                    -default => 'ice cold'),
        br(),
        'I will learn more about Perl and CGI: ',
        checkbox(-name    => 'learnmore',
                 -value   => 'yes',
                 -label   => 'Yes',
                 -checked => 1),
        br(),
        'I will use this operating system: ',
        popup_menu(-name   => 'operating_system',
                   -values => ['Linux', 'Solaris', 'HPUX'],
                   -size   => 1),
        br(),
        'My favorite animal(s): ',
        scrolling_list(-name     => 'animal',
                       -values   => ['Penguin', 'Camel', 'Llama',
                                     'Panther'],
                       -size     => 3,
                       -multiple => 1),
        br(),
        br(),
        submit(-value => 'Submit Form'),
        ' ',
        reset(-value => 'Reset Form'),
        end_form();
}
```

Here the various CGI.pm functions are used to produce the HTML for this form.

> **N** Notice that `action="/cgi-bin/widgets.cgi"` was not set in the `start_form()` method. CGI.pm is smart enough to set the action to the name of the CGI program it is used within.

CGI.pm offers these other methods to create form widgets:

- `start_multipart_form()`—beginning tag for a multipart form
- `defaults()`—tag for a defaults button
- `password_field()`—tag for a password field (a text field containing data that won't be displayed—it will be starred-out)
- `checkbox_group()`—tags for a group of check boxes
- `filefield()`—tag for a file upload widget (must use `start_multipart_form()`)
- `hidden()`—tag for a hidden field
- `image_button()`—tag for an image button
- `button()`—tag for a generic button

See the CGI.pm documents for further information.

7.9 CGI SECURITY CONSIDERATIONS

Although CGI programming is not inherently insecure, insecure CGI programs are easy to write. In this section, we discuss some of the most common security issues with CGI programs. If you heed these suggestions, you will be a long way toward being secure, or at least you will not be an easy target.

7.9.1 Avoid Shipped and Downloaded CGI Programs

We mentioned this before in Chapter 3, but it deserves mention again: Do not trust preshipped CGIs. Before developing your own CGI scripts, remove all the ones you find in `cgi-bin`, or if you want to keep them around, change their permissions so that they are not executable.

And never download CGI programs from source code web sites. Many contain *serious* security problems. Besides, now that you know how to write them, you don't need to download them. Why should you deprive yourself of the fun of writing them yourself? At the very least, be very sure you understand what any CGI script you download does, in detail, before you use it.

7.9.2 Never Assume Anything

It is very easy for a savvy cracker (or a not so savvy script kiddy, for that matter) to pass to your CGI program fields that you did not expect. As an example, this script executes the `nameage.cgi` script and passes it an unexpected field:[6]

```
#! /usr/bin/perl

use HTTP::Request::Common 'POST';
use LWP::UserAgent;

use strict;

my $ua = LWP::UserAgent->new();
my $req = POST 'http://www.opensourcewebbook.com/cgi-bin/nameage.cgi',
          [ yourname => 'John Doe', age => 95, baddata => 'gotcha' ];

my $content = $ua->request($req)->as_string;
print $content;
```

The bogus field name "baddata" is sent with the bogus data "gotcha." Easy to do, and done all the time.[7] Don't assume that you get only what you expect.

7.9.3 Always Check Data, Including the Length

To quote a former president, "Trust, but verify." He was speaking of the former USSR and nuclear weapons, but the philosophy is the same. The Cold War now is between you and crackers. To deal with the reality that

---

[6]The code may look a bit complex to you, but we bet you could figure out how to take its content and modify it a bit to abuse your favorite CGI program. But we know you would not do this maliciously. We certainly don't suggest you do it.

[7]In the example, sending this data to `nameage.cgi` is not a big deal, because it is essentially ignored; but you can see how easy it would be to send bogus posted data to a CGI program.

you should never trust what you receive, always verify what you have. For instance, if you expect a valid first name, you should verify that you get one:

```
if ($firstname =~ /^[\w\. ]+$/) {
    # all is well
} else {
    # there is a problem
}
```

This regular expression checks to see if $firstname contains only word characters ([a-zA-Z0-9_]), spaces, or periods. No other characters are allowed.

Checking the length of the data is a snap:

```
$name = param('name') || 'John Doe';

if (length($name) > 60) {
    # someone is being nasty
}
```

7.9.4 Never Trust Hidden Fields

This distrust of what you receive applies to hidden fields as well. Let's say that a form to purchase a new pair of shoes has the name of the shoes and the price of the shoes in hidden fields:

```
<input type="name" price="NewShoes">
<input type="hidden" price="149.00">
```

A cracker (or someone who wants a deal on a new pair of shoes, and don't we all?) could post the price as:

```
$req = POST 'http://www.example.com/cgi-bin/checkout.cgi',
        [ price => '0.00', name => 'NewShoes' ];
```

Now that is a good price![8]

---

[8]A similar scam has been worked on PayPal even though this kind of exploit is extremely well known.

One of the most common exploits in practice today, and not just of CGI scripts, is buffer overflows. If you write a CGI program that expects a name, you might write that name to a database (see Chapter 5). If someone were to send you 50MB of data for a name, putting that data in the database would use excessive amounts of disk space or worse. A number of exploits of many different programs have relied on buffer overflows to start their nastiness. Programmers of every stripe must learn to check input data for reasonable lengths in every application—don't be lazy. Do it not just in this application, but everyplace in this book where you accept data from the outside world.

7.9.5 Don't Trust Filenames

The trust issue is magnified many times when it comes to filenames. Never trust data you receive if you are using data to open files. A classic example is that of "magic opens"—for example, a remote mail reader that does an `open MAIL, "/var/mail/$USERNAME"`. This sort of thing has caused many exploits because of applications opening attachments, as you probably know.

7.9.6 Don't Trust Referer Headers

The referer information is sent in through the header. The header can be constructed to be whatever the evil person wants, so don't trust it. Referer information is useful when you want to know from whence a user is coming, but don't put too much trust into it.

7.9.7 Don't Trust Cookies or JavaScript Preprocessing

Cookies are small tokens of information that reside on the client computer and send information back to the server. Examples are the cookie that remembers your password for the *New York Times* and the cookie that tells Amazon who you are so that you can get back to the half-finished order you started yesterday—very convenient, but also powerful and insecure.

Because they are sent in the header, they can be constructed to be whatever a less than honorable person wants. Don't trust them completely. On the server side, always double-check cookie information.

JavaScript preprocessing of data is nice, but don't assume it has taken place. Always check your data.

> **Be Paranoid.** That says it all. If you are going to put your server out in the big bad world and accept bits from the madding crowds, don't blindly accept what they send you. Be cautious, be paranoid, and expect to not think of everything. Check your logs. Watch the skies!

7.10 A NOTE ABOUT die()

In Chapter 4, we learned that when things go disastrously wrong in a Perl program, the situation should be dealt with by terminating the program with the `die()` function. This function prints a message to the standard error output, cleans up nicely, and exits the program with a nonzero exit status.

In CGI programs, if the `die()` function is executed, we may think that the string passed to the function will end up in the browswer. However, standard error output is not sent on to the client that requested the CGI program; instead, it is written to the error log file (here, `/var/www/logs/error_log`). For instance, if the CGI program `test.cgi` contains this line:

```
open FH, '/var/www/data/mydata.dat' or die "File not opened: $!";
```

Let's say that the file `/var/www/data/mydata.dat` doesn't exist. When the client tries to open it, the `open()` fails, causing the `die()` function to be executed. The `die()` generates text that resembles the following:

```
File not opened: No such file or directory at /var/www/cgi-bin/test.cgi
line 10.
```

At first glance, one would think that this output would be sent on to the client, informing it of our problem. However, this is not true. A quick check of the log file would show this output was sent there.

So if you want to handle error conditions cleanly with CGI programs, don't use `die()` to do it. Instead, consider rolling your own error handler, as we do in the following project.

7.11 PROJECT—CGI/MySQL/DBI

Now we have all the necessary tools to do what we came here to do: hook DBI into CGI programs. We'll create a CGI program that displays the current contents of the `age_information` table like that created in Chapter 5. It also presents the user with a form to fill out, and if the user submits the form, the data submitted is added to the database table.

The program is in the file /var/www/cgi-bin/age.cgi. The entire contents can be found at either http://localhost/mysql/age.cgi or www.opensourcewebbook.com/mysql/age.cgi.

This program generates a page that has the look and feel of our web site, so it builds a bunch of HTML code. We put this code into two functions, `top_html()` and `bottom_html()`, to build the HTML for the top of the page and the bottom of the page, respectively. The HTML for the top of the page is quite involved because it includes the <head> information (such as metainformation) and the links along the left rail.

The first thing seen in **age.cgi** is the subroutine `top_html()`, which is one big **here** document. This is followed by the code for `bottom_html()`, which is one small **here** document.

This program is a bit more complicated than the other CGI examples we've shown, and as a result, more things can go wrong. If they do, the script needs to do more things to clean up. It needs a subroutine to do that:

```
####
#
# handle_error() - a subroutine we can use to handle any error
#         conditions
#
####
sub handle_error {
    my $msg = shift ||' ';
    my $dbh = shift ||' ';
    my $sth = shift ||' ';

    print <<EOHTML;
Content-type: text/html

<head>
<title>Age Information Error</title>
</head>
<body bgcolor="#ffffff">
There was an error: <b>$msg</b>
```

```
</body>
</html>
EOHTML

    # finish the state handle and disconnect, if necessary
    $sth->finish()    if $sth;
    $dbh->disconnect() if $dbh;
    exit 0;
}
```

The subroutine `handle_error()` is defined at the top of this program. It takes up to three arguments: `$msg`, a message is printed to the browser; `$dbh`, a database handle; and `$sth`, a statement handle. These values are shifted from `@_` into `my()` variables. After printing HTML telling the user what went wrong, the subroutine finishes the statement handle, if there is one, and then disconnects from the database, if it needs to. This means that this subroutine can be called with a statement handle and/or a database handle, if it is appropriate. It then exits the CGI program gracefully, so nothing else happens.

A subroutine to process the form data is then defined:

```
####
#
# process_form_data() - subroutine to process the form data:
#     we get the posted data, check to make sure we have received
#     what we need, do some sanity checking on the data, then insert
#     the data into the table
#
####
sub process_form_data {
    # get the argument passed in, the database handle
    my $dbh = shift;

    # get the posted data
    my $lname = param('lname') || ' ';
    my $fname = param('fname') || ' ';
    my $age   = param('age')   || 0;

    # check to be sure we have all the fields
    unless ($lname and $fname and $age) {
        handle_error('You need to enter last name, first name and age!',
                $dbh);
    }

    # check the length of the data
    if (length($lname) > 20 or length($fname) > 20 or length($age) > 3) {
        handle_error('The length of your data is too long!', $dbh);
    }
```

```
    # error out if the age is not numeric (contains a character which is
    # not a digit
    if ($age =~ /\D/) {
        handle_error('Your age is not numeric!', $dbh);
    }

    # ok, now insert data
    my $sth = $dbh->prepare('INSERT INTO age_information
                    (lastname, firstname, age) VALUES (?,?,?)')
            or handle_error("Can't prepare SQL: " . $dbh->errstr(), $dbh);

    $sth->execute($lname, $fname, $age)
            or handle_error("Can't execute SQL: " . $dbh->errstr(),
                        $dbh, $sth);
}
```

The subroutine `process_form_data` takes one argument, the opened database handle `$dbh`. The posted data is then grabbed and stored into three variables: `$lname`, `$fname`, and `$age`. Then, three very important checks are made. First, the program checks to see that it has received the proper number of parameters. Also, for good style (security is always good style), it checks to see that none of the data exceeds the length that can be stored in the database. This is necessary because anyone can send this program posted data that exceeds 20 characters of text—especially critical if our MySQL data type is TEXT or BLOB. It then checks to make sure that the age passed in is numeric—if not, it is not an age. If any of these checks fail, call `handle_error()` to handle the error.

But you might say, "Hey, didn't we limit the amount of text the user can enter into the form by setting the text widget's `maxsize` to 20 characters?" Yes, but this program can easily be called directly by not using this form, or it would be simple to create our own form that would allow us to enter more than 20 characters. Once the data has been checked, it can be inserted into the database.

And now for the main code:

```
####
#
# herein begins the main code
#
####

# connect to the MySQL server
my $dbh = DBI->connect('DBI:mysql:people', 'apache', 'LampIsCool')
        or handle_error("Can't connect..." . DBI->errstr());
```

```
# if param() returns true, we have parameters, so process them
if (param()) {
    process_form_data($dbh);
}

# here we query the db for the data that is to be
# displayed in a table
my $sth = $dbh->prepare('SELECT lastname, firstname,
                         age FROM age_information')
        or handle_error("Can't prepare SQL" . $dbh->errstr(), $dbh);

$sth->execute()
        or handle_error("Can't execute SQL" . $sth->errstr(), $dbh, $sth);
```

After the definition of these subroutines, the script connects as usual, but now if there is an error, handle_error() is called, not die().

The checks we make in this program are only moderately important for this application. If we failed to make these checks, DBI would do the right thing for us, given the database. Our table was defined so that the first and last names were both 20 characters in length, and the age was an integer. If we received a first or last name that exceeded 20 characters, DBI would store only the first 20 in the database, and if we received an age that was not numeric, the value 0 would be used. We check because we would like to tell the user that they have entered incorrect or missing data. We also check because it is a good habit to get into.

The code if (param) checks to see if any posted data has been received. If so, the script calls process_form_data() to gather the posted data and add it to the database.

```
# now, create HTML for the table and the form
# first, use CGI methods and the defined subroutines
# to build HTML
print
    header(),
    top_html(),    # this is the subroutine defined above
    <<EOHTML;
<h2>Current Name/Age Information</h2>
<table border="1">
<tr><th>Last Name</th><th>First Name</th><th>Age</th></tr>
EOHTML
```

The script then prints the header and start of the HTML, including the start of the table that displays the information in the MySQL table.

```
# and print the records in the table
my($ln,$fn,$age);
while (($ln,$fn,$age) = $sth->fetchrow()) {
    print "<tr><td>$ln</td><td>$fn</td><td>$age</td></tr>\n";
}
```

Next, the script grabs all the information from the database, looping through the result of the SELECT query and printing each record as a row in the table.

```
# print the end of the table, then the form using a
# here document
print
    <<EOHTML;
</table>
<hr>
<h2>Enter New Name/Age Information</h2>
If you enter your name and age, you will be added to the database
and will be displayed above.
<form action="/cgi-bin/age.cgi" method="post">
<table border="0">
  <tr>
    <td>Last name:</td>
    <td><input type="text" name="lname" maxsize="20" value=""></td>
  </tr>
  <tr>
    <td>First name:</td>
    <td><input type="text" name="fname" maxsize="20" value=""></td>
  </tr>
  <tr>
    <td>Age:</td>
    <td><input type="text" name="age" maxsize="20" value=""></td>
  </tr>
  <tr>
    <td><input type="submit" value="Submit Data"></td>
    <td><input type="reset" value="Reset Form"></td>
  </tr>
</table>
</form>
EOHTML
```

The next step is to print the form that collects information from the user to be added to the MySQL table if the client fills it out and clicks the submit button.

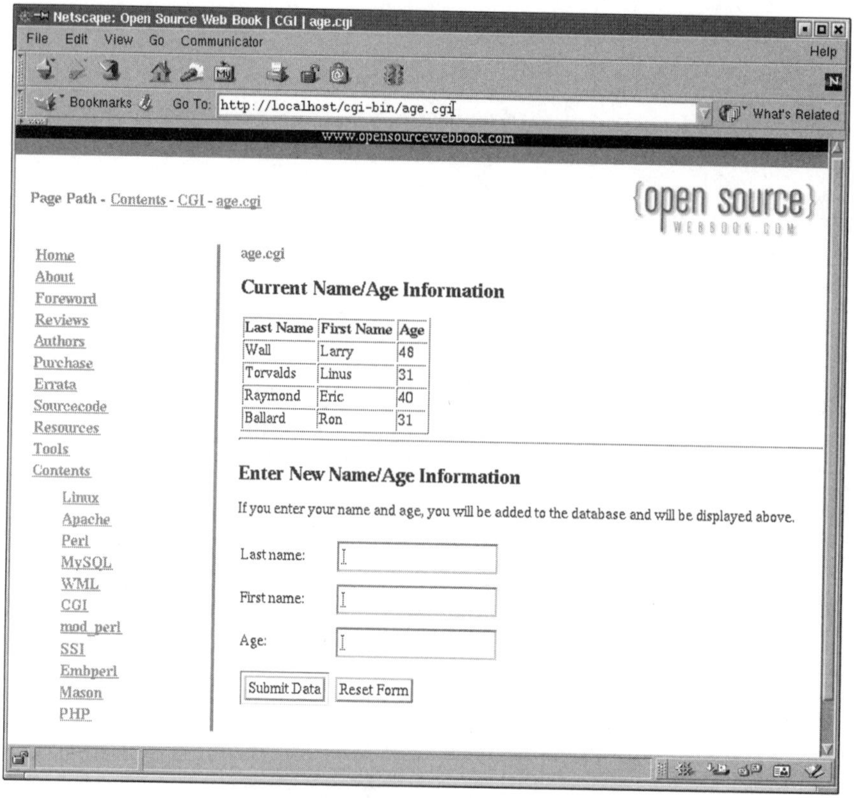

Figure 7.14   Age information, before adding a new entry

```
print
    bottom_html();  # this is the subroutine defined above

# clean up
$sth->finish();
$dbh->disconnect();
```

And finally, the bottom HTML is printed, and the program cleans up by finishing the state handler and disconnecting the database handle. To execute this code, load one of these URLs into your browser: `http://localhost/cgi-bin/age.cgi` or `www.opensourcewebbook.com/cgi-bin/age.cgi`. You should see Figure 7.14.

Now, add the following information:

```
Last name:  Kedzierski
First name: John
Age:        23
```

Enter this data and click the submit button to produce the output shown in Figure 7.15.

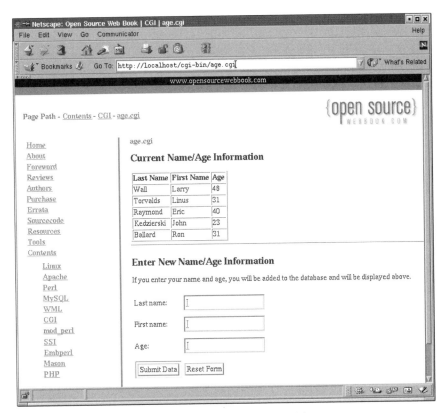

Figure 7.15   Age information, after adding a new entry

This program uses both forms of printing HTML to the browser: The first part of the program uses CGI.pm modules such as `start_html()` and `h1()`; the latter part uses a short `here` document. This is fine—programs can use both styles. The style chosen for any application is a matter of suitability, programming style, and the specific application—TMTOWTDI.

7.12 SUMMARY

CGI is arguably the simplest way to generate dynamic HTML. There are other ways (mod_perl), which we explore later in the book, that trade the simplicity of this method for speed and flexibility at the price of complexity. CGI is commonly used, so this chapter should help you understand the syntax if you see it in someone else's web page and help you create simple programs simply.

7.13 RESOURCES

Books

[Boutell 96] Boutell, Thomas. *CGI Programming in C and Perl.*

[Guelich+ 00] Guelich, Scott, Shishir Gundavaram, Gunther Birznieks, and Linda Mui. *CGI Programming with Perl, Second Edition.*

[Meltzer+ 01] Meltzer, Kevin, and Brent Michalski. *Writing CGI Applications with Perl.*

[Stein 97] Stein, Lincoln D. *How to Set Up and Maintain a Web Site, Second Edition.* One of the best books written about creating and maintaining a web site.

[Stein 98] Stein, Lincoln. *Official Guide to Programming with CGI.pm.* The title says it all.

Web Sites

The Idiot's Guide to Solving Perl CGI Problems: `www.perl.com/pub/doc/FAQs/cgi/idiotsguide.html`—Not only for idiots; full of useful information and gotchas.

Perl CGI FAQ: `www.perl.com/pub/doc/FAQs/cgi/perl-cgi-faq.html`— A must-read for all new CGI programmers.

The WWW Security FAQ: `www.w3.org/Security/Faq/`—Details about writing secure web programs.

8

mod_perl

8.1 INTRODUCTION

mod_perl is another, better way to create dynamic web pages. It is faster and far more flexible than CGI and has the advantage of being based on Perl. Thus it provides the dual benefit of building on the knowledge base you've gained by studying Perl, and taking advantage of the entire Perl base.

mod_perl is a fully functional Perl interpreter embedded in the Apache webserver, making the Perl interpreter always available for CGI programs—there is no extra step to load Perl into memory. Also, mod_perl is smart enough to cache CGI programs in memory, so if a CGI program is run multiple times, it is compiled only once. The result is a considerable improvement in speed.

Speed is not the only advantage of mod_perl. It also gives you increased power, flexibility, and the ability to customize Apache. Because Perl is built into Apache, Perl is available to the server at all times. So you can write Perl code that performs customized processing during any phase of Apache's processing, from the request phase to the authentication phase to the logging phase (to name just a few).

Another feature of mod_perl is that with the `Apache::Registry` module, you can instantly turn your existing CGI programs into mod_perl programs. Your existing CGI programs will run considerably faster, with no rewriting.

You can also write pure mod_perl programs ("pure" meaning using the mod_perl API instead of the CGI.pm module). These programs generally run faster than CGI programs because they use the native mod_perl API instead of a module.

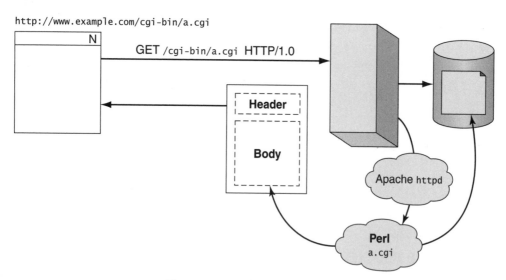

Figure 8.1   CGI execution

8.1.1 How It's Faster

Figure 8.1 depicts what happens when a CGI program is executed, as explained in Chapter 7. When the request is made for the CGI program, `a.cgi`, the `httpd` child process that is handling the request discovers that the CGI program is to be executed by Perl (it learns this from the first line of `a.cgi`: `#!/usr/bin/perl`). Therefore, the child process first loads `perl` into memory (this takes some work and time to do). Then, the `perl` process executes `a.cgi` by first compiling it into an internal byte-code representation (this compilation takes some work and time to do) and then executing it.

If `a.cgi` is executed multiple times a day (let's say a million, for a nice round number), this loading of Perl/compilation/execution must be repeated a million times a day. This is inefficient. Instead, wouldn't it be nice to be able to eliminate the first two steps by loading Perl only once and compiling `a.cgi` only once, leaving only the execution of `a.cgi`? If this could be done, the execution of `a.cgi` could be sped up significantly. mod_perl *can* do this!

When you want to use mod_perl to execute `a.cgi`, the scenario looks like Figure 8.2. With mod_perl, the `httpd` child process has Perl embedded within it, so there is no need to load Perl when `a.cgi` is to be executed,

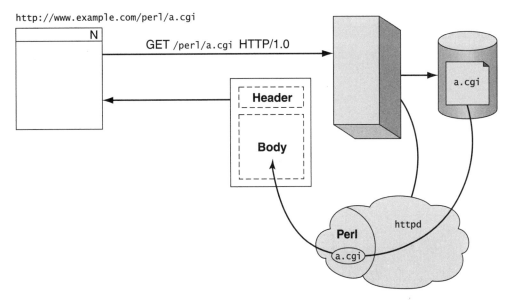

Figure 8.2 Execution of mod_perl

thereby eliminating the need for the first step of the load/compile/execute process. The first time a.cgi is requested by the child process, the process compiles it and then caches it within itself so that subsequent executions of a.cgi are like executing a function. Thus a.cgi does not need to be compiled again for that child process (eliminating the need for the second step of the load/compile/execute process). When a.cgi is requested, it is simply executed. Quite zippy!

8.2 CONFIGURATION

First, make a directory for mod_perl programs. This directory can be anywhere, except that it's a bad idea to put it in the Apache document tree starting with /var/www/html for the same reasons that it is a bad idea to do so for CGI programs. Let's choose /var/www/mod_perl. Create the directory with the appropriate permissions:

```
# mkdir /var/www/mod_perl
# chmod a+rx /var/www/mod_perl
```

Apache needs to be configured appropriately to use mod_perl effectively. We start by creating a Perl script that Apache runs each time it starts up (or more precisely, each time the Apache configuration file is reread). Name this program `startup.pl`, since it runs when Apache starts up, and put it in the Apache configuration directory **/etc/httpd/conf**:

```
#! /usr/bin/perl

# tell Perl where to find our modules
use lib '/var/www/mod_perl';

# use some common modules
use Apache::Registry();
use Apache::Constants();
use CGI ':standard';
use DBI;

# add other modules here...

# the file needs to end with 1;
1;
```

The `use lib` statement tells Apache (really Perl that is built into Apache) where to find the mod_perl modules that we will write—in this case, the newly minted **/var/www/mod_perl** directory.

The next four `use` statements preload four commonly used Perl modules. Preloading at server start-up speeds up loading the individual modules when they are used in the mod_perl programs[1]—if this start-up script weren't used, the modules would have to be loaded the first time each mod_perl program executed, while the client waited for a response from the server.

The last line must be `1;`—strange, but important. This program, and all Perl modules, must end in `1;` so that when they are used via the `use` pragma (`use CGI;`), the `use` must evaluate to 1 (true). To accomplish that, simply make the last line of the module `1;`. This needs to be done for all the mod_perl modules.

Then configure Apache to execute the start-up script by adding these lines at the end of the Apache configuration file **/etc/httpd/conf/httpd. conf**:

```
PerlRequire conf/startup.pl
PerlFreshRestart On
```

---

[1]As you go along, add any other commonly used modules as needed.

Restart Apache to test the start-up script:

/etc/init.d/httpd graceful

and check the log file for error messages:

tail -f /var/log/httpd/error_log

If you see no errors, all is well with the start-up script.

8.3 TURNING CGIs INTO mod_perl PROGRAMS

One immediate benefit of mod_perl is to cache the compilation of CGI
programs. They are compiled once and thereafter executed from memory,
hence the speed of these programs increases substantially. Now we can
use the benefits of mod_perl to execute our current CGI programs as they
are written. The good news is that the CGI programs do not need to be
modified—all it takes is an Apache configuration change.

There are two approaches to using mod_perl to run CGI programs:
`Apache::Registry` and `Apache::PerlRun`.

8.3.1 Apache::Registry

The beauty of the `Apache::Registry` module is that it takes plain-Jane CGI
programs, like those written in Chapter 7, and automatically makes them
mod_perl programs by compiling the programs only the first time they
are called, caching the compilation for subsequent executions. In other
words, CGI programs become sort of like function calls because the code is
compiled and ready to execute. The only thing that needs be done to apply
the `Apache::Registry` module to the CGI programs is to alter the Apache
configuration.

To illustrate that existing CGI programs can be run under mod_perl, as
usual the first step is to create a new directory to hold these CGI programs,
`/var/www/perl`:

mkdir /var/www/perl
chmod a+rx /var/www/perl
cd /var/www/perl

Copy the CGI programs written in Chapter 7 into the new directory:

```
# cp ../cgi-bin/* .
```

Configure Apache to run these programs using mod-perl by adding this to the `httpd.conf` file:

```
Alias /perl/ /var/www/perl/
<Location /perl>
   SetHandler          perl-script
   PerlHandler         Apache::Registry
   PerlSendHeader      On
   Options             +ExecCGI
</Location>
```

Now if Apache sees a URI starting with /perl/, it will look for that file in /var/www/perl/. Then, with the `<Location>` directive, Apache knows that anything accessed in the /perl directory should be handled by the `perl-script` handler—in other words, executed by Perl built into Apache. `Apache::Registry` is set to be the module that handles requests for files in this part of the document tree. Because this module is applied to this directory, each program within it is compiled as the body of a Perl subroutine and then executed. Each Apache child process compiles the program the first time it is executed, caching it for later executions. If the file is changed on disk, it is recompiled for each child process that executes it, being cached again after the first compilation.

The `PerlSendHeader` is set to `On`, which tells mod-perl to intercept anything that looks like a header and turn it into a validly formatted header line. The `+ExecCGI` option is used by `Apache::Registry` to make sure you really know what you are doing. It requires that all programs in the directory be executable—an added step you have to take to make sure this works.

Load the changed Apache configuration file by restarting it:

```
# /etc/init.d/httpd graceful
```

Now it is time to try one of the CGI programs. Load one of these URLs into your browser: `http://localhost/perl/hello.cgi` or `www.opensourcewebbook/perl/hello.cgi`. You should see Figure 8.3.

Although `Apache::Registry` is magic when it comes to existing CGI programs, instantly converting them to mod-perl programs, existing scripts

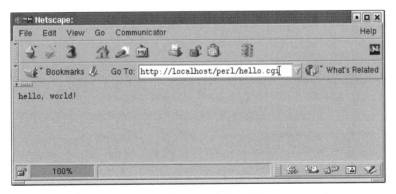

Figure 8.3 hello, world! with mod_perl

may need to be modified slightly if they are written "sloppily." This is because a "normal" CGI program has a short life span: from when it is requested to when it finishes executing.

This is in contrast to a mod_perl program, which has a life span the same as the Apache child process. For instance, using global variables in plain-Jane CGIs is no big deal, because once the program finishes executing, the globals go away. But for a mod_perl CGI program using `Apache::Registry`, the global variables live as long as the Apache child process lives, which can cause serious bugs (imagine a variable's value persisting from one execution of the CGI to the next, without designing it this way).

So, the rule of thumb is, if you use `Apache::Registry`, your script may need to be modified slightly, but it will run much quicker! Or if you are lazy and don't want to modify the scripts that you have (yes, we understand), see Section 8.3.3, `Apache::PerlRun`, later in the chapter.

8.3.2 A Speed Example or Two

You may notice that the program runs much faster than as a normal CGI program. Here is a little Perl script that simulates 1,000 requests for plain CGI and mod_perl CGI, and times how long it takes. This program is called `hitit.pl`. It makes requests to the `localhost` server, so there is minimal network lag.

```perl
#!/usr/bin/perl -w
# hitit.pl

use LWP::Simple;

# the URLs to request
$CGIURL     = 'http://localhost/cgi-bin/hello.cgi';
$MODPERLURL = 'http://localhost/perl/hello.cgi';

# initialize to empty string
$content    = ' ';

# the time() function returns the number of seconds
# since January 1, 1970
$start_time = time();
print "Start CGI: ", $start_time, "\n";
# loop 1000 times
foreach (1..1000) {
    unless (defined ($content = get($CGIURL))) {
        die "could not get $CGIURL\n";
    }
}
$end_time = time();
print "End CGI: ", $end_time, "\n";
print "CGI difference: ", $end_time - $start_time, "\n";

$start_time = time();
print "Start mod_perl: ", $start_time, "\n";
foreach (1..1000) {
    unless (defined ($content = get($MODPERLURL))) {
        die "could not get $MODPERLURL\n";
    }
}
$end_time = time();
print "End mod_perl: ", $end_time, "\n";
print "mod_perl difference: ", $end_time - $start_time, "\n";
```

This program uses the `LWP::Simple` module, which provides simple functions using Perl to interface to the World Wide Web. One of those functions, `get()`, makes an HTTP request to get the web page that is its argument. Two variables are defined: `$CGIURL`, the URL for the CGI version of `hello.cgi`, and `$MODPERLURL`, the URL for the mod_perl version.

Then, for the CGI version, the `time()` function is called. This function returns the number of seconds since the Epoch—January 1, 1970.[2] After the time is printed, the program loops 1,000 times, calling the CGI program using the `get()` function from `LWP::Simple`. The result of the `get()`, which

---

[2]The beginning of time for Unix, or for us geeks, the beginning of life as we now understand it.

is the output of the CGI program, is stored in $content. But we don't care too much about the output in this program, so we simply ignore it. Then the end time is computed and printed, and the difference between the start time and end time is reported. This action is repeated for the mod_perl program.

Here is the output of this program on one of our machines (a dual 450MHz server with 512MB of memory):

```
$ ./hitit.pl
Start CGI: 1017758223
End CGI: 1017758259
CGI difference: 36
Start mod_perl: 1017758259
End mod_perl: 1017758265
mod_perl difference: 6
```

Thirty-six seconds for CGI, six seconds for mod_perl—not bad. Of course, YMMV.[3]

Since TMTOWTDI, here is another Perl program that times the execution of 1,000 get() calls for both the CGI and mod_perl URLs. It is called hitit2.pl:

```
#!/usr/bin/perl

use LWP::Simple;
use Benchmark;

# the URLs to request
$CGIURL     = 'http://localhost/cgi-bin/hello.cgi';
$MODPERLURL = 'http://localhost/perl/hello.cgi';

timethese(1000, {
        CGI     => q{ $content = get($CGIURL); },
        MODPERL => q{ $content = get($MODPERLURL); },
    }
);
```

This program uses the Benchmark module, included in the Perl distribution, which provides a method named timethese() that times blocks of code. Here we call timethese() with two arguments: The first is the number of times (1000) the code will be executed in the next argument; the second is an anonymous hash, the values of which are code that will be executed

---

[3]Your Mileage May Vary.

1000 times.[4] The `timethese()` method then prints some information about how long it takes to execute these two blocks of code. The `Benchmark` module simplifies the previous example greatly.

Executing `hitit2.pl` produces this output:

```
$ ./hitit2.pl
Benchmark: timing 1000 iterations of CGI, MODPERL...
     CGI: 35 wallclock secs ( 2.70 usr + 1.17 sys = 3.87 CPU)
                              @ 258.40/s (n=1000)
 MODPERL:  6 wallclock secs ( 2.25 usr + 1.00 sys = 3.25 CPU)
                              @ 307.69/s (n=1000)
```

Remember the programs from Chapter 7 that displayed the client/server information? That information is available to mod_perl too. Try one of these URLs: `http://localhost/perl/info4.cgi` or `www.opensourcewebbook.com/perl/info4.cgi`.

You may be curious about the improvement for this program because it is much more involved than the earlier `hello.cgi` example. In `hitit.pl` and `hitit2.pl`, we changed the two URL variables to the following:

```
$CGIURL     = 'http://localhost/cgi-bin/info4.cgi';
$MODPERLURL = 'http://localhost/perl/info4.cgi';
```

We then reran the program on the same computer and got this result:

```
$ ./hitit.pl
Start CGI: 1017758565
End CGI: 1017758764
CGI difference: 199
Start mod_perl: 1017758764
End mod_perl: 1017758773
mod_perl difference: 9
$ ./hitit2.pl
 Benchmark: timing 1000 iterations of CGI, MODPERL...
     CGI: 199 wallclock secs ( 2.68 usr + 1.23 sys = 3.91 CPU)
                              @ 255.75/s (n=1000)
 MODPERL:   8 wallclock secs ( 2.39 usr + 1.07 sys = 3.46 CPU)
                              @ 289.02/s (n=1000)
```

Either way you look at it, that's a huge improvement.

---

[4]Anonymous hashes are beyond the scope of this book—just type the curly braces where you see them, and you will create this interesting and powerful data type. For more information, see the Camel Book [Wall+ 00].

Posted data can be handled with mod_perl just as it was with CGI. To see how, create a directory:

```
$ cd /var/www/html
$ mkdir mod_perl
$ chmod a+rx mod_perl
$ cd mod_perl
```

Insert the following HTML into /var/www/html/mod_perl/nameage.html:

```
<html>
<head>
<title>Enter Your Name and Age</title>
</head>
<body bgcolor="#ffffff">
<form action="/perl/nameage.cgi" method="post">
Name: <input type="text" name="yourname">
<br>
Age: <input type="text" name="age">
<br>
<input type="submit" value="Click to Submit">
</form>
</body>
</html>
```

This HTML is similar to the example in Chapter 7, but the action= parameter to the <form> tag is different—it points to /perl/nameage.cgi instead of /cgi-bin/nameage.cgi.

Try this example with one of these two URLs: http://localhost/ mod_perl/nameage.html or www.opensourcewebbook.com/mod_perl/nameage. html. If you submit the form, you can see that the Apache::Registry mod_perl program handles form data exactly like the CGI version.

Curious about the speed advantage of using mod_perl with CGI programs that handle posted data? We modified hitit.pl and hitit2.pl by changing the URL variables to the following (wrapped here so that it fits on the page):

```
$CGIURL     = 'http://localhost/cgi-bin/nameage.cgi?
              yourname=Ron+Ballard&age=31';
$MODPERLURL = 'http://localhost/perl/nameage.cgi?
              yourname=Ron+Ballard&age=31';
```

Executing the program produces this:

```
$ ./hitit.pl
Start CGI: 1017759184
End CGI: 1017759377
CGI difference: 193
Start mod_perl: 1017759377
End mod_perl: 1017759384
mod_perl difference: 7
$ ./hitit2.pl
 Benchmark: timing 1000 iterations of CGI, MODPERL...
       CGI: 192 wallclock secs ( 2.77 usr + 1.23 sys = 4.00 CPU)
                                @ 250.00/s (n=1000)
   MODPERL:    8 wallclock secs ( 2.43 usr + 1.14 sys = 3.57 CPU)
                                @ 280.11/s (n=1000)
```

Once again, quite a nice improvement in speed. All that gain with such a simple change!

8.3.3 Apache::PerlRun

Apache::Registry speeds things up because programs are compiled only once, the first time they are executed, but there are other issues besides speed to worry about. As we mentioned, if the program is badly (or sloppily) written, you can still get into trouble.

One typical problem seen in ill-considered mod_perl CGI programs is the use of global variables. After the CGI program is compiled the first time, the program remains in memory inside Apache, and any global variables are reused each time that instance of httpd is used. Usually, this is not such a good idea, because the variable value persists from one execution to another.

You might have some legacy CGI programs that are written somewhat sloppily (although we would never expect you to admit it), but you still want to use them and have them run as fast as possible. The solution is Apache::PerlRun. It compiles the script each time it is run, and all variables exist only for the life of the script.

You may think, "Hey, if the program is compiled each time, then how can using Apache::PerlRun be faster than plain-Jane CGI?" The answer to this good question is that because Perl is already within Apache, loading Perl is not necessary. Also, the CGI program can use preloaded modules that we add to script.pl without loading them for each execution of the script.

To apply Apache::PerlRun to a directory of CGI programs, create a directory and add something similar to this to /etc/httpd/conf/httpd.conf:

```
Alias /sloppyperl/ /var/www/sloppyperl/
<Location /sloppyperl>
   SetHandler         perl-script
   PerlHandler        Apache::PerlRun
   PerlSendHeader     On
   Options            +ExecCGI
</Location>
```

Now, all CGI scripts under the URI /sloppyperl/ will be executed with Apache::PerlRun, so any ill effects from sloppy programming will be minimized. Better yet, rewrite the thing!

8.4 PURE mod_perl PROGRAMMING

Although speed is always desirable, the real power of mod_perl comes in using the mod_perl API to process system information, path information, and posted form data. But the best part is something that can't be done with plain-Jane CGI—mod_perl allows you to modify the guts of Apache to perform unique and specific tasks during different phases of the Apache request handling process. These phases include access control, authentication, and logging (to name just a few).

The first example, as you might guess, prints "hello, world!" First, create a Perl module. This file must be in a directory that Perl knows about. Earlier we discussed the Apache startup.pl script, and this was one line of that script:

```
use lib '/var/www/mod_perl';
```

This line directs Perl to check for modules. Go into that directory:

$ cd /var/www/mod_perl

Create a file named /var/www/mod_perl/HelloWorld.pm (the .pm filename extension means "Perl module"). These are the contents of this file:

```
package HelloWorld;
# file: HelloWorld.pm

use strict;
use Apache::Constants ':common';

# the handler() method
sub handler {
    # shift the argument into $r
    my $r = shift;
```

```
    # set the content type and send the header
    $r->content_type('text/html');
    $r->send_http_header();

    # print the HTML to say hello
    $r->print(<<EOHTML);
<html>
<head>
<title>hello, world with mod_perl</title>
</head>
<body bgcolor="#ffffff">
<h1>hello, world!</h1>
hello, world! with mod_perl
</body>
</html>
EOHTML

    # return OK to Apache so that it knows
    # to continue as normal
    return OK;
}

1;
```

The first line of this file is `package HelloWorld;`. This creates a *package* (also known as a *namespace* in some languages) named `HelloWorld`. This line makes sure that any variables and subroutines we define will not clash with those from other mod_perl programs. All mod_perl programs are created as modules. This package begins with the first line and extends to the end of the file. This file will be called `HelloWorld.pm`.

It's always a good idea to `use strict` in modules. This enforces good programming style by forcing the declaration of all the variables as `my` variables (hence no globals), thus eliminating many pesky problems caused by global variables. Global variables have their uses, but one should think carefully before using them.

The `Apache::Constants` module contains some useful constant values (such as `OK`). When Apache receives a request that is associated with a mod_perl program, it invokes the `handler()` method, passing it an Apache request object that is stored in `$r`. This object has available to it the many methods defined in the mod_perl API.

The first request object method executed is `content_type()`, which tells Apache that the content type is `text/html`. The HTTP header is sent with `send_http_header()`. The HTML content is generated using the `print()`

method that prints a `here` document. Finally, the `handler()` subroutine returns the value `OK`, which tells Apache that all is well and to continue as normal.

Again, like all modules we write, the `HelloWorld.pm` module must end with `1;`.

Make sure this file is readable (you must do this for all the `.pm` files described in this chapter):

```
$ chmod a+r HelloWorld.pm
```

We need to tell Apache how to use this file. Add the following to the bottom of `/etc/httpd/conf/httpd.conf`:

```
<Location /helloworld>
  SetHandler    perl-script
  PerlHandler   HelloWorld
</Location>
```

This Apache directive says that when the `/helloworld` URI is requested, Apache should execute the Perl module `HelloWorld` (stored in the file `HelloWorld.pm` in the directory `/var/www/mod_perl`). Restart Apache:

```
# /etc/init.d/httpd graceful
```

and load it in the browser via either `http://localhost/helloworld` or `www.opensourcewebbook.com/helloworld`. You should see Figure 8.4.

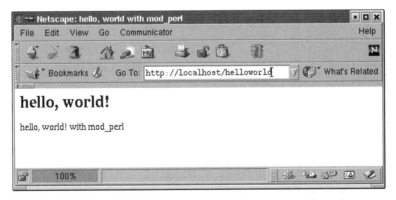

Figure 8.4   hello, world! with pure mod_perl

8.4.1 An Important Note about mod_perl

Because mod_perl modules are compiled into Apache the first time they are executed, every time a module changes, the server has to be restarted. Even if the program file changes on disk, mod_perl will not recompile it for us. This can be a drawback because it's a hassle to restart the server every time the code is changed. So this is the trade-off you make to get the speed of compiled, persistent code—you have to restart the server when you change something versus compiling Perl code every single time it's called. Once the program is developed and working properly, restarting for this reason becomes less of an issue.

8.4.2 Handling Posted Form Data with mod_perl

As you have seen, a major task of CGI programs is handling posted form data. mod_perl programs need to be able to perform the same task. Using mod_perl is a bit different from CGI.pm because we use the mod_perl API.

Let's see an example. Place the following in /var/www/mod_perl/ HandleCGIData.pm:

```perl
package HandleCGIData;
# file: HandleCGIData.pm

use strict;
use Apache::Constants ':common';

sub handler {
    # shift the argument into $r
    my $r = shift;

    # initialize %params, then assign
    # it the form data depending on
    # the method used
    my %params = ();
    if ($r->method() eq 'POST') {
        %params = $r->content();
    } else {
        %params = $r->args();
    }

    # set the content type and send the
    # header
    $r->content_type('text/html');
    $r->send_http_header();

    # print initial HTML
    $r->print(<<EOHTML);
```

```
<html>
<head>
<title>Processing CGI Parameters</title>
</head>
<body bgcolor="#ffffff">
<h1>Processing CGI Parameters</h1>
EOHTML

    # loop through the sorted keys of
    # %params, printing the key (form
    # widget name) followed by the
    # value (form widget value)
    foreach my $key (sort keys %params) {
        print "$key: <b>$params{$key}</b><br>";
    }

    # print the final HTML, return OK
    $r->print(<<EOHTML);
</body>
</html>
EOHTML

    return OK;
}

1;
```

The `handler()` subroutine is invoked to handle the request, so it gets the data and processes it. First the hash `%params`, which holds the form data received, is declared and initialized. The hash `%params` is assigned based on the method used to send the data to the program: either `POST` or `GET`, to call either `content()` (for `POST`) or `args()` (for `GET`). The end result of both these methods is the same: a list of the parameter names and values. So if the program were invoked with:

```
http://localhost/cgidata?name=John+Doe%21&abc=def&ghi=923
```

the hash `%params` would be assigned this data:

```
name    => ´John Doe!´,
abc     => ´def´,
ghi     => ´923´
```

N Both `content()` and `args()` automatically decode the URL or posted data for you. In this case, the "+" is converted to the space character, and %21 is converted to "!".

After the parameters and their values are received, the content type is set, and the header and the starting HTML are printed.

The posted data in %params is processed using a foreach loop, printing the parameter names and their values, sorted by the names. The closing HTML is then printed, OK is returned to Apache, and the file ends with the ubiquitous 1;.

To tell Apache about this new module, we add the following to /etc/httpd/conf/httpd.conf:

```
<Location /cgidata>
  SetHandler    perl-script
  PerlHandler   HandleCGIData
</Location>
```

and restart:

```
# /etc/init.d/httpd graceful
```

You can see the result by loading either one of the following URLs: http://localhost/cgidata?name=John+Doe%21&abc=def&ghi=923 or www.opensourcewebbook.com/cgidata?name=John+Doe%21&abc=def&ghi=923. You should see Figure 8.5. Remember, the Perl motto is TMTOWTDI—There's More Than One Way to Do It. We could have written the if statement where we assign %params as follows:

```
my %params = ($r->args(), $r->content());
```

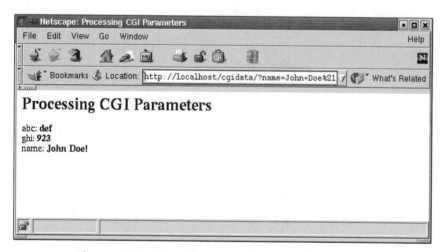

Figure 8.5 Handling CGI data with mod_perl

There is one limitation with the approach we've taken so far: If any of the parameters have more than one value (such as if you have a scrolling list box where more than one choice can be selected), only the last value will be used. To deal with this, we can use the following:

```
my %params;
my @args = ($r->args(),$r->content());
while (my($name,$value) = splice(@args, 0, 2)) {
    push @{$params{$name}}, $value;
}
```

To get at the value for a particular parameter, we do this:

```
@values = @{$params{$parameter_name}};
```

There's one problem with this: It's way too complicated![5] As you might expect, those canny Open Source hackers have come up with a better way, a slight variation on how we write basic CGI programs—Apache::Request.

8.4.3 Apache::Request

To use Apache::Request, you must install it, because the module is not installed by default. This is a simple process.

Download the latest version of the module. This module is part of a package called libapreq, and the latest version as of the writing of this book is 0.33 (as usual, this is likely to change over time). You can download the tarball from www.cpan.org/modules/by-module/Apache/libapreq-0.33.tar.gz into a convenient directory—a good place for this is /tmp. Follow these simple steps to install the module (or use the CPAN modules as shown in Chapter 4):

```
$ cd /tmp
$ tar xzvf libapreq-0.33.tar.gz
$ cd libapreq-0.33
$ perl Makefile.PL
$ make
$ su
# make install
```

Voilà! You just installed the module. By the way, this does not require us to restart Apache; like all other Perl modules (as opposed to mod_perl modules), this module is loaded when asked with use Apache::Request.

---

[5]This code is dereferencing an array reference, copying its contents into @values. Array references (and hash references, for that matter) are very interesting, fun, and powerful. Unfortunately, they are beyond the scope of this book.

To show an example using this module, we return to our directory of mod_perl modules:

```
$ cd /var/www/mod_perl
```

Create the file HandleCGIData2.pm and put the following code in it:

```perl
package HandleCGIData2;
# file: HandleCGIData2.pm

# use statements, including
# our new Apache::Request module
use strict;
use Apache::Constants ':common';
use Apache::Request;

sub handler {
    # shift the argument and pass it into
    # the new() method in the Apache::Request
    # class
    my $r = Apache::Request->new(shift);

    # we can now call param() with the Apache::Request
    # object in a similar way to using CGI.pm
    my $name = $r->param('name') || 'John Doe';
    my $age  = $r->param('age')  || 50;

    # set the content type and send the header
    $r->content_type('text/html');

    $r->send_http_header();

    # print the HTML, including our variables
    # $name and $age
    $r->print(<<EOHTML);
<html>
<head>
<title>Using Apache::Request</title>
</head>
<body bgcolor="#ffffff">
<h1>Using Apache::Request</h1>
name = $name<br>
age = $age
</body>
</html>
EOHTML

    return OK;
}

1;
```

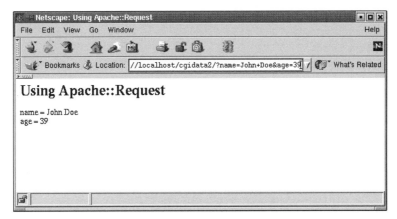

Figure 8.6 Handling CGI data with mod_perl
using `Apache::Request`

The difference in this version of `handler()` with `Apache::Request` is in how the data passed into the program is obtained. We no longer need to call either `content()` or `args()`—`$r->param()` is called in a way that is similar to the way `param()` was called using CGI.pm. The program then prints the HTML, returns `OK`, and ends with `1;`.

The next thing to do is tell Apache about this new module by adding the following to `/etc/httpd/conf/httpd.conf`:

```
<Location /cgidata2>
   SetHandler    perl-script
   PerlHandler   HandleCGIData2
</Location>
```

Restart Apache:

 # /etc/init.d/httpd graceful

Then load one of these two URLs: `http://localhost/cgidata2?name=John+Doe&age=39` or `www.opensourcewebbook.com/cgidata2?name=John+Doe&age=39`. You should see Figure 8.6.

8.4.4 Getting the Path Information

The path information can be obtained simply by calling the `path_info()` method as shown in the following example contained within `PathInfo.pm`:

```perl
package PathInfo;
# file: PathInfo.pm

use strict;
use Apache::Constants ':common';

sub handler {
    # the argument into $r
    my $r = shift;

    # call the path_info() method to get
    # the path information
    my $path_info = $r->path_info();

    # set the content type and send the header
    $r->content_type('text/html');
    $r->send_http_header();

    # print the HTML
    $r->print(<<EOHTML);
<html>
<head>
<title>Path Information with mod_perl</title>
</head>
<body bgcolor="#ffffff">
<h1>Path Information with mod_perl</h1>
We were passed this path information: <b>$path_info</b>
</body>
</html>
EOHTML

    return OK;
}

1;
```

As shown in the `handler()` method, to obtain the path information (everything after the /pathinfo URI and before the ?), we execute the `path_info()` method.

Again, Apache must be reconfigured for this new module. Modify the Apache configuration file by adding this to /etc/httpd/conf/httpd.conf:

```
<Location /pathinfo>
   SetHandler     perl-script
   PerlHandler    PathInfo
</Location>
```

Load the altered Apache configuration file:

 # /etc/init.d/httpd graceful

Then load one of these two URLs: `http://localhost/pathinfo/hello/world` or `www.opensourcewebbook.com/pathinfo/hello/world`. What other path information would we send but /hello/world? We should see Figure 8.7.

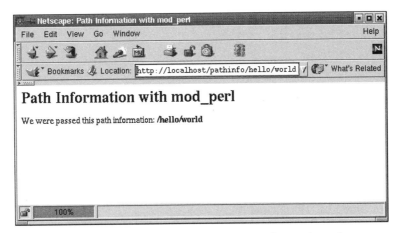

Figure 8.7   Path information with mod_perl

8.5 PROJECT: MySQL, DBI, AND mod_perl

We now have enough information to put all the ideas we have discussed into practice by combining mod_perl, MySQL, and DBI.

We start by developing a mod_perl program that displays to the visitor a list of available books about interesting computer subjects. Each book in the list will have a link taking the user to a page describing the details about the book, including the publisher and the price.

The collection will number approximately 75 books. With a database of such a small number of books, a possible solution would be to use a flat file to store the data, such as can be found in the file `/var/www/misc/book_data.txt`. A line of the file is a tab-delimited record containing the following:

- ISBN
- Author
- Title

- Publisher
- Date
- Description
- Price

This is an example line of the file:

```
0596000278 <tab> Larry Wall, Tom Christiansen, Jon Orwant <tab>
Programming Perl (3rd Edition)  <tab> O'Reilly & Associates <tab>
July 2000 <tab> The best book about Perl
written by Larry Wall, the creator of Perl. <tab> $49.95
```

The fields are separated by a single tab character, represented here by `<tab>` because invisible tab characters are hard to see in a book.

For this program, we will create two pages. The first page will show a brief listing of all the books from the file in groups of ten. When a user clicks on one of the books, a second page will load that shows a verbose listing of that book's information.

We will also show how to customize Apache's logging phase for each of these pages. The information will be logged to `access_log` as normal, but we will add functionality to send an e-mail for each access.

The first page is a listing of all the books in our database, showing ten books at a time. Since we can have more than ten books (in our example file, we will have more than 75 books), we want to give the user the ability to navigate to another page of ten, so we'll provide links to the remaining pages. This sort of display should be familiar to anyone who's used a search engine, so this example should show how useful this type of code is.

Although implementing this program with MySQL would be the best approach in the long term, especially if our database grows to thousands of books or more, this program can be implemented by reading the data directly from the text file. This flat-file approach is OK for small databases because it is simple to code—just read from a file and you are ready to go. If you want to see this flat-file solution, check out `/var/www/mod_perl/BookListing.pm` and `/var/www/mod_perl/BookDetail.pm`. You can view these files at `http://localhost/mod_perl/BookListing.pm`, `www.opensourcewebbook.com/mod_perl/BookListing.pm`, `http://localhost/mod_perl/BookDetail.pm`, or `www.opensourcewebbook.com/mod_perl/BookDetail.pm`.

To make these work, the following must be added to `httpd.conf`:

```
<Location /booklisting>
  SetHandler        perl-script
  PerlHandler       BookListing
</Location>

<Location /bookdetail>
  SetHandler        perl-script
  PerlHandler       BookDetail
</Location>
```

To see it in action, go to one of these URLs: www.opensourcewebbook. com/booklisting, http://localhost/booklisting, www.opensourcewebbook. com/bookdetail?isbn=0072127732, or http://localhost/bookdetail?isbn= 0072127732.

Because we recommend using MySQL, we won't discuss the flat-file solution any further but leave it as an exercise for the reader.

The first step in implementing this project in MySQL is to create the tables that will hold the information. Log in to the MySQL server as `root` and create a new database and table:

```
# mysql -u root -p
Enter password:
Welcome to the MySQL monitor.  Commands end with ; or \g.
Your MySQL connection id is 114 to server version: 3.23.36

Type 'help;' or '\h' for help. Type '\c' to clear the buffer

mysql> CREATE DATABASE books;
Query OK, 1 row affected (0.00 sec)

mysql> USE books;
Reading table information for completion of table and column names
You can turn off this feature to get a quicker startup with -A

Database changed
mysql> CREATE TABLE book_information (
    ->     isbn        CHAR(10) PRIMARY KEY NOT NULL,
    ->     author      CHAR(100),
    ->     title       CHAR(100),
    ->     publisher   CHAR(100),
    ->     date        CHAR(20),
    ->     description TEXT,
    ->     price       FLOAT
    -> );
Query OK, 0 rows affected (0.00 sec)
```

```
mysql> DESCRIBE book_information;
+-------------+---------------+------+-----+---------+-------+
| Field       | Type          | Null | Key | Default | Extra |
+-------------+---------------+------+-----+---------+-------+
| isbn        | varchar(10)   |      | PRI |         |       |
| author      | varchar(100)  | YES  |     | NULL    |       |
| title       | varchar(100)  | YES  |     | NULL    |       |
| publisher   | varchar(100)  | YES  |     | NULL    |       |
| date        | varchar(20)   | YES  |     | NULL    |       |
| description | text          | YES  |     | NULL    |       |
| price       | float         | YES  |     | NULL    |       |
+-------------+---------------+------+-----+---------+-------+
7 rows in set (0.00 sec)
```

N We created the table `book_information` with a *key*, or a field that has a unique value relative to all other values for this field. We decided to use ISBNs as the key (`isbn`) because they are unique and so are quite suitable for this purpose, almost as if they were designed for it.

Grant the `apache` user permission for this new database:

```
mysql> USE mysql;
Reading table information for completion of table and column names
You can turn off this feature to get a quicker startup with -A

Database changed
mysql> GRANT SELECT,INSERT,UPDATE,DELETE
    ->      ON books.*
    ->      TO apache@localhost;
Query OK, 0 rows affected (0.00 sec)
```

Note that the GRANT command does not need IDENTIFIED BY to set the password this time—we already set the `apache` MySQL user password the first time we executed GRANT back in Chapter 5.

OK, now that the tables are ready, they need to be populated. We already have a flat file of all the books, which we went to quite a bit of trouble to type in, so it would be nice to be able to transfer that data to the database. Never fear—Perl and DBI to the rescue! Reformatting and transferring data is one thing that Perl excels at.[6]

The program `book.pl` puts the contents of the flat file of book information in the database:

---

[6]We could have entered the data using the `mysqlimport` command because `book_data.txt` is a well-formed, tab-delimited file. But using Perl is much more fun. See `mysqlimport --help` for details.

```perl
#!/usr/bin/perl -w
# book.pl

use strict;
use DBI;

# connect to the database
my $dbh = DBI->connect('DBI:mysql:books', 'apache', 'LampIsCool')
        or die "Can't connect: " . DBI->errstr();

# open the data file
open FH, '/var/www/misc/book_data.txt' or die $!;

my($line, $sth);
# loop through each line of the file
while ($line = <FH>) {

    chomp($line);

    # split the line into some variables
    my($isbn, $author, $title, $publisher, $date,
       $description, $price) = split /\t/, $line;

    # remove the $ from $price
    $price =~ s/^\$//;

    # prepare SQL for insert
    $sth = $dbh->prepare('INSERT INTO book_information
                (
                    isbn,
                    author,
                    title,
                    publisher,
                    date,
                    description,
                    price
                )
                VALUES
                (
                    ?,
                    ?,
                    ?,
                    ?,
                    ?,
                    ?,
                    ?
                )')
                or die "Can't prepare SQL: " . $dbh->errstr();
```

```
        # execute the query, passing the variable values so they
        # can fill the ? placeholders in the query
        $sth->execute($isbn, $author, $title, $publisher, $date,
                $description, $price)
            or die "Can't execute SQL: " . $sth->errstr();

}

# close the file, finish and disconnect
close FH;

$sth->finish();
$dbh->disconnect();
```

The script first tells Perl it needs the DBI module; then it connects
to the `books` database and `die()`s if it can't. It opens the file containing the book information with the `open()` function, and if the open fails,
it `die()`s.

The script then loops through the input file, inserting the data into
the database after `chomp()`ing the newline character and `splitting` on a tab
character. Because the price has a leading dollar sign, it is removed with
the `s///` statement.

The script then constructs the SQL query to insert the data into the
database and calls `execute()` with the proper variables to plug into the "?"
placeholders in the query.

Finally, in good style, the input file is closed, the statement handle
finished, and the database disconnected. Run the program now:

$ book.pl $ ./book.pl

The database should now be populated, so it is time to talk about the
mod_perl programs to display the database information.

First, look at the code to generate the list of books in the
file `/var/www/mod_perl/BookListingMysql.pm`. For the complete code, see
`http://localhost/mod_perl/BookListingMysql.pm` or `www.opensourcewebbook.`
`com/mod_perl/BookListingMysql.pm`.

'The purpose of this code is to display the data in a nice, readable
fashion in a table. The program does so by first connecting to the MySQL
server, querying the database to read the information for a subset of the
book data (because there are too many books to display at once, we will
show ten books at a time), and building a table of the information. We will

also add a row of links allowing us to navigate to different subsets of book data, just for fun.

First, at the top, put the appropriate package name:

```
package BookListingMysql;
# file: BookListingMysql.pm
```

We must use the DBI module, so add this among other use pragmas:

```
use DBI;
```

A simple error-handling routine is added to this module, much like the one you saw in Chapter 7, age.cgi:

```
####
#
# handle_error() - subroutine to handle any errors
#
####

sub handle_error {
    my $r      = shift;
    my $msg    = shift;
    my $dbh    = shift;
    my $sth    = shift;

    $r->print(<<EOHTML);
ERROR: <font color="#ff0000">$msg</font>
EOHTML

    print bottom_html();

    $sth->finish()      if $sth;
    $dbh->disconnect() if $dbh;

    return OK;
}
```

This handle_error() subroutine is similar to the ones used previously, but this time it returns OK instead of exiting so that Apache can be given a return value that tells it to continue processing the request—this way, Apache handles failure gracefully. The subroutine takes four arguments: $r, the request object; $msg, the error message; $dbh, the database handle object; and $sth, the statement handle object. Then some helpful HTML code is printed, followed by what bottom_html() returns (the bottom HTML code, natch). The statement is finished, if necessary, and the database connection is disconnected, if necessary. Then OK is returned.

The next bit of code defines the top_html() function. In this function, one big here document is returned:

```
####
#
# top_html()
#
# a subroutine that will return the HTML for the top of
# the page - this will create a look and feel like the
# rest of the website
#
####

sub top_html {
    return <<EOHTML;
<html>

...

EOHTML
}
```

The top_html() function returns the HTML for the top of the page (clever name, eh?). It includes the HTML for the top and left rail.

Following is the bottom_html() function, which prints, as you might guess, the HTML for the bottom of the page:

```
####
#
# bottom_html()
#
# a subroutine that will return the HTML for the bottom of
# the page
#
####

sub bottom_html {
    return <<EOHTML;
</td>
<td width="65"> </td>
</tr>
</table>
</body>
</html>
EOHTML
}
```

We then see the definition of the handler() function, which works as follows:

```
####
#
# handler()
#
####

sub handler {
    # shift the argument and pass it into
    # the new() method in the Apache::Request
    # class
    my $r = new Apache::Request(shift);
```

The first thing this function does is create an Apache::Request by passing the first argument of handler() to the Apache::Request constructor (using shift). We create an Apache::Request object so that we can obtain the ISBN of the first book passed in with $r->param('first'). This first ISBN tells us which book to start displaying—the first book (first is 1), the eleventh book (first is 11), etc.

We then see this code:

```
# set the number of books to 10, and
# grab the value posted with 'first'
# (defaulted to 0)
my $NUM_BOOKS = 10;
my $first_book = $r->param('first') || 0;
```

The variable $NUM_BOOKS is assigned the value 10. This variable specifies the number of books to show at one time. A different number could be shown by choosing something else; it's not too difficult to imagine that this number might be chosen by the client as a parameter, but this is left as an exercise for the student. The variable $first_book has the value of the first parameter passed in. This value is the first book in the list of books shown, and it defaults to 0. We do this because we only want to show ten books per page; otherwise, our table would show 70-plus books—way too many!

```
# set the content type and send the header
$r->content_type('text/html');
$r->send_http_header();

# print the initial HTML
$r->print(top_html());
```

Next, the content type is set to text/html, the header is sent, and the top_html() function is called to build the HTML for the top and left rail; then that HTML is printed.

Now comes the code where we connect to the database, and we get all the ISBNs:

```
# connect to the database, and if the connect fails,
# call handle_error(), returning what it returns: OK
my $dbh = DBI->connect('DBI:mysql:books', 'apache', 'LampIsCool')
        or return handle_error($r, 'Connecting to db failed.'.
                            DBI->errstr());

# first, we need to get all the ISBN numbers so we can
# grab our page of them -
# prepare the SQL, handling the error if failure - we are
# passing handle_error the variable $dbh so it can disconnect
# from the database
my $sth = $dbh->prepare('SELECT isbn FROM book_information
                    ORDER BY isbn')
        or return handle_error($r, 'Prepare of SQL failed'.
                        $dbh->errstr(), $dbh);

# execute the query, and it if fails, call handle_error()
# passing it $dbh and $sth
$sth->execute()
        or return handle_error($r, 'Execute failed'. $sth->errstr(),
                        $dbh, $sth);

# declare some variables
my(@isbn) = ();
my($isbn);

# fetch each row
while (($isbn) = $sth->fetchrow()) {
    push @isbn, $isbn;
}
```

The first DBI action is to connect to the database and retrieve the ISBNs for all the books. All of them are stored in @isbn so that a range of them (such as numbers 30–39) can be grabbed.

```
# this code prints the navigation for all the pages
# of book information - the HTML will resemble:
#     1 | 2 | 3 | 4 | 5
# if the user clicks on '3', they will go to the third
# page of books
my $bgcolor = '';
for (my $i = 0; ($i+1)*$NUM_BOOKS <= $#isbn; $i++) {
    if ($i != 0) {
```

```
        $r->print('|');
    }
    if ($i * $NUM_BOOKS == $first_book) {
        $r->print($i + 1);
    } else {
        $r->print("<a href=\"/booklistingmysql?first=",
                $i*$NUM_BOOKS, "\"><font color=\"#999966\"><b>",
                $i + 1, "</b></font></a>");
    }
}
```

This code prints the HTML for page navigation. These will be links to other pages of book information (such as books 1–10, 11–20, etc.). In this example, we query the database for the ISBNs, loop through the result of the query, and push each ISBN onto @isbn.

```
    # print the intial HTML for our table
    $r->print(<<EOHTML);
<table border="0" cellspacing="0" cellpadding="3">
<tr><th>Title</th><th>Author(s)</th><th>Price</th></tr>
EOHTML
```

The beginning of the table that holds the information for all the books can be printed, and all the book information for this range (such as 1–10) processed:

```
    # this for loop loops through this page of book information -
    # if the user has asked for the 3rd page of books, we start
    # with book 30 (0-based) in @isbn and loop for 10 books
    for (my $i = $first_book;
            $i < ($first_book + $NUM_BOOKS) and $i <= $#isbn;
                $i++) {

        # get this book's information based on the ISBN
        $sth = $dbh->prepare('SELECT title, author, price
                        FROM book_information WHERE isbn = ?')
            or handle_error($r, 'Prepare of SQL failed'.
                        $dbh->errstr(), $dbh);
        $sth->execute($isbn[$i])
            or handle_error($r, "</table>Execute failed: $isbn[$i]" .
                        $dbh->errstr(), $dbh, $sth);

        # fetch the title, author, price from the row
        my($title, $author, $price) = $sth->fetchrow();

        # this sets the background color for the row -
        # even rows are grayish, odd rows are white -
        # this makes reading easier
        if ($i % 2 == 0) {
            $bgcolor = '#DDDDDD';
```

```
        } else {
            $bgcolor = '#FFFFFF';
        }

        # print the HTML for the row
        $r->print(<<EOHTML);
<tr bgcolor="$bgcolor"><td valign="top"><i>
<a href="/bookdetailmysql?isbn=$isbn[$i]"><font
color="#999966"><b>$title</b></font></a></i></td>
<td>$author</td><td valign="top">\$$price</td></tr>
EOHTML
    }
```

It first prints the HTML for the beginning of the table. Then, for each of the books in the range of the array requested, the database is queried for each book's specific information, and the HTML to build a table row for each book is printed. For readability, we set the row background colors to alternate between gray and white.

```
    # print the end of the table of books
    $r->print("</table>");

    # print the last of the HTML
    $r->print(bottom_html());

    # finish, disconnect, return
    $sth->finish();
    $dbh->disconnect();

    return OK;
}
```

Finally, the script finishes the necessary HTML for the table and the bottom of the page, finishes the statement handle, disconnects from the database, and returns OK.

To configure Apache to use this new module, add the following to httpd.conf:

```
<Location /booklistingmysql>
   SetHandler        perl-script
   PerlHandler       BookListingMysql
</Location>
```

Then restart Apache with /etc/init.d/httpd graceful. To view the page, go to http://localhost/booklistingmysql/ or www.opensourcewebbook.com/ booklistingmysql/. If all works well, you should see a page that resembles Figure 8.8. Feel free to cruise through the different groups of books by clicking on the link to page 2 or 3 or any others.

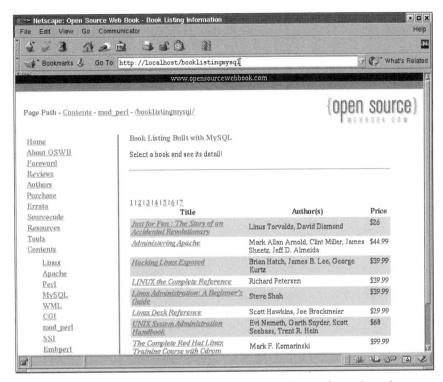

Figure 8.8   Book listing using MySQL and mod_perl

Notice that for each book there is a link to that book's details; now look at the code for generating the details. This code is in /var/www/mod_perl/ BookDetailMysql.pm. To see the complete code, look at either http:// localhost/mysql/BookDetailMysql.pm or www.opensourcewebbook.com/mysql/ BookDetailMysql.pm.

First, at the top, is the appropriate package name:

```
package BookDetailMysql;
# file: BookDetailMysql.pm
```

Then, of course, there is the database interface module, among other use pragmas:

```
use DBI;
```

The same as in BookListingMysql.pm, there is an identical error-handling function:

```
####
#
# handle_error() - subroutine to handle any errors
#
####

sub handle_error {
    my $r      = shift;
    my $msg    = shift;
    my $dbh    = shift;
    my $sth    = shift;

    $r->print(<<EOHTML);
ERROR: <font color="#ff0000">$msg</font>
EOHTML

    print bottom_html();

    $sth->finish()     if $sth;
    $dbh->disconnect() if $dbh;

    return OK;
}
```

The top and bottom HTML is generated in `top_html()` and `bottom_html()`, as before.

As usual, the `handler()` function is where the action is. First, here is the top of the function:

```
####
#
# handler()
#
####

sub handler {
    # shift the argument and pass it into
    # the new() method in the Apache::Request
    # class
    my $r = new Apache::Request(shift);

    # get the ISBN number posted
    my $isbn = $r->param('isbn') || 0;
```

Again, the request object is obtained first. The variable `$isbn` is set to the ISBN sent to the program through the `isbn` parameter (which defaults to 0). This variable is the book for which the detailed information will be displayed.

```
# set the content type and send the header
   $r->content_type('text/html');
   $r->send_http_header();

   $r->print(top_html());
```

The content type is sent, the header sent, and the beginning HTML printed. These are the goods:

```
# connect to the database, and if the connect fails,
# call handle_error(), returning what it returns: OK
my $dbh = DBI->connect('DBI:mysql:books', 'apache', 'LampIsCool')
        or return handle_error($r, 'Connecting to db failed.'
                                . DBI->errstr());

# prepare the SQL, handling the error if failure - we are
# passing handle_error the variable $dbh so it can disconnect
# from the database
my $sth = $dbh->prepare('SELECT
                        author, title, publisher, date, description,
                        price FROM book_information WHERE isbn = ?')
        or return handle_error($r, 'Prepare of SQL failed'.
                                $dbh->errstr(), $dbh);

# execute the query, and if it fails, call handle_error()
# passing it $dbh and $sth
$sth->execute($isbn)
        or return handle_error("Execute failed for $isbn" .
                                $sth->errstr(), $dbh, $sth);

# fetch the row and assign the data to some variables
my($author, $title, $publisher, $date, $desc, $price)
                = $sth->fetchrow();
```

This time, after connecting to the database, the script creates a query asking for the record of the ISBN passed in and executes the query. The correct row is fetched and the data stored in variables.

```
# this if is one way to check to see that we recevied some
# data from our query, if so, print the information,
# if not, call handle_error()
if (defined $author) {
    $r->print(<<EOHTML);
<table align="center">
<tr><th align="left">ISBN</th><td>$isbn</td></tr>
<tr><th align="left" valign="top">Author</th><td>$author</td></tr>
<tr><th align="left" valign="top">Title</th><td><i>$title</i></td></tr>
<tr><th align="left" valign="top">Publisher</th><td>$publisher</td></tr>
<tr><th align="left">Date</th><td>$date</td></tr>
<tr><th align="left" valign="top">Description</th><td>$desc</td></tr>
<tr><th align="left">Price</th><td>\$$price</td></tr>
</table>
```

```
<hr>
Click
<a href="/booklistingmysql/"><font color="#999966"><b>here</b></font></a>
to find another book.
EOHTML
    } else {
        return handle_error($r, "ISBN $isbn not found...\n",
                                $dbh, $sth);
    }
```

If the data is good ($author is defined), the data is printed in a table; otherwise, the error is dealt with.

```
# print the final HTML, finish, disconnect, return OK
$r->print(bottom_html());

$sth->finish();
$dbh->disconnect();

return OK;
```

Exiting gracefully, the script prints the last bit of HTML to finish the page and returns OK so that Apache will move on to the next thing.

We need to tell Apache about the new modules, so add the following to the Apache configuration file /etc/httpd/conf/httpd.conf, and reload the new configuration file:

```
<Location /bookdetailmysql>
   SetHandler        perl-script
   PerlHandler       BookDetailMysql
</Location>
```

To see this code, drill down on one of the book titles. If you click the first title, *Open Source Web Development with LAMP,* you should see Figure 8.9.

We also want to add some functionality to the normal logging phase of Apache. In our example, we want to not only log but also send an e-mail each time either the /booklistingmysql/ or /bookdetailmysql/ page is hit. We need to write a module to do the work. Of course, the server must be configured to use the new module.

Create the file /var/www/mod_perl/BookMailLog.pm. Its contents can be found at http://localhost/mod_perl/BookMailLog.pm or www.opensourcewebbook. com/mod_perl/BookMailLog.pm. The beginning of the file looks like our other examples. The handler() method begins as follows:

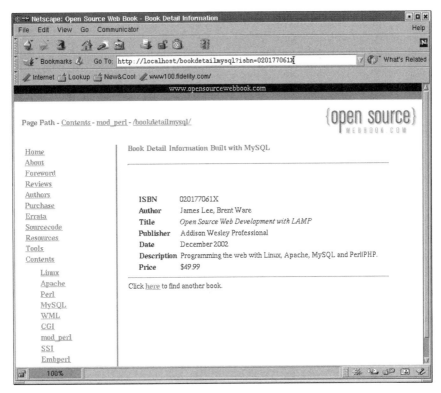

Figure 8.9 Book detail using MySQL and mod_perl

```
sub handler {
    # shift the argument into $r
    my $r = shift;

    # get the date/time
    my $date         = localtime();

    # get some of the request information
    # including the remote host, the URI,
    # the query string and the number of
    # bytes sent to the mod_perl program
    my $remote_host  = $r->get_remote_host();
    my $uri          = $r->uri();
    my $query_string = $r->query_string();
    my $num_bytes    = $r->bytes_sent();
```

To e-mail information about the request, the program calls some rather obvious methods to learn about who and what asked for the information. These methods include get_remote_host(); uri(); query_string() (gets the query string—all the stuff after the "?"); and bytes_sent(). Most of these are self-explanatory.

```
# check for nastiness - first, is
# the query string too big?
if (length($query_string) > 100) {
    return OK;
}

# now check to see if the query string
# contains anything besides word characters
# ([a-zA-Z0-9_]) or the equal sign (=)
unless ($query_string = ~ /^[\w=]+$/) {
    return OK;
}
```

The program then does something crucial—it does a sanity check of the data to make sure someone is not calling our program with less than honorable intent. First it checks that the query string is not huge—this makes sure a devious person hasn't invoked this program with a giant query string (which could fill our e-mail spool file quite rapidly). Then it checks to see that the query string contains valid characters (word characters or "="). These measures are important! Even though we haven't put them in every example we've discussed, every working program you write should contain similar precautions.

```
# ok so far, so open a pipe to sendmail,
# and if it opens ok, send text into it -
# this text will be an e-mail message
if (open SM, '| /usr/sbin/sendmail -t -oi') {
    print SM <<EOM;
From: mod_perl email log <log\@opensourcewebbook.com>
To: log_notification\@opensourcewebbook.com
Subject: Book Listing/Detail was accessed

Time:              $date
Remote host:       $remote_host
Requested URI:     $uri
Query string:      $query_string
Bytes transferred: $num_bytes

EOM

    close SM;
}
return OK;
}

1;
```

If everything is fine with this data, the program opens a *pipe* into the sendmail program. A pipe is a connection to a program, such as sendmail, that reads from its standard input.[7] For this application, sendmail is invoked with a few options: -t means the To: list will be read from the header, and -oi means that lines with a single period on them will not terminate the input. The program then builds the mail header, followed by an all-important blank line, before the body of the e-mail is built. The e-mail is sent to the recipient(s) when the pipe is closed (close()).

Apache needs to be configured to use this code during the logging phase. To do that, the /booklisting/ and /bookdetail/ sections of /etc/httpd/conf/httpd.conf must be modified to have the following content:

```
<Location /booklisting>
   SetHandler        perl-script
   PerlHandler       BookListing
   PerlLogHandler    BookMailLog
</Location>

<Location /bookdetail>
   SetHandler        perl-script
   PerlHandler       BookDetail
   PerlLogHandler    BookMailLog
</Location>
```

The addition of the PerlLogHandler lines tells Apache to use this module during the logging phase. Normally, the logging phase simply logs to the access_log file, but we are adding functionality to send an e-mail. We can add just about anything in the logging phase: log to another file, execute system programs, or add data to an SQL database.

Remember to reload the new Apache configuration file by restarting the server. When this page is requested, e-mail is sent. Here is an example of what might be sent by this program:

---

[7]Sendmail is an Open Source program that comes with Linux that manages e-mail. It happens to be the program that routes more than 75 percent of all the e-mail on the Internet, so we are happy to use it here.

```
From apache@www.opensourcewebbook.com Wed Jun 20 16:13:48 2001
Date: Wed, 20 Jun 2001 16:14:19 -0500
From: mod_perl email log <log@opensourcewebbook.com>
To: log_notification@opensourcewebbook.com
Subject: Book Listing/Detail was accessed

Time:              Wed Jun 20 16:14:19 2001
Remote host:       127.0.0.1
Requested URI:     /bookdetail
Query string:      isbn=1565922433
Bytes transferred: 720
```

Having an e-mail sent every time a page is requested is a questionable activity for a web page that is accessed often. Imagine, if your web page were hit a million times a day, you would get a million e-mails telling you so! Of course, if your web page had a million hits a day, you could make some serious money selling banner ad space to all those companies that like to advertise on the Web (fewer today than in years past, we are sorry to say—or are we?). So, if a web page gets a lot of traffic, don't send yourself e-mail. This is just an example of what's possible.

8.6 OTHER STUFF YOU CAN DO

Because mod_perl gives us access to the internals of Apache, the things that can be done with mod_perl are almost endless. This list gives you a flavor.

- Enhance access control during the access control phase.
- Perform specific authentication above and beyond `.htaccess` during the authentication phase.
- Enhance logging during the logging phase.
- Use Perl Server Side Includes, which resemble the basic Apache Server Side Includes (see Chapter 9).

8.7 SUMMARY

mod_perl is a powerful way to create dynamic HTML web pages. It has all the power of Perl and gives access to the internals of Apache, allowing you to perform specific tasks for your particular application. It is much faster, once written, than CGI. It also makes it possible to completely customize mod_perl and Apache for your Web application, making for a very efficient and powerful dynamic webserver. mod_perl also speeds up legacy CGI scripts by compiling them once and keeping them cached in memory.

8.8 RESOURCES

Books

[Conway 99] Conway, Damian. *Object-Oriented Perl.* An excellent book describing object-oriented programming using Perl, from the basics to advanced topics—a must-read!

[Stein+ 99] Stein, Lincoln, and Doug MacEachern. *Writing Apache Modules with Perl and C.* All the details of writing mod_perl programs can be found in this book.

[Wall+ 00] Wall, Larry, Jon Orwant, and Tom Christiansen. *Programming Perl, Third Edition.*

Web Sites

mod_perl home page: `perl.apache.org/`

mod_perl guide: `perl.apache.org/guide/`

Writing Apache Modules with Perl and C web site: `www.modperl.com/`

Part IV
Embedded

9

Server Side Includes

9.1 INTRODUCTION

Server Side Includes (SSI) provides a simple way to *embed* executable code into a web page. The advantages of SSI are that it is simple to use and easy to learn, and sometimes simplicity is its own reward. The main drawback of SSI is that because of its simplicity, it is limited in what it can do.[1]

SSI is not CGI (see Chapter 7)—that is, it is not a program that is executed to generate HTML text, so one needn't be a Perl hacker to use it. Rather, SSI is a collection of directives that can be embedded in an HTML file and processed by Apache. A directive has this form:

```
<!--#directive param1="value1"
            param2="value2"... -->
```

which is simply an HTML comment with a "#" escape to SSI.

Among other things, SSI allows you to

- Display variables
- Include contents of files
- Display information such as the date and filename
- Execute programs or commands
- Create variables
- Use simple conditional expressions

SSI is not intended to be used to perform sophisticated programming tasks. It is mainly used to do simple includes (thus the name) of basic information.

---

[1]Gödel raises his head again [Hofstadter 99].

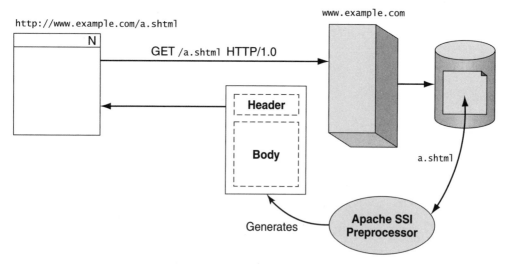

Figure 9.1   How SSI works

For anything more complex, other things you learn about elsewhere in this book are better choices. But you don't need a cannon to kill a gnat, so SSI has some useful applications if gnats are what need to be swatted.

9.1.1 How It Works

As Figure 9.1 shows, when the user requests a file that ends in the `.shtml` extension, the Apache server runs the text through the Server Side Includes preprocessor. This processes the SSIs, converting all SSI directives into the appropriate text. The resulting text is then sent back to the browser.

9.1.2 Configuration

If you installed Linux as suggested in Chapter 2, Apache should already be configured to support SSI. To check, make sure these two lines of the Apache configuration file (`/etc/httpd/conf/httpd.conf`) are uncommented:

```
AddType text/html .shtml
AddHandler server-parsed .shtml
```

These directives add a type of file with the suffix `.shtml`, whose content is to be treated as HTML and whose file is to be server-parsed, or preprocessed, by the Apache server before being served up. All files with the

.shtml suffix are preprocessed, so don't name normal non-SSI HTML files with the .shtml extension—that only slows down the webserver, because it will preprocess files that do not require it.

As always, if you change the Apache configuration file, restart the server.

9.1.3 Tutorial

SSI is relatively simple to learn, and we can give a short tutorial of its important aspects in just a few pages. SSI consists of a few directives, which implement its functionality.

echo Directive

The echo directive instructs the server to insert (*echo*) the value of a variable at that point in the HTML file. It has this syntax:

```
<!--#echo var="variable"-->
```

The variables that can be echoed are

- DOCUMENT_NAME—the name of the document
- DOCUMENT_URI—the virtual path to the document
- DATE_LOCAL—the local date and time
- DATE_GMT—the date and time in Greenwich Mean Time
- LAST_MODIFIED—the last modification date for the document
- QUERY_STRING_UNESCAPED—an undecoded query string with all shell metacharacters escaped with a backslash

Let's show an example. First, make a directory for the SSI work, giving it the proper permissions:

```
$ cd /var/www/html
$ mkdir ssi
$ chmod a+rx ssi
$ cd ssi
```

Call this example echo.shtml and make sure it is readable (with chmod a+r echo.shtml—be sure to do this for all the examples in this chapter). Put the following code in it:

```html
<html>
<head>
<title>Server Side Includes: echo Directive</title>
</head>
<body bgcolor="#ffffff">
<h1>Examples of the echo directive</h1>
Filename: <b><!--#echo var="DOCUMENT_NAME"--></b>
<br>
URI: <b><!--#echo var="DOCUMENT_URI"--></b>
<br>
Local time: <b><!--#echo var="DATE_LOCAL"--></b>
<br>
GMT: <b><!--#echo var="DATE_GMT"--></b>
<br>
Last modified: <b><!--#echo var="LAST_MODIFIED"--></b>
</body>
</html>
```

There are several `echo` directives, which result in a web page like Figure 9.2. To see for yourself, go to one of these URLs: `http://localhost/ssi/echo.shtml` or `www.opensourcewebbook.com/ssi/echo.shtml`.

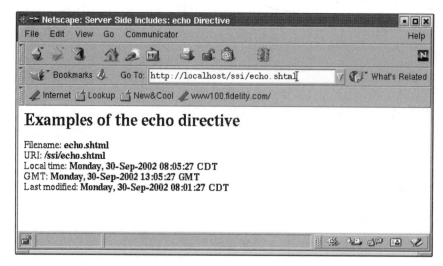

Figure 9.2   echo SSI directive

include Directive

The `include` directive allows you to include the contents of another file in the current document. This is convenient if you want every page to have the same header and/or footer. Let's say we have this HTML in the file `header.html`:

```
<html>
<head>
<title>Server Side Includes: include Directive</title>
</head>
<body bgcolor="#ffffff">
<h1>You are at www.opensourcewebbook.com</h1>
```

and this HTML in the file `footer.shtml`:

```
<hr>
<a href="http://www.opensourcewebbook.com/">
http://www.opensourcewebbook.com/</a>
<br>
Date: <!--#echo var="DATE_LOCAL"-->
</body>
</html>
```

We can wrap header and footer HTML around any HTML (`include.shtml`):

```
<!--#include file="header.html"-->

Here is the stuff between what was included.

<!--#include file="footer.shtml"-->
```

Load this page by going to one of these URLs: `http://localhost/ssi/include.shtml` or `www.opensourcewebbook.com/ssi/include.shtml`. The result is Figure 9.3. Notice that the footer filename, `footer.shtml`, ends in `.shtml`, which caused it to be preprocessed as well, showing the local date.

fsize and flastmod Directives

The `fsize` directive inserts the size of the file specified. This is its syntax:

```
<!--#fsize file="filename"-->
```

By default, the size is rounded to the next kilobyte. To change the output format, use the `config` directive:

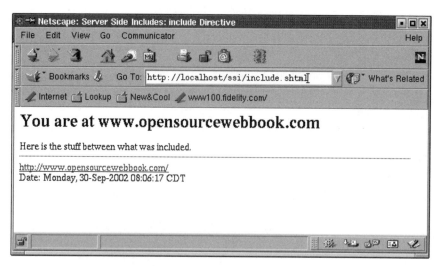

Figure 9.3 include SSI directive

```
<!--#config sizefmt="bytes"-->
```

The `flastmod` directive inserts the last modification date of the specified file. Its syntax is:

```
<!--#flastmod file="filename"-->
```

As an example, put this code into `file.shtml`:

```
<html>
<head>
<title>Server Side Includes: fsize and flastmod Directives</title>
</head>
<body bgcolor="#ffffff">
<h1>Examples of the fsize and flastmod directives</h1>
The file <tt>echo.shtml</tt> was last modified
<!--#flastmod file="echo.shtml"-->
<br>
Its size is <!--#fsize file="echo.shtml"-->
bytes.
<br>
<!--#config sizefmt="bytes"-->
The size can also be displayed as
<!--#fsize file="echo.shtml"--> bytes.
</body>
</html>
```

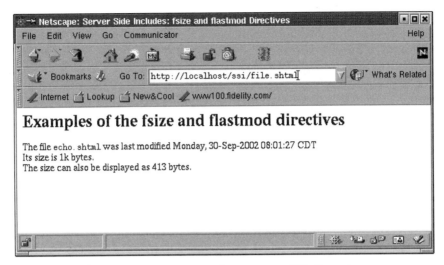

Figure 9.4 `fsize` and `flastmod` SSI directives

Then go to one of these URLs—`http://localhost/ssi/file.shtml` or `www.opensourcewebbook.com/ssi/file.shtml`—and get Figure 9.4.

exec Directive

The `exec` directive inserts the output of a command or CGI script. This is useful for executing a shell command or CGI script via an SSI directive:

```
<!--#exec cmd="command"-->
<!--#exec cgi="cgiscript"-->
```

This example can be found in `exec.shtml`:

```
<html>
<head>
<title>Server Side Includes: exec Directive</title>
</head>
<body bgcolor="#ffffff">
<h1>Examples of the exec directive</h1>
Here is the disk usage summary for <tt>/home</tt>:
<pre>
<!--#exec cmd="/bin/df /home"-->
</pre>
</body>
</html>
```

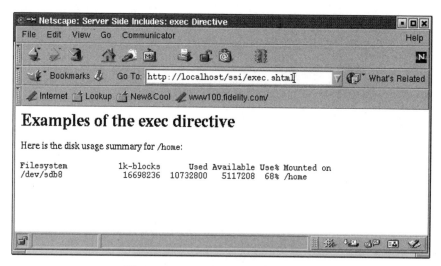

Figure 9.5   exec SSI directive

You can view this by going to either `http://localhost/ssi/exec.shtml` or `www.opensourcewebbook.com/ssi/exec.shtml`. This results in Figure 9.5.

config Directive

The `config` directive can be used to change the configuration of SSI output. If an error occurs during the processing of an SSI directive (for instance, including a file that does not exist), the following default error output is displayed:

```
[an error occurred while processing this directive]
```

This output can be changed with the `config` directive:

```
<!--#config errmsg="Error, contact webmaster@opensourcewebbook.com"-->
```

Earlier in this section, we changed the default output of the `fsize` directive. The default behavior of many of the directives can be similarly changed. For instance, the time format can also be changed in a number of ways:

```
<!--#config timefmt="format"-->
```

If you want to know more about all the possible configurations of the timefmt directive, check out `man strftime`.

set Directive

The set directive allows us to create variables. Its syntax is:

```
<!--#set var="varname" value="varvalue"-->
```

Here is an example:

```
<!--#set var="name" value="Ron"-->
Name is: <!--#echo var="name"-->
```

This SSI code produces the text "`Name is: Ron.`"

if Directive

Simple conditional expressions are available with the `if/elsif/else/endif`. This is the syntax:

```
<!--#if expr="expression1"-->
    text generated if expression1 is true
<!--#elsif expr="expression2"-->
    text generated if expression2 is true
<!--#else-->
    text generated if expression1 is false and expression2 is false
<!--#endif-->
```

Here is a simple example that tests whether the $DATE_LOCAL SSI variable contains the text "AM" (if so, it is morning):

```
<!--#config timefmt="%p" -->
<!--#if expr="$DATE_LOCAL = /AM/" -->
    <p>Good Morning!</p>
<!--#endif -->
```

First, the time format is configured to display "AM" or "PM". Then, the variable $DATE_LOCAL is checked to see whether it matches the regular expression /AM/, and if so, the expression is true. We could have checked to see whether the variable did not match the regular expression /PM/ with:

```
<!--#if expr="$DATE_LOCAL != /PM/" -->
```

9.2 SECURITY CONSIDERATIONS

SSI directives are as secure as you are. Don't execute any commands that might do bad things or provide too much information. We suggest that directives like this *not* be included:

```
<!--#exec cmd="/bin/cat /etc/passwd"-->
```

On the other hand, SSI doesn't let the client do anything not specifically allowed by the server, so it's relatively harmless. But don't do anything stupid, anyway.

9.3 SUMMARY

SSI is a simple way to embed executable code within HTML. There are other ways (Embperl, Mason, and PHP), which trade the simplicity of this method for power, speed, and flexibility at the price of complexity. SSI is commonly found in the wild, so this chapter should also help you understand the syntax if you see it in someone else's web page.

9.4 RESOURCES

Books

[Hofstadter 99] Hofstadter, Douglas R. *Gödel, Escher, Bach: An Eternal Golden Braid, Twentieth Anniversary Edition.*

[Stein 97] Stein, Lincoln D. *How to Set Up and Maintain a Web Site, Second Edition.* One of the best books written about creating and maintaining a web site.

Web Sites

The official Apache SSI page: `httpd.apache.org/docs/howto/ssi.html`

An extensive tutorial from Bignosebird.com: `www.bignosebird.com/ssi.shtml`

A tutorial from the folks at NCSA: `hoohoo.ncsa.uiuc.edu/docs/tutorials/includes.html`

10

Embperl (HTML::Embperl)

10.1 INTRODUCTION

`HTML::Embperl` (aka Embperl) is a Perl module that allows the execution of server-side programming code by embedding Perl code into HTML files. Embperl, written and maintained by Gerald Richter, can be found at `http://perl.apache.org/embperl/`.

A powerful feature of Embperl is that it is hooked into mod_perl. Most mod_perl features apply to Embperl, so if you know mod_perl, you need know only a bit more to use Embperl. As in mod_perl, the code in the page is compiled only the first time it is called (or when the file is modified), as is the case with `Apache::Request` programs with mod_perl.

The result of the compilation is cached so that the next time the page is requested, the Perl code does not need to be recompiled. It is the Perl code compilation that is cached, *not* the generated HTML code. This means that the next time the page is requested, the Perl code reexecutes (but does not recompile) to generate the HTML for that request. If the HTML file is modified, a recompile is forced, but that is a good thing because we want the changes to take effect. After the recompile, the Perl code is again cached. This makes for efficient execution. Also, as in mod_perl, the internals of Apache are available to use if we want them, so Embperl can hook into Apache's different phases (such as authentication and logging) if the application warrants it.

Embperl is basically Perl code—and you know how we feel about Perl. You can write Perl server-side programs embedded within HTML files. Mmmm, Perl...

10.2 INSTALLING EMBPERL

Embperl does not come standard on Red Hat (yet), so you need to install it. Get the latest source from `ftp://ftp.dev.ecos.de/pub/perl/embperl/`. As of this writing, the latest beta release was 2.0b3,[1] so the file we want is `HTML-Embperl-2.0b3.tar.gz`. Save it in `/tmp`.

Change directory to `/tmp` and do the following:

```
$ cd /tmp
$ tar xzf HTML-Embperl-2.0b3.tar.gz
$ cd HTML-Embperl-2.0b3
$ perl Makefile.PL
```

You will then be prompted for some site-specific information. The important information you need is the locations of the following files:

- `httpd.h`—located at `/usr/include/apache/httpd.h`

- `httpd`—located at `/usr/sbin/httpd`

- `mod_env.so`—located at `/usr/lib/apache/mod_env.so`

Check that these files can be found at these locations on your machine. If you find them in a different location, make the necessary adjustments in the following responses (wrapped for readability):

```
Build with support for Apache mod_perl?(y/n) [y]y
Searching for Apache sources...
Look at ..
Look at ../src
Look at ./src
Apache source not found, enter path name or q to quit
  []/usr/include/apache
Searching for Apache sources...
Look at /usr/include/apache
Use /usr/include/apache as Apache source(y/n) [y]y
Will use /usr/include/apache for Apache Headers
Enter path and file to start as httpd [/usr/include/apache/httpd]
  /usr/sbin/httpd
Apache Version Server version: Apache/1.3.19 (Unix) (Red-Hat/Linux)
Library for mod_env.c not found, please enter path to mod_env.so
  []/usr/lib/apache
  .
  .
  .
```

---

[1]The latest stable release was 1.3.4, but the new release, version 2, will probably be the stable release when this book is printed, so we will install version 2.

Now make, test, and install:

```
$ make
$ make test
$ su
# make install
```

That's it, assuming no errors—Embperl is installed. Make sure by checking the online documentation:

```
$ perldoc HTML::Embperl
```

You should see the HTML::Embperl man page.

10.3 APACHE CONFIGURATION

Apache needs to be reconfigured to use Embperl to process HTML files. This requires a decision about how to use this module: whether to process every file with Embperl or to tag Embperl files with a special extension (.epl is commonly used) so that only those files are processed.

Processing only the files with the different filename extension is more efficient. The drawbacks are that the extension gives out information about the server, and URLs aren't uniform, which presents a human factors issue—people remember .html and don't remember .epl.

There is another good reason not to use special filenames. Suppose you have a page that has no Embperl and is linked everywhere else in your site. If you decide that page needs Embperl, it must be renamed, and all references to that file changed everywhere on your site. If that page is linked externally, it will be wrong on all the search engines.

If you do decide to create a special filename extension such as .epl, add this to Apache's configuration file:

```
<Files *.epl>
  SetHandler  perl-script
  PerlHandler HTML::Embperl
  Options     ExecCGI
</Files>

AddType text/html .epl
```

We choose to not use a special extension. Instead, we'll limit the use of Embperl to a certain directory within the web document tree for only HTML files (files ending in .html).

By limiting it to one directory, only the .html files under that directory and its subdirectories will be processed by Embperl—.html files in other directories will not be affected by Embperl. This is a good compromise.

Make a directory for the Embperl stuff:

```
$ mkdir /var/www/html/embperl
$ chmod a+rx /var/www/html/embperl
```

As root, add the following to the bottom of /etc/httpd/conf/httpd.conf:

```
SetEnv EMBPERL_DEBUG 2285
PerlSetEnv EMBPERL_LOG /var/log/embperl.log

<Directory /var/www/html/embperl>
  <Files *.html>
    SetHandler    perl-script
    PerlHandler   HTML::Embperl
    Options       ExecCGI
  </Files>
</Location>
```

The SetEnv directive sets the variable EMBPERL_DEBUG to the value 2285. This sets the debugging level to a very high value, causing a great deal of output to be written to the log file (here configured to be /var/log/embperl.log).

To have a minimal amount of log information, set EMBPERL_DEBUG to 1. More is good for now—you can change it later after you get used to using it. For fun, run tail -f /var/log/embperl.log in a terminal to see the debug information as it is generated.

Configuring the log file to be in /var/log/embperl.log requires that the webserver apache be able to write to this file.[2] So, as root, execute these commands to create the file and give it the proper owner and permissions:

```
# touch /var/log/embperl.log
# chmod gw-rwx /var/log/embperl.log
# chown apache /var/log/embperl.log
```

The <Directory> directive says that for the directory /var/www/html/embperl and its subdirectories, the following specifications are applied. The <Files *.html> directive tells Apache to process only .html files with

---

[2]The Embperl default is /tmp/embperl.log, which is a security problem because anyone else who uses your machine can write to this file; so don't use it.

HTML::Embperl! Files with .txt and .jpg extensions in these directories are normal files that should not processed by Embperl and should be served up plain. See perldoc HTML::Embperl for all the different ways to configure this directory.

Now, load the changed Apache configuration file:

```
# /etc/init.d/httpd graceful
```

10.4 A QUICK EXAMPLE

Let's start with a quick example to display "hello, world!" with Embperl (what else?). Create the file /var/www/html/embperl/index.html with the following contents (remember to chmod a+r index.html[3]):

```
[-
    $msg = ´hello, world!´;
-]

<html>
<head>
<title>hello, world with Embperl</title>
</head>
<body bgcolor="#ffffff">
[+ $msg +]
</body>
</html>
```

To see the result of this page, load one of the following into your browser: http://localhost/embperl/ or www.opensourcewebbook.com/embperl/. You should see something like Figure 10.1.

The first part of index.html is an Embperl command denoted by [- ... -]. We discuss this later in this chapter, but for now suffice it to say that the code within this command is executed as Perl code. In this example, $msg is set to a familiar message that is included in the HTML within the <body> tags.

To include the contents of the variable $msg, use the Embperl command [+ $msg +]. This command is replaced by the value of the variable $msg. This value is then displayed in the browser.

---

[3]In general, if you have any problems, check your permissions. Don't make us say this again.

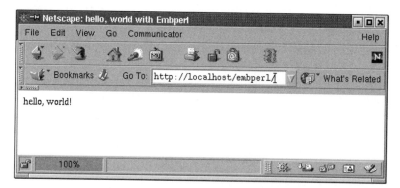

Figure 10.1   hello, world! with Embperl

10.5 EMBPERL COMMANDS

As we saw earlier, Embperl commands start with a "[" and end with a "]". Because "[" has a special meaning, to put a "[" on your web page, you must write it as "[[".

10.5.1 [+ Perl Code +]

The code within [+ ... +] is executed, and the result is that the command is replaced with what the code evaluates to. Thus [+ "hello!" +] is the same as `print "hello!"` in a normal CGI program. For example:

```
<p>Hello [+ $name +]</p>
```

If the value of $name is "Gerald Richter", the result of the previous command after Embperl is through processing it is this:

```
<p>Hello Gerald Richter</p>
```

A command can contain any Perl expression, including array elements, hash elements, and function calls:

```
[+ $i+1 +]
[+ $a[$i] +]
[+ $info{name} +]
[+ generate_link() +]
```

Figure 10.2 Generating a link in Embperl

Embperl can be used to create links.[4] Check out /var/www/html/embperl/link.html:

```
[-
    $url = ´http://www.opensourcewebbook.com/´;
-]

<html>
<head>
<title>The World of Open Source Web Development</title>
</head>
<body bgcolor="#ffffff">
The fun begins here:
<a href="[+ $url +]">[+ $url +]</a>
</body>
</html>
```

The first part of this HTML file is similar to the previous example, but the URL shown on the web page is inserted via the variable $url in this file.

The line beginning with <a href executes the Embperl code. The code [+ $url +] is evaluated within the double quotes first and evaluated within the >...< a second time. This creates the following valid HTML link:

```
<a href="http://www.opensourcewebbook.com/">
        http://www.opensourcewebbook.com/</a>
```

This example can be seen by loading one of these URLs into your browser: http://localhost/embperl/link.html or www.opensourcewebbook.com/embperl/link.html. This generates Figure 10.2. Of course, much more

---

[4] "Ha! Big deal!" you might think. "I can do that with regular HTML." Of course you can, but with Embperl, you can generate links dynamically.

fun is to be had if you click the link on the page and go down that rabbit hole.

10.5.2 [- Perl Code -]

In the previous examples, we've used the construct [- ... -] repeatedly. This command executes the Perl code, but the return value of the code isn't printed into the HTML, as it is with the [+ ... +] construct. However, if you `print()` within the [- ... -], that printed text does find its way onto the HTML page. The easy way to remember this is that the results of whatever you put inside the [+ ... +] end up in the browser, while that inside [- ... -] doesn't (unless you `print()`).

Here is one example we have already seen:

```
[-
    $msg = 'hello, world!';
-]
```

This assigns a value to the variable `$msg` but doesn't generate any output that would be displayed by the browser.

This command can be used to execute arbitrary code, such as:

```
[-
    # connect to a MySQL database
    use DBI;

    $user = 'someuser';
    $pass = 'somepassword';

    $dbh = DBI->connect('DBI:mysql:somedb', $user, $pass);
-]
```

That code does a lot of database things that might need to be done, but it does not generate any HTML that is sent to the browser.

10.5.3 [! Perl Code !]

This command is the same as [- ... -] except that the Perl code within is executed only the first time the page is requested (or when the page is modified). Recall that in Embperl, the page is compiled the first time it is requested, and then it is cached for quick execution for all following requests.

This command is useful for defining subroutines or initializing variables. Here is an example:

```
[!
    sub create_link {
        my($url) = @_;

        return "<a href=\"$url\">$url</a>";
    }

    $HOME_URL = ´http://www.opensourcewebbook.com/´;
!]
```

10.5.4 [# Some Text #]

This is a comment block. Everything between [# ... #] is removed from the output.

Because the pages we discuss here are being processed by Embperl, [# ... #] can be used instead of the HTML comment marks <!-- ... -->.

10.5.5 [$ Command Arguments $]

The [$ ... $] *metacommand* contains Perl commands such as the flow control constructs if, while, and foreach. This is the syntax for the if metacommand:

```
[$ if (condition) $] ... [$ endif $]
```

It includes the contents of the if section if the *condition* is true. For example:

```
[$ if ($day eq ´Monday´) $]
Today is <b>Monday</b>, so my condolences.<br>
[$ endif $]
```

The [$ elsif $] and [$ else $] are optional and work similarly. An example is in /var/www/htdocs/embperl/if.html:

```
[-
    # assign date the current date/time (as if we
    # executed `date`)
    $date = localtime();
-]

<html>
<head>
```

```
<title>Embperl if</title>
</head>
<body bgcolor="#ffffff">
Today's date is: <b>[+ $date +]</b>.
<hr>

[# check to see if $date begins with `Mon´   #]
[# if so, it is Monday                        #]
[$ if ($date =~ /^Mon/) $]
  Today is <b>Monday</b>, so my condolences.
[# check to see if $date begins with `Sat´   #]
[# or `Sun´, if so, it is the weekend         #]
[$ elsif ($date =~ /^(Sat|Sun)/) $]
  Today is a <b>weekend day</b>, so take the day off!
[# otherwise, just a normal work day          #]
[$ else $]
  Today is an <b>acceptable weekday</b>, so get some work done.
[$ endif $]

</body>
</html>
```

To view the result, load one of these URLs into your browser: `http://localhost/embperl/if.html` or `www.opensourcewebbook.com/embperl/if.html`. You should see something similar to Figure 10.3.

In addition to the condition `if` construct, Embperl has looping constructs. This is the syntax for the `while` metacommand:

```
[$ while (condition) $] ... [$ endwhile $]
```

The `while` loop behaves like Perl's `while` loop—it includes the contents of the `while` section as long as *condition* is true. In the following example,

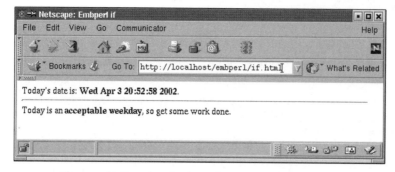

Figure 10.3   An Embperl `if` metacommand

the `while` loop prints all of Apache's environment variables stored within `%ENV`. Note that the code within [- ... -] is embedded in the middle of the HTML document—Embperl commands can be anywhere within the HTML document.

```
<html>
<head>
<title>Embperl while</title>
</head>
<body bgcolor="#ffffff">
<h1>Environment Variables</h1>

[-
    # initialize $i, the loop control variable
    # used within the while loop below
    $i = 0;

    # grab the keys and sort them, storing them
    # in @k
    @k = sort(keys(%ENV));
-]

[# loop through @k, printing the variable names #]
[# and their values                            #]
[$ while ($i <= $#k) $]
  [+ $k[$i] +] = [+ $ENV{$k[$i]} +]<br>
  [- $i++; -]
[$ endwhile $]

</body>
</html>
```

Again, note that there are [- ... -] commands in the middle of the page, including [- $i++; -] inside a [$ ... $] command.

To see the result, look at either `http://localhost/embperl/while.html` or `www.opensourcewebbook.com/embperl/while.html`. You should see something similar to Figure 10.4.

Embperl has a `foreach` loop similar to Perl's `foreach` loop, passing the *control_var* through *list* and executing the body for each of the elements. This is the syntax:

```
[$ foreach control_var (list) $] ... [$ endforeach $]
```

The `while` loop in the previous example, which prints the environment variables, is better written with `foreach`:

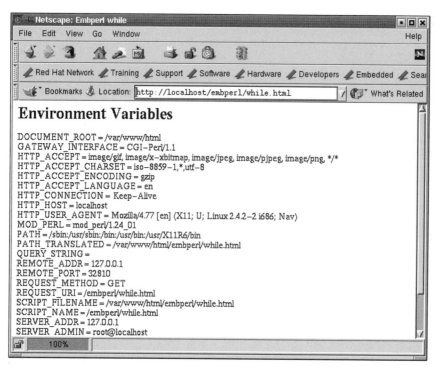

Figure 10.4   Displaying environment variables with
Embperl's `while` command

```
<html>
<head>
<title>Embperl foreach</title>
</head>
<body bgcolor="#ffffff">
<h1>Environment Variables Redux</h1>

[# loop through the sorted keys of %ENV, printing #]
[# the keys and their values                       #]
[$ foreach $key (sort keys %ENV) $]
  [+ $key +] = [+ $ENV{$key} +]<br>
[$ endforeach $]

</body>
</html>
```

Executing this code produces the same result as the `while` loop, as seen in
Figure 10.4.

You can see it by going to either of these URLs: `http://localhost/`
`embperl/foreach.html` or www.opensourcewebbook.com/embperl/foreach.html.

Embperl Language Notes

There is not a [$ for ... $] metacommand in Embperl. The [$ while ... $] command can be used instead (as it can in every other language with those constructs also).

There is a [$ do $] ... [$ until condition $] metacommand. We don't use it much—we rarely find much application for do ... while or do ... until loops in HTML pages. If you care to, you can read about these things at the Embperl web site, http://perl.apache.org/embperl/Embperl.pod.cont.html, or perldoc HTML::Embperl.

10.6 POSTED DATA AND %fdat

Posted data—that is, data posted to the server by the client browser (this data was obtained using the param() function in the CGI and mod_perl chapters)—is accessed by Embperl programs through the variable %fdat. Each form widget name is a key in %fdat, and the widget value is the value of that key.

Here's a simple example. First, there's a form to collect some data (/var/www/html/embperl/fdat1.html):

```
<html>
<head>
<title>Form to Demonstrate %fdat</title>
</head>
<body bgcolor="#ffffff">

<h1>A Form to Demonstrate %fdat</h1>

<form action="/embperl/fdat2.html" method="post">
Name:  <input type="text" name="name"> <br>
Age:   <input type="text" name="age"> <br>
Phone: <input type="text" name="phone"> <br>
<input type="submit">
</form>

</body>
</html>
```

There is nothing new about this; it is simply a form with three text input fields. No Embperl here. Still, Apache processes it with HTML::Embperl because it is under the /embperl subdirectory of the /var/www/html/ directory.

This is a consequence of the earlier decision to process all `.html` files under `/embperl` with HTML::Embperl, at a slight reduction in processor efficiency (but one hopes, an increase in programmer efficiency). This might be a bad choice if you're writing a server for `HugeOnlineRetailer.com`, but in that case, you'd probably know to make a different choice.

In this form, the action is `/embperl/fdat2.html`, an Embperl HTML file. Even though data is posted, we don't need CGI, as we did in Chapter 7. Embperl allows us to accomplish the same thing within an HTML page.

This is the page that processes the posted data (`/var/www/html/embperl/fdat2.html`):

```
[-
    # grab the posted data from %fdat
    $name  = $fdat{name}  || ´´;
    $age   = $fdat{age}   || ´´;
    $phone = $fdat{phone} || ´´;
-]
<html>
<head>
<title>Processing %fdat</title>
</head>
<body bgcolor="#ffffff">
<h1>Processing %fdat</h1>

[$ if ($name ne ´´ and $age ne ´´ and $phone ne ´´) $]
    [# all the fields were filled out! #]
Thank you for filling out the form!  You entered:
<br>Name = <b>[+ $name +]</b>
<br>Age = <b>[+ $age +]</b>
<br>Phone = <b>[+ $phone +]</b>

[$ else $]
    [# uhoh, not all the fields were filled out #]

Sorry, but you need to go back and fill out all the fields.

[$ endif $]

</body>
</html>
```

At the beginning of this file, the script gets the data from `%fdat`. When the data is posted, the value of the widget `name` is stored into `$fdat{name}`, the value of the widget `age` is stored into `$fdat{age}`, and the value of the widget `phone` is stored into `$fdat{phone}`.

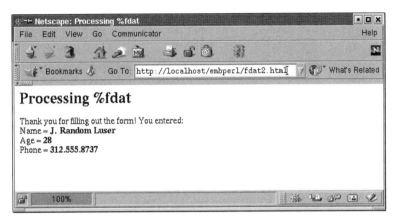

Figure 10.5 Using %fdat

Then, in the body of the HTML file, the script uses a [$ if ... $] command to check that it received values for all three widgets. If so, the data is printed to the user. If not, the script tells the client that they need to go back and correctly fill out the form.

To try this program, check either of these URLs: http://localhost/embperl/fdat1.html or www.opensourcewebbook.com/embperl/fdat1.html. If you enter some information into this form and click the submit button, you should see a result that resembles Figure 10.5.

10.7 OTHER EMBPERL VARIABLES—$row AND $col

Embperl can generate one- or two-dimensional tables dynamically with the use of $row and/or $col. If either $row or $col (or $cnt) is used within a <table>, Embperl repeats the text between <table> and </table> as long as the expression that includes $row/$col does not evaluate to undef.

For instance, if a program has this code:

```
[- @nums = (1..5); -]
<table>
  <tr><td>[+ $nums[$row] +]</td></tr>
</table>
```

this means start the table and then use $row to loop through @nums, one element at a time. And because it is $row, each element is treated as a row, so it repeats `<tr><td>` ... `</td></tr>`. Therefore, this is the result of this code:

```
<table>
  <tr><td>1</td></tr>
  <tr><td>2</td></tr>
  <tr><td>3</td></tr>
  <tr><td>4</td></tr>
  <tr><td>5</td></tr>
</table>
```

Changing the code to this:

```
[- @nums = (1..5); -]
<table>
  <tr><td>[+ $nums[$col] +]</td></tr>
</table>
```

loops through `@nums`, and because we use `$col`, each element is treated as a column, so it repeats `<td>` ... `</td>`. Therefore, this is the result of this code:

```
<table>
  <tr><td>1</td><td>2</td><td>3</td><td>4</td><td>5</td></tr>
</table>
```

Cool HTML table magic!

As an example, we display the environment variables in a table. First, we show how the table might be built without the magic and then how more magic makes life better. This code can be found in /var/www/html/embperl/rowcol.html:

```
<html>
<head>
<title>Using $row and $col</title>
</head>
<body bgcolor="#ffffff">
<h1>Using a <tt>foreach</tt></h1>

<table border="1">

[# loop through the sorted keys of %ENV, #]
[# printing the keys and their values     #]

[$ foreach $key (sort keys %ENV) $]
  <tr><th> [+ $key +] </th><td> [+ $ENV{$key} +] </td></tr>
[$ endforeach $]

</table>
```

```
<h1>Using the Magical <tt>$row</tt> and <tt>$col</tt></h1>

[# grab the sorted keys of %ENV, put them in @k       #]
[# then, define one row in the table, and $row will   #]
[# magically take on the values of the indices of @k #]

[- @k = sort keys %ENV -]

<table border="1">
  <tr><th> [+ $k[$row] +] </th><td> [+ $ENV{$k[$row]} +] </td></tr>
</table>

</body>
</html>
```

Try this program by going to one of these URLs: `http://localhost/embperl/rowcol.html` or `www.opensourcewebbook.com/embperl/rowcol.html`. You should see something that resembles Figure 10.6.

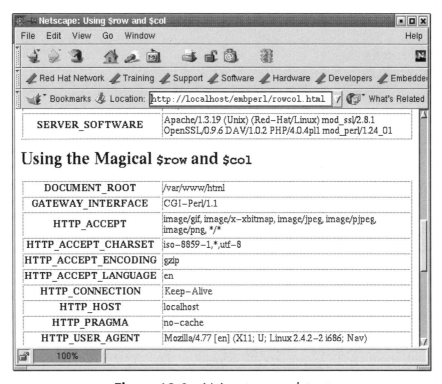

Figure 10.6 Using $row and $col

10.8 EMBPERL PROJECT

Now you know enough to have some real fun, so we'll do a real Embperl project—a product filtering system.

10.8.1 The Problem

We will create two web pages: The first enables the user to filter a list of products, narrowing the selected items based on three criteria: the manufacturer's city, the manufacturer's name, or the product category (the user can select any combination of these three categories); the second page provides details for a selected product.

For a sneak preview, see `http://localhost/embperlproject/productfilter/` or `www.opensourcewebbook.com/embperlproject/productfilter/`. These Embperl pages are built from a MySQL database, so the first step is to create the tables and populate them with data.

We will have two tables: a table of manufacturers and a table of products. Each manufacturer has a unique manufacturer ID, and each product relates to a manufacturer through this ID.

The manufacturers table (named `manufacturers`, strangely enough) has the following fields:

- `man_id`—the manufacturer ID, a 10-character string (the key to the table)
- `name`—a 60-character string
- `address`—a 60-character string
- `city`—a 60-character string
- `state`—a 2-character string
- `zip`—a 10-character string

The products table (named `products`, strangely enough) has the following fields:

- `prod_id`—the product ID, a 10-character string (the key to the table)
- `man_id`—the ID of the manufacturer of the product
- `name`—a 60-character field that is the product name
- `category`—a 30-character field that is the category for the product
- `description`—a `BLOB` describing what the product is and what it does
- `price`—a double

Now we need to log in to MySQL to create the tables and insert some data. One way to accomplish this is for us to show you the commands and have you type them in. If we were mean, we would do this. However, there is another approach: Create the tables and insert the data using a text file that contains the table definition and the MySQL insert commands, and use a single, simple command to build the tables.

We're not mean, so we have created this file for you. You can find it at /var/www/misc/product_database.sql or online at http://localhost/embperl/ product_database.sql or www.opensourcewebbook.com/embperl/product_ database.sql.

To magically build this, first log in to MySQL and create the database:

```
$ mysql -uroot -p
Enter password:
Welcome to the MySQL monitor. Commands end with ; or \g.
Your MySQL connection id is 3 to server version: 3.23.36

Type 'help;' or '\h' for help. Type '\c' to clear the buffer

mysql> CREATE DATABASE product_database;
Query OK, 1 row affected (0.00 sec)

mysql> USE mysql;
Reading table information for completion of table and column names
You can turn off this feature to get a quicker startup with -A

Database changed
mysql> GRANT SELECT,INSERT,UPDATE,DELETE
    -> ON product_database.*
    -> TO apache@localhost;
Query OK, 0 rows affected (0.00 sec)
```

Execute this shell command from directory that contains this text file:

```
$ mysql -uapache -p product_database < product_database.sql
Enter password:
```

Like magic, the database is created and populated. You're welcome!

10.8.2 Creating a Consistent Look and Feel

Before we get into the nitty-gritty of the project, let's talk in general about some options we can use to create a web site with a consistent look and feel (such as www.opensourcewebbook.com/).

There are several ways to create such a web site with a consistent look and feel to all the web pages.

1. Hard-code all the HTML pages—bad idea; it's static and hard to maintain.

2. Use WML (see Chapter 6) to create a static look and feel—better, but not dynamic.

3. Use CGI (see Chapter 7)—a little better; easy to do, certainly.

4. Use mod_perl (see Chapter 8)—better still, but a bit too complicated, perhaps.

5. Use Embperl and write functions to return top and bottom—much better.

6. Use Embperl and EmbperlObject—best!

Method 1: Hard-Code HTML Files

All the pages can be hard-coded with the same HTML. Although this seems like the simplest thing to do, it isn't a great idea—if any content changes in the common parts, such as adding a link or changing the placement of a logo, every page has to be modified. Yuck. Good programmers are lazy, so a little work up front can save a lot of work later.

Method 2: Use WML to Create HTML Files

Using WML, as in Chapter 6, is much better than hard-coding HTML files. Creating a template for a look and feel is possible, so when (not if) changes to the look and feel occur, the changes need only be made once and will apply to all the HTML files. This is fine for static pages.

WML can be used with Embperl because WML has the `<protect>` tag, which makes WML ignore all the content within. Thefore, the WML files can be used to generate HTML, and that HTML can also contain Embperl code. We don't discuss this here because, in practice, wrapping `<protect>` ... `</protect>` around all the Embperl code can cause us to have dozens of protected blocks, and that is not pleasant. We don't go into this except to mention it here, but keep in mind that you can use WML and Embperl to create a consistent look and feel. TMTOWTDI in all things LAMP.

Method 3: Use CGI

We can certainly use CGI to create dynamic web sites; we did so in Chapter 7. Just take the HTML created by the web designers, add a bunch of `print()` functions, add our code to do the dynamic stuff (such as reading from a database), and we can solve the problem. But this requires us to transform the HTML files into Perl programs. Sometimes this is more work than we want—remember, good programmers are lazy.

Method 4: Use mod_perl

mod_perl, discussed in Chapter 8, is great for many uses, especially if we want to access Apache directly or if we want to speed up the CGIs. But,

as in CGI, creating mod_perl pages means we convert the HTML into a
program. And as we mentioned earlier, most of the features of mod_perl
are available to our Embperl programs (such as speed of execution because
of caching and access to Apache internals), so why convert?

Method 5: Use Embedded Programs to Build HTML

We can create a couple of functions to generate the HTML for the top and
the bottom of the HTML. Then, in the HTML files, we can have Embperl
code that calls these functions to generate the HTML for the look and feel.
As you might have guessed, because this is the Embperl chapter, this is
the method we talk about here.

To illustrate, we'll create a file to hold functions for the top and bottom of the HTML. We'll put the code in a file not within the document
tree—put it in /var/www/lib/emberl_template.pl. Hey, did you notice this
is outside the web document tree /var/www/html? That is good security
because the program is not viewable by someone visiting the web site, and
therefore we don't show them the internals of how we are building the web
pages. The less information we give crackers, the better.

First create this directory, make it accessible by user apache, and then
create the file within it that is readable by apache:

```
# mkdir /var/www/lib
# chmod a+rx /var/www/lib
# cd /var/www/lib
# vi emberl_template.pl
# chmod a+r emberl_template.pl
```

These are the contents of emberl_template.pl:

```
# file: /var/www/lib/emberl_template.pl

##
## the subroutine to return the HTML for the top
## of the page
##

sub top {
    return <<EOHTML;
<html>
<head>
<title>Embperl Project Take 1</title>
</head>
<body bgcolor="#ffffff">
<h1>A First Stab at Our Embperl Project</h1>
EOHTML
}
```

```
##
## the subroutine to return the HTML for the
## bottom of the page
##

sub bottom {
    return <<EOHTML;
</body>
</html>
EOHTML
}

1;   # don't forget this line!
```

This file simply defines two functions: top() and bottom(). The top() function returns the HTML for the top of the HTML, and the bottom() function returns the bottom of the HTML.

Two things to note: First, there is no shebang (#!/usr/bin/perl) in this file because it is not an executable file but a file that defines a couple of functions that are used by other programs; second, the file must end with 1;. This is the same syntactical Perl requirement seen in Chapter 8; the file must evaluate to true in the end, or the compilation fails, and the easiest way to guarantee a true value is by ending the program with 1;.

Now create a file that will source these two functions. Go to the directory with all of the Embperl code, /var/www/html/embperl, and create the file take1.html:

```
[-
    require '/var/www/lib/embperl_template.pl';

    $escmode = 0;
-]

[+ top() +]

This is a test of the Embperl Project Take 1

[+ bottom() +]
```

Load one of these URLs: http://localhost/embperl/take1.html or www.opensourcewebbook.com/embperl/take1.html. You should see Figure 10.7.

At the top of take1.html is a [- ... -] command; the Perl code within will be executed. The first line of this Perl code is a require. This statement

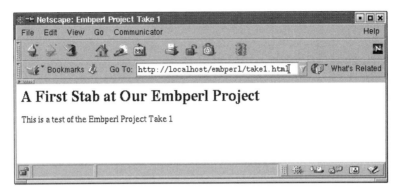

Figure 10.7 Embperl project take 1

will go out, find the file in question (the `embperl_template.pl` file containing the `top()` and `bottom()` function definitions), source that file, and compile the functions. Then, we see `$escmode = 0;`.

This is an important statement and deserves some discussion. When Embperl generates output, as with the `top()` function, Embperl automatically HTML- and URL-escapes it. In other words, if the Embperl code generates <hr>, it is escaped to be <hr>, which is displayed in the browser as the characters <hr>, not as the horizontal rule we wanted. There are several solutions to this problem, including escaping the characters we don't want to be HTML-escaped or URL-escaped with the backslash, as in \<hr\>. You can imagine that this could become a real drag if a whole mess of HTML is generated.

The better solution is to assign `$escmode` the value 0, which turns off this HTML- and URL-escape behavior. If this is turned off, when <hr> is generated, it indeed becomes a horizontal rule.

But there is a drawback to using `require` in this manner. Before we describe the problem click the Reload button on the browser a couple of times to reload this page (so that some of the many `httpd` processes will read in and compile the `top()` and `bottom()` functions).

Modify the `top()` function to add more HTML. Change the definition of `top()` to:

```
##
## the subroutine to return the HTML for the top
## of the page
##
```

```
sub top {
    return <<EOHTML;
<html>
<head>
<title>Embperl Project Take 1</title>
</head>
<body bgcolor="#ffffff">
<h1>A First Stab at Our Embperl Project</h1>
Here is some text followed by a horizontal rule.
<hr>
EOHTML
}
```

We simply added some text followed by a <hr> tag. Reload take1.html, then reload several more times. Chances are that sometimes you will see the new HTML, and sometimes the old. Why?

When new httpd processes are started, they compile the new definition. But the existing httpd processes do not recompile them, because Embperl has cached the compiled code. Embperl recompiles the Perl byte code if the Embperl file (take1.html) has changed, but in our case it hasn't—only the template file embperl_template.pl has changed. Moreover, once the Apache child process has compiled embperl_template.pl, it won't recompile it even if its contents change—the only file that is recompiled is the page that is requested (in our example, take1.html), not the pages that they require. Remember, because this speeds up execution time, this is one of the advantages of Embperl!

How do we force the existing versions of httpd to recompile the changed functions? Reload Apache. This is not ideal, because one has to be root to reload, which makes it a pain during code development.

To prove this actually solves the problem, reload Apache (as root, of course):

```
# /etc/init.d/httpd graceful
```

Now, reload the page as many times as you like, and you will see the new content on all the pages. All the versions of httpd have the new definition of top().

Method 6: Use HTML::EmbperlObject

There's a more powerful way to build a web site with Embperl: HTML::EmbperlObject, aka EmbperlObject. This Perl module allows the creation of templates for the entire web site or for portions thereof, and simple modifications to the HTML in the templates take effect immediately—there is no reason to restart the server.

It works like this: When an .html file is requested, a base file (call it base.html, configured in httpd.conf) is searched for in the directory that contains the file requested. This base.html contains HTML for the look and feel of the web site—the top, left rail, and bottom HTML. If base.html is not found in that directory, EmbperlObject looks in directories up the tree until it finds one named base.html. If EmbperlObject searches up to the directory root (/var/www/html, in these examples) and does not find a base.html, the user sees a "Not Found" error.

We start with a simple example to illustrate the concepts and then move on to implement a project. First we must create a new directory because the examples and project must be told to use the EmbperlObject module. Create a new directory:

```
# mkdir /var/www/html/embperlproject
# chmod a+rx /var/www/html/embperlproject
```

Next, reconfigure Apache so it knows about the new part of the web site. As root, add the following to the bottom of Apache's configuration file:

```
<Directory /var/www/html/embperlproject>
  PerlSetEnv    EMBPERL_OBJECT_BASE base.html
  <Files *.html>
    SetHandler    perl-script
    PerlHandler   HTML::EmbperlObject
    Options       ExecCGI
  </Files>
</Directory>
```

This directive tells Apache that under the directory /var/www/html/ embperlproject, the EmbperlObject base file, or template file, is named base.html. Then, for all files that end in .html, process them with the handler HTML::EmbperlObject. As mentioned before, this directory is configured this way because Apache should serve up .txt, etc., from this directory as normal files. See the docs (perldoc HTML::Embperl) for all the different ways to configure this directory.

When this is done, load the altered Apache configuration file:

```
# /etc/init.d/httpd graceful
```

A Simple Example

The base file is named base.html. You can create one in /var/www/html/embperlproject with this content:

```
<html>
<head>
<title>A Simple EmbperlObject Example</title>
</head>
<body bgcolor="#ffffff">
<h1>This is a simple EmbperlObject Example</h1>
This text, and the following horizontal rule, is in
base.html.
<hr>

[# the following will include the contents of the      #]
[# HTML file requested - `*´ means the requested file #]
[- Execute (´*´) -]

<hr>
The above horizontal rule, and this text, is in
base.html.
</body>
</html>
```

The line [- Execute (´*´) -] is important here—it means, "Include the content of the file that the user has requested (such as index.html)." So, in essence, the contents of base.html are wrapped around the contents of the requested file.

The requested file is the last part of the URL. The first example of this, and the file that should be created, is (as usual) index.html, the file that is delivered if no specific .html file is requested. It is in the directory /var/www/html/embperlproject and has the following content:

```
<i>This text, and the following message, is in
index.html.</i>
<br>
<i><b>Hello, world!</b></i>
<br>
```

Simple enough. The desired result would be to see the previous HTML in the middle of the template base.html.

Now give it a try by loading either of these URLs: http://localhost/embperlproject/ or www.opensourcewebbook.com/embperlproject/. You should see something like Figure 10.8.

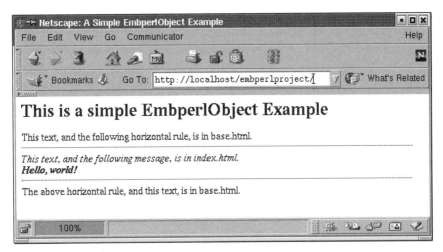

Figure 10.8 EmbperlObject simple example

The beauty of this is that if either base.html or index.html is changed, the effect is seen immediately without the need to restart Apache. Give it a try—alter the content of base.html, see the change, and change it back to the content shown previously.

Create another file in /var/www/html/embperlproject named cool.html:

```
<h4>Why Open Source is Cool (in the file cool.html)</h4>

<ul>
<li>It is open, so you have all the code available - reading
the code is a good way to spend a rainy day</li>
<li>The programs are free</li>
<li>The people involved in Open Source are cool, smart, and
all around "good people"</li>
<li>It is a movement bigger than any individual and more
than the sum of its parts</li>
</ul>
```

To see this (important) content wrapped within the template, request cool.html with either http://localhost/embperlproject/cool.html or www.opensourcewebbook.com/embperlproject/cool.html. The content will show up within the template as in Figure 10.9.

This template is applied to subdirectories under the directory that includes base.html. As an example, make a new directory:

```
$ mkdir /var/www/html/embperlproject/sub1
$ chmod a+rx /var/www/html/embperlproject/sub1
```

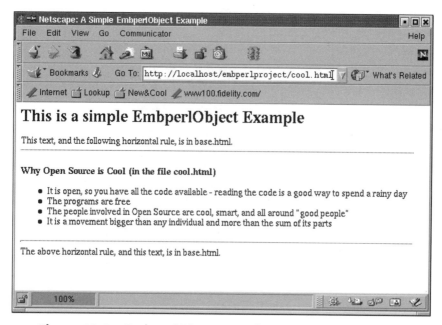

Figure 10.9   EmbperlObject simple example—`cool.html`

Within this new directory, create a new file named `index.html` with this content:

```
This is <i>index.html</i> within the subdirectory
<i>sub1</i>.  Requesting this file will use the
template <i>base.html</i> located in the parent
directory <i>/var/www/html/embperlproject</i>,
since there is no <i>base.html</i> in this
directory.
```

Look at this new file by asking for one of these URLs: `http://localhost/embperlproject/sub1/` or `www.opensourcewebbook.com/embperlproject/sub1/`. The template defined in `base.html` in the parent directory is wrapped around the content of the new `index.html` in subdirectory `sub1`. It looks like Figure 10.10.

You can redefine the template for a specific subdirectory—you don't have to use the same template for all the subdirectories. Create another subdirectory under `/var/www/html/embperlproject`:

```
$ mkdir /var/www/html/embperlproject/sub2
$ chmod a+rx /var/www/html/embperlproject/sub2
```

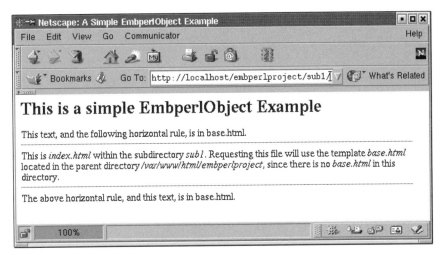

Figure 10.10 Using base.html in the parent directory

Now define a new template within the file base.html. Make sure that this new file is created within the new subdirectory—don't overwrite base.html in the parent directory.

```
<html>
<head>
<title>sub2 Template</title>
</head>
<body bgcolor="#ffffff">
<h1>sub2 Template</h1>

This is the template for all files within
<i>/embperlproject/sub2</i>.
<hr>

[- Execute (´*´) -]

<hr>
Back to the template.  Hey, check it out, we are
including a footer file below!  Perhaps it contains
HTML that will be the bottom of the page?

[- Execute (´bottom.html´) -]
```

There's something interesting at the end of this example: [- Execute (´bottom.html´) -]. One might surmise that this will source the file bottom.html located in the same directory, and that is exactly what it does. EmbperlObject files can include other EmbperlObject files. One can have a file for the top of the page, another for the navigation for the page, another for the bottom of the page, and so on.

The file `bottom.html` is located in the same directory:

```
<hr>
We are at the bottom of the page.
<br>
For comments, please email
<a href="mailto:webmaster@opensourcewebbook.com">the
webmaster</a>.

</body>
</html>
```

The contents of `index.html` in the subdirectory `sub2` is simply this:

```
<i>The contents of index.html.</i>
```

To see the result of these three files, load either one of these URLs: `http://localhost/embperlproject/sub2/` or `www.opensourcewebbook.com/embperlproject/sub2/`. You should see Figure 10.11.

Now, one more thing is needed for this example to be really useful: the ability to pass information into the files in question so that things can change dynamically, such as the title. In the base file, we can define

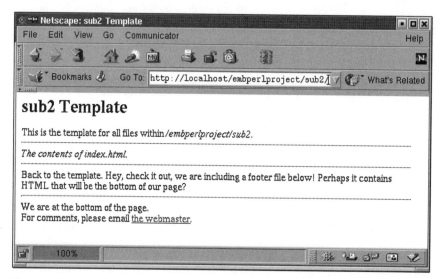

Figure 10.11   Using `base.html` in the same directory, plus a footer

a method; then, in other files, the same function can be redefined. The function names must be the same in all the redefinitions. The base file uses the latest function definition.

To illustrate this, create a third subdirectory, named sub3:

```
$ mkdir /var/www/html/embperlproject/sub3
$ chmod a+rx /var/www/html/embperlproject/sub3
```

Create a very simple base.html including only the barest of HTML—note the value of the title within the <title> tags:

```
[!
    # remember that code in these types
    # of commands is executed only when
    # the file is first requested or after
    # the file is modified

    sub title {
        return 'The Default Title';
    }
!]

[-
    # now, each time the page is requested,
    # get the first argument passed in (it
    # is the request object)
    # we will then be able to call the
    # title() function above using our
    # request object

    $req = shift;
-]

<html>
<head>

[# the code $req->title() below executes the title() #]
[# function defined in the file requested, or this   #]
[# file by default                                   #]

<title>[+$req->title()+]</title>
</head>
<body bgcolor="#ffffff">

[- Execute ('*') -]

</body>
</html>
```

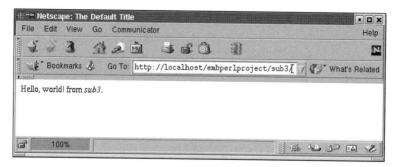

Figure 10.12   Using the default title

The content of `index.html` is simply this:

```
Hello, world! from <i>sub3</i>.
```

This file does not redefine the `title()` function, so it uses the default definition found in `base.html`. Load this page in `http://localhost/embperlproject/sub3/` or `www.opensourcewebbook.com/embperlproject/sub3/`. The file `index.html` uses the default title as shown in Figure 10.12.

Now create a file that redefines the `title()` function. Call it `newtitle.html`, located in `sub3`:

```
[!
    # we redefine title(), so that base.html
    # will use this definition when this page
    # is requested

    sub title {
        return 'The title for newtitle.html';
    }
!]
```

```
This is the content of <i>newtitle.html</i>.
```

Have a look at `http://localhost/embperlproject/sub3/newtitle.html` or `www.opensourcewebbook.com/embperlproject/sub3/newtitle.html`. The new title returned from `title()`, defined in `newtitle.html`, is shown in Figure 10.13.

Now all the pieces needed to do some serious web development are in place. You now can create templates that can be given specific information for the page requested, and the server doesn't have to be restarted every time something changes.

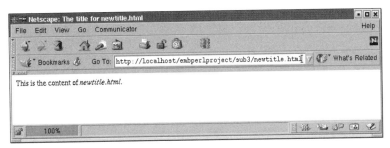

Figure 10.13 Using the title redefined in `newtitle.html`

10.8.3 Product Filter

Now you have the tools to code the product filter. Recall that we created a database of manufacturer and product information. We will now create two Embperl pages: `/embperlproject/productfilter/index.html`, to filter the list of products, and `/embperlproject/productfilter/productdetail/index.html`, to display the details of a specific product.

A `base.html` file would be helpful to define the web site look and feel, so look at the file `/var/www/html/embperlproject/productfilter/base.html`, also found by clicking `http://localhost/embperlproject/productfilter/base.html.txt` or `www.opensourcewebbook.com/embperlproject/productfilter/base.html.txt`.

We don't cover all of this file—it is a bit too big—but you can find its contents at `www.opensourcewebbook.com`.

First, see the `[! ... !]` command:

```
[!
    # the default title
    sub title {
        return 'Product Filter Embperl Style';
    }

    # the default bread crumb string
    sub bread_crumb {
        return 'productfilter';
    }
!]
```

This defines the functions to be used for the default title placed between the `<title> ... </title>` tags and the bread crumb text, which is processed in the following block of code:

```
[-
    # get the request object
    $req = shift;

    # we are building a string with HTML in it, so turn off
    # HTML- and URI-escaping
    $escmode = 0;

    # get the bread crumb string and split it on the colon
    @crumbs = split /:/, $req->bread_crumb();

    # build the bread crumb string - grab each pair of URI/text,
    # build the link
    $bread_crumb_text = '';
    while (@crumbs > 1) {
        $href = shift(@crumbs);
        $text = shift(@crumbs);
        $bread_crumb_text .= "\<a href=\"$href\">\
                             <font color= \"#999966\">\<b>$text\
                             <b>\</font>\</a> ";
    }

    # add the last text in the bread crumb string
    $bread_crumb_text .= $crumbs[0];
-]
```

First, the request object is gotten and assigned to `$req`. Then `$escmode` is set to 0 to turn off HTML- and URI-escaping because we are going to build some HTML to be included in the output. Then the bread crumb string is generated by calling the function `bread_crumb()` defined either in this file (the default) or a file that uses this base (which will override the default).

The elements of the string are then processed. For each URI/text pair, the `href` and text are shifted out of `@crumbs`, and an HTML link is created and concatenated to `$bread_crumb_text`. When all the URI/text pairs are processed, the last text is concatenated onto `$bread_crumb_text`.

Later we see the inclusion of the title defined in the `title()` function:

```
<title>Open Source Web Book - [+$req->title()+]</title>
```

Still later, we see the inclusion of the bread crumb string:

```
- [+$bread_crumb_text+]
```

Then, buried in all the HTML that builds the links on the left rail and other fun things, the statement that includes the HTML file uses this template:

```
[- Execute (´*´) -]
```

Now we come to the page that builds the filter form. It is in the file `/var/www/html/embperlproject/productfilter/index.html` at either `http://localhost/embperlproject/productfilter/index.html.txt` or at `www.opensourcewebbook.com/embperlproject/productfilter/index.html.txt`.

The beginning `[- ... -]` command works pretty hard.

```
use DBI;

# connect to the database
$dbh = DBI->connect(´DBI:mysql:product_database´,
                    ´apache´,´LampIsCool´);
```

A connection is made to the database. Then we see the following code:

```
# grab the posted data
$posted_city        = $fdat{city}         || ´´;
$posted_manufacturer = $fdat{manufacturer} || ´´;
$posted_category    = $fdat{category}     || ´´;

# make sure that the posted data contains the data we want
# (no nasty characters) and the length we expect - if the
# data looks bad, set variable to empty string
unless ($posted_city =~ /^[\w ´\.]+$/) {
    $posted_city = ´´;
}
if (length($posted_city) > 60) {
    $posted_city = ´´;
}
```

This code grabs the posted data and does some sanity checks on its contents (we show only the sanity checking of `$posted_city`; the other variables are similar).

```
# $sql_cond will contain the conditions that we will use for
# the SQL query - if we received any posted data, then we need
# to append to $sql_cond the appropriate SQL text and we will
# add the value of the variable to the array of execute()
# arguments
$sql_cond = ´´;
@execute_args = ();

if ($posted_city or $posted_manufacturer or $posted_category) {
    if ($posted_city) {
        $sql_cond .= ´ AND manufacturers.city = ?´;
        push @execute_args, $posted_city;
```

```
    }
    if ($posted_manufacturer) {
        $sql_cond .= ´ AND manufacturers.name = ?´;
        push @execute_args, $posted_manufacturer;
    }
    if ($posted_category) {
        $sql_cond .= ´ AND products.category = ?´;
        push @execute_args, $posted_category;
    }
}
```

The preceding code builds a string named $sql_cond, the text of which is included in the SQL query, and @execute_args, an array of values that is plugged into the "?" in the query.

```
        <select name="city">

[# for each of the posted variables, generate the select #]
[# box HTML - this will include an SQL query to get the  #]
[# data out of the database                              #]

        <option value="">Select One</option>
        <option value="">-------</option>

[-
    $sth = $dbh->prepare(´SELECT DISTINCT city FROM manufacturers
                        ORDER BY city´);
    $sth->execute();
-]

[$ while (($city) = $sth->fetchrow()) $]
  [$ if ($posted_city eq $city) $]
        <option value="[+ $city +]" selected>[+ $city +]</option>
  [$ else $]
        <option>[+ $city +]</option>
  [$ endif $]
[$ endwhile $]

        </select>
```

The preceding code builds the city selection button (there is similar code to build the button to select the manufacturer and the category). Then the database is queried for all the cities, and for each city, an option is added, marking the posted city selected, if appropriate.

Notice that the Select One option and the ----- option both have the value of empty string (""). This ensures that if the user selects one of these, the value will be empty string, so that category will not be used in the filter.

```
[# now build the table - this query will include any conditions #]
[# that we have based on the posted data from the filter        #]
[# options - we will then loop through the results, building     #]
[# the rows of the table                                        #]
[-
    $sth = $dbh->prepare('SELECT products.prod_id,products.name,
                                products.category,products.price
                        FROM manufacturers, products
                        WHERE manufacturers.man_id = products.man_id '
                        . $sql_cond .
                        ' ORDER BY products.category, products.name');

    $sth->execute(@execute_args);

    $i = 0;
-]
```

The preceding code queries the database for all products that match the filter criteria, including the selected city, manufacturer, and category, that were set in $sql_cond and @execute_args.

```
[$ while (($prod_id,$name,$category,$price) = $sth->fetchrow()) $]
  [-
    if ($i % 2 == 0) {
        $bgcolor = "#ffffff";
    } else {
        $bgcolor = "#cccccc";
    }
    $i++;
  -]
  <tr bgcolor="[+ $bgcolor +]">
    <td>
      <a href="/embperlproject/productfilter/productdetail/
              ?prod_id=[+ $prod_id +]"><font color="#999966">
              <b>[+ $name +]</b></font></a></td>
    <td>[+ $category +]</td>
    <td>$[+ $price +]</td>
  </tr>

[$ endwhile $]
```

In the preceding code, the background color alternates between white and gray on each loop, making the table more readable. A link is created for the product detail page (wrapped for readability), passing the product ID into its %fdat, and then the data is displayed.

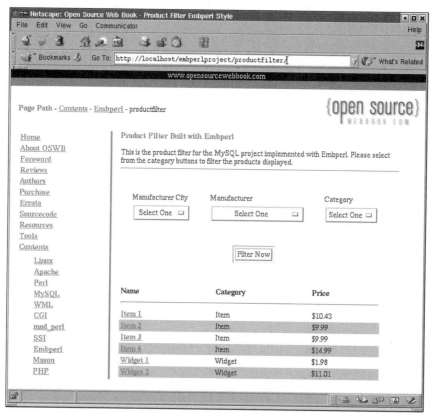

Figure 10.14   Product filter with Embperl

Check page by clicking http://localhost/embperlproject/productfilter/ or www.opensourcewebbook.com/embperlproject/productfilter/. You should see a page that resembles Figure 10.14. Feel free to experiment with the filter.

Next, we come to the page that displays the product detail. When the product link is clicked, the page grabs the query string and prints the information to the user. It starts with:

```
[!
    , # define a title to override the default in base.html
    sub title {
        return 'Product Detail Embperl Style';
    }

    # define a bread crumb string to override the default
    # in base.html
```

```
    sub bread_crumb {
        return '/embperlproject/productfilter/:/productfilter/
          :productdetail';
    }
!]
```

The preceding code defines the functions that overide the default definitions in `base.html` in the parent directory—defining the title and bread crumb string (wrapped for readability).

```
[-
    use DBI;

    # connect to the database
    $dbh = DBI->connect('DBI:mysql:product_database',
                        'apache','LampIsCool');

    # grab the posted data
    $prod_id = $fdat{prod_id} || '';

    # make sure the product id is what we expect and the
    # length is within expected limits
    unless ($prod_id =~ /^[\w]+$/) {
        $prod_id = '';
    }
    if (length($prod_id) > 4) {
        $prod_id = '';
    }
-]
```

The preceding code connects to the database and then grabs the product ID that was sent through the query string and assigned to `%fdat`. Then the data is tested to be sure it contains only word characters (alphas, digits, or underscores), and the length of the product ID is checked—good for security!

```
[$ if ($prod_id) $]

    [# we have a good product id, so query the database and generate #]
    [# the output                                                    #]

    [-
        $sth = $dbh->prepare('SELECT products.name, products.category,
                              products.description,products.price,
                              manufacturers.name,
                              manufacturers.address,
                              manufacturers.city,
                              manufacturers.state,
                              manufacturers.zip,
```

```
                    manufacturers.man_id
              FROM manufacturers, products
              WHERE manufacturers.man_id = products.man_id
                AND products.prod_id = ?
              ORDER BY products.category, products.name´);

    $sth->execute($prod_id);

    ($name,$category,$description,$price,$man_name,
     $address,$city,$state,$zip,$man_id) = $sth->fetchrow();
  -]
```

Next we check to make sure we have a product ID. If so, the database is queried, and we grab most of the data in it for that product ID. Then the result of the query is assigned to several variables, such as $name.

```
  [$ if ($name) $]

    [# $name has a value, so we have a record!  display it #]
<font color="#ff0000"><b>Product: [+ $prod_id +]</b></font><br>
<table border="0" cellspacing="0" cellpadding="0">
<tr><th align="left">Name</th><td>  </td><td>
[+ $name +]</td></tr>
<tr><th align="left">Category</th><td>  </td><td>
[+ $category +]</td></tr>
<tr><th align="left">Description</th><td>  </td><td>
[+ $description +]</td></tr>
<tr><th align="left">Price</th><td>  </td><td>
$[+ $price +]</td></tr>
<tr><th align="left"
valign="top">Manufacturer</th><td>  </td><td>
ID: [+ $man_id +]<br>
[+ $man_name +]<br>
[+ $address +]<br>
[+ $city +], [+ $state +] [+ $zip +]
</td></tr>
</table>

  [$ else $]

    [# oops, the record wasn't in the database, so say so #]
Product ID <b>[+ $prod_id +]</b> not found in the database.

  [$ endif $]
```

The program then checks to see whether it received a name—if so, $name would have a value. If it has a name, the product information is displayed

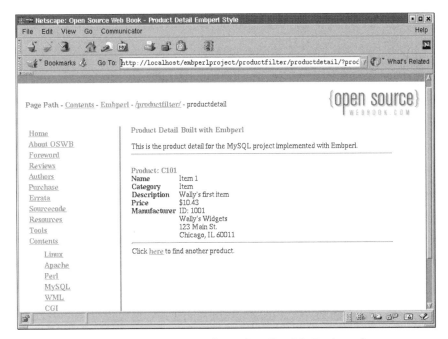

Figure 10.15 Product detail with Embperl

in the browser. If not, it prints a message saying that the product ID was not found. Finally, we have:

```
[$ else $]
```

```
[# oops, the user didn't give us a good product ID, so say so #]
```

```
Please enter a valid product ID.
```

```
[$ endif $]
```

This `else` occurs when there is a bad product ID. The program just prints a nice message (we *did* say please).

When you click one of the product links, you should see a page that resembles Figure 10.15.

10.9 WHAT WE DIDN'T TALK ABOUT

There is much more to Embperl that we didn't discuss. Here are a few topics that you might investigate as you proceed in your Open Source web development career.

10.9.1 Persistent Database Connections

In this project, each time one of the pages is requested, a new database connection is made. This can generate a lot of overhead, especially if the page receives a lot of hits. Embperl can use `Apache::DBI` to maintain persistent connections to the MySQL database. For more information, check out `Apache::DBI` at CPAN.

10.9.2 Session Handling with %udat and %mdat

Embperl allows you to easily track sessions with `%udat`, `%mdat`, and `Apache::Session`. The module `Apache::Session` must be installed for the session handling to work.

The hash `%udat`, if used within an HTML page, creates a session for the user and sends session information to the user via a cookie. This session is then remembered the next time the user visits the site, restoring `%udat` to the value from the last visit.

The hash `%mdat`, if used with an HTML page, stores persistent data for the page/module that was requested. This information is restored into `%mdat` the next time the page is requested, regardless of which user requests it.

For more information, see `perldoc HTML::Embperl`.

10.9.3 Tons of Variables

Many more Embperl variables are available. The following list is just a sample. For a complete list, check out the Embperl web page or `perldoc`.

@ffld An array containing the fields in the form that was posted (usually in the same order as they appear in the form).

$maxrow, $maxcol The maximum number of rows or columns to display in a table. These variables help prevent infinite loops when creating tables while using `$row` and `$col` (the default for `$maxrow` is 100 and for `$maxcol` is 10).

$cnt The number of table cells currently displayed (used with `$row` and `$col`).

$tabmode A value that affects how the end of table creation is determined when using `$row` and `$col`.

$escmode A value that affects HTML- and URL-escaping.

LOG The log file filehandle—print to this filehandle to add to the log file (`/tmp/embperl.log` by default).

OUT Embperl's output stream—anything printed to it ends up being sent out by the server (the same as a `[+ ... +]` block).

%http_headers_out A hash containing keys and values that are sent in the header. A redirect can be accomplished with `[- $http_headers_out{Location} = "http://www.onsight.com/"; -]`.

10.9.4 XML and XSLT Support

Starting with version 2.0b4, Embperl integrates with XML and XSLT. See the Embperl web page or `perldoc` for details.

10.10 SUMMARY

Embperl is a flexible and moderately simple way to implement embedded server-side web pages. It's based on Perl and similar to mod_perl, so it builds on an excellent knowledge base. It is useful but not that much different from things you already know. However, there is more than one way to do it, as we saw with SSI, and there are a couple of other ways to do embedded HTML programming, so read on before you decide what to use in your system.

10.11 RESOURCES

Web Sites

Embperl home page: `perl.apache.org/embperl/`

Embperl German home page: `www.ecos.de/embperl/`

11

Mason (HTML::Mason)

11.1 INTRODUCTION

`HTML::Mason` (aka Mason—see www.masonhq.com/) is a Perl module created by Jonathan Swartz. Its function is similar to Embperl: to include Perl code within an HTML page. The following are some of the features of Mason:

- Simple embedded Perl syntax—An HTML file can harness the power of Perl, including variables (scalar, arrays, hashes, etc.), complex data types, and flow-control constructs.

- Modular pages with components—Create subroutine-like code, known as components, to generate headers, footers, menus, and so on.

- Parameter handling—It provides easy access to `GET/POST` parameters, including assigning default values and triggering error conditions.

- Templates and filters—A template can be created and applied to the entire site or a portion of the site.

- Object-oriented techniques—The power of Perl and its object-oriented features can be used.

- Caching—When the code on a page or component is cached, the next time the page or component is requested, the cached version is executed.

- Previewing—A built-in previewer can be used to review a page, using a number of client and request conditions.

- Staging/production modes—Mason can be configured to use a staging server or staging area for development.

11.1.1 Mason Compared with Embperl

Mason and Embperl are similar: Both embed Perl code directly into HTML pages. This allows the creation of a web page to be divided into two parts: the web designers (graphic artists) can concentrate on creating the page with static (and easy to use) HTML, and the programmers can focus on adding the programming code.

Both Embperl and Mason allow the use of Perl variables, complex data types, and Perl classes and objects (if we want to use Perl's obect-oriented features). Both provide an interface to `Apache::Session` to create user sessions and the ability to create templates to apply to the entire web site or portions of the web site. Both cache the compiled Perl code within the HTML, recompiling only when the file timestamp changes.

Why have both? The answer is TMTOWTDI. One of the benefits of Open Source is that we have choices, so here again we have the choice of Embperl or Mason (or `Apache::ASP`, or eperl, or ...).

We will try to point out some differences between these two approaches, but we think the most important difference lies in this simple idea: It is a matter of style and preference. Because almost every situation encountered in developing a web site is solvable by either Embperl or Mason, the choice comes down to which you prefer. Given that, here are some differences between the two.

Embperl's focus is on easily generating HTML. It is known for its speed and ease of use. Its syntax is straightforward and clean, and there is an easy-to-use `Apache::Session` interface. It is tightly integrated with HTML, allowing the programmer to dynamically create tables and escape HTML and URLs (with `$escmode`), and its form widgets are sticky.

Mason is geared toward a more sitewide approach—it is more than a template tool. Mason's approach aims less toward making it easy to use and more toward a system that is very flexible and allows the programmers to code "my way" at the cost of being a bit more complicated. An example is that the interface to `Apache::Session` is not built in—programmers must add the code to hook into this module; but that enables programmers to do what they want with this module instead of relying on Mason to do it for them. Mason can be a bit more complicated and intimidating to new users, but good online documentation and a helpful user community go a long way toward helping new programmers learn the rich feature set.

An important feature of Mason is that with a special syntax tag (`<%init>`—more on this later), executable code can exist at the bottom of the HTML page, yet be executed first thing. The model here is that in a web design shop, HTML is created by graphic designers; then programmers come in and add code. With Mason, much of that code can simply be added at the bottom of the HTML file, so when the graphic designers update the HTML, they don't have to contend with the Mason code.

11.2 INSTALLATION

Mason is not installed on many distributions, including Red Hat (yet), so we'll go through the the drill of installing it manually. First though, two other modules must be installed: `MLDBM` (Multi-Level DataBase Manager) and `Params::Validate`. `MLDBM` is a Perl module that allows the storage and retrieval of multidimensional data structures. Mason uses `MLDBM` to store its cache files.

To install `MLDBM`, get the latest version (as of the writing of this book, 2.00) from `www.cpan.org/modules/by-module/MLDBM/`. Save `MLDBM-2.00.tar.gz` to `/tmp`. Then, as `root`:

```
# cd /tmp
# tar xzvf MLDBM-2.00.tar.gz
# cd MLDBM-2.00
# perl Makefile.PL
# make
# make test
# make install
```

Next install `Params::Validate`. Mason uses this module to validate function call arguments. Get the latest version available (as of this writing, version 0.07) from `www.cpan.org/modules/by-authors/id/D/DR/DROLSKY/`. Next, download `Params-Validate-0.07.tar.gz`, and save it to `/tmp`. Then, as `root`:

```
# cd /tmp
# tar xzvf Params-Validate-0.07.tar.gz
# cd Params-Validate-0.07
# perl Makefile.PL
# make
# make test
# make install
```

Now your system is prepped for `HTML::Mason`. The latest version (as of this writing, version 1.04) can be found at `www.cpan.org/modules/`

by-module/HTML/. Get `HTML-Mason-1.04.tar.gz`, and save it to /tmp. Then, as root:

```
# cd /tmp
# tar xzvf HTML-Mason-1.04.tar.gz
# cd HTML-Mason-1.04
# perl Makefile.PL
Checking for MLDBM...ok
Checking for Data::Dumper...ok
Checking for Params::Validate...ok
--------------------
Creating Mason configuration file.
Checking for existing configuration...not found.
```

More stuff is printed, and then we are prompted for information:

```
For testing purposes, please give the full path to an httpd
with mod perl enabled. The path defaults to $ENVAPACHE, if present.
 [/usr/sbin/httpd] ('!' to skip): <ret>
Search existing config file for dynamic module dependencies? [y]: <ret>
  Config file [/etc/httpd/conf/httpd.conf]: <ret>
...
User to run tests under [nobody]: apache
Group to run tests under [nobody]: apache
Port to run tests under [8228]: <ret>

# make
# make test
# make install
```

If you've gotten something like this and had no errors installing the previous Perl modules, everything is installed and you're good to go.

11.3 APACHE CONFIGURATION

Apache must be configured to handle Mason much as with Embperl. We will choose a directory and for all .html files under that directory, have Mason process them (for the same reasons, too).

First, create a directory for the Mason work:

```
$ mkdir /var/www/html/mason
$ chmod a+rx /var/www/html/mason
```

As root, add the following to /etc/httpd/conf/httpd.conf:

```
PerlSetVar MasonCompRoot /var/www/html/mason
PerlSetVar MasonDataDir /var/www/misc/mason
```

```
PerlModule HTML::Mason::ApacheHandler
<Directory /var/www/html/mason>
    SetHandler perl-script
    PerlHandler HTML::Mason::ApacheHandler
</Directory>
```

The first line sets the Mason component root directory to /var/www/html/mason. This tells Mason where to find the components (more on these later). The data directory is set to /var/www/misc/mason. The Mason data directory should not be under the HTML root directory (/var/www/html), because we want to hide the Mason data files from the Web surfer visiting our site. The data directory contains data files that Mason uses, so we have picked an innocuous place for Mason to put them. You do not have to create this directory; it and all of its subdirectories are magically created for you.

Apache directives should be defined for the directory /var/www/html/mason. They tell Apache to set the handler to perl-script and to use the HTML::Mason::ApacheHandler module for all files in the /var/www/html/mason directory.

Load the altered Apache configuration file:

 # /etc/init.d/httpd graceful

11.4 A QUICK EXAMPLE

Let's show an example. We create the file /var/www/html/mason/test.html and place the following contents within it:[1]

```
% my $name = 'John Doe';

<html>
<head>
<title>Mason Example</title>
</head>
<body bgcolor="#ffffff">

Hello, <% $name %>!
<br>2 + 3 = <% 2 + 3 %>

</body>
</html>
```

---

[1]Set the permissions to 644, but you already knew that, right?

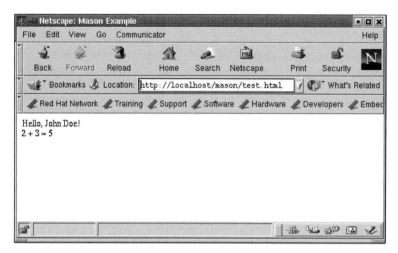

Figure 11.1 Mason example

You will notice right away that our first Mason example is *not* "hello, world!". We apologize for the inconsistency.

At the top of this file is `% my $name = ´John Doe´;`. The character "%" indicates that this line is Perl code to be executed.[2] The variable `$name` is defined using the `my()` function. Global variables in Mason must be `my()` variables—if they are not declared with `my()`, a syntax error is generated.

The Perl code within `<% ... %>` is executed, and what that code evaluates to is replaced in the HTML file (much like Embperl's `[+ ... +]`). Therefore, `<% $name% >` is replaced with the value `John Doe`, and `<% 2 + 3 %>` is replaced with the result 5.

Try this page by loading either of the following URLs: `http://localhost/mason/test.html` or `www.opensourcewebbook.com/mason/test.html`. This should display a page similar to Figure 11.1.

11.5 INLINE PERL SECTIONS

There are several different ways to embed Perl code into the Mason pages: `<% ... %>` sections, "%" lines, and `<%perl> ... </%perl>` blocks. The next sections explore these.

---

[2]For lines that begin with "%," that "%" must be the first character in the line.

11.5.1 The <% ... %> Tag

These tags are useful for generating the values of variables and complex expressions. This example code generates HTML using these tags:

```
Name: <% $name %>
Age:  <% $age %>
Address: <% %address %>
Price : <% $price * (1 + $tax) %>
```

The HTML generated is the result of the evaluation of the variables within the tags, including the evaluation of the final arithmetic expression.

11.5.2 % Lines

This type of Perl code is most useful for creating global variables and for embedding conditional and looping constructs.

Put this example in /var/www/html/mason/percent.html:

```
% my $client = $ENV{REMOTE_ADDR};

<html>
<head>
<title>Percent Lines with Mason</title>
</head>
<body bgcolor="#ffffff">

Hello <% $client %>!

<hr>

% if ($client =~ /127\.0\.0\.1/) {
We are called from localhost.
% } else {
We are called from elsewhere.
% }

<hr>

% my $i = 0;
% while ($i < 10) {
<tt>$i == <% $i %></tt>
<br>
%    $i++;
% }

</body>
</html>
```

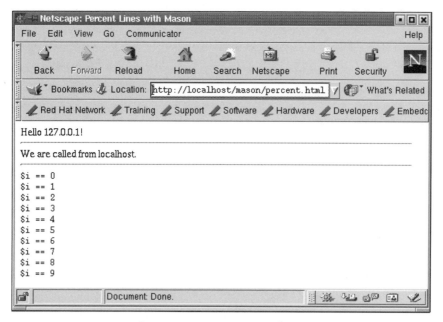

Figure 11.2   Mason % lines

The file begins by setting $client to the client IP address stored in %ENV (notice that Mason has access to the Apache environment variables stored in %ENV). Within the body of the HTML is the code <% $client %>, which is replaced with the client IP address—if this program is accessed by a client that is the localhost, this address will be 127.0.0.1.

An if statement checks the client IP address. If it is 127.0.0.1, the localhost, the program says so. Otherwise, it prints a statement saying the program was called from elsewhere.

The code then loops from 0 to 9, including the values of the integers (such as $i = 0) in the HTML. Again, $i must be declared as a my() variable. To view this file, load either of these URLs: http://localhost/mason/percent.html or www.opensourcewebbook.com/mason/percent.html. You should see something that resembles Figure 11.2.

More on Perl Constructs

All of Perl's constructs can be embedded in a Mason HTML file. Next we demonstrate the syntax for each construct and then show a complete example illustrating each construct.

The if Statement This is the syntax for the if:

```
% if (condition) {
% } elsif {
% } elsif {
% } else {
% }
```

As usual, the elsif and the else are optional.

The unless Statement This is the syntax for the unless:

```
% unless (condition) {
% } else {
% }
```

The else is optional.

Put the following code in /var/www/html/mason/cond.html as an example of these two conditional constructs:

```
<html>
<head>
<title>Mason Conditional Constructs</title>
</head>
<body bgcolor="#ffffff">

<h3><tt>if</tt> Statement</h3>

% if ($ENV{HTTP_USER_AGENT} =~ /mozilla/i) {
Hello Mozilla browser!
% } else {
You are not the Mozilla browser.
% }

<h3><tt>unless</tt> Statement</h3>

Today is <% scalar(localtime()) %>
% unless (localtime() =~ /^(Sat|Sun)/) {
and it is NOT a weekend.
% } else {
and it is a weekend!
% }
</table>
</body>
</html>
```

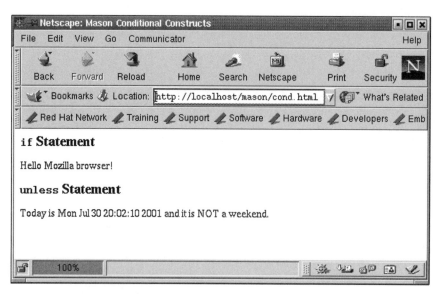

Figure 11.3   Mason conditional statements

To view the result of this block of code, load one of these URLs: `http://localhost/mason/cond.html` or `www.opensourcewebbook.com/mason/cond.html`. This should produce a page that resembles what is shown in Figure 11.3.

The while Loop   The syntax for the `while` loop is:

```
% while (condition) {

% }
```

The for Loop   This is the syntax for the `for` loop:

```
% for (init_expression; condition; step_expression) {

% }
```

The foreach Loop   The syntax for the `foreach` loop is:

```
% foreach my variable (list) {

% }
```

We'll show examples of each these looping constructs. Put the following code into the file /var/www/html/mason/loop.html:

```
<html>
<head>
<title>Mason Looping Constructs</title>
</head>
<body bgcolor="#ffffff">

<h3><tt>while</tt> Loop</h3>

<table border="1">
  <tr><th>number</th><th>squared</td></tr>

% my $i = 1;
% while ($i <= 5) {
    <tr><td><% $i %></td><td><% $i ** 2 %></td></tr>
%   $i++;
% }

</table>

<h3><tt>for</tt> Loop</h3>

% for (my $j = 10; $j > 5; $j--) {
    $j = <% $j %><br>
% }

<h3><tt>foreach</tt> Loop</h3>

<table border="1">
  <tr><th>Variable</th><th>Value</th></tr>

% foreach my $var (sort keys %ENV) {
  <tr><td><% $var %></td><td><% $ENV{$var} %></td></tr>
% }

</table>
</body>
</html>
```

To view the result, load either of these URLs: http://localhost/mason/loop.html or www.opensourcewebbook.com/mason/loop.html. This produces a page similar to Figure 11.4.

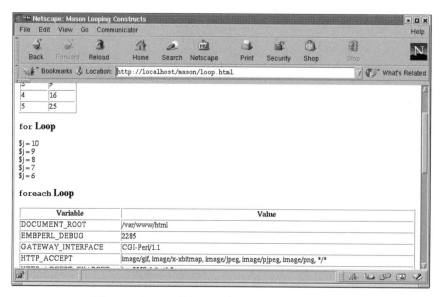

Figure 11.4   Mason looping statements

11.5.3 The <%perl> ... </%perl> Tag

The <%perl> ... </%perl> tags can be used to execute arbitrary amounts of Perl code. These tags can occur anywhere within the HTML file and can contain comments, functions, and variable assignments—essentially anything Perl.

This example is in /var/www/html/mason/perl.html:

```
<html>
<head>
<title>Mason &lt;%perl&gt; Block</title>
</head>
<body bgcolor="#ffffff">

<%perl>
  # we can put arbitrary amounts of Perl
  # code within these tags

  # these tags can be embedded anywhere within the HTML

  # remember that all variables must be my() variables

  my $client = $ENV{REMOTE_ADDR};
  my $agent  = $ENV{HTTP_USER_AGENT};
  my $method = $ENV{REQUEST_METHOD};
  my $time   = localtime();
```

```
   # we can also include function definitions - this function
   # is called in the HTML below

   sub hello_world {
       return "hello, world!"
   }
</%perl>

Hello <b><% $client %></b>. <br>
You are using <b><% $agent %></b>. <br>
The local time is <b><% $time %></b>. <br>
Your request method is <b><% $method %></b>. <br>
A message: <b><% hello_world() %></b>.
</table>
</body>
</html>
```

To see the result of this code, load one of the following URLs into your browser: `http://localhost/mason/perl.html` or `www.opensourcewebbook.com/mason/perl.html`. This page generates an output that resembles Figure 11.5.

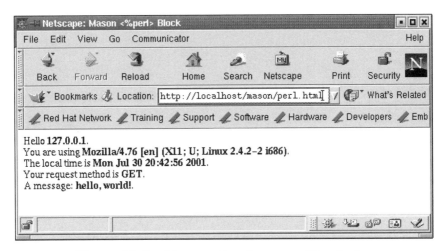

Figure 11.5 Mason <%perl> ... </%perl> tag

11.6 HANDLING POSTED DATA WITH %ARGS AND <%args>

Mason handles posted form data similarly to Embperl. All form data widget names and their values are stored in the hash %ARGS. Let's say a form is posted to a Mason page with the form widget named city. To obtain the value of the form widget, include this code in a Mason page:

```
<%perl>
    my $city;
    if (!exists $ARGS{´city´}) {
        die "no value sent for required parameter ´city´";
    } else {
        $city = $ARGS{´city´});
    }
</%perl>
```

Using this code, the my() variable $city contains the value posted in the form for the widget named city.

In practice, %ARGS is generally not used. Instead, Mason programmers use <%args> ... </%args>.

11.6.1 The <%args> ... </%args> Tag

The following tag, included anywhere in the Mason page, is used to grab posted data:

```
<%args>
$city
</%args>
```

This tag checks for the existence of the posted city parameter and calls the die() function if it doesn't exist, otherwise assigning the value to $city. Thus, using the <%args> ... </%args> block is a convenient shorthand for declaring variables and assigning them the value of posted form data.

The next example shows the passing of form data using this tag. Put this form in the file /var/www/html/mason/form.html. This is just pure HTML, no Mason code. However because this file is under the /mason/ directory, it is processed by Mason even though there is no Mason code within it.

```
<html>
<head>
<title>Mason Form Example</title>
</head>
<body bgcolor="#ffffff">
<h3>Mason Form Example</h3>
<form action="/mason/handleform.html">
Name:    <input type="text" name="name"> <br>
Address: <input type="text" name="address"> <br>
```

```
City:      <input type="text" name="city"> <br>
State:     <input type="text" name="state" size="2"> <br>
Zip:       <input type="text" name="zip" size="10"> <br>
<input type="submit"> <input type="reset">
</form>
</body>
</html>
```

Load this form in the browser by going to either one of these URLs: `http://localhost/mason/form.html` or `www.opensourcewebbook.com/mason/form.html`. An example of this page with example data entered can be seen in Figure 11.6.

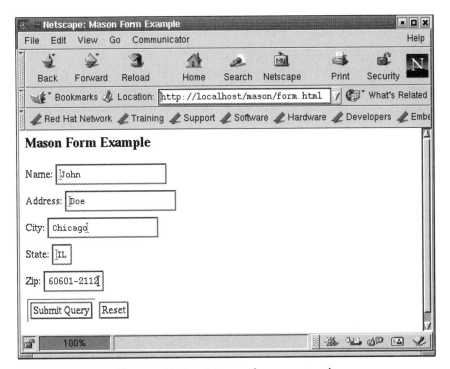

Figure 11.6 Mason form example

When the form is submitted, it invokes the action specified in the form: `/mason/handleform.html`. This corresponds to the file `/var/www/html/mason/handleform.html`, which has the following contents:

```
<html>
<head>
<title>Mason Form Handling Example</title>
</head>
<body bgcolor="#ffffff">

<h3>Mason Form Handling Example</h3>

You entered the following in the form:

<br><br>
Name: <b><% $name %></b> <br>
Address: <b><% $address %></b> <br>
City: <b><% $city %></b> <br>
State: <b><% $state %></b> <br>
Zip: <b><% $zip %></b> <br>
</body>
</html>

<%args>
    # within this block we "declare" all our variables
    # that will contain the posted data - the name of
    # the variable is the name of the widget in the form -
    # for instance the city widget is named "city", so
    # the corresponding variable is $city

    # the location of this block is arbitrary - it can
    # be at the top of the page or at the bottom or
    # anywhere in between - by convention it is at the
    # bottom

    $name
    $address
    $city
    $state
    $zip
</%args>
```

The important addition to this HTML page is the <%args> tag. This tag can occur anywhere within the HTML file. Here it is placed at the bottom of the page, but it could be at the top or anywhere else. By convention, most Mason programmers place this tag at the bottom of the HTML page, because this puts the programming stuff, which is less likely to be altered, at the bottom of the page and leaves the graphic design stuff (which, experience has proved, is more likely to be tinkered with) at the top.

Within this tag are listed several variables, all of which are assigned their respective form data values. For example, $address is assigned the

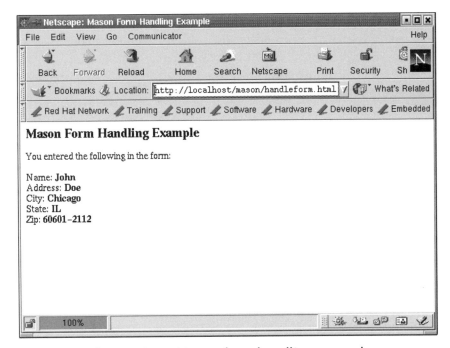

Figure 11.7 Mason form handling example

value from the form for the widget named address. We then include the variable's value in the HTML with <% $address %>.

If you enter the information as shown in Figure 11.6 and click Submit Query, you should see a result much like Figure 11.7.

In the next section, you will see that the <%args> ... </%args> block is also used with Mason components. If a variable listed in the <%args> tag has not been posted to the Mason program, the program will die(). For instance, in the form.html example, there was no widget named phone, so if we include that in the <%args> tag:

```
<%args>
$city
$phone
</%args>
```

Mason will complain with a runtime error indicating that $phone is not set. Feel free to try this: Change handleform.html by adding $phone to the <%args> tag and resubmit the form data—the related Mason error should show up.

Not so good, eh? Having an error occur by default is bad behavior. This error can be prevented by providing defaults for elements that may not be supplied by the browser. Providing defaults may not be necessary in all instances, but it's usually good practice to think about the consequences of incorrectly posted data. Here's an example:

```
<%args>
$city
$phone => ´847-555-1234´
</%args>
```

The default is indicated by the => ´847-555-1234´ syntax. If the parameter named phone is posted to the program, that value is used; otherwise, the default 847-555-1234 is used. So any or all of the variables declared can be made defaults within the <%args> tag:

```
<%args>
$name
$address
$city  => ´Chicago´
$state => ´IL´
$zip   => ´60601-0001´
$phone => ´847-555-1234´
</%args>
```

This example provides defaults for the last four variables. The default values are overridden when the values for those parameter names are posted.

Now we have the basics of Mason—embedding Perl code into our pages and retrieving the posted form data—and we can move on to one of the more powerful features of Mason: components.

11.7 MASON COMPONENTS

Mason allows construction of complex web sites through the notion of components. A Mason component is a file with any combination of HTML, Perl, and Mason code.

For a simple example, we will create a header file and footer file that will be applied across the web site.

First, we'll create some header HTML and put it in the file /var/www/ html/mason/_header. The following HTML is the beginning HTML for the example:

```
<html>
<head>
<title>Mason Component Example</title>
</head>
<body bgcolor="#ffffff">
<i>This text is in the header.</i>
<hr>
```

Don't panic[3]—this is just basic HTML. No new stuff here. This illustrates that a Mason component need not contain any Mason at all—plain HTML is fine. This HTML is then included when the component is used.

And now for the footer (/var/www/html/mason/_footer):

```
% my $url   = 'http://www.opensourcewebbook.com/';
% my $email = 'webmaster@opensourcewebbook.com';

<hr>
Website: <a href="<% $url %>"><% $url %></a>
<br>
Comments: <a href="mailto:<% $email %>"><% $email %></a>
</body>
</html>
```

This file does indeed contain Mason code. The variables $url and $email are defined. The component then generates a bit of HTML, using both variables.

The name of each of these two component files starts with the underscore character. We'll explain why in a bit.

To use these header and footer components, create the file /var/www/html/mason/components.html:

```
<& _header &>

<i>this text is in components.html:</i> <b>hello, world!</b>

<& _footer &>
```

The new tag in this example is <& ... &>, which reads in the component within. For instance, <& _header &> reads in the _header component, and <& _footer &> reads in the _footer component. If one loads components.html, it reads in the header and footer to create this HTML (lines wrapped for readability):

---

[3]Excellent all-purpose advice from the late Douglas Adams, RIP.

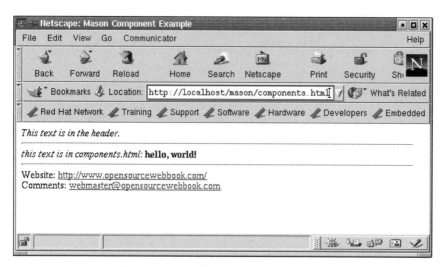

Figure 11.8 Mason components

```
<html>
<head>
<title>Mason Component Example</title>
</head>
<body bgcolor="#ffffff">
<i>This text is in the header.</i>
<hr>
<i>this text is in components.html:</i> <b>hello, world!</b>

<hr>
Website: <a href="http://www.opensourcewebbook.com/">
                http://www.opensourcewebbook.com/</a>
<br>
Comments: <a href="mailto:webmaster@opensourcewebbook.com">
                webmaster@opensourcewebbook.com</a>
</body>
</html>
```

To view the result, load either of these URLs into the browser: `http://localhost/mason/components.html` or `www.opensourcewebbook.com/mason/components.html`. This produces Figure 11.8.

11.7.1 Components and <%args>

Variables and their values can be passed into components and then accessed using `<%args>` much as if they were posted data. As an example, create the file /var/www/html/mason/components2.html. It will be a duplicate of the preceding example, with two differences:

```
<& _header2, title => 'The Second Component Example' &>

<i>this text is in components2.html:</i> <b>hello, world!</b>

<& _footer2, url   => 'http://www.opensourcewebbook.com',
             email => 'webmaster@opensourcewebbook.com' &>
```

The change you probably noticed right away occurs within the <& ... &> tags. In this example, the component included is _header2 (as opposed to _header), and a name/value pair is passed into the component:

```
title => 'The Second Component Example'
```

This name/value pair is passed into the component just as posted data would be passed in. In this example, the key title and its value The Second Component Example are passed in. This value can be accessed using the <%args> tag just as if it were posted data. Look at the new _header2 component (found in the file /var/www/html/mason/_header2):

```
<html>
<head>
<title><% $title %></title>
</head>
<body bgcolor="#ffffff">
<i>This text is in the header.</i>
<hr>

<%args>
$title => 'Mason Component Example'
</%args>
```

Notice the addition of the <%args> ... </%args> tag. This assigns $title the value "posted" (or in the example, the value passed in when we ask for the component), defaulting to the string Mason Component Example. The variable $title is then used within the <title> ... </title> tag.

Because a default has been provided to the variable $title, we can ask for this component without providing a title:

```
<& _header2 &>
```

In this case, the default string Mason Component Example is used for the title.

Another difference in `components2.html` is in the included `_footer2` component:

```
<& _footer2, url   => ´http://www.opensourcewebbook.com´,
             email => ´webmaster@opensourcewebbook.com´ &>
```

This requests the component `_footer2`, passing data to the component. The values of the arguments are contained within the `<%args>` tag in the `_footer2` component. This component is contained in the file `/var/www/html/mason/_footer2`:

```
<hr>
Website: <a href="<% $url %>"><% $url %></a>
<br>
Comments: <a href="mailto:<% $email %>"><% $email %></a>
</body>
</html>

<%args>
$url   => ´http://www.onsight.com/´
$email => ´webmaster@onsight.com´
</%args>
```

At the bottom of this file, `$url` is assigned the value passed into the component, or it defaults to `http://www.onsight.com/`. The variable `$email` is handled similarly. When the `components2.html` page is requested, it generates this HTML (links are wrapped for readability):

```
<html>
<head>
<title>The Second Component Example</title>
</head>
<body bgcolor="#ffffff">
<i>This text is in the header.</i>
<hr>
<i>this text is in components2.html:</i> <b>hello, world!</b>

<hr>
Website: <a href="http://www.opensourcewebbook.com">
              http://www.opensourcewebbook.com</a>
<br>
Comments: <a href="mailto:webmaster@opensourcewebbook.com">
              webmaster@opensourcewebbook.com</a>
</body>
</html>
```

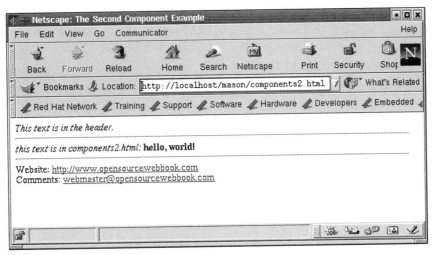

Figure 11.9 Mason components, take

To view the result, load one of these URLs: `http://localhost/mason/components2.html` or `www.opensourcewebbook.com/mason/components2.html`. The result should be similar to Figure 11.9.

11.7.2 The <%init> ... </%init> Section

Recall the _footer example:

```
% my $url   = 'http://www.opensourcewebbook.com/';
% my $email = 'webmaster@opensourcewebbook.com';

<hr>
Website: <a href="<% $url %>"><% $url %></a>
<br>
Comments: <a href="mailto:<% $email %>"><% $email %></a>
</body>
</html>
```

At the top of this file is some executable Perl code: the declaration of the variables `$url` and `$email`. Having Perl code at the top of the file is fine, but remember, in Mason the convention is to put the code at the bottom of the file instead of the top. How can we include code that must be executed *before* the HTML is processed, yet have it be physically *after* said HTML? The answer is the <%init> block.[4]

The <%init> ... </%init> block is a block of Perl code that is executed first,[5] before anything else in the file is processed. So if you want to have a block of Perl code that has to be executed first but have it at the bottom of the file, this block can be used. The _footer file can be rewritten as:

```
<hr>
Website: <a href="<% $url %>"><% $url %></a>
<br>
Comments: <a href="mailto:<% $email %>"><% $email %></a>
</body>
</html>

<%init>
my $url   = ´http://www.opensourcewebbook.com/´;
my $email = ´webmaster@opensourcewebbook.com´;
</%init>
```

11.7.3 The <%once> ... </%once> Section

The <%once> ... </%once> tag defines a block of code that is executed only once, when the component is first loaded. Variables and functions that are declared/defined in this block can be seen in all the component's code and persist for the entire life of the component in the httpd process. This block is useful for declaring persistent component-scoped lexical variables and for defining functions. For example:

```
<%once>
my $var = ´this is a test´;

sub important {
    ...
}
</%once>
```

11.7.4 A Note about Mason Security

This method of including components is fine, as far as it goes, but it has one major flaw: Apache serves up the components as simple text files. To

---

[4]The things we do for stylistic consistency!

[5]Well, after the <%args> block, anyway.

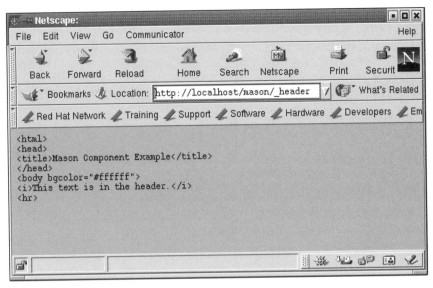

Figure 11.10 Serving up Mason components

prove this, try loading the URL `http://localhost/mason/_header`. You'll see Figure 11.10. D'oh! Our Mason component source code is being served up on a platter, thereby making our Mason component source code available. A cracker may be able to learn something about how our site works and perhaps leverage that knowledge in an attack.

There are several ways of securing the Mason components (see `www.masonhq.com/docs/manual/Admin.html#securing_top_level_components`). One method, the one we'll use, is to deny access to files in the Mason directory that start with the underscore character (`_foo.bar`). Now the reason Mason files are named with a leading underscore becomes clear. Here we used the underscore character, but one could as well choose to prefix the files with "." The advantage of the underscore is that files still show up with the standard `ls` command—`ls -a` is not necessary to see the Mason files in the directory.

To implement this security measure, modify the Apache configuration for Mason:

```
PerlSetVar MasonCompRoot /var/www/html/mason
PerlSetVar MasonDataDir /var/www/misc/mason
PerlModule HTML::Mason::ApacheHandler
<Directory /var/www/html/mason>
```

```
    SetHandler perl-script
    PerlHandler HTML::Mason::ApacheHandler
    <Files ~ "^_">
        SetHandler perl-script
        PerlInitHandler Apache::Constants::NOT_FOUND
    </Files>
</Directory>
```

Here the <Files> directive is added. This directive instructs Apache to handle all files that begin with an underscore and to send the response that that file is not found.

Alternatively, access to the file could have simply been denied by modifying the preceding Apache configuration as follows:

```
<Files ~ "^_">
    Order allow,deny
    Deny from all
</Files>
```

This directive tells Apache to deny access, which is printed on the browser as "Forbidden". This is fine because it doesn't serve up the file, but it tells the user that the file is there and they cannot access it. But why tell a would-be cracker that the component actually exists at all?[6] Instead, trick them into thinking that the component is not found, and give no information about the component's state of existence.

So, we will stick with this:

```
<Files ~ "^_">
    SetHandler perl-script
    PerlInitHandler Apache::Constants::NOT_FOUND
</Files>
```

After changing the configuration file, restart Apache:

 # /etc/init.d/httpd graceful

Now, loading the URL http://localhost/mason/_header produces Figure 11.11.

---

[6]This sort of "reject rather than deny" approach is good practice in many applications of security. If a cracker is trying to probe your system, make them wait for a time-out or a file-not-found message rather than send them a message that they've hit the right thing but simply don't have the right access—too much information.

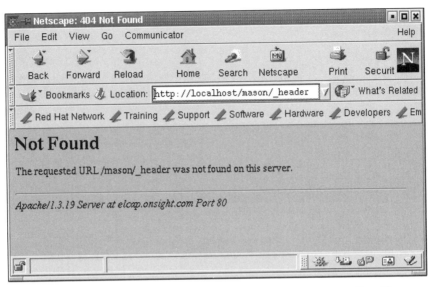

Figure 11.11 Serving up Mason components—fixed!

11.8 MASON PROJECT

In the Embperl chapter, we did a project that displayed a list of products and filtered that list based on the manufacturer's city, name, or product type. We will now develop a Mason back end that enables the addition and modification of manufacturers and their products.

This back end will consist of three pages: one to allow the user to select an action (add a manufacturer, modify a manufacturer, add a product, or modify a product), one to allow the user to enter the data for either a manufacturer or a product, and one that thanks the user for the addition or modification and allows them to select another action.

Before we show each of the three pages, we need to discuss the components involved in creating our now familiar look and feel.

The first component generates the top HTML for our pages and is named, believe it or not, _top. Its contents can be found in the file /var/www/html/mason/productbackend/_top online at either http://localhost/mason/productbackend/top or www.opensourcewebbook.com/mason/productbackend/top. The filename in those URLs is top, not _top. We copied _top into top so that the webserver would serve it up, allowing you to view its contents as examples. Remember, Apache is configured to not serve up files in this part of the document tree whose names begin with the underscore.

Looking first at the bottom of the file (where all the Mason goodies are), you will see:

```
<%args>
    $title      => ''
    $breadcrumb => ''
</%args>
```

These are the title in the title bar and the bread crumb trail. These components, when called from elsewhere, might have these two variables defined. So these should be declared in the `<%args>` tags, with simple defaults, as in the preceding code. You should then see this:

```
<%init>
    # get the bread crumb string and split it on the colon
    my @crumbs = split /:/, $breadcrumb;

    # build the bread crumb string - grab each pair of URI/text,
    # build the link
    my $bread_crumb_text = '';
    while (@crumbs > 1) {
        my $href = shift(@crumbs);
        my $text = shift(@crumbs);
        $bread_crumb_text .= "<a href=\"$href\"><font color=\"#999966\">
                       <b>$text</b></font></a> - ";
    }

    # add the last text in the bread crumb string
    $bread_crumb_text .= $crumbs[0];
</%init>
```

Recall that the `<%init>` block is executed first (after `<%args>`, that is). This block of code generates bread crumb links much as in the Embperl chapter (see Chapter 10). The bread crumb string is split on the colon, and each pair of href/text is looped through, appending onto $bread_crumb_ string the proper HTML for the link. This component builds all the HTML up to and including the bread crumb path and the logo.

We also will create a component for the left rail called, surprisingly, _leftrail. Its contents can be found in the file /var/www/html/mason/ productbackend/_leftrail at either http://localhost/mason/productbackend/ leftrail or www.opensourcewebbook.com/mason/productbackend/leftrail. Close examination of this component shows that it is simply HTML, which is fine for components, but not exciting enough to describe in detail.

We now need a component for the bottom, called, cleverly enough, _bottom. Its contents can be found in /var/www/html/mason/productbackend/ _bottom at either http://localhost/mason/productbackend/bottom or www. opensourcewebbook.com/mason/productbackend/bottom. It is so simple that we can show it here without taking up too much space:

```
</td>
<td width="15"> </td>
</tr>
</table>
</body>
</html>
```

Again, it's only HTML.

The code to use these three components to create a bare page with no content in the main section would look like the contents of file /var/www/ html/mason/productbackend/bare.html:

```
<& _top, title => ´Bare Example´,
      breadcrumb => ´/contents/:Contents:/contents/mason/:Mason:Bare´ &>
<& _leftrail &>

<& _bottom &>
```

This demonstrates that a file can contain only Mason commands— no HTML and no Perl! Here we use the _top component, assigning the $title within it to the text Bare Example and the bread crumb variable $breadcrumb to a string of two href/text pairs and the text Bare.

Try it out at http://localhost/mason/productbackend/bare.html or www. opensourcewebbook.com/mason/productbackend/bare.html. You should see something resembling Figure 11.12. Now this page has the look and feel but no content.[7]

One more component is needed to build the first page—this one will allow the selection of an action to take. This component will generate the form that presents the user with several options to add or modify a manufacturer and add or modify a product. We will create a component for this form because it will be reused later. It is called _select_form and

---

[7]That's common enough on the Internet, but we hope the other pages on our web site don't fall into this category.

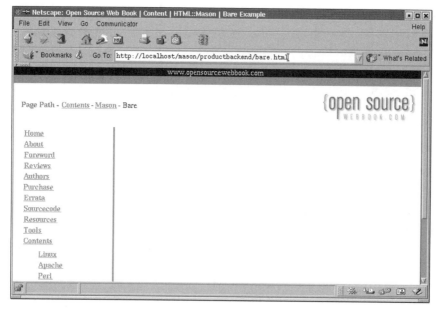

Figure 11.12 A bare page using project components

can be found in the file /var/www/html/mason/productbackend/_select_form at www.opensourcewebbook.com/mason/productbackend/select_form or http://localhost/mason/productbackend/select_form.

As before, look at the bottom first and find:

```
<%init>
use DBI;

my $dbh = DBI->connect('DBI:mysql:product_database',
                       'apache','LampIsCool');

my $manid;
my $prodid;
my $cursor;
</%init>
```

Again, this block is executed first. It uses the DBI module and then connects to the product database. Then three variables are declared with my(), to be used within the previous Perl and HTML code.

The top part of this file contains the HTML that builds the form. The form allows the user to choose one of four actions—four radio buttons and two select buttons are created. Let's look at the code that creates the first one:

```
<select name="manid">
% $cursor = $dbh->prepare('SELECT man_id
%                         FROM manufacturers
%                         ORDER BY man_id');
% $cursor->execute();
% while (($manid) = $cursor->fetchrow()) {
        <option value="<% $manid %>"><% $manid %></option>
% }
</select>
```

The first character in the line, "%", means that this is a line of Perl code to execute.[8] The first line creates an SQL query to grab all the manufacturer IDs from the manufacturers table. Notice that the query is broken into three lines for clarity. That's fine, as long as each line begins with the percent character. The query is then executed, and the result is looped through; and for each ID, an option is created in the select button. The result is a select widget with all the manufacturer IDs in the database.

Similar code is used to generate a button of all the product IDs.

To use this component, simply add `<& _select_form &>`, and there it is. We do exactly that in `index.html`. Its contents can be found in the `/var/www/html/mason/productbackend/index.html` file at http://localhost/mason/productbackend/index.html.txt or www.opensourcewebbook.com/mason/productbackend/index.html.txt. And it's short enough to show here:

```
<& _top, title => 'Project',
        breadcrumb => '/contents/:Contents:/contents/mason/
                        :Mason:Product Backend' &>
<& _leftrail &>

<p><font color="#FF0000"><b>Product Backend</b></font><br></p>

<& _select_form &>

<& _bottom &>
```

The `_top` component, with a title and bread crumb string, is called; then `_leftrail` is called to build the left rail. Next there is some HTML, followed by a call to the `_select_form` component, and finally the `_bottom` component.

---

[8]Don't forget—it must be the first character!

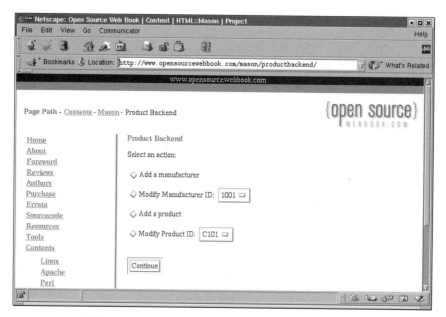

Figure 11.13　Mason project select page

Loading this page generates something resembling Figure 11.13. If you look carefully at the form built by `_select_form`, you can see that the action is `/mason/productbackend/continue/`. This means that regardless of the selection made, the data will always post to the same page, `index.html` under the `continue` directory.

There is another option: Each of the four choices could go to its own page. This is often a good idea, especially if the options are sufficiently dissimilar. In this example, it makes sense for the options to post to the same page.

In any case, the page that the data is posted to will have to look at the action chosen and execute the necessary code to build the proper form.

Look at `continue/index.html`. Its contents can be found in the file `/var/www/html/mason/productbackend/continue/index.html`, or online at `http://localhost/mason/productbackend/continue/index.html.txt` or `www.opensourcewebbook.com/mason/productbackend/continue/index.html.txt`. Its contents are as follows (`breadcrumb` is wrapped for readability):

```
<& ../_top, title => ´Project | Continue´,
          breadcrumb => ´/contents/:Contents:/contents/mason/
                        :Mason:/mason/productbackend/:Product Backend
                        :Continue´ &>

<& ../_leftrail &>

<p><font color="#FF0000"><b>Product Backend - Continue</b></font><br></p>

% if ($action eq ´addman´ or $action eq ´modman´) {
<& _man_form, action => $action,
              manid  => $manid &>
% } elsif ($action eq ´addprod´ or $action eq ´modprod´) {
<& _prod_form, action => $action,
               prodid => $prodid &>
% } else {
Please go back and choose an action.
% }

<& ../_bottom &>

<%args>
$action => ´´
$manid  => ´´
$prodid => ´´
</%args>
```

The components _top, _leftrail and _bottom are used as before. Mason needs to be told where to find the components by using the relative path, such as ../_top. At the bottom, the <%args> block shows the posted variables, any combination of $action, $manid, or $action.

This code hinges on the if statement—here the value of $action is checked to find out what the user wants to do. If it involves either adding or modifying a manufacturer, the component named _man_form builds the form for the manufacturer, given the values of $action and $manid that are passed into this component. If it involves either adding or modifying a product, the necessary variables are passed to the component _prod_form.

Note that if there is an unexpected action, the program generates a nice message asking the user to go back and choose an action.

Next we'll examine _man_form. Its contents are in the /var/www/html/mason/productbackend/continue/_man_form file online at http://localhost/mason/productbackend/continue/man_form or www.opensourcewebbook.com/mason/productbackend/continue/man_form. At the bottom, you'll see this:

```
<%args>
    $action => ´´
    $manid  => ´´
</%args>
```

This component is used with:

```
<& _man_form, action => $action,
              manid  => $manid &>
```

where the action and manufacturer ID are passed in.

Next is a <%once> block with a function definition:

```
<%once>
# define a function to make sure our manid is well formed
sub check_man_id {
    my $manid  = shift;
    my $action = shift;

    if ($manid) {
        if (length($manid) <= 4 and $manid =~ /^\d+$/) {
            # all is well, return an empty string
            return ´´;
        } else {
            return ´Manufacturer id is not properly formatted
                    as up to 4 digit characters.´;
        }
    } elsif ($action eq ´modman´) {
        return ´Please go back and enter a manufacturer id to modify.´;
    } else {
        # all is well, return an empty string
        return ´´;
    }
}
</%once>
```

Here a function is defined: check_man_id(). Its job is to take the manufacturer ID and the action and check that the ID is well formed and that there is an ID if the manufacturer is being modified. If this function finds anything wrong, it returns a string that is not empty. This nonempty string is used to find out if there is an error condition.

This function is defined within the <%once> block. This function could have been defined as a component, but using <%once> is an alternative. We chose this method to show the use of this type of block.

```
<%init>
use DBI;

my $name    = ´´;
my $address = ´´;
my $city    = ´´;
my $state   = ´´;
my $zip     = ´´;
```

```
# first things first, if we are not modifying a manufacturer,
# then we don't need a manufacturer id
if ($action ne 'modman') {
    $manid = '';
}
```

In the <%init> block, we use DBI and declare some variables. The code checks that $manid has no value if the manufacturer is not being modified, just to be sure.

```
my $result = '';
unless ($result = check_man_id($manid, $action)) {
    if ($manid) {
        # we have a manid, so query the database
        my $dbh = DBI->connect('DBI:mysql:product_database',
                                'apache','LampIsCool');
        my $cursor = $dbh->prepare('SELECT name, address, city,
                                            state, zip
                                    FROM manufacturers
                                    WHERE man_id = ?');
        $cursor->execute($manid);

        ($name,$address,$city,$state,$zip) = $cursor->fetchrow;
    }
}
</%init>
```

The function check_man_id() is called and the result stored in $result. If the function returned an empty string (in other words, a false value), the unless block is executed. Within it the code checks to see if there is a manufacturer ID. If one is passed, a manufacturer is being modified, and the program queries the database so that the stored values are displayed in the updated form presented to the user after the changes.

Returning to the top of the file _man_form, we see:

```
% if ($result) {
    <% $result %>
% } else {
```

Here the value of $result is checked. Remember, it was set in the <%init> block—if it has a nonempty string, or a true value, there was some sort of error condition. Thus, if it has a value, that error is reported to the user.

If there is not an error, the form is built in the `else` block. The form has several widgets that resemble the following:

```
<tr>
  <td>Name:</td>
  <td><input type="text" name="name" value="<% $name %>" size="4"></td>
</tr>
```

The value of the widget is `<% $name %>`, the value of the `name` field that was grabbed from the database, if the database was queried. If the database wasn't queried, the value of the widget is blank.

Next comes this code:

```
% if ($action eq 'modman') {
<input type="submit" value="Modify">
% } else {
<input type="submit" value="Add">
% }
```

This displays the proper text in the submit button: "`Modify`" when modifying, otherwise "`Add`".

```
<input type="hidden" name="action" value="<% $action %>">
```

Finally, we have this hidden field. The purpose of this widget is to pass along to the next page the action being taken. This allows the finished page to perform the proper action based on the selection from the previous page.

So check this one out. Go to the form page and select, from the selection menu, modification of a manufacturer (we choose manufacturer ID 1001). When Modify a Manufacturer ID is selected with the value 1001, a page like Figure 11.14 shows up. The values of the fields can be changed, and when the user clicks the Modify button, the database is updated with changes.

Moving on to the product form. Its contents can be found in the file `/var/www/html/mason/productbackend/continue/_prod_form` online at either `http://localhost/mason/productbackend/continue/prod_form` or at www.opensourcewebbook.com/mason/productbackend/continue/prod_form.

We don't show this code here, because it is very similar to `_man_form`. A quick check of the differences shows that this code expects to receive two posted variables: `$action` and `$prodid`. In the `<%init>` block, it assigns the empty string to `$prodid` if a product is not modified. It defines, using a `<%once>` block, a function named `check_prod_id()` that makes sure the

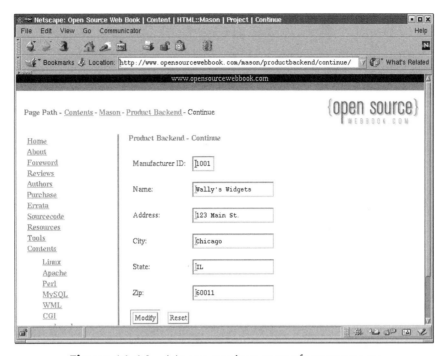

Figure 11.14 Mason project manufacturer page

product ID is well formed and that returns error messages if it finds anything it does not expect. Then the check_prod_id() function is invoked, its result is stored in $result, and if the function returns the empty string (all is well), a query is made of the database if there is a product ID (which means that a product is being modified).

In the top part of the file, $result is examined, and if it is not the empty string, an error is printed. If it is the empty string, a form is built for the product information. As with the manufacturer form, the values are set if anything was grabbed from the database. Also, as before, the correct button text is generated, either "Modify" or "Add", and a hidden field is generated that notifies the next Mason page of what action to take.

Let's try this one out. Go back to the selection Modify a Product and choose product ID C101. It should generate a form that resembles Figure 11.15.

So now we can fill out a form to add a manufacturer, modify a manufacturer, add a product, and modify a product. What happens when these

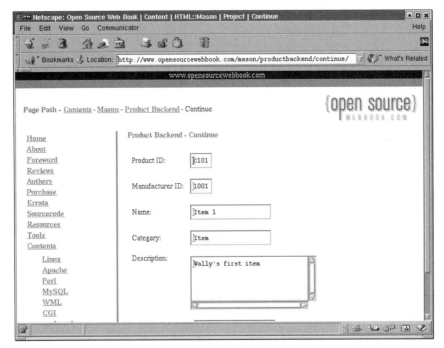

Figure 11.15 Mason project product page

forms are submitted? The HTML in both _man_form and _prod_form shows that the form action is set to /mason/productbackend/finished/, which posts the data to index.html within that directory. So let's examine this file. Its contents can be found in the /var/www/html/mason/productbackend/ finished/index.html file online at http://localhost/mason/productbackend/ finished/index.html.txt or www.opensourcewebbook.com/mason/productbackend/ finished/index.html.txt.

Go immediately to where the action is, the <%args> block. There are a bunch of variables here, but remember, this file is used to handle posted data for both a manufacturer and a product, so these variables handle both forms. All the variables default to the empty string because in any case chosen, several will not be assigned a posted value.

Next is the <%init> block. First, the familiar use of DBI is seen and then the connection to the product database. The remainder of the <%init> block consists of a big if .. elsif .. else like this:

```
if ($action eq 'addman' or $action eq 'modman') {

    ...

} elsif ($action eq 'addprod' or $action eq 'modprod') {

    ...

} else {
    $error = 'Invalid action.';
}
```

The decision that this code makes is based on the action that was posted to this page (through the hidden field `action`). Note that an error condition results if an unexpected action is received.

The variable `$error` plays an important role in this file: It is assigned a string if an error or unexpected condition is found. Near the top of the file, this value is checked (more on this later). The two blocks in the `if/elsif` are very similar, so we will look at only one in detail: the section that handles the action of either adding or modifying a manufacturer.

First, the program does a sanity check on the data:

```
unless ($name and $address and $city and $state and $zip) {
    $error = 'Please go back and fill out all fields.';
} else {

    # now, check to see if the data is ok
    # is $manid properly formed?
    unless (length($manid) <= 4 and $manid =~ /^\d+$/) {
        $error = 'Manufacturer ID is not properly formatted
                  as up to 4 digit characters';
    } else {
        # check each of the other variables for valid characters
        foreach my $var ($name, $address, $city, $state, $zip) {
            unless ($var =~ /^[\w\s\.\-']+$/) {
                $error = "One or more fields contain invalid characters:
                          $var";
                last;
            }
        }
    }
}
```

It first verifies that all the fields have been filled out. If not, `$error` is assigned a string that is used to inform the user of their mistake.[9]

---

[9]Remember, `$error` is assigned a value if there is some unexpected condition; otherwise, it is as empty string.

If all the fields are filled out, the manufacturer ID is checked to see that it is well formed: no more than four word characters. If the manufacturer ID checks out OK, the other variables containing the posted data are checked. If any of this posted data contains an illegal character (the legal characters are word characters, space characters, periods, dashes, or single quotes— this set may need to be expanded based on the data that you allow), $error is assigned.

If all the data checks out as OK, $error is assigned its original empty string, or false value.

```
unless ($error) {
    if ($action eq 'addman') {
        my $cursor = $dbh->prepare('INSERT INTO manufacturers
                                    (man_id, name, address, city, state,
                                    zip)
                                    VALUES (?, ?, ?, ?, ?, ?)');
        $cursor->execute($manid, $name, $address, $city, $state, $zip);

        # check for an error message
        $error = $cursor->errstr();
```

If $error is false, the program goes on. There are two options: either adding or modifying a manufacturer. In the case of adding a manufacturer, an SQL query is created to insert data into the manufacturers table. The value in errstr() is assigned to $error—either the error that just happened or the empty string if there is no error.

```
    } elsif ($action eq 'modman') {
        my $cursor = $dbh->prepare('SELECT name FROM manufacturers
                                    WHERE man_id = ?');
        $cursor->execute($manid);

        # check for an error message
        unless ($error = $cursor->errstr()) {
            # check to see if record is in the database
            my($name_in_db) = $cursor->fetchrow();
            unless ($name_in_db) {
                $error = 'Trying to modify a Manufacturer ID that is not
                        in the database.';
            } else {
                # we found the record, so let's modify it
                my $cursor = $dbh->prepare('REPLACE INTO manufacturers
                                            (man_id, name, address, city,
                                            state, zip)
                                            VALUES (?, ?, ?, ?, ?, ?)');
```

```
                    $cursor->execute($manid, $name, $address, $city, $state,
                                     $zip);

                    # check for an error message
                    $error = $cursor->errstr();
                }
            }
        }
    }
```

The modification of a manufacturer requires a bit more work. First, check to see if the manufacturer to be modified exists in the database—this is done with the SELECT query. If the query is executed correctly (errstr() returns false), the name queried is assigned to $name_in_db. If this variable is false, the manufacturer is not in the table, so an appropriate error message is assigned to $error. If the name is found, the REPLACE command is executed, which replaces the current record for that manufacturer ID or inserts it if it doesn't exist (but it previously determined that it indeed does exist).

Now that the bottom of the file has been explored, check out the top of the file. The components _top and _leftrail are used. Then, after a bit of HTML:

```
% if ($error) {
<p>
There was a problem <font color="#ff0000"><% $error %></font>
</p>
% } else {
<p>
Thank you.
</p>
<hr>
<& ../_select_form &>
% }
```

This checks to see if $error has been assigned, and if so, reports the value to the user. If not, a thank-you message is reported, and the _select_form component is executed. This builds the form, allowing the user to add or modify a manufacturer, or add or modify a product.

To show the result, try changing one of the manufacturers and clicking the Modify button. You should see a page resembling Figure 11.16.

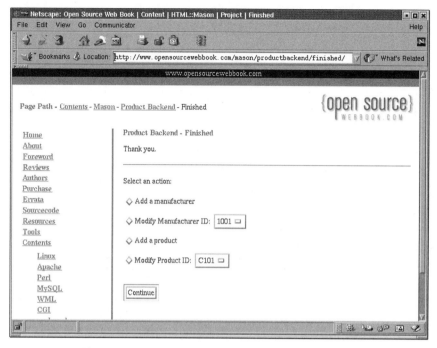

Figure 11.16   Mason project finished page

11.9 WHAT WE DIDN'T TALK ABOUT

As with many of the other topics in this book, we could write another volume describing all the features of Mason; we have only scratched the surface here (the 80/20 rule). Although it's not essential, you may want to explore the following topics as you learn more about how you can develop web sites with Mason.

11.9.1 Tags for Initialization and Cleanup

Mason provides tags that contain blocks of Perl code to be executed at specific times. For details, see `www.masonhq.com/docs/manual/Devel.html#initialization_and_cleanup`.

The `<%cleanup>` Tag

The `<%cleanup> ... </%cleanup>` tag defines a block of code that is executed just before the component exits. For example:

```
<%cleanup>
$dbh->disconnect();
</%cleanup>
```

This is equivalent to having a <%perl> ... </%perl> tag at the end of the file.

The <%shared> Tag

The <%shared> ... </%shared> tag is similar to <%once> in that all variables declared within it can be seen in the entire component, but <%shared>, unlike <%once>, is executed for each request.

11.9.2 Session Handling

The hash %session is a global variable that can contain the session information for the current user. If you assign a value to %session, a session is created for this user (the Apache::Session module must be installed for this to work).

A session ID is a commonly used value placed in the %session hash and then accessed on the user's next visit. You can ensure that the user has a session ID with code like this:

```
unless ($session{session_id}) {
    $session{session_id} = generate_new_session_id();
}
```

11.9.3 Request API

Mason provides an extensive API for the Mason Request object. This API allows you to access and change cache information, examine the component call stack, call components directly (for example, $m->comp()), use the long version of the <& ... &>, and much more. For details, www.masonhq.com/docs/manual/Request.html.

11.9.4 Component Class API

Mason provides methods to examine and report on the components that are used in the generation of the web page. See www.masonhq.com/docs/manual/Component.html for details.

11.9.5 Top-Level Components

Mason has a feature that enables a web page to be created even though the requested page, or even the directory, does not exist. In other words, let's say the user requests www.example.com/reports/2002/March/. Under normal conditions, Apache would serve up the file index.html under the directory reports/2002/March/. However, in this example, the directory 2002 doesn't exist. Moreover, neither does March. So, what happens?

Mason, properly configured, searches for the index.html and if it is not found, it then begins to search for *dhandlers,* or default handles, in the desired directory and up the directory tree. For instance, with the preceding request, Mason looks for, in order, the following:

```
/reports/2002/March/index.html
/reports/2002/dhandler
/reports/dhandler
/dhandler
```

The first file found is the one used. Let's say that the files /reports/2002/March/index.html and /reports/2002/dhandler are not found, and the first file found is /reports/dhandler. That file is used to generate the HTML. Its contents could be this:

```
<& _header &>
<h1>Report for <% $month %>, <% $year %></h1>
<% $report_contents %>
<& _footer &>

<%init>
# get the path, or the stuff asked for
my $arg = $m->dhandler_arg;
# split on the /, getting the year and the month
my($year,$month) = split("/",$arg);    # split out pieces

# do whatever is necessary to get the report content,
# perhaps reading from a database, assign it to $report_contents
my $report_contents = 'All the good content of the report';
</%init>
```

The <%init> section, the first code executed, grabs the contents of the path below /reports/—in this case, 2002/March. This text is stored in $arg, which is then split on the slash and stored in $year and $month. Then, by some means (perhaps a database is queried or a text file is read), the contents of the March 2002 report are read and stored in $report_contents.

Then, at the top of the file, we call the _header component to build the header; then we create an <h1> tag with the month and year in question. The contents of the report are included with <% $report_contents %>, followed by the _footer component.

As this example shows, depending on the report contents read, we can have the same default handler take care of all the following URLs and then some:

```
http://www.example.com/reports/2002/March/
http://www.example.com/reports/2002/February/
http://www.example.com/reports/2002/January/
http://www.example.com/reports/2001/December/
http://www.example.com/reports/2001/November/
```

For more information on default handlers, see the Mason documents at www.masonhq.com/docs/manual/Bevel.html/top_level_components.

11.10 SUMMARY

Mason is similar to Embperl—it enables executable code to be placed into HTML pages to transform static web pages into live ones. Most things that can be done with Embperl can be done with Mason, and vice versa. So why have both? TMTOWTDI, of course! All this may not be necessary if you are just building your own web site. You can just pick one of these, stick with it, and never worry about the others. But if you move on to a career as a web programmer, it's good to be familiar with all the tools you might run into in your career.

TMTOWTDI, and there is another way of doing what Mason and Embperl can do—PHP, coming right up.

11.11 RESOURCES

Web Site
Mason headquarters: www.masonhq.com/

12
PHP

12.1 INTRODUCTION

PHP is one of the Ps in LAMP (Perl and PHP). Its function is similar to that of `HTML::Embperl` and `HTML::Mason`—it uses executable code embedded in HTML to create dynamic web pages. In the last chapter, we compared Embperl and Mason, and saw that they are similar in purpose. Both can handle most any situation one would come across when developing a web site. Whether one chooses PHP over Embperl or Mason is a matter of personal preference. There are differences, and we try to point them out. The choice is yours. TMTOWTDI (not just with Perl, but with LAMP and Open Source in general). Choice is good!

PHP is another of those recursive initialisms beloved of a certain portion of the hacker community[1]; it's short for PHP: Hypertext Preprocessor. It was developed by Rasmus Lerdorf, Zeev Suraski, Andi Gutmans, and others. The first version was released in 1994; PHP is currently up to version 4.1.1 (as of this writing), while the version released with Red Hat 7 is version 4.0.4.

PHP has many built-in functions that perform important and common requests: It can connect to databases (many types, including MySQL, which we cover here), send e-mail, create PDFs, and more. PHP is widely used,[2] and there are plenty of tutorials, examples, and help available on the Web.

The syntax is similar to Perl, C, and C++, so learning it is not a stretch for the experienced programmer. The ubiquitous flow-control constructs (`if`, `switch`, `while`, `for`, and `foreach`, among others) are available. Grabbing

---

[1] Re: GNU: GNU's Not Unix.

[2] Especially in Europe, where LAMP usually stands for Linux, Apache, MySQL and PHP. In the states, due to the popularity of `www.onlamp.com`, it is usually more broadly taken to be Linux, Apache, MySQL and Perl—Python—PHP.

posted data is simple, so form data can be processed easily. The syntax is a bit simpler than Perl. Like Perl, PHP is object oriented, so you can create classes, methods, etc.

PHP does have some limitations. For one thing, PHP requires that you learn YAPL.[3] Although PHP has numerous built-in functions to do most things we would need to do, it is not Perl based, as are Embperl and Mason. With Embperl and Mason, you can download and install modules from CPAN and then use them, making Embperl and Mason programs more flexible and extensible. PHP is more self-contained and is *slightly* more limited than Perl (that's a bit of an understatement—no reflection on PHP, but Perl is a big language with which one can literally do most anything computer related).

Hard-core Perl programmers are likely to stay with Embperl or Mason. Others may choose PHP. Try them all and make your own choice.

12.2 EMBEDDING PHP INTO HTML

There are several ways to embed PHP code into HTML documents. One way is to put the PHP code within the tags <? ... ?>:

```
<? echo "hello, world!"; ?>
```

Most PHP programmers choose this syntax. If PHP is combined with XML, however, there are conflicts with this syntax. In XML the <? ... ?> construct is a special thing called a *processing instruction*. If PHP and XML are needed in the same file, one can use the alternative PHP tag <?php ... ?>:

```
<?php echo "hello, world!"; ?>
```

Some HTML editors (such as FrontPage) don't like processing instructions, so another alternative is to use the <SCRIPT> tag. This is the syntax:

```
<SCRIPT LANGUAGE="php"> echo "hello, world!"; </SCRIPT>
```

And last but not least, the final way is to use a style similar to one in Mason: the <% ... %> tag:

```
<% echo "hello, world!"; %>
```

---

[3]Yet Another Programming Language—but for us nerds, learning another language is a good thing. Imagine how much better your resume would look if you added PHP!

We are not using XML in these examples, so we don't need to use the `<?php ... ?>` syntax. Also, because our favorite HTML editors are vi and emacs, we don't need the `<script>` syntax (we don't use FrontPage or other HTML editors—if you do, plan accordingly). We use the first style in our examples.

12.3 CONFIGURATION

If you installed Linux as suggested in Chapter 2, Apache is already configured for PHP. To use PHP, simply name the PHP files with the `.php` extension.

You might note that this approach is contrary to that used for Embperl and Mason, where we decided against using a separate extension for those files. The logic was to not provide too much information about our site and to keep a clean URL look throughout the site (all pages are accessed through an `.html` extension). But because Apache is configured to use `.php` files out of the box, we'll stick with it out of sheer laziness (one of the desirable properties of a good programmer).

There is a way to configure Apache so that all `.html` files in a directory are processed by PHP. See the docs for more information.

12.4 A COUPLE OF QUICK EXAMPLES

We'll start with two quick examples. Create a new directory for PHP work and `cd` into it:

```
$ mkdir /var/www/html/php
$ chmod a+rx /var/www/html/php
$ cd /var/www/html/php
```

Create a PHP file named `hello.php`:[4]

```
<html>
<head>
<title>Hello, world! with PHP</title>
</head>
<body bgcolor="#ffffff">
<? echo "hello, world!" ?>
</body>
</html>
```

---

[4]Remember the permissions, 644.

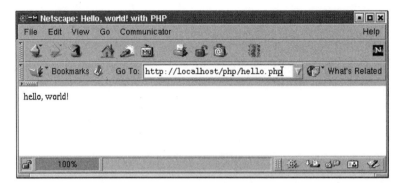

Figure 12.1   hello, world! with PHP

To view the result of this file, load either one of these URLs: `http://localhost/php/hello.php` or `www.opensourcewebbook.com/php/hello.php`. The result can be seen in Figure 12.1.

The PHP code is embedded in the HTML within the <? ... ?> tag. In this example the PHP code simply echoes (displays) the string "hello, world!". The `echo` PHP statement outputs a string that eventually is rendered in the browser.

Now that the obligatory "hello, world!" example has been done with PHP, try a built-in function that does a lot of work: `phpinfo()`. Place this code into `phpinfo.php`:

```
<html>
<head>
<title>PHP Information</title>
</head>
<body bgcolor="#ffffff">
<? phpinfo() ?>
</body>
</html>
```

The function `phpinfo()` builds a page with a wealth of useful information on how PHP was built, the PHP environment, etc. To view the result, load either of these URLs: `http://localhost/php/phpinfo.php` or `www.opensourcewebbook.com/php/phpinfo.php`. The result of this can be seen in Figure 12.2.

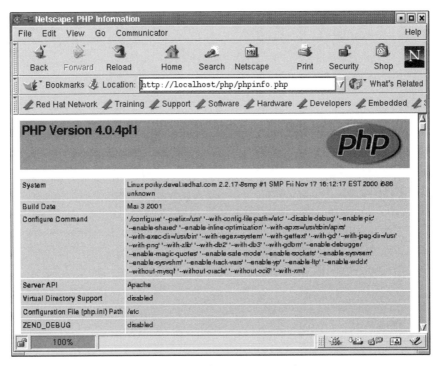

Figure 12.2   PHP information with `phpinfo()`

12.5 LANGUAGE SYNTAX

Like the other languages we've studied (and most easy-to-use languages), PHP is whitespace-insensitive. Therefore, this statement:

```
<? $title="PHP is cool";echo "<title> $title </title>"; ?>
```

might be clearer if written as this:

```
<?
    $title = "PHP is cool";
    echo "<title> $title </title>";
?>
```

Variable names in PHP are case-sensitive—`$a` is different from `$A`. Function names (including user-defined functions) are case-insensitive—`rose()` is equivalent to `ROSE()` is equivalent to `Rose()`.

As in C, C++, Java, and Perl, statements are terminated by a semi-colon. Also as in C, C++, and Java (but not Perl), single-line bodies do not require the curly braces ({}), while multiline bodies do:

```
<?
    // one-line bodies do not require the curlies,
    // but using them would be ok
    if ($num > 10)
        echo "\$num is greater than 10";

    // in this example, the curlies are required
    if ($name == "John Doe") {
        echo "You say your name is John Doe";
        echo "Are you sure that is your name?";
    }
?>
```

PHP supports three types of comments:

```
# Perl/sh style - comment until end of line
/* C style */
// C++ style (preferred for one-line comments)
```

C-style comments can span more than one line:

```
/*
    the following code is so cool,
    it almost doesn't need to be
    commented
*/
```

12.5.1 Variables

All variable names (including arrays) begin with a dollar sign ($) followed by an alpha (A–Z, a–z) or underscore (_), followed by zero or more alphanumeric characters or underscores (there is no limit on variable name length):

```
$i
$_1st_name
$array[0]
```

As in other scripting languages, such as Perl and shell scripts, variables do not need to be declared.

12.5.2 Data Types

Primitive Data Types

PHP has three primitive data types: integers, floats, and strings.

- Integers: long ints (32 bits)
  - Decimal: 10
  - Hexadecimal: 0x2A
  - Octal: 025

```
<?
    // these all represent the same value
    $myint = 69;     // decimal
    $myint = 0x45;   // hexadecimal
    $myint = 0105;   // octal
?>
```

- Floats:
  - Standard: 4.745
  - Scientific: 12.3E-4

```
<?
    // these both represent the same value
    $myfloat = 169.345;
    $myfloat = 1.69345e2;
?>
```

- Strings (like Perl):
  - Single quotes:

```
<?
    $os = 'Linux';
    echo 'Favorite OS\t$os\n';
    // outputs: Favorite OS\t$os\n
?>
```

  - Double quotes:

```
<?
    $os = "Linux";
    echo "Favorite OS\t$os\n";
    // outputs:  Favorite OS<tab>Linux<ret>
?>
```

  - Escape characters:

```
\n     newline
\t     tab
\r     carriage return
\\     backslash
\$     dollar sign
```

Data Type Examples

This example shows how PHP uses the various data types. This code can be found in the file /var/www/html/php/variables.php:

```
<?
    // assign some variables the different data types
    $integer = 12;
    $float1  = 1.345e23;
    $float2  = 4995.392;
    $string1 = 'My favorite number is $integer';
    $string2 = "I am this big: $float1 or $float2";
?>
<html>
<head>
<title>Integers, Floats and Strings in PHP</title>
</head>
<body bgcolor="#ffffff">
Integer: <b><? echo $integer; ?></b><br>
Float 1: <b><? echo $float1; ?></b>
<i>note that the format is *almost* the same as assigned</i><br>
Float 2: <b><? echo $float2; ?></b>
<i>the format is the same as assigned</i><br>
String 1: <b><? echo $string1; ?></b><br>
String 2: <b><? echo $string2; ?></b>
</body>
</html>
```

An integer, two floats, and two strings are demonstrated.

The two floats are assigned in a different format, and PHP maintains that format (well, almost—our lowercase "e" is replaced with an uppercase "E"). The difference between single quotes and double quotes is demonstrated.

To view the result of this program, load in either http://localhost/php/variables.php or www.opensourcewebbook.com/php/variables.php. This produces Figure 12.3.

Arrays

To index a PHP array, use the syntax $array[n], where [n] is an integer beginning at 0, as in Perl. But when referring to the entire array, use the dollar sign ($)—sort($array)—not the at sign (@array) of Perl. PHP arrays can be treated in one of two ways: as enumerated arrays or as associative arrays.

Enumerated Arrays Enumerated arrays are zero-based arrays indexed with integer values—$array[0]:

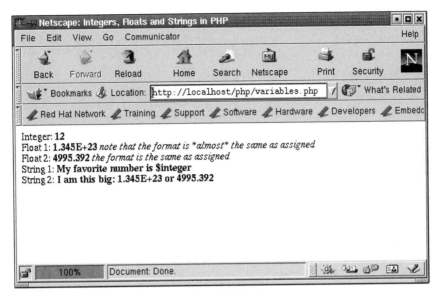

Figure 12.3 PHP data types

```
<?
    $a[0] = 10;
    $a[1] = 4 * 4;
    $a[2] = 12;

    echo $a[0] + $a[1] + $a[2];
    // echoes 38
?>
```

Enumerated arrays can be created as shown by simply assigning values to each array index, or they can be created with the `array()` function, which returns an array of values:

```
<?
    $a = array(2, 4, 6, 8);
    echo $a[0];
    // echoes 2

    $b = array("foo", "bar", "blah");
    echo $b[1];
    // echos bar
?>
```

Associative Arrays Associative arrays are indexed with unique strings— `$array["key"]`—like Perl hash variables:

```
<?
    $capital["Illinois"]   = "Springfield";
    $capital["California"] = "Sacramento";
    $capital["Texas"]      = "Austin";
    $capital["Wisconsin"]  = "Madison";

    $state = "Illinois";
    echo "$state: $capital[$state]";
    // echoes "Illinois: Springfield"
?>
```

Associative arrays can be created by assigning values individually to keys as just shown, or they can be created with the `array()` function:

```
<?
    $capital = array(
        "Illinois"   => "Springfield",
        "California" => "Sacramento",
        "Texas"      => "Austin",
        "Wisconsin"  => "Madison"
    );

    $state = "Illinois";
    echo "$state: $capital[$state]";
    // echoes "Illinois: Springfield"
?>
```

The `array()` function is useful. PHP has many more built-in functions to process arrays. We examine some of these later in the chapter.

12.5.3 Web Variables

PHP can be used to process data that is submitted via forms; such data is accessible in several ways. To illustrate this, create a simple form in `/var/www/html/php/form1.html`:

```
<html>
<head>
<title>PHP Form Example 1</title>
</head>
<body bgcolor="#ffffff">
<form action="/php/form1.php">
Var 1: <input type="text" name="var1">
<br>
Var 2: <input type="text" name="var2">
<br>
<input type="submit">
</form>
</body>
</html>
```

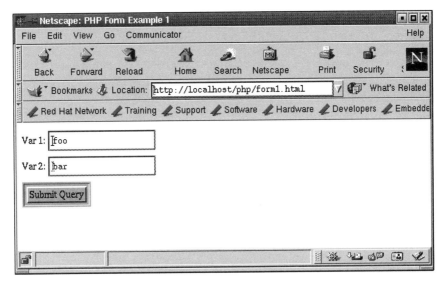

Figure 12.4   PHP form 1

The result of using this form, with example data entered into the widgets, is shown in Figure 12.4. When the form is submitted, the form data is passed to the PHP program in several ways.

When the data is posted to the PHP program specified in the `action=` form attribute (`/php/form1.php` in this example), PHP variables are automatically created in that PHP script when it executes. These variables have the same name as the form elements, preceded by "**$**". In this form, there are two fields—`var1` and `var2`—so PHP creates two variables in `/php/form1.php`: `$var1` and `$var2`.

An Important Security Consideration

This "feature" of PHP can create a huge security hole. Consider this code:

```
if (something_important()) {
    $authenticated = true;
}
```

Here we are relying on `something_important()` to verify that we can set the authentication flag to true. We can assume `something_important()` does, er, something important to authenticate the user. However, it would be easy to pass a parameter to this program using the name/value pair that we want, as in:

`http://localhost/php/big_security_hole.php?authenticated=true`

Doing this would magically set `$authenticated` to true. Therefore, even if `something_important()` returned false, the very important flag `$authenticated` would be assigned true—very bad.

Therefore, we *strongly suggest* that you turn off this feature for PHP. You can do so for the entire site or for a specific directory. Because this is a nasty problem, we suggest that you turn it off for the whole site by adding this line to `/etc/httpd/conf/httpd.conf`:

`php_flag register_globals Off`

To turn it off for only a specific directory in the web document tree, add this to the configuration file:

```
<Directory /var/www/html/php>
    php_flag register_globals Off
</Directory>
```

Load the new config file:

 # /etc/init.d/httpd graceful

Now that PHP is more secure, let's talk about how to grab the posted data. PHP Version 4.1.0 has added a new and strongly suggested approach to grabbing the posted data. However, as of this writing, version 4.1.0 had just been released, and Red Hat had not yet released a binary for it. Therefore, we first discuss how to use the pre-4.1.0 approach and then discuss the 4.1.0 way.[5]

Pre–PHP Version 4.1.0

PHP has two special array variables that are magically assigned the data passed into the program: `$HTTP_GET_VARS` and `$HTTP_POST_VARS`.

All the data passed in using the GET method is stored in the array `$HTTP_GET_VARS`, so the value of the field `var1` can be accessed with `$HTTP_GET_VARS["var1"]`. If the data were passed to the program using POST

---

[5]Fear not! The pre-4.1.0 approach still works in 4.1.0. As with most tools, PHP makes a great effort to be backward compatible, which means that this book has to be backward compatible too.

instead of GET, the data would be passed into the array $HTTP_POST_VARS instead, so the data could be accessed with $HTTP_POST_VARS["var1"].

It is useful have both variables because we can post data through the form and at the same time use the GET method to pass the data through the URL. The parameters can have the same names (not always a good idea, but it can be done) and grab the posted data from $HTTP_POST_VARS and the URL data from $HTTP_GET_VARS.

The file that processes the form data from the previous form, /php/ form1.php, looks like this:

```
<html>
<head>
<title>PHP Form 1 Result</title>
</head>
<body bgcolor="#ffffff">
Using $var1: <b> <? echo $var1; ?> </b>
<br>
Using $var2: <b> <? echo $var2; ?> </b>
<br>
Using $HTTP_GET_VARS:
<b> <? echo $HTTP_GET_VARS["var1"]; ?> </b>,
<b> <? echo $HTTP_GET_VARS["var2"]; ?> </b>
</body>
</html>
```

This program produces Figure 12.5.

The good news is that $var1 and $var2 are not magically assigned (because we turned off register_globals—you can see that there is nothing echoed out by <? echo $var1; ?>). This is a good thing.

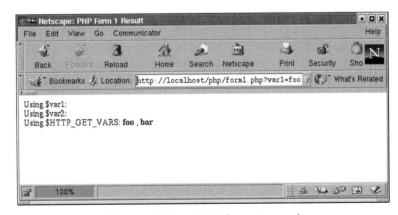

Figure 12.5 PHP form 1 result

Post–Version 4.1.0

Version 4.1.0 adds a new, improved, and strongly suggested approach to grabbing the posted data. Because Red Hat version 7 does not include PHP version 4.1.0, we will only discuss it here—the remaining examples use the pre-4.1.0 method. In the future, you should use the new way.

PHP version 4.1.0 has added several new global variables:

- $_GET—an array of the data sent with GET (replaces $HTTP_GET_VARS)
- $_POST—an array of the data sent with POST (replaces $HTTP_POST_VARS)
- $_COOKIE—HTTP cookie variables
- $_REQUEST—a merge of the GET, POST, and cookie data

Version 4.1.0 introduces some other helpful variables:

- $_SERVER—the Apache server environment variables, such as REMOTE_ADDR
- $_ENV—the environment variables
- $_SESSION—data registered by the session module

Therefore, the preceding example could change to this:

```
Using $_GET:
<b> <? echo $_GET["var1"]; ?> </b>,
<b> <? echo $_GET["var2"]; ?> </b>
```

or this:

```
Using $_REQUEST:
<b> <? echo $_REQUEST["var1"]; ?> </b>,
<b> <? echo $_REQUEST["var2"]; ?> </b>
```

12.5.4 Operators

PHP operators are similar to the ones available in Perl, including precedence (see www.php.net/manual/en/language.operators.precedence.php). One exception is that there are no string comparison operators. The comparison operators (==, <, etc.) are used to compare both numbers and strings, as in $name == "Joe".

The or and and Operators

Like Perl, PHP has the or and and operators, often used with short-circuited evaluation:

```
$name == "Joe" or print "Name is not Joe";
```

You can also write this logic with the and, but this is less common:

```
$name != "Joe" and print "Name is not Joe";
```

12.5.5 Flow-Control Constructs

PHP's constructs are similar to those of C and Perl. However, for most of the constructs, PHP has two preferred syntax forms. The first is C-like and is suggested when the entire block is contained within a single PHP block. The second is useful when the PHP code is embedded within a large block of HTML.

As in C, C++, and Java (but not Perl), the curly braces are optional for the bodies of the constructs if the body is one statement.

```
if/elseif/else
```

Here are the two PHP syntaxes for an if:

```
if (condition) {
    statements
} elseif (condition) {
    statements
} else {
    statements
}
```

and:

```
if (condition) :
    statements
elseif (condition) :
    statements
else :
    statements
endif;
```

As an example (this can be found in the file named /var/www/html/php/if.php):

```php
<?
    $name = $HTTP_GET_VARS["name"];
    $age  = $HTTP_GET_VARS["age"];

    // this syntax is recommended when the entire if
    // is contained within a PHP block like this one

    $msg = "You $name are ";
    if ($age < 13) {
        $msg = $msg . "a child";
    } elseif ($age < 18) {
        $msg = $msg . "a teenager";
    } elseif ($age < 62) {
        $msg = $msg . "an adult";
    } else {
        $msg = $msg . "a senior";
    }

    // the syntax of the if statement below is
    // recommended if you have embedded PHP code
?>
<html>
<head>
<title>PHP if statement</title>
</head>
<body bgcolor="#ffffff">
<? echo $msg; ?>
<hr>
<? if ($name < "N") : ?>
Your name begins with A through M
<? else: ?>
Your name begins with N through Z
<? endif; ?>
</body>
</html>
```

The result of this code can be examined by invoking the program and passing data into it through either of these URLs so that it is treated as GET data: http://localhost/php/if.php?age=39&name=John+Doe or www.opensourcewebbook.com/php/if.php?age=39&name=John+Doe. The result can be seen in Figure 12.6.

switch

Like C and C++, PHP has a switch statement. Like the PHP if, it has two different syntaxes:

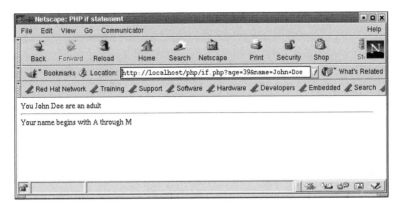

Figure 12.6 PHP if example

```
switch (expression) {
    case expr:
        statements
        break;
    case expr:
        statements
        break;
    default:
        statements
        break;
}
```

and:

```
<?
    switch (expression) :
        case expr:
            statements
            break;
        case expr:
            statements
            break;
        default:
            statements
            break;
    endswitch;
?>
```

As in C and C++, the break in each branch is crucial. If it weren't there, program execution would just flow through each executable statement in the switch construct following the valid one, not just the ones related to the specific case.

The `switch` is often used to replace the nested `if` where each conditional expression compares the same variable against a value. An `if` statement:

```
<?
    if ($i == 0) {
        statements0
    } elseif ($i == 1) {
        statements1
    } elseif ($i == 2) {
        statements2
    } elseif ($i == 3) {
        statements3
    } elseif ($i == 4) {
        statements4
    }
?>
```

can be rewritten as a switch:

```
<?
    switch ($i) {
        case 0:
            statements0
            break;
        case 1:
            statements1
            break;
        case 2:
            statements2
            break;
        case 3:
            statements3
            break;
        case 4:
            statements4
            break;
    }
?>
```

`while` Loop

PHP's `while` loop is C-like, and as one might expect, also has two syntaxes:

```
while (condition) {
    statements
}
```

and the second one:

```
while (condition) :
    statements
endwhile;
```

Like C, C++, and Java, PHP allows one to break out of a loop with `break` and go to the next iteration with the `continue` statement.

do ... while Loop

PHP also has a do ... while loop:

```
do {
    statements
} while (condition);
```

for Loop

PHP has a C-like `for` loop with two syntax options:

```
for (start_expr; condition; step_expr) {
    statements
}
```

and:

```
for (start_expr; condition; step_expr) :
    statements
endfor;
```

foreach Loop

PHP has a Perl-like `foreach` loop, which iterates through arrays in two distinct ways. Each `foreach` method has two syntax variations.

The first method returns only the value and is used to iterate through enumerated arrays. The syntax is:

```
foreach (array_expr as variable) {
    statements
}
```

or:

```
foreach (array_expr as variable) :
    statements
endforeach;
```

These constructs loop through the array represented by *array_expr*, assigning the variable *variable* the value of that element. The following is an example:

```
<?
    $array = array(2, 4, 6, 8);
    foreach ($array as $value) {
        echo "$value ";
    }

    // echoes "2 4 6 8 "
?>
```

Here, $value takes on each value of the array $array, and the body is executed for each of those values. The variable $value is first 2, then 4, then 6, and finally 8.

The second foreach method returns both the key and the value, which is used to iterate through associative arrays. It has this syntax:

```
foreach (array_expr as key => value) {
    statements
}
```

or:

```
foreach (array_expr as key => value) :
    statements
endforeach;
```

Unlike in Perl, key/value arrays are not stored in an apparent random order (based on how the keys hash). They are stored in the order created.

This version of foreach loops through array_expr, assigning the next key/value pair to key, value. Here is an example:

```
<?
    $array = array(
        "name"  => "John Doe",
        "age"   => 39,
        "phone" => "555-1234"
    );

    foreach ($array as $k => $v) {
        echo "$k: \t $v \n";
    }

    // echoes:
    //     name:      John Doe
    //     age:       39
    //     phone:     555-1234
?>
```

Note that the `foreach` that iterates through an associative array can be used to iterate through enumerated arrays. The indices 0, 1, and so on are treated as the keys:

```
<?
    $a = array(2, 4, 6, 8);
    foreach ($a as $k => $v) {
        echo "$k = $v";
    }
    // echoes:  0 = 2
    //          1 = 4
    //          2 = 6
    //          3 = 8
?>
```

The following example shows the various looping constructs and can be found in `/var/www/html/php/loops.php`. It shows how to loop through an enumerated array using `while`, `for`, and `foreach`. It then demonstrates iteration through an associative array with a `foreach`.

```
<?
    // enumerated array of numbers
    $nums = array(2, 4, 6, 8);

    // associative array of names and ages
    $ages = array(
        "Ron"  => 31,
        "Gail" => 26,
        "Al"   => 38,
        "Tom"  => 36
    );
?>
<html>
<head>
<title>Examples of PHP Loops</title>
</head>
<body bgcolor="#ffffff">

<h3>Loop through $nums with the while loop</h3>
<?
    $i = 0;
    while ($i < 4) {
        echo "$nums[$i] ";
        $i++;
    }
?>

<h3>Loop through $nums with the for loop</h3>
<?
    for ($i = 0; $i < 4; $i++) {
        echo "$nums[$i] ";
    }
?>
```

```
<h3>Loop through $nums with the foreach loop</h3>
<?
    foreach ($nums as $v) {
        echo "$v ";
    }
?>

<h3>Display ages in a table using the foreach loop</h3>
<table border="1">
<?
    foreach ($ages as $k => $v) {
        echo "<tr><th>$k</th><td>$v</td></tr>";
    }
?>
</table>

</body>
</html>
```

To give this code a test drive, put one of the following URLs into your browser: `http://localhost/php/loops.php` or `www.opensourcewebbook.com/php/loops.php`. The proof is in the pudding, in Figure 12.7.

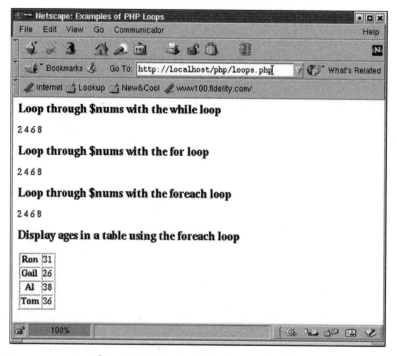

Figure 12.7   PHP loops example

12.5.6 Writing PHP Functions

The syntax to declare a function is:

```
function function_name(variable_list) {
    statements
}
```

The syntax to call a function is:

```
function_name(variable_list);
```

Look in `/var/www/html/php/function1.php` for the familiar `hello, world!` example:

```
<?
    function print_hello () {
        echo "hello, world!";
    }
?>
<html>
<head>
<title>PHP Functions - Part 1</title>
</head>
<body bgcolor="#ffffff">

<? print_hello(); ?>

</body>
</html>
```

This program defines the function `print_hello()`, which, as you might guess, prints "hello, world!". The function is defined within the `<? ... ?>` tags, just like any other PHP code. It is then invoked within the `<body>` tags with `<? print_hello(); ?>`. The result can be seen by loading one of these URLs: `http://localhost/php/function1.php` or `www.opensourcewebbook.com/php/function1.php`. The result will be the familiar, hypnotic, spiritual "hello, world!" displayed in the browser.

PHP functions can return values (covered next) and take arguments (covered later).

Return Values

A PHP function can return a single value or an array of values. The `return` statement returns the value from the function to the caller. This example illustrates the return of a string, an array of integers, and an associative array. This code can be found in /var/www/html/php/function3.php:

```php
<?
    function return_string() {
        // return a string
         return "hello, world!";
    }

    function return_array1() {
        // return an array of integers
         return array(2, 4, 6, 8);
    }

    function return_array2() {
        // return a more complicated array
        $a = array(
            "one"   => "first",
            "two"   => "second",
            "three" => "third"
        );
        return $a;
    }
?>
<html>
<head>
<title>PHP Functions</title>
</head>
<body bgcolor="#ffffff">

<?
    // echo the return value from return_string()
    echo return_string();
?>

<hr>

<?
    // grab the array returned from return_array1()
    // foreach through it, echoing the value
    $array1 = return_array1();
    foreach ($array1 as $value) {
        echo "$value <br>";
    }
?>

<hr>

<?
    // grab the array returned from return_array2()
    // foreach through it, echoing the keys and values
    $array2 = return_array2();
```

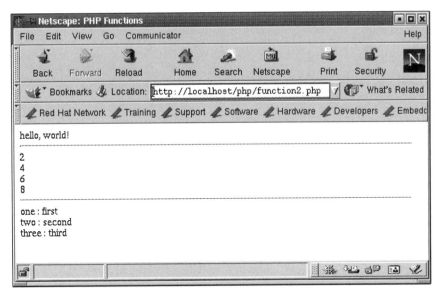

Figure 12.8 PHP function2 example—return values

```
    foreach ($array2 as $k => $v) {
        echo "$k : $v <br>";
    }
?>

</body>
</html>
```

Notice the variable $a within the function return_array2()? It is by definition locally scoped. All variables within a function are by default locally scoped to the function in which they are used.[6]

To try this program, load in either http://localhost/php/function2. php or www.opensourcewebbook.com/php/function2.php. You should see something like Figure 12.8.

Function Arguments

As in all other languages, arguments can be passed to PHP functions, as follows:

---

[6]To enable a global variable to be accessed with the function, declare it as global $a. You can also create static variables, but that is a bit beyond our scope.

```
function no_default_args($a, $b, $c) {
    echo "<hr>";
    echo "no_default_args(): \$a : $a <br>";
    echo "no_default_args(): \$b : $b <br>";
    echo "no_default_args(): \$c : $c <br>";
}
```

This function is called no_default_args solely because it does not have default argument values. It accepts three arguments: $a, $b, and $c. It then prints an <hr> tag, followed by the value of the three variables. As with all variables within a function, the three variables in this function are by default locally scoped.

To call this function, simply put the arguments within the parentheses:

```
no_default_args("foo", $variable_name, 4.9485);
```

If this function were called with fewer than three arguments, a warning message would be displayed, and the function would execute with the variables that were not passed a value being given the value of the empty string. If this function were called with more than three arguments, the extra arguments would be ignored.

This invites the question, "Can a function be written so that the arguments are given default values if values are not provided?" The answer is, of course, yes.[7] In this sort of application, in which unknown users will be passing information into your system, all values should have default, sane values.

To provide default arguments to a function, simply assign the variable within the parentheses in the function definition:

```
function default_args($a = 2, $b = 4, $c = 6) {
    echo "<hr>";
    echo "default_args(): \$a : $a <br>";
    echo "default_args(): \$b : $b <br>";
    echo "default_args(): \$c : $c <br>";
}
```

In this function, $a accepts the value of the argument passed to it, or it defaults to 2 if no value is given. If the function is called as:

```
default_args("foo", "bar", 10.498);
```

---

[7]Perhaps you saw this coming, given the name of the last example: no_default_args().

$a receives the value "foo", $b receives value "bar", and $c receives the value 10.498. If the function is called as:

```
default_args("foo");
```

$a receives the value "foo", but $b receives its default value, 4, and $c receives its default value, 6. If the function is called as:

```
default_args();
```

each variable receives its default value.

Arguments can be dropped only at the end of the list, not at the beginning.[8] Thus default_args(,"bar"); is a syntax error. You must provide the value for the first argument:

```
default_args(2, "bar");
```

Let's look at a complete example. It illustrates the two preceding concepts plus it shows that a function can receive as its argument an array variable. The example can be found in /var/www/html/php/function3.php:

```php
<?
    function no_default_args($a, $b, $c) {
        echo "<hr>";
        echo "no_default_args(): \$a : $a <br>";
        echo "no_default_args(): \$b : $b <br>";
        echo "no_default_args(): \$c : $c <br>";
    }

    // this function is defined so that the arguments
    // have default values
    function default_args($a = 2, $b = 4, $c = 6) {
        echo "<hr>";
        echo "default_args(): \$a : $a <br>";
        echo "default_args(): \$b : $b <br>";
        echo "default_args(): \$c : $c <br>";
    }

    // this function accepts an array
    function expects_array($a) {
        echo "<hr>";
```

---

[8]This makes sense because how would the program know that an argument was dropped at the beginning? This would require telepathy on the part of the function, and this is not yet implemented in PHP. Perhaps in the next version.

```
        foreach ($a as $k => $v) {
            echo "expects_array(): $k : $v <br>";
        }
    }
?>
<html>
<head>
<title>PHP Functions - Arguments</title>
</head>
<body bgcolor="#ffffff">

<?
    // no_default_args() expects 3 arguments
    no_default_args("foo", "bar", 20);
    no_default_args(10, 48*23, 1.884e-23);
    // this one only passes in 2 args, but the function
    // expects 3 - a warning message is generated and
    // the last arg gets empty string
    no_default_args(1,2);

    // use the defaults
    default_args();
    // override the first two defaults, use the third default
    default_args("foo","bar");

    // create an array to pass into expects_array()
    $array = array(
        "one"   => "first",
        "two"   => "second",
        "three" => "third"
    );

    // pass in an array because that is what it expects
    expects_array($array);

    // pass in a string, yet it expects an array - warning message!
    expects_array("foo");
?>
</body>
</html>
```

As the comment implies, calling no_default_args() without three arguments generates a warning message. Calling expects_array(), a function that expects its argument to be an array, with an argument that is not an array produces a warning message.

To try this program, load in either http://localhost/php/function3.php or www.opensourcewebbook.com/php/function3.php. The resulting error messages can be seen in Figure 12.9.

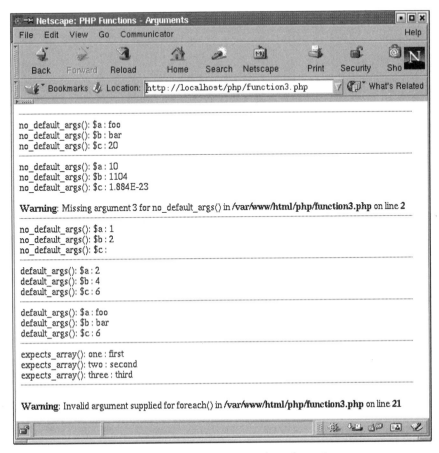

Figure 12.9   PHP `function3` example—function arguments

12.6 BUILT-IN PHP FUNCTIONS

PHP has a number of built-in functions. We sample a few, but there is no way we can cover all of them in this overview. See the documents (`www.php.net/manual/en/funcref.php`) or a suggested book for a complete list.

12.6.1 Important Functions

Let's start with two important functions: `print()` and `die()`.

print()

This function outputs a string that ends up being displayed in the browser. For example:

```
print "<h1>PHP Results</h1>";
print "$name : $age : $result[0]";
print "<hr>";
```

The print() function is essentially the same as the echo statement. These two do the same thing—they both produce the text "hello, world!":

```
echo "hello, world!";
print "hello, world!";
```

die()

PHP also has the die() function, which outputs a string and then exits the script. It is usually used to output an error message when something unexpected happens. For example:

```
if ($name == "") {
    die("the name field was not entered in the form");
}
```

12.6.2 Array Functions

PHP has a number of functions that can be used to manipulate arrays. Many of these have some similarities to Perl array functions—for instance, there are functions to push onto PHP arrays (array_push()), reverse an array (array_reverse()), sort an array (sort(), rsort(), and others), and many more.

The following is a description of some of the array functions. For an exhaustive discussion, see the documents.

array_push(), array_pop(), array_unshift(), and array_shift()

These four functions are similar to the Perl functions push(), pop(), unshift(), and shift(), as discussed in Chapter 4.

To add elements to the right side, use array_push(). Use array_pop() to remove the rightmost element.

To add elements to the left side, use `array_unshift()`. Use `array_shift()` to remove the leftmost element. Here is an example:

```
<?
    $languages = array("C", "C++", "Java");

    $lang1 = array_pop($languages);
    // $lang1 is: "Java"
    // $languages is now: ("C", "C++")

    array_push($languages, "Perl");
    // $languages is now: ("C", "C++", "Perl")

    $lang2 = array_shift($languages);
    // $lang2 is: "C"
    // $languages is now: ("C++", "Perl")

    array_unshift($languages, "PHP", "Python");
    // $languages is now: ("PHP", "Python", "C++", "Perl")
?>
```

sort() and rsort()

These functions sort an enumerated array in ASCII ascending order (`sort()`) and ASCII descending order (`rsort()`):

```
$names = array("Ryan", "Christian", "Madeline", "Reegen");

sort($names);
// $names is now: ("Christian", "Madeline", "Reegen", "Ryan")

$numbers = array(10, 3, 49, 4, 1, 30, 22);

rsort($numbers);
// $numbers is now: (49, 30, 22, 10, 4, 3, 1)
```

As you can see, these functions sort numerically if the elements are numeric. You can force these functions to sort in a specific way by using either SORT_REGULAR, SORT_NUMERIC, or SORT_STRING as the second argument:

```
rsort($numbers, SORT_STRING);
```

asort(), arsort(), ksort(), and krsort()

These functions sort associated arrays. The functions `asort()` and `arsort()` sort by value in ascending or descending order, respectively. The functions `ksort()` and `krsort()` sort by key in ascending or descending order, respectively:

```
$person = array(
    "firstname" => "John",
    "lastname"  => "Doe",
    "phone"     => "555-1234",
    "address"   => "123 Main St.",
    "city"      => "Chicago",
    "state"     => "IL"
);

asort($person);
// ascending by value
// $person is now: "address"   => "123 Main St."
//                 "phone"     => "555-1234"
//                 "city"      => "Chicago"
//                 "lastname"  => "Doe"
//                 "state"     => "IL"
//                 "firstname" => "John"

arsort($person);
// descending by value
// $person is now: "firstname" => "John"
//                 "state"     => "IL"
//                 "lastname"  => "Doe"
//                 "city"      => "Chicago"
//                 "phone"     => "555-1234"
//                 "address"   => "123 Main St."

ksort($person);
// ascending by key
// $person is now: "address"   => "123 Main St."
//                 "city"      => "Chicago"
//                 "firstname" => "John"
//                 "lastname"  => "Doe"
//                 "phone"     => "555-1234"
//                 "state"     => "IL"

krsort($person);
// descending by key
// $person is now: "state"     => "IL"
//                 "phone"     => "555-1234"
//                 "lastname"  => "Doe"
//                 "firstname" => "John"
//                 "city"      => "Chicago"
//                 "address"   => "123 Main St."
```

count()

The function `count()` returns the number of elements of its argument. If it is passed the value of a scalar variable, it returns 1. If it is passed the value of an array, it returns the number of things in the array:

```
$nums = array(2,4,6,8);
echo count($nums);
// echoes 4

$stuff = array(
    "one"   => "first",
    "two"   => "second",
    "three" => "third"
);
echo count($stuff);
// echoes 3

$name = "John Doe";
echo count($name);
// echoes 1
```

array_keys() and array_values()

These return the keys and the values of an associative array, like the Perl functions keys() and values():

```
$person = array(
    "firstname" => "John",
    "lastname"  => "Doe",
    "phone"     => "555-1234",
    "address"   => "123 Main St.",
    "city"      => "Chicago",
    "state"     => "IL"
);

$p_keys = array_keys($person);
// $p_keys is: ("firstname", "lastname", "phone", "address",
//             "city", "state")

$p_values = array_values($person);
// $p_values is: ("John", "Doe", "555-1234", "123 Main St.",
//                "Chicago", "IL")

$numbers = array(2, 4, 6, 8);
$n_keys = array_keys($person);
// $n_keys is:  (0, 1, 2, 3)

$n_values = array_values($person);
// $n_values is: (2, 4, 6, 8)
```

array_reverse()

This function returns the values of its arguments in reverse order. It does not return the keys or indices. As an example:

```
$person = array(
    "firstname" => "John",
    "lastname"  => "Doe",
    "phone"     => "555-1234",
    "address"   => "123 Main St.",
    "city"      => "Chicago",
    "state"     => "IL"
);

$new_person = array_reverse($person);
// $new_person is: ("IL", "Chicago", "123 Main St.", "555-1234",
//                  "Doe", "John")

$numbers = array(2, 4, 6, 8);
$new_numbers = array_reverse($numbers);
// $numbers is: (8, 6, 4, 2)
```

12.6.3 String Functions

PHP has a multitude of string functions. Here are but a few of them. There are far too many to talk about in detail, but keep this idea in mind: If you want to process text, there is probably a built-in function to do what you want to do.

printf()

PHP's `printf()` outputs a string that ends up being displayed in the browser. It works much like C's (and Perl's) `printf()` function:

```
printf "Integer: %d, Float: %6.2f", $i, $f;
```

PHP also has the `sprintf()` function, which returns a string in the format specified.

join()

The `join()` function joins array elements into a string:

```
$array = array(2, 4, 6, 8);
$string = join(":", $array);
// $string is now "2:4:6:8"
```

substr()

This function returns a portion of a string from a character index (zero-based), for a number of characters:

```
$string = "hello, world!";
$substring = substr($string, 2, 6);
// $substring is "llo, w"
```

trim()

The `trim()` function removes whitespace from each end of a string and returns the result:

```
$string = "   hello, world!\n\n\n";
$string2 = trim($string);
// $string2 is "hello, world!"
```

12.6.4 Other Functions

PHP has a large number of built-in functions. There is not enough space in this chapter to discuss them all. See the docs for more information (`www.php.net/manual/en/funcref.php`). Another helpful place to start that shows all the functions is `www.php.net/quickref.php`.

12.7 PHP AND MySQL

Now that we have covered the basics of PHP, we get to the good stuff. PHP provides built-in functions to connect to and query a MySQL database. This is one of the main benefits of using PHP. Many Web programmers turn to PHP for a seamless interface between their web pages and MySQL.

12.7.1 MySQL Functions, Part 1

We'll start with the basic PHP functions necessary to connect to the MySQL server, execute a simple database query, and display the result.

Most of these functions have default values for the arguments. One such default argument is the empty string for a password. That's just plain silly! We will not discuss the arguments in detail—if you are interested in all the details, check out `www.php.net/manual/en/ref.mysql.php`.

mysql_connect()—Connect to the MySQL Server

This function returns a MySQL link identifier on success or an error message on failure:

```
<?
    $mysql = mysql_connect("localhost", "apache", "LampIsCool")
        or die("could not connect to mysql");
?>
```

`mysql_close()`—Close a MySQL Server Connection
This functions closes the connection to the MySQL server:

```
<?
    mysql_close($mysql);
?>
```

`mysql_db_query()`—Execute a Query
This function executes a query for the specified database. It returns a result identifier on success or returns false on error. The result identifier is used to retrieve the result from the query:

```
$result = mysql_db_query($db, $query)
```

`mysql_num_rows()`—Return the Number of Rows Selected
This function returns the number of rows selected by a query:

```
<?  echo mysql_num_rows($result); ?>
```

`mysql_fetch_row()`—Fetch a Row as an Enumerated Array
This function returns the next row as an enumerated array. Each column is stored as an array element, indexing starting with 0:

```
<?
    $array = mysql_fetch_row($result);
    echo "First column:  $array[0]";
    echo "Second column: $array[1]";
?>
```

`mysql_errno()` and `mysql_error()`—Return MySQL Errors
The `mysql_errno()` function returns the error number of the most recent function call or 0 if there was no error. The `mysql_error()` function returns the error text of the most recent function call or the empty string if there was no error:

```
<?
    $result = mysql_db_query($db, $query)
        or die("query failed - " . mysql_errno() . ": "
             . mysql_error());
?>
```

Putting It All Together
Let's put all these functions together and create a simple example. To demonstrate connecting to a database and executing basic queries, we use the existing "books" database from Chapter 8.

This example connects to the MySQL server (mysql_connect()), queries the database (mysql_db_query()), reports any errors (mysql_errno() and mysql_error()), shows the number of rows that are returned by the query (mysql_num_rows()), and returns each row (mysql_fetch_row()). When the query is finished, the program closes the connection (mysql_close()).

```
<?
    // connect to the mysql server on localhost
    $mysql = mysql_connect("localhost", "apache", "LampIsCool")
        or die("could not connect to mysql");

    // execute the MySQL query, grab the result in $result
    $result = mysql_db_query("books", "SELECT * FROM book_information")
        or die("query failed - " . mysql_errno() . ": " . mysql_error());

?>
<html>
<head>
<title>PHP and MySQL</title>
</head>
<body bgcolor="#ffffff">
We executed: <b>SELECT * FROM book_information</b>
<hr>
We found <b><? echo mysql_num_rows($result); ?></b> rows.

<h3>Query result</h3>

<?
    //loop through each row
    while ($array = mysql_fetch_row($result)) {
        // foreach column in the row
        foreach ($array as $f) {
            print "$f :: ";
        }
        print "<hr>";
    }
?>

</body>
</html>
<?
    // we are all done, so close the MySQL connection
    mysql_close($mysql);
?>
```

To see the result of this program, go to either http://localhost/php/mysql1.php or www.opensourcewebbook.com/php/mysql1.php. The result can be seen in Figure 12.10.

The output in mysql1.php is displayed, after a fashion, but we can do better by putting it in a table. We show only the ISBN, the author, and the

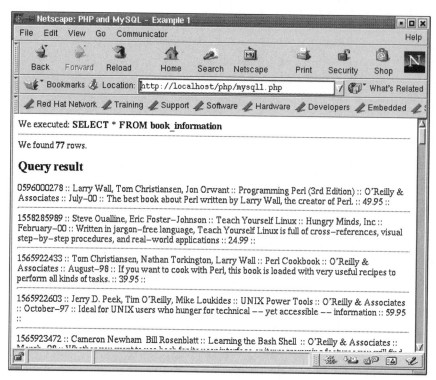

Figure 12.10   PHP `mysql` example 1

title by indexing into the array. Here are the contents of `/var/www/html/php/mysql2.php`.

```
<?
    // connect to the mysql server on localhost
    $mysql = mysql_connect("localhost", "apache", "LampIsCool")
        or die("could not connect to mysql");

    // execute the MySQL query, grab the result in $result
    $result = mysql_db_query("books", "SELECT * FROM book_information")
        or die("query failed - " . mysql_errno() . ": " . mysql_error());
?>
<html>
<head>
<title>PHP and MySQL - Example 2</title>
</head>
<body bgcolor="#ffffff">
<table border="1">

  <tr>
    <th>ISBN</th>
```

```
      <th>Author(s)</th>
      <th>Title</th>
  </tr>

<? while ($array = mysql_fetch_row($result)) : ?>
  <tr>
    <td><? echo $array[0]; ?></td>
    <td><? echo $array[1]; ?></td>
    <td><? echo $array[2]; ?></td>
  </tr>
<? endwhile; ?>

</table>
</body>
</html>
<?
    // we are all done, so close the MySQL connection
    mysql_close($mysql);
?>
```

To view the result of this program, go to either `http://localhost/php/mysql2.php` or `www.opensourcewebbook.com/php/mysql2.php`. The result can be seen in Figure 12.11.

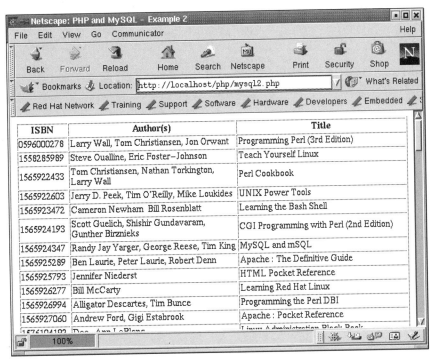

Figure 12.11 PHP `mysql` example 2

12.7.2 MySQL Functions, Part 2

`mysql_select_db()`—Select a Database

One might grow weary of specifying the database each time it's called; luckily the developers of PHP did also. This function selects a database that is used by all subsequent `mysql_query()` function calls. The function returns true if successful, false on error:

```
mysql_select_db("books")
    or die("select failed - " . mysql_errno() . ": " . mysql_error());
```

`mysql_query()`—Query a Selected Database

This function queries the currently selected database and returns true if successful, false on error:

```
mysql_query("SELECT * FROM books")
    or die("query failed - " . mysql_errno() . ": " . mysql_error());
```

`mysql_fetch_array()`—Fetch a Row as an Associative Array

This function returns the next row as an associative array with the table field names as the array keys and the table values as the array values. It returns the fetched row or false if there are no more rows. Each column is stored as an array element, where the field name is used as the key:

```
<?
    $array = mysql_fetch_array($result)
    echo "ISBN: " . $array["isbn"];
    echo "Title: " . $array["title"];
?>
```

`mysql_affected_rows()`—Return the Number of Affected Rows

This function returns the number of affected rows from the last INSERT, UPDATE, or DELETE MySQL query:

```
<?
    $result = mysql_query("DELETE FROM books WHERE isbn = '0596001320' ");
    echo "This should be 1: " . mysql_affected_rows($mysql);
?>
```

`mysql_free_result()`—Free the Result Memory

This function frees the memory used by the result. If you do not call this function, all the memory used by the result is deleted when the script finishes running. This function is needed only if you are concerned about memory as your script is running:

```
<?
    mysql_free_result($result);
?>
```

Putting It All Together, V2.0

As a third example of MySQL functions, we query the book database again. This example selects only three fields: `isbn`, `title`, and `price`. The result of the query is obtained by calling `mysql_fetch_array()`, which returns an associative array of data. The elements in the array are accessed by indexing with the key, as in `$array["isbn"]`.

The code can be found in /var/www/html/php/mysql3.php file or online at `http://localhost/php/mysql3.php` or www.opensourcewebbook.com/php/mysql3.php. This example is a bit long, so we talk about it in chunks. The code is first, followed by an explanation.

```
<?
    // connect to the mysql server on localhost
    $mysql = mysql_connect("localhost", "apache", "LampIsCool")
        or die("could not connect to mysql");

    // select the "books" database
    mysql_select_db("books")
        or die("select failed - " . mysql_errno() . ": " . mysql_error());

    // execute the MySQL query, grab the result in $result
    $result = mysql_query("SELECT isbn,title,price FROM book_information")
        or die("query failed - " . mysql_errno() . ": " . mysql_error());

?>
```

At the top of the file, the PHP code connects to the database, selects the proper database and makes our query (starts with `// execute . . .`).

```
<html>
<head>
<title>PHP and MySQL - Example 3</title>
</head>
<body bgcolor="#ffffff">
```

```
<table border="1">
  <tr>
    <th>ISBN</th>
    <th>Title</th>
    <th>Price</th>
  </tr>
```

That is the top of the HTML (pretty boring stuff), but this is more interesting:

```
<?
  // a different way to build the HTML, using print()
  // function calls within a while loop (echo could have
  // been used

  // $array is indexed as an associative array

  while ($array = mysql_fetch_array($result)) {
    print "  <tr>";
    print "    <td>" . $array["isbn"] . "</td>";
    print "    <td>" . $array["title"] . "</td>";
    print "    <td>" . $array["price"] . "</td>";
    print "  </tr>";
  }

  // free memory
  mysql_free_result($result);

  // we are all done, so close the MySQL connection
  mysql_close($mysql);
?>
```

The preceding PHP code loops through the result of the SQL query and prints the HTML for each row of data. After each row is printed, the memory is freed and the MySQL connection is closed. And finally, here is the ending HTML:

```
</table>

</body>
</html>
```

To see the result of this code, go to either this URL, http://localhost/php/mysql3.php, or www.opensourcewebbook.com/php/mysql3.php. The result can be seen in Figure 12.12.

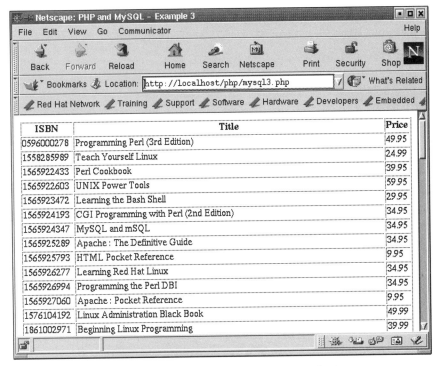

Figure 12.12   PHP `mysql` example 3

12.7.3 More PHP MySQL Functions

There are more MySQL functions that we did not talk about (see the docs for a complete list). Here are a few to pique your curiosity—see the documentation for the proper arguments.

- `mysql_change_user()`—Change the logged-in user.
- `mysql_create_db()`—Create a new database.
- `mysql_data_seek()`—Move the result pointer.
- `mysql_drop_db()`—Drop a database.
- `mysql_fetch_field()`—Get a field from a query result.
- `mysql_field_name()`—Get the name of a field.
- `mysql_field_table()`—Get the name of the table the field is in.
- `mysql_field_type()`—Get a field's type.

- `mysql_list_dbs()`—List the databases available on the server.
- `mysql_list_fields()`—List the fields in a result.
- `mysql_list_tables()`—List the tables in a database.

12.8 PROJECT

The PHP project is a simple journal-entry manager. Several PHP pages are implemented: a launching point, a page to add an entry, a page to view the last ten entries with the option of searching for matching entries, and a page to view the details about a specific entry. The journal entries are stored in a MySQL database and dynamically displayed in the PHP pages.

12.8.1 Journal MySQL Database

First, the database is created. The database is named `journal`, and there is one table named `entries`. The `entries` table has four fields:

- **id**—This is a unique integer to identify the entry that the user wants to see displayed; it is an `auto_increment` field (discussed later) and the key into the table.
- **date**—This is the date and time the item was entered into the table; we discuss this data type later.
- **title**—This is the title of the entry, a 60-character text field.
- **text**—This is the text of the entry, a `BLOB`.

The `id` is defined as an `auto_increment` integer. This is a special type of integer that does not need to be assigned a value when a row is entered in the table—it automatically takes the value of the most recent (or highest) value in the table plus 1.

For instance, when the first record is added, `id` is automatically assigned 1. When the second record is added, it is assigned 2, and so on for all the records. This data type ensures a sane unique value for each key entered into the table, and the programmer doesn't have to do any extra work to ensure that it receives a good value.

The `date` is defined as a `datetime` data type, which is a string that resembles `2002-04-19 07:36:09`, or the year-month-day hour:minute:second. Each record is stamped with the time that it was entered into the database, so the most recent entries can easily be grabbed by selecting them ordered by date in descending order. This field also tells the user when the entry was added. MySQL has many built-in commands to process dates, the most important of which is the `now()` function, which returns the current date/timestamp. Here is an example of the output of this function:

```
mysql> select now();
+---------------------+
| now()               |
+---------------------+
| 2002-04-20 13:14:24 |
+---------------------+
1 row in set (0.00 sec)
```

To create the database, log in as the **root** MySQL user:

```
$ mysql -uroot -p
Enter password:
Welcome to the MySQL monitor. Commands end with ; or \g.
Your MySQL connection id is 998 to server version: 3.23.41

Type 'help;' or '\h' for help. Type '\c' to clear the buffer.

mysql> CREATE DATABASE journal;
Query OK, 1 row affected (0.00 sec)

mysql> GRANT SELECT,INSERT,UPDATE,DELETE,CREATE
    -> ON journal.*
    -> TO apache@localhost;
Query OK, 0 rows affected (0.03 sec)

mysql> QUIT
Bye
```

Here we create the new database and grant the `apache` user privileges to create, insert, etc.

Now, in the `apache` persona, we can create the table. We could show you the MySQL commands necessary to create the table, but in the spirit of laziness, we have provided the database for you to create it from the command line:

```
$ cd /var/www/misc
$ mysql -uapache -pLampIsCool journal < journal.sql
```

Now that the database is created (including some helpful entries), we can work on the PHP pages to display it.

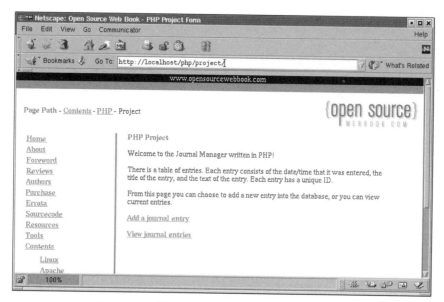

Figure 12.13   PHP project launch page

12.8.2 Project Pages

First, we have the launching page. This page contains a brief description of the journal manager, and two links. One link goes to the page to add an entry, and the other link goes the page to view the entries.

You can view this page by checking out `www.opensourcewebbook.com/php/project/` or `http://localhost/php/project/`. The result can be seen in Figure 12.13.

This page requires no PHP code because it is just text and two links, so there is no reason to show the code. However, if you want to see it, check out `/var/www/html/php/project/index.html`.

Next, we have the page to add an entry. To see the page, go to `www.opensourcewebbook.com/php/project/add/` or `http://localhost/php/project/add/`, shown in Figure 12.14.

The content of this file is in `/var/www/html/php/project/add/index.php`. Note that Apache comes configured in Red Hat 7 to serve up `index.php` in the `add` directory by default (if there is no `index.html`, the normal default).

The user is presented with a form in which they can add the new journal entry. Also, there is a link at the bottom of the page to view the journal entries. Supposedly, if the user requests this page, they want to add

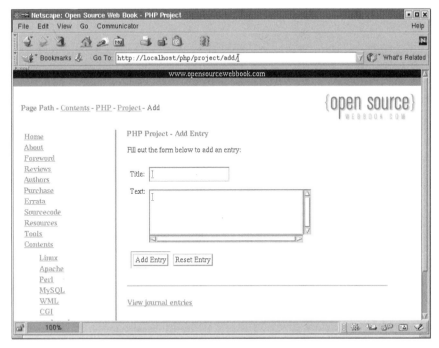

Figure 12.14   PHP poject add page

an entry, so let's add one. We enter the title "PHP Project" and the text "A journal entry for the PHP Project." Clicking the Add button posts the data to the same page (add/index.php, as specified in the <form> tag). A response is given so that the user knows the data was entered correctly, and then the form is displayed again so another entry can be added.

That's how it's supposed to work; now it's time to look at the code. First, we have the form:

```
<form action="/php/project/add/" method="post">
<table>
  <tr>
    <td>Title:</td>
    <td><input type="text" name="title" width="60">
  </tr>
  <tr>
    <td valign="top">Text:</td>
    <td><textarea name="text" cols="40" rows="5"></textarea></td>
  </tr>
  <tr>
    <td colspan="2">
```

```
        <input type="submit" value="Add Entry">
        <input type="reset" value="Reset Entry">
    </td>
  </tr>
</table>
</form>
```

The action is /php/project/add/, which is the index page in that directory, or in this case, the same file in which this form resides. Then two fields are created: a text field that is named title and a text area field named text. These two widgets are posted to our program, so we need to grab their values. Also, the method for this form is post, so our program must grab the posted data. It does so at the top of the file:

```
<?
    $title = $HTTP_POST_VARS["title"];
    $text  = $HTTP_POST_VARS["text"];
```

Here is the section of PHP code where the values in the title and text fields are put into variables named $title and $text.

This is followed by the code to insert the data into the table:

```
if ($title and $text) {
    // we have posted data -- first check its length
    // so no one nasty is posting a 10meg text value
    if (strlen($title) < 60 and strlen($text) < 1000) {

        // connect to the server
        $mysql = mysql_connect("localhost", "apache", "LampIsCool")
                    or die("could not connect to mysql");

        // select the "journal" database
        mysql_select_db("journal")
          or die("select failed - " . mysql_errno() . ": " .
              mysql_error());

        // insert into the table
        mysql_query("INSERT INTO entries (title,text,date)
                VALUES ('$title','$text',now())")
          or die("query failed - " . mysql_errno() . ": " .
              mysql_error());
    } else {
        // clear out the title and the text
        $title = "";
        $text  = "";
    }
}
?>
```

First, the code checks to see whether it has received the title and the entry text in posted data with `if ($title and $text)`. If so, it does a sanity check on the data, making sure that the length of the input data is not too big. Then, a connection is made to the server, selecting the `journal` database. We then insert the title, the entry text, and the current date/timestamp (the result of the `now()` function).

"Hey," you say to yourself, "isn't there a potential problem with how we are inserting?" We use `$title` in the `INSERT` command, but what if the user enters a string into the title widget such as "I'm hacking PHP code?" Won't the single quote in the string break the MySQL command because the string itself is contained in single quotes? Nope, because PHP automagically escapes single quotes. PHP escapes double quotes as well.

The last bit of interesting code in this page is found right above the form tag:

```
<?
    if ($title and $text) {
        print "<p>Entry added!  Fill out the form below to add another
            entry.";
        print "Or, click the link below to see the added entry.</p>";
    } else {
        print "<p>Fill out the form below to add an entry:</p>";
    }
?>
```

This code determines whether a title and an entry text have been given. If so, give the user a nice message saying that all is well. Otherwise, the original message is shown.

By the way, the preceding code could have been written as:

```
<?  if ($title and $text) : ?>
<p>Entry added!  Fill out the form below to add another entry.
Or, click the link below to see the added entry.</p>
<? else : ?>
<p>Fill out the form below to add an entry:</p>
<? endif; ?>
```

TMTOWTDI in PHP as in all things LAMP.

Now, we have the view page. To see the page, go to either www.opensourcewebbook.com/php/project/view/ or http://localhost/php/project/view/. This resembles Figure 12.15. The contents of the page can be found in the file /web/www/html/php/project/view/index.php. This page presents the user with an option to search the entries to narrow the search results. The fields searched for the data are `title` and `text`.

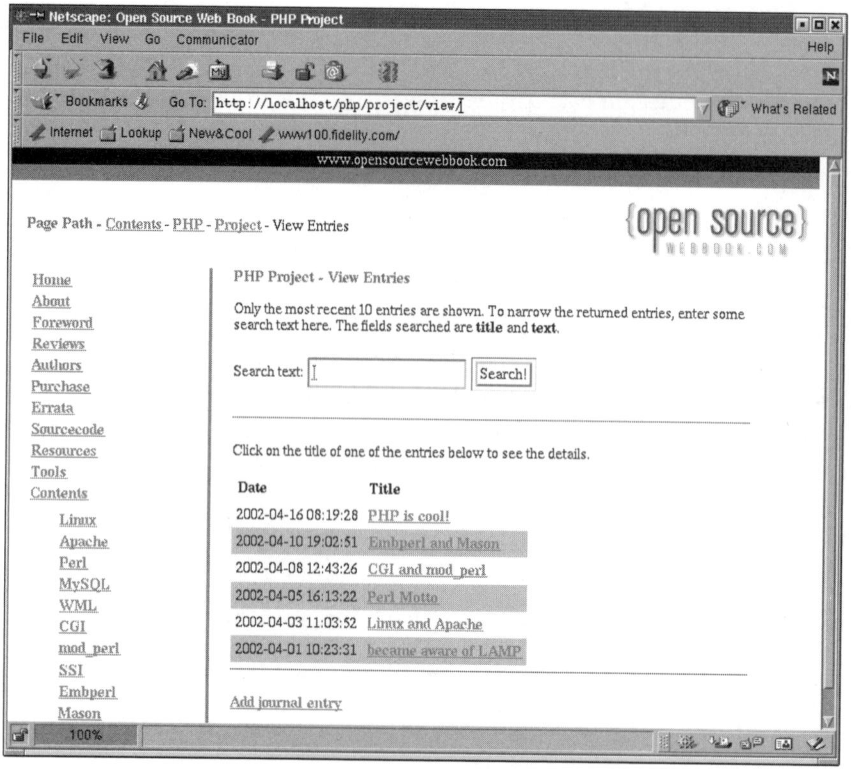

Figure 12.15 PHP project view page

Then a list of all entries matching the search string (or all the entries if there is no search string) is shown. Actually, only the ten most recent entries are shown, because eventually there might be hundreds of journal entries.

The data displayed is the entry's date and title. Clicking the title shows the details for the specific entry (we'll look at that page in a bit).

This code is found at the top of the file:

```
<?
$search = $HTTP_POST_VARS["search"];

// connect
$mysql = mysql_connect("localhost", "apache", "LampIsCool")
    or die("could not connect to mysql");

// select the "journal" database
mysql_select_db("journal")
    or die("select failed - " . mysql_errno() . ": " . mysql_error());
```

```
    if ($search) {
        $query = "SELECT id,date,title
                    FROM entries
                    WHERE title LIKE '%$search%'
                        OR text LIKE '%$search%'
                    ORDER BY date DESC
                    LIMIT 10";
    } else {
        $query = "SELECT id,date,title
                    FROM entries
                    ORDER BY date DESC
                    LIMIT 10";
    }
    // execute the MySQL query, grab the result in $result
    $result = mysql_query($query)
        or die("query failed - " . mysql_errno() . ": " . mysql_error());

?>
```

First, `$search` is assigned the search string (if any) entered into the search string widget. Then a connection is made to the server, and the `journal` database is selected.

If a search string is entered and stored in `$search`, a query is made that includes `WHERE title LIKE '%$search%' OR text LIKE '%$search%'`. This query uses the `WHERE ... LIKE` clause. If we say `WHERE title LIKE '%$search%'`, the `LIKE` pattern works just like a shell glob, where "%" is like "*". So, `%foo%` means "any text followed by `foo` followed by any text," much as we would say in the shell as *foo*.

Therefore, our `LIKE` clause reads as "where the field `title` matches the pattern `'%$search%'`, or any text followed by the value of the variable `$search` followed by any text." Or, more simply, match a title that contains our search string somewhere in it.

The search string in the `text` field is also checked. If either of those fields contains the search pattern, the item is selected.

This query returns the ten (with `LIMIT 10`) most recent (with `ORDER BY date DESC`) entries. If no search string is stored in `$search`, the query simply returns the ten most recent entries.

Later in the page you see this code:

```
<?
  if ($search) {
    print "<p>Search string: <b>" . $search . "</b></p>";
  }
?>
```

The purpose of this is to tell the user what search criteria they entered. It's just a nice habit to verify such things.

Then we see this code:

```
<? if (mysql_num_rows($result) > 0) : ?>
   .
   .
   .
<? else : ?>
<p>Sorry, no records found.  Please try again.</p>
<? endif; ?>
```

If the query returned at least one row of data (meaning the search returned some records), display the result (shown next). Otherwise, tell the user that no records were found. Here is the code to display the table (contained in the if block):

```
<p>Click on the title of one of the entries below to see the details.</p>
<table border="0" cellspacing="0" cellpadding="5">
  <tr>
    <th align="left">Date</th>
    <th align="left">Title</th>
  </tr>
<?
  $i = 0;
  while ($array = mysql_fetch_array($result)) {
    if ($i % 2 == 0) {
        $bgcolor = "#ffffff";
    } else {
        $bgcolor = "#cccccc";
    }
    print "  <tr bgcolor=" . $bgcolor . ">";
    print "    <td>" . $array["date"]  . "</td>";
    print '    <td valign="top"><a href="/php/project/view/entry/?id='
        . $array["id"] . '"><font color="#999966"><b>'
        . $array["title"] . '</b></font></a></td>';

    print "  </tr>";
    $i++;
  }
}
```

This prints the HTML to start the table and for the first row of the table. Then, the records that were returned by the SELECT are looped through, printing the HTML for the record, including different background colors for the even elements and the odd elements. The HTML for each entry includes a link to /php/project/view/entry/ passing the ID into that page. Then we see this code:

```
<?
    // free memory
    mysql_free_result($result);

    // we are all done, so close the MySQL connection
    mysql_close($mysql);
?>
```

Here the MySQL connection is cleaned up nicely. Finally, the following code is seen:

```
<?
    if ($search) {
        print "<p><a href=\"/php/project/view/\">
                <font color=\"#999966\">";
        print "<b>View all entries</b></font></a>";
        print "<hr>";
    }
?>
```

The purpose of this code is to provide a link to the user who entered the search string. This link goes to the view page with no search string, thereby showing all entries (or at least the last ten entries) without searching.

The final page to examine is the page displaying the detail of one of the entries. For an example, go to www.opensourcewebbook.com/php/project/view/entry/?id=6 or http://localhost/php/project/view/entry/?id=6. This resembles Figure 12.16. You can find this file online at /var/www/html/php/project/view/entry/index.php.

This page is the detail information for journal entry 6. It displays the date the entry was added, its title, and its text. At the top of this page is the following PHP code:

```
<?
    $id = $HTTP_GET_VARS["id"];

    // flag to tell us if the record was found
    $found = 0;

    if ($id > 0) {
        // we have an id number, so first
        // connect
        $mysql = mysql_connect("localhost", "apache", "LampIsCool")
            or die("could not connect to mysql");
```

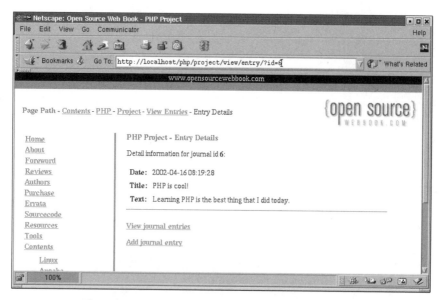

Figure 12.16   PHP project view entry page

```php
    // select the "journal" database
    mysql_select_db("journal")
        or die("select failed - " . mysql_errno() . ": " .
                mysql_error());

    // execute the MySQL query, grab the result in $result
    $result = mysql_query("SELECT title,text,date
                            FROM entries
                            WHERE id = $id")
        or die("query failed - " . mysql_errno() . ": " .
                mysql_error());

    // see if we found a record
    if (mysql_num_rows($result) == 1) {
        // grab the result in $array
        $array = mysql_fetch_array($result);

        // we found a record, so set the flag
        $found = 1;
    }

    // free memory
    mysql_free_result($result);

    // we are all done, so close the MySQL connection
    mysql_close($mysql);
}
?>
```

First, the ID number for the journal entry is stored in $id. Then, if there is an ID number and it is greater than 0, we connect to the server, select the journal database, and grab the title, text, and date from the record for the given id. Then, we make sure we have a record, and if so, the data is stored in $array and the flag is set to true. Then the connection is cleaned up.

Later in the page, there is this code:

```
<? if ($found) : ?>
<table border="0" cellspacing="0" cellpadding="5">
  <tr><th valign="top">Date:</th><td><? echo $array["date"]; ?></td></tr>
  <tr><th valign="top">Title:</th><td><? echo $array["title"];
                    ?></td></tr>
  <tr><th valign="top">Text:</th><td><? echo $array["text"]; ?></td></tr>
</table>
<? else :?>
<p>Sorry, id <b><? echo $id; ?></b> was not found.</p>
<? endif; ?>
```

This code checks to see whether a record was found. If so, a table is built displaying the date, title, and text values for that entry, each of which is stored in the variable $array. If the record was not found, the user is told, sorry, better luck next time.

12.9 SUMMARY

PHP is an excellent alternative to the Perl-based programs Embperl and Mason, doing similar things but not requiring Perl knowledge. PHP provides an excellent way to interface to databases, e-mail programs, forms, and more.

12.10 RESOURCES

Books

[Atkinson 01] Atkinson, Leon. *Core PHP Programming.*

[Greenspan+ 01] Greenspan, Jay, and Brad Bulger. *MySQL/PHP Database Applications.*

[Lea+ 00] Lea, Chris, et al. *Beginning PHP4.* PHP for beginners.

[Lerdorf 00] Lerdorf, Rasmus. *PHP Pocket Reference.* A handy little book to have for a quick reference.

[Meloni 02] Meloni, Julie C. *PHP Fast & Easy Web Development, Second Edition.*

[Welling+ 01] Welling, Luke, and Laura Thomson. *PHP and MySQL Web Development.* A thorough discussion of PHP and MySQL.

Web Sites

PHP central: `www.php.net`

Tons of PHP scripts and articles: `www.phpbuilder.com`

Lots of good information: `www.phpwizard.net`

Online PHP manual: `www.php.net/manual/en`

Bibliography

[Atkinson 01] Atkinson, Leon. *Core PHP Programming: Using PHP to Build Dynamic Web Sites, Second Edition.* Upper Saddle River, NJ: Prentice Hall PTR, 2001.

[Aulds 00] Aulds, Charles. *Linux Apache Web Server Administration (Linux Library).* Alameda, CA: Sybex, 2000.

[Boutell 96] Boutell, Thomas. *CGI Programming in C and Perl.* Reading, MA: Addison-Wesley, 1996.

[Christiansen+ 98] Christiansen, Tom, and Nathan Torkington. *Perl Cookbook.* Sebastapol, CA: O'Reilly, 1998.

[Conway 99] Conway, Damian. *Object-Oriented Perl.* Greenwich, CT: Manning Publications, 1999.

[DuBois+ 99] DuBois, Paul, and Michael Widenius. *MySQL.* Indianapolis, IN: New Riders, 1999.

[Engelschall+ 01] Engelschall, Ralf. *Apache Desktop Reference.* Boston: Addison-Wesley, 2001.

[Friedl 02] Friedl, Jeffrey F. *Mastering Regular Expressions.* Sebastopol, CA: O'Reilly, 2002.

[Greenspan+ 01] Greenspan, Jay, and Brad Bulger. *MySQL/PHP Database Applications.* New York: Wiley, 2001.

[Guelich+ 00] Guelich, Scott, Shishir Gundavaram, Gunther Birznieks, and Linda Mui. *CGI Programming with Perl, Second Edition.* Sebastapol, CA: O'Reilly, 2000.

[Hall+ 98] Hall, Joseph N., and Randal Schwartz. *Effective Perl Programming: Writing Better Programs with Perl.* Reading, MA: Addison-Wesley, 1998.

[Hatch+ 02] Hatch, Brian, James Lee, and George Kurtz. *Hacking Linux Exposed: Linux Security Secrets and Solutions, Second Edition.* New York: McGraw-Hill/Osborne, 2002.

[Himanen+ 01] Himanen, Pekka, Manuel Castells, and Linus Torvalds. *The Hacker Ethic.* New York: Random House, 2001.

[Hofstadter 99] Hofstadter, Douglas R. *Gödel, Escher, Bach: An Eternal Golden Braid, Twentieth Anniversary Edition*. New York: Basic Books, 1999.

[Kofler 99] Kofler, Michael. *Linux: Installation, Configuration, and Use, Second Edition*. Reading, MA: Addison-Wesley, 1999.

[Laurie+ 02] Laurie, Ben, Peter Laurie, and Robert Donn (Eds.). *Apache: The Definitive Guide, Third Edition*. Sebastapol, CA: O'Reilly, 2002.

[Lea+ 00] Lea, Chris, Wankyu Choi, Allan Kent, Ganesh Prasad, and Chris Ullman. *Beginning PHP4*. Chicago: Wrox, 2000.

[Lerdorf 00] Lerdorf, Rasmus. *PHP Pocket Reference*. Sebastapol, CA: O'Reilly, 2000.

[Lerdorf+ 02] Lerdorf, Rasmus, and Kevin Tatroe. *Programming PHP*. Sebastapol, CA: O'Reilly, 2002.

[McCarty 02] McCarty, Bill. *Learning Red Hat Linux: A Guide to Red Hat Linux for New Users, Second Edition*. Sebastapol, CA: O'Reilly, 2002.

[Meloni 02] Meloni, Julie C. *PHP Fast & Easy Web Development, Second Edition*. Stamford, CT: Premier Press, 2002.

[Meltzer+ 01] Meltzer, Kevin, and Brent Michalski. *Writing CGI Applications with Perl*. Boston: Addison-Wesley, 2001.

[Musciano+ 02] Musciano, Chuck, and Bill Kennedy. *HTML and XHTML: The Definitive Guide, Fifth Edition*. Sebastapol, CA: O'Reilly, 2002.

[Nemeth+ 01] Nemeth, Evi, Garth Snyder, Scott Seebass, and Trent R. Hein. *UNIX System Administration Handbook, Third Edition*. Upper Saddle River, NJ: Prentice Hall PTR, 2001.

[Nemeth+ 02] Nemeth, Evi, Garth Snyder, Trent R. Hein, and Adam Boggs. *Linux Administration Handbook*. Upper Saddle River, NJ: Prentice Hall, 2002.

[Niederst 02] Niederst, Jennifer. *HTML Pocket Reference, Second Edition*. Sebastapol, CA: O'Reilly, 2002.

[Powers+ 02] Powers, Shelley, Jerry Peek (Eds.), with Tim O'Reilly, Mike Loukides, Laurie Petrycki. *Unix Power Tools, Third Edition*. Sebastapol, CA: O'Reilly, 2002.

[Raggett+ 97] Raggett, Dave (Ed.), with Jenny Lam, Ian Alexander, and Michael Kmiec (Contributors). *Raggett on HTML 4, Second Edition*. Reading, MA: Addison-Wesley, 1997.

[Raymond+ 97] Raymond, Eric S., and Bob Young. *The Cathedral and the Bazaar: Musings on Linux and Open Source*. Sebastopol, CA: O'Reilly, 1997.

[Schilli 99] Schilli, Michael. *Perl Power!: A JumpStart Guide to Programming with Perl 5*. Reading, MA: Addison-Wesley, 1999.

[Schneier 00] Schneier, Bruce. *Secrets and Lies: Digital Security in a Networked World.* New York: Wiley, 2000.

[Schwartz+ 01] Schwartz, Randal L., and Tom Phoenix. *Learning Perl: Making Easy Things Easy and Hard Things Possible, Third Edition.* Sebastapol, CA: O'Reilly, 2001.

[Siever 00] Siever, Ellen (Ed.), with Jessica P. Hekman, Stephen Figgins, and Stephen Spainhour. *Linux in A Nutshell: A Desktop Quick Reference, Third Edition.* Sebastapol, CA: O'Reilly, 2000.

[Stein 97] Stein, Lincoln D. *How to Set Up and Maintain a Web Site, Second Edition.* Reading, MA: Addison-Wesley, 1997.

[Stein 98] Stein, Lincoln. *Official Guide to Programming with CGI.pm.* New York: Wiley, 1998.

[Stein 99] Stein, Lincoln, and Doug MacEachern. *Writing Apache Modules with Perl and C.* Sebastapol, CA: O'Reilly, 1999.

[Stein 01] Stein, Lincoln D. *Network Programming with Perl.* Boston: Addison-Wesley, 2001.

[Thomas+ 02] Thomas, Deepak, et al. *Professional PHP4 Programming.* Chicago: Wrox, 2002.

[Torvalds+ 01] Torvalds, Linus, and David Diamond. *Just for Fun: The Story of an Accidental Revolutionary.* New York: HarperBusiness, 2001.

[Wainwright+ 02] Wainwright, Peter, with Afrasiab Ahmad, Michael Link, and Poornachandra Sarang (Contributors). *Professional Apache 2.0.* Chicago: Wrox, 2002.

[Wall+ 00] Wall, Larry, Jon Orwant, and Tom Christiansen. *Programming Perl, Third Edition.* Sebastapol, CA: O'Reilly, 2000.

[Welling+ 01] Welling, Luke, and Laura Thomson. *PHP and MySQL Web Development.* Indianapolis, IN: Sams, 2001.

[Welsh+ 99] Welsh, Matt, Matthias Kalle Dalheimer, and Lar Kaufman. *Running Linux, Third Edition.* Sebastapol, CA: O'Reilly, 1999.

[Yarger+ 99] Yarger, Randy Jay, George Reese, and Tim King. *MySQL and mSQL.* Sebastapol, CA: O'Reilly, 1999.

Index

A

@ character, array names beginning with, 64

Access, and files ending in .wml, 134

Access control
  with .htaccess, 50–55
  mod_perl and enhancement of, 272
  and mod_perl programming, 243

AccessFileName directive, 43

access_log, 254, 272

Accounts, Linux, 18–19

a.cgi, mod_perl used for executing, 232–233

a.cgi program, 6

action= form attribute, 387

$action, 366

address field, in manufacturers table, 304

Advanced Package Tool (APT), 12

age.cgi, 223

Age information
  before adding new entry, *228*
  after adding new entry, *229*

age_information table, 223
  in MySQL, 112
  records in, 124

AIDE program, 30

Aliased commands, 27

AllowOverride directive, 190

Ampersand (&), in format of query string, 208

and operator, in PHP, 391

-a option, for building WML files in directory, 136

Apache, xxix, xxviii, xxx, 10, *34*, 37, 130, 187, 264, 310, 374
  configuration files, 271
  configuration of, 39–40, 190–191, 355–356
  Embperl and configuration of, 289–291
  EmbperlObject and configuration file in, 311
  functionality added to normal logging phase of, 268
  and HelloWorldPerl module, 245
  Mason and configuration of, 334–335
  modifying default configuration, 39–40
  mod_perl and configuration of, 233–234, 235
  and note about mod_perl, 246
  and PerlLogHandler lines, 272
  and PHP, 379
  and root account, 19
  Server Side Includes processed by, 277
  and SSI configuration, 278
  starting, stopping, and restarting, 36–39
  versatility with, 55
  welcome page, *36*
  and WML chapter, 134

Apache::Constants module, 244

Apache::DBI, 328

Apache environment variables, Mason access to, 338

Apache log files and access control with .htaccess, 50–55

Apache::PerlRun, 242–243

Apache::Registry, 231, 235–237, 241

Apache::Request, 249–251, 287

Note: Italicized page locators refer to figures.

437

Apache security, 41–45
  access to local documentation, 42
  disable CGI programs, 45
  disallow directory indexes, 44
  disallow public_html web sites, 42
  disallow symbolic links, 44
  .htaccess, 43
  proxy server warning, 44–45
  reload configuration file, 45
  remove online manuals, 41–42
  server-status and server-info removal, 43
  set user and group, 41
Apache Server Side Includes, 272
Apache::Session, 332
apache user
  and DBI module, 123
  mysql database, 120, 121
  permission granted to, 256
  privileges with PHP pages, 421
Apache Web Server, 5, 33–55, 231
Apache web site creation, 46–49
Applets, 4, 9
Application Program Interface (API), 109
apt-get mechanism, 12
$arg, 374
<%args> tag, 350–353, 358
%ARGS, posted data handled with, 343–344
<%args ... %args> tag, posted data grabbed
    with, 344–348
Arguments
  concatenating with CGI.pm HTML
    shortcut, 200
  passing to PHP functions, 401–404
Arithmetic operators, Perl, 71–72
$array, 431
Array elements
  accessing, 65
  and Embperl commands, 292
array() function, 385, 386
Array functions, 66–67
  in PHP, 406–410
array_keys() function, in PHP, 409
array_pop() function, in PHP, 406
array-push() function, in PHP, 406
array_reverse() function, in PHP, 409–410
Arrays
  associative, 67, 384, 386, 396, 397, 416
  enumerated, 384, 385, 396, 397, 407, 412

array_unshift() function, in PHP, 406
array_values() function, in PHP, 409
Array variables, 64–66
  files read into, 97
  reading input into, 94
Arrow notation, methods invoked with, 105
arsort() function, in PHP, 407
asort() function, in PHP, 407
Assignable lists, 106
Assignment operator (=), 73
Associative arrays, 67
  fetching row as, 416
  in PHP, 384, 386, 396, 397
Asterisk (*)
  and navigation bar definition, 153
  and SELECT command, 115
  as wildcards, 26, 159
Attributes
  for multiple cells, 159
  in navigation bar definition, 153
  tag, 172
%attributes variable, 172
Authentication
  and Embperl, 287
  and mod_perl, 243, 272
$(author) variable, in WML template file, 141
Autodecrement operator (–), 75
auto_increment integer, 420
Autoincrement operator (++), 75
awk, 28, 57, 87

B
Background color
  in Embperl project, 323
  and readability, 264, 323
  setting in CGI.pm program, 199
  in page tag, 148
  in WML template files, 140–141, 142
Backquotes, 104
Backticks, 64
  commands bracketed by, 195
Backups, in Linux, 14, 15
Bandwidth, xxvii
Banner ads, getting rid of, 30
Banners, 187
Bare page, with Mason project
    components, *360*
Base files, 311, 312

base.html, 311, 312, 313, 315, *316*, 325
bash, 22, 27
Benchmark module, 239, 240
Berners-Lee, Tim, 33n
better1.html, HTML file in, 166–167
BIGINT, in MySQL, 113
Binary Large Object (BLOB), 113, 114, 225
/bin directory, 28
bk2site program, 30
Blank lines
    after mail header, 271
    in CGI programs, 188, 189, 190, 192, 195
Body, with CGI program, 188, 189, 190
<body> tag, 142, 147, 148
book_information table, 256
BookListingMysql.pm, 265
book.pl program, flat file of book
        information in, 257
Books database
    book information processed in, 263–264
    and MySQL functions, 412–415
    and PHP mysql example 3, 417–418, *419*
/boot directory, 29
Borders, for tables, 159
.bottom component, in Mason project, 359,
        361, 363
bottom() function, 308, 309
bottom.html, 223, 259, 260, 266, 316
Brackets ([]), Embperl commands starting
        and ending with, 292
bread_crumb() function, 320
Bread crumbs, *179*
Bread crumb strings, 320, 325
Bread crumb text, 319
$bread_crumb_text, 320
Bread crumb trails, 176
    generating for www.opensourcewebbook.
        com, 180–181
    in Mason project, 358
break, in PHP switch statement, 393
Browsers, 3, 35, 189
BSD, xxxii, xxxiii
BSD-type Open Source license, 33
Buffer overflows, 221
Bugs, xxix
    security, xxxi
    and template files, 165
Bugtraq, xxxi

Built-in functions in PHP, 405–411
    array functions, 406–410
    important functions, 405–406
    string functions, 410–411
button(), for form widget creation, 218
Byte code, 60
bytes_sent(), 270

C
C, 61, 377, 382, 391
C++, 377, 382, 391
Caching, with Mason, 331
Camel Book, 57, 81, 106
Caret character (^), 83
Case sensitivity
    with PHP, 381
    and SQL commands/subcommands, 111
category field, in products table, 304
cd ~/bin command, 25
cd ./bin, 25
cd command, standard shortcuts, 25–26
Cells, for tables, 158
CERN, 33n
CGI. *See* Common Gateway Interface
cgi-bin, removing CGI scripts in, 218
cgi-bin directory, 190
CGI data, handling with mod_perl using
        Apache::Request, *251*
CGI.pm, 105, 187, *198*
    introduction to, 197–200
CGI.pm HTML shortcuts, 200–202
    and named parameters *versus* ordered
        arguments, 202
    nesting of, 201
    using, 200–201
CGI programming, 105
CGI programs
    disabling with Apache, 45
    downloading advice for, 188
    information received by, 202–216
    path information received by, 205–206
    posted form data received by, 206–216
    session information received by, 202–204
CGI script, and exec directive, 283
$CGIURL variable, 238
Character and string substitution phase
        (Pass 6), in WML, 137
Character classes, in Perl, 82–83

Characters, in Perl, 82
Character strings, in MySQL, 112
CHAR data type, in MySQL, 113
Check box, in posted form data, 211
checkbox(), for widget creation, 216
checkbox_group, for form widget creation, 218
check_man_id(), in Mason project, 364, 365
check_prod_id() function, in Mason, 367
Checks, for CGI/MySQL/DBI program, 226
chkconfig, as root, 110
chkconfig command, 27
chmod, 23
chomp() function, 95, 98, 126, 258
chomping, of returned newlines, 195
chown command, 23
chsh command, 22
city field, in manufacturers table, 304
Cleanup tags, in Mason, 372–373
CLI. *See* Command line interface
Client, and Apache log, 40
Client-server relationship, 10
Client-side browser, 133
Closed-source software, xxxiii
Closed systems, xxix
close() function, 97
Closing tags, in HTML, 170, 171
Cluster software, 18
cmp, 74
$cnt variable, in Embperl, 328
Code, spacing dialog inside, 223
$col, and dynamic table generation, 301, *303*
Colons, value separated by, 153
Color, background, 140–141, 142, 148, 199, 264, 323
Columns, 159
combined format, 40
combined output, 50
[$ Command Arguments $] Embperl command, 295–298
Command line interface, 15
    Linux used through, 20, *21*
Commands
    Embperl, 292–299
    and SSI, 277
Comment blocks, in Embperl, 295
Comments
    in hello, world program, 59
    in PHP, 382
    with WML, 144–146

comment style, 144
COM1, 3
Common Gateway Interface, 4, 122, 133, 188–190, *189*, 273
    Apache configuration, 190–191
    CGI/MySQL/DBI project, 223–230
    and CGI.pm, 197–200
    CGI.pm HTML shortcuts, 200–202
    for dynamic website creation, 306
    errors with programs in, 196–197
    execution, *232*
    first program with, 191–196
    form widget methods, 216–218
    information, *204*
    information received by CGI program, 202–216
    mod_perl *versus,* 231
    note about die(), 222
    path information, *206*
    security considerations, 218–222
Compare operator (=), 73, 74
Comparison operators, in PHP, 390
Complex data types, 107
Component class API, in Mason, 373
Components, in Mason, 335
Comprehensive Perl Archive Network, 45, 59, 105, 107, 328, 378
COM2, 3
Conditional constructs, 77–81, 337
Conditional expressions, and SSI, 277
Conditional statements, Mason, *340*
config directive, 281, 284–285
Configuration file, reloading with Apache, 45
connect() method, 123, 124
content_type(), 244
continue statement, in PHP, 395
$_COOKIE, 390
Cookies
    controlling, 30
    distrust of, 221
Cool.html file, EmbperlObject example, 313, *314*
count() function, in PHP, 408
CPAN. *See* Comprehensive Perl Archive Network
CPAN module, 106
cp command, 26
Crackers, 219, 220, 307, 355, 356

Cracking, 9
  hacking *versus,* xxx
CREATE DATABASE command,
      in MySQL, 111, 121
CREATE TABLE command,
      in MySQL, 112, 122
csh, 22
CUPS, 30
Curly braces ({ }), 69, 77
  for bodies of PHP constructs, 391
  in PHP multiline bodies, 382
Customization, with mod_perl, 231
CustomLog options, with Apache, 40
Custom tags, 170, 184
CVS, xxxii, xxxiii

D
Daemons, 23, 33
Darwin, xxxiii
Dash (-), for specifying a range, 82
Data
  checking for security
          reasons, 219–220
  and table joins, 127
Database handle, 123
DataBase Independent interface, 109,
      122–127, 130
  hooking into CGI program, 223
  ISBN retrieval with, 262–263
  and Mason project, 368
Databases
  connecting to in Perl, 122
  loading and dumping, 129–130
  in MySQL, 111
  querying selected, 416
  and SELECT command, 115
  selecting, 416
Data directory, Mason, 335
$DATA_LOCAL variable, 285
Data types
  examples in PHP, 384
  in MySQL, 112
  in PHP, 383
DATE, in MySQL, 113
Date
  and Apache log, 40
  display of in CGI program, *194*
  and SSI, 277
$date, 201

date field, in journal MySQL database, 420
DATE_GMT variable, and echo
      directive, 279
DATE_LOCAL variable, and echo
      directive, 279
DATETIME, in MySQL, 113
$dbh value, 224, 259
DBI. *See* DataBase Independent interface
DBI method, 123
DBI module, for book listing, 265
D character, and standard input, 95
dd(), in CGI.pm, 200
Debian GNU/Linux, 12
DECIMAL, in MySQL, 113
Decrement operators (--), in Perl, 75–76
Default arguments, providing to functions
      in PHP, 402
defaults(), for form widget creation, 218
Default values, for variables assigned with
      posted data, 212
<define-tag> macro, 170
DELETE command, in MySQL,
      118–119, 122
DELETE MySQL query, 416
DELETE query, and DBI, 122
DESCRIBE command, in MySQL, 114, 122
description field, in products table, 304
Design, of navigation bars, 152
/dev directory, 29
df command, 26
dhandlers (or default handlers), and Mason,
      374, 375
die, scripts and, 123, 124
die() function, 96
  and book database, 258
  note about, 222
  in PHP, 405, 406
  and %args ... %args tag, 344, 347
"Digital divide," xxvii
Digital Millennium Copyright Act
      (DMCA), 16
digit character (\d), 83
Directory directive, 290
Directives, with Server Side Includes, 277
Directories
  for mod_perl programs, 233
  searching with WML, 138
Directory indexes, disallowing in Apache, 44
Directory listing sample, *23*

Directory permissions, and server errors, 197
disconnect() method, 123
Disk Druid, 17
DIVERSION, 163
Diversion filter phase (Pass 5), in WML, 137
Diversions, 162–164, 182
divert Name, 163
dl(), in CGI.pm, 200
DNS, 55
do ... while loop, in PHP, 395
doctype, 48
DOCUMENT_NAME variable, and echo directive, 279
Document Object Model (DOM), 6
Document root, 34, 47
DOCUMENT_URI variable, and echo directive, 279
Dollar sign ($), 61
    and non-root user, 19
    variable names in PHP beginning with, 382
Dotfile generator, 22
Dotfiles, 22
DOUBLE, in MySQL, 113
Double parentheses, with wml::fmt::xtable, 158
Double quotes, 64, 196
    in Perl, 178
    and PHP, 425, 383
    string literals created with, 63
    and WML, 138, 140
[do]...[$ until condition $] metacommand, in Embperl, 299
Downloaded CGI programs, avoiding, 218–219
-DROOT~, 176
DROP TABLE command, in MySQL, 112
Dual booting, 15
du command, 26
Dumping databases, 130
dvipdf, xxxii
Dynamic clickable menus, 6
Dynamic content, 4
Dynamic data, serving up, 6
Dynamic HTML, 6, 229
Dynamic HTML web pages, mod_perl and creation of, 272

Dynamic web pages, 187
    and embedded HTML, 7
    mod_perl and creation of, 231
    PHP and creation of, 377
Dynamic web sites, 133
    and structural portion of LAMP, 130

E
echo directive, 279–*280*
echo PHP statement, 380
echo statement, 406
else part, 217
emacs, xxxii, xxxiii, 379
e-mail, xxx, 271
    PHP and sending of, 377
    and web page traffic, 272
Embedded content, 4
Embedded HTML, serving up content with, 7–8
Embedded programming, approaches to, 7
Embedded programs, for building HTML, 307
Embedded web sites, and structural portion of LAMP, 130
Embperl, 7, 8, 122, 133, 174, 184, 286, 287–329, 378, 379
    and Apache configuration, 289–291
    commands in, 292–299
    "hello, world!" with, 291, *292*
    installing, 288–289
    introduction to, 287
    Mason compared with, 332–333, 375
    and persistent database connections, 328
    PHP as alternative to, 431
    posted data and %fdat, 299–301
    project with, 304–327
    $row and $col, 301–303
    sample list of variables in, 328–329
    session handling with %udat and %mdat, 328
    XML and XSLT support with, 329
Embperl commands, 292–299
    [$ command arguments $], 295–298
    [! Perl Code !], 294–295
    [+ Perl Code +], 292–294
    [− Perl Code −], 294
    [# some text #], 295
    [$ while $], 299
EMBPERL_DEBUG, 290

EmbperlObject, 306
Embperl project, 304–327
  CGI used in, 306
  consistent look and feel created
      in, 305–306
  embedded programs for building HTML
      in, 307–310
  hard-code HTML files, 306
  HTML::EmbperlObject used in, 310–318
  mod_perl used in, 306–307
  problem defined for, 304–305
  product filter in, 319–327
  WML used to create HTML files, 306
embperl_template.pl, contents of, 307
Empty strings, 178
Empty string values, 322, 323
__END__ file, markers added to, 144
end_form(), for widget creation, 216
end_html() method, in CGI.pm program, 199
__END__ marker, 145
End-of-diversion marker, 163
End Of HTML (EOHTML), 196
End-of-line, 144
Engelschall, Ralf, 133
entries table, in journal MySQL
      database, 420
Enumerated arrays
  fetching row as, 412
  in PHP, 384, 385, 396, 397
  sorting in ASCII ascending/descending
      order, 407
Environment variables, 24, 25
  displaying in HTML table, 302
  displaying with Embperl's while
      command, 298
  UNIX, 24, 25
$_ENV variable, 390
eperl, 136–137, 174–179
.epl extension, 289
Equal sign (=), in format of query
      string, 208
Equal-tilde (=~), 81
Equivalence operator (==), 73
$error, 371
Error handler, rolling, 222
Errors, 37
  fixing, 38
  server, 190, 192

$error variable, 369, 370
Escape characters, in PHP, 383
$escmode, 320, 329
$escmode = 0; statement, 309
/etc directory, 29
/etc/init.d directory, 29
/etc/X11 directory, 29
etherape program, 30
Ethernet, 3
Examples
  Embperl, 291
  EmbperlObject, 312, 313, 314
  Mason, 335–336
  PHP, 379–380
Exclamation point character (!), 94, 208
.exe, xxviii
+ExecCGI option, and Apache::Registry, 236
exec directive, 283–284
exec.html, 283
@execute_args, 322
execute() method, 125, 126
expects_array() function, 404
Expression modifiers, in Perl, 100
Extensible Markup Language, 8–9
  Embperl integrated with, 329
  PHP combined with, 378

F
False values, in Perl, 73
FAT filesystem, 16
%fdat, 323, 325
  posted data and, 299–301
  using, 301
fetchrow() method, 125
@ffld variable, in Embperl, 328
FH variable, 96
Fields, in MySQL, 111
__FILE__, 145
File contents, and SSI, 277
filefield(), for form widget creation, 218
Filehandles, 96, 98
File information, with WML,
      143–144
File I/O, with Perl, 93–98
Filenames
  distrust of, 221
  and SSI, 277
__FILE__ , 136, 143

File permissions
   changing, 23
   and server errors, 197
Files *.html directive, 290
Files, and Perl, 95–98
Files directive, 43, 134, 356
file.shtml, 282
File slurp, 97
Filesystem Hierarchy Standard, 13
Filters, with Mason, 331
finish() method, 125
fips, 16
Firewalled router, 20
Firewalls, 20, 55
Firewire, 3
flastmod directive, 282, *283*
Flat-file solutions, for small databases,
   254–255
FLOAT, in MySQL, 113
Floating points, in MySQL, 113
Floats, 63, 383
Flow-control constructs,
   in Perl, 77–81
   in PHP, 377, 391–398
_footer component, 375
Footer file, in Mason, 348, 349
Footers, 165, 166
   for base.html, *316*
   in "hello, world!", 138, 139
   and navigation bar definition, 153
   in WML template file, 375
footer2 component, in Mason, 352
foreach loop, 80–81, 248
   in Mason, 341
   in PHP, 395–398
Foreach metacommand, in Embperl, 295
for loop, 79
   in Mason, 340
   in PHP, 395
Form data
   processing with PHP, 378
   subroutines for processing,
      224–225
Forms interfaces, 187
Forms, PHP data processing submitted
   via, 386–387
<form> tag, and PHP project
   add page, 423

Form widgets, *210*, 216–218
freetable, warning about tables generated by,
   157, 160, 161
FrontPage, 378, 379
fsize directive, 281, *283*, 284
Function arguments, in Perl, 90–93
Function calls, and Embperl commands,
   292
Function names, in PHP, 381
Functions
   array, 66–67
   hash, 70–71
   string, 107
   user-defined, 87

G
Galeon, 3
Game-boxes, 11
GET, 247
get() function, 238
GET method, 208, 388, 389
get_remote_host(), 270
$_GET variable, 390
Ghostview, xxxii
Gimp, xxix
gkrellm program, 30
Global variables, 89
   caution in use of, 244
   in ill-considered mod_perl
      CGI programs, 242
   in Mason, 336, 337, 373
   and mod_perl programs using
      Apache::Registry, 237
   in PH version 4.1.0, 390
Gnome, 18, 20
Google, 25, 38
GPL license listing, xxx
graceful option, 38
GRANT command, 122, 256
Graphical user interfaces (GUI), 18
Graphic designers, 7
   and Mason, 332, 333
grep command, 26, 87
Groups
   setting in Apache, 41
   and UNIX, 22
GUI configuration programs, with
   Red Hat, 30–31

H

Hacking, cracking *versus,* xxx
HAKMEM, xxx
HandleCGIData.pm, 246
HandleCGIData2.pm, 250
handle_error(), 225, 226
handle_error subroutine, 224, 259
handler() function, 261, 266
handler() method, 244, 252, 269
handler() subroutine, 245, 247
Hard-coding HTML files, 306
Hash character (#), with Unix root
    accounts, 19
Hash elements, and Embperl
    commands, 292
Hashes, creating, 68
Hash functions, 70–71
Hash variables, 67–69, 175
_header component, in Mason, 375
Header file, in Mason, 348
header() method, 105, 199
Headers, 35, 50, 165, 146, 166
    with CGI program, 188, 189, 190, 192
    in "hello, world!", 138, 144
    in navigation bar definition, 153
    referer information sent through, 221
    in tables, 156
<head> information, 223
<head> tag, in wml::std::page, 147
head.wml, 140
"Hello, world!", *49,* 59–60
    CGI program, 191–196, *192, 193, 194*
    with Embperl, 291, *292*
    with mod_perl, 237
    with PHP, *380*
    with pure mod_perl, 243–244, *245*
    version with WML, 138, 139, *140*
    version 2 with WML, 142
    version 3 with WML, 144–146, *147*
hello.cgi, creating, 191
hello.php file, 379–380
hello2.cgi program, 192
HelloWorld package, 244
HelloWorld.pm module, 245
here document, 195, 196, 215, 216, 223,
    229, 245, 260
hidden(), for form widget creation, 218
Hidden fields, distrust of, 220

High-level macro construct expansion phase
    (Pass 2), in WML, 136
hitit.pl program, 237, 241
hitit2.pl program, 239, 240, 241
<hN> tags, with wml::std::toc, 149, 150
/home directory, 28
h1() method, 229
    in CGI.pm program, 199, 200
<h1> tag, 375
Horizontal rule, 309
$host, 201
Hostname
    and CGI.pm program, 201
    display in CGI program, *194*
hr() method, in CGI.pm program, 198, 199
htaccess directive, uncommented, 43, 51
.htaccess, 43, 50–55, 190
h3() method, in CGI.pm, 300
HTML
    for components2.html, 352
    embedded programs used for building, 307
    and eperl, 174, 175, 176, 178
    for navigation bar rendering, 154
    PHP embedded into, 378–379
    SSI and embedding executable
        code within, 286
    and text diversion filter, 162
    with wml::std::page, 148
    in wml::std::toc, 150
HTML code, 137, 138
HTML editors, 378, 379
HTML::Embperl, 287, 289, 299, 300, 377
HTML::EmbperlObject, 310–311
.html extension, 289, 379
HTML files
    for Apache, 34
    building for WML, 135–136
    and dynamic data, 6
    hard-coding, 306
    Server Side Includes embedded in, 277
    and static data, 5
    %args tag in, 346
HTML lists, methods for generation of, 204
HTML::Mason, 331, 333, 377
HTML pages, Mason and Embperl and, 332
HTML tables, cells formatted in, 158
<html> tag, in wml::std::page, 147
HTML tags, closing tags required by, 171

httpd file, location of, 288
httpd.h file, location of, 288
httpd PIDs, 37
$HTTP_GET_VARS, 388, 389
%http_headers_out, in Embperl, 329
$HTTP_POST_VARS, 388, 389
HTTP requests, 3, 35
HTTPS, 53
h2() method, in CGI.pm, 200
HyperText Transfer Protocol (HTTP), 33

I
ICANN, 55
$id, 431
IDENTIFIED BY clause,
        in SQL command, 121
id field, in journal MySQL database, 420
if condition, PHP syntaxes for, 391–392
ifconfig, netstat command, 27
if directive, 285
if metacommand, in Embperl, 295, *296*
if statement, 57, 77, 100
    in Mason, 339
    in Mason project, 363
    in PHP, 394
    widgets.cgi modified by, 213
image_button(), for form widget creation, 218
Image rollovers, 6, 9, 151
Images, 4
images subdirectory, of HTML root
        directory, 169
$(IMG), 169
imgbase attribute, in navigation
        bar definition, 153
imgstar, in navigation bar definition, 153
Immunix, 13
#include, 143, 144
include directive, 280–281, *282*
Include directories, 170
include (-I), in WML, 138
Increment operators, in Perl, 75–76
index.html file, 47, 313, 314
    and Mason top-level components, 374
    simple, 51
Infinite loops, preventing, 328
Informix, 109
<info> tag, 143, 144, 146, 179
info.wml file, 143

<%init> block, 365
    in Mason, 368
    in Mason project, 358
<%init ... %init> tag, in Mason, 353–354
<%init> section, and top-level
        components, 374
Initialization tags, in Mason, 372
Inner HTML, and templates, 163
Input, reading with, 106
INSERT command, in MySQL,
        114–115, 122
INSERT INTO, 115
INSERT MySQL query, 416
INSERT query
    and DBI, 122
    SQL prepared for, 126
INTEGER, in MySQL, 113
Integers, 63
    in MySQL, 112
    in PHP, 383
International characters, 137
Internet, 9
    and Open Source programs, xxx
Internet address, 3
Internet protocol (IP), xxvii
Internet service provider (ISP), xxvii
int() function, 72
-I option, 136, 138
IP addresses, and Apache log files, 55
IP port numbers, 3
IP verification, and .htaccess file, 53
@isbn, ISBNs pushed onto, 262, 263
ISBNs, 266, 267
    and Apache::Request object, 261
    retrieving in books database, 262
$isbn variable, 266

J
Java programming language, 9, 61, 382, 391
Java applets, 4
JavaScript, 4, 6, 9, 154, 155
JavaScript preprocessing, distrust of,
        221–222
JavaServer Pages (JSP), 9
join() function, in PHP, 410
journal database, 425, 431
Journal MySQL database, 420–421
.jpg extension, 291

K

kbdconfig program, 31
KDE, 18, 20
Key, book_information created
    with, 256
Keys() function, 70, 409
killall command, 24, 38
killall foo, 24
kill command, 24, 38
kill -9 command, 38
Konquerer, 3
krsort() function, in PHP, 407, 408
ksh, 22
ksort() function, in PHP, 407, 408

L

LAMP, xxviii, xxxiii
    PHP within, 377
    programs, xxxii
    structural portion of, 130
Language notes, Embperl, 299
Language syntax, for PHP,
        381–404
LAST_MODIFIED variable, and echo
        directive, 279
LaTeX, xxxii, xxxiii
Left rail, 223, 260, 262
    for www.opensourcewebbook.com, 181
.leftrail component, in Mason project,
        358, 361, 363
_leftrail component, in Mason, 371
Legacy CGI scripts, mod_perl and
        speeding up of, 273
Less-than symbol (<), 96
LGPL license listing, xxx
libapreq package, 249
/lib directory, 28
Licenses, Open Source, xxix
li(), 200, 204
__LINE__, 136, 143, 145
% Lines, in Mason, 337
Link identifier, in MySQL, 411
Links, 3
    in Embperl, *293*
    to eperl web sites, 176
    in PHP project launch page, 422
    rolling over, 151
<link> tag, 172, 179

Linux, xxviii, xxix, xxxi, xxxii, 10, 11–31,
        109, 130, 278
    accounts, 18–20
    and Apache configuration, 190
    decisions about installation of, 15–16
    distributions, 11–13
    download and install, 14–15
    installation CD, 18
    partition sizes, 16–18
    and PHP, 379
    recommended partition sizes, *17*
    root user, 110
    security and, 20
    useful programs, 30–31
linuxconf program, 30
linuxconfig System, 31
Linux Documentation Project, 38
Linux Filesystem Standard, 13
Linux Security HOWTO, 9
Lists, in CGI.pm, 200
LiveScript, 4*n*
ln command, 26
Loading databases, 129
Local documentation, access to in Apache, 42
localtime() function, 201
Local variables, in Perl, 89–90
locate command, 26
Locations, and diversion filter, 137
Locked accounts, 41
LOG, in Embperl, 329
Log file, in MSQL, 110
Logging
    and Embperl, 287
    mod_perl and enhancement of, 272
    and mod_perl programming, 243
Logical and operator, 76
Logical and operator (&&), 76
    short-circuited nature of, 101, 102
Logical not operator (!), 76
Logical operators, in Perl, 76–77
Logical or operator (||), 76, 209
    short-circuited nature of, 101, 102
Logic operators, short-circuited, 101–103
Log monitoring program, 53
logrotate, 50
Log-watching program, 20
LONGBLOB, in MySQL, 114
LONGTEXT, in MySQL, 114

Looping constructs, 77–79
    embedding in Mason, 337
    in Embperl, 296
Looping statements, in Mason, *342*
Low-level macro construct expansion phase
        (Pass 4), in WML, 137
ls command, 26
LWP::Simple module, 238
Lynx, 3

M

Macros, creating in WML, 170–174
Mail header, 271
make capacity, of WML, 184
make-like command, 133
man command, 20, 25
Mandrake, 12
_man_form, in Mason project, 363–364,
        365, 368
man function, 24
man_id field, 304
man-k best guess at a useful function, 24
man -k command name, 20
man -k foo command, 25
man man command, 20, 25
man mysqldump, 130
man pages, 57
man strftime, 285
Manufacturer IDs
    in Mason, 370
    in Mason project, 361, 364, 366, *367*
Manufacturers, modifying in Mason
        project, 371
Manufacturers table in Embperl project,
        fields in, 304
Markup code fixup phase (Pass 7),
        in WML, 137
markup code splitting and output generation
        phase (Pass 9), in WML, 138
Markup code stripping phase (Pass 8),
        in WML, 137
Mason, 7, 8, 122, 133, 184, 286, 331–375,
        377, 378, 379
    Apache configuration with, 334–335
    component class API, 373
    components, *350*
    components in, 335, 348–356
    conditional statements, *340*

Embperl compared with, 332–333, 375
examples in, 335–336, *345*, *347*
and inline Perl sections, 336–343
installation of, 333–334
introduction to, 331
% lines in, *338*
looping statements in, *342*
PHP as alternative to, 431
posted data handled with %ARGS and
        %args in, 343–348
project, 357–371, *372*
request API with, 373
security with, 354–356
serving up components in, *355*
session handling with, 373
tags for initialization and cleanup in,
        372–373
top-level components in, 374–375
Mason Request object, API for, 373
matches_class() function, 91
$maxcol, in Embperl, 328
$maxrow, in Embperl, 328
maxsize, 225
%mdat, session handling with, 328
MEDIUMBLOB, in MySQL, 114
MEDIUMINT, in MySQL, 113
MEDIUMTEXT, in MySQL, 114
Memory, and Perl, 85–87
Metacommands, in Embperl, 295
Metainformation, 223
Metalanguage, 133
method="POST", 208
Methods, 104
Microsoft Windows, and dual booting
        with Linux, 15
MIME. *See* Multipurpose Internet
        Mail Extensions
mkdir command, 26
MLDBM. *See* Multi-Level DataBase Manager
/mnt directory, 29
mod_env.so file, location of, 288
Modify button, in Mason, 371
mod_perl, 6, 122, 133, 187, 188, 229,
        231–273, *265*, *269*, 329
    CGI data handled with, *248*
    CGI data handled with using
        Apache::Request, *251*
    CGIs turned into programs in, 235–243

configuration of, 233–235
embperl hooked into, 287
introduction to, 231–233
MySQL, DBI and mod_perl project,
    253–272
other capabilities with, 272
path information with, *253*
pure programming in, 243–253
speed examples in, 237–242
for web page creation, 306–307
mod_perl programs, turning CGIs into,
    235–243
$MODPERLURL, 238
Modular pages, with Mason, 331
Modules
    installing, 105, 106
    strict used in, 244
mod_user module, 42
Month, 374
more command, 27
Mouse clicks, and navigation bar
        definition attributes, 153
mouseconfig, 31
Mozilla, xxix, 33*n*, 50
[+ $msg +] Embperl command, 291
$msg, 224, 259, 291, 294
mSQL, 109
Multi-Level DataBase Manager,
        installing, 333
multiple attribute set, 212
Multiple disks, dual boot installation
        option, 16
Multipurpose Internet Mail
        Extensions, 193
munge_phone() function, 91
mv command, 26
Mv -i option, 26
my() function, 89
my() operator, 69
MySQL, xxviii, 109–130, *265*, *269*, 377
    administrative details with, 119–121
    CREATE DATABASE command
        in, 111
    CREATE TABLE COMMAND
        in, 112
    and Database Independent interface,
        122–127
    DELETE command in, 118–119

DESCRIBE command in, 114
implementing book program in, 255
INSERT command in, 114–115
insert commands in, 305
loading and dumping a database in,
    129–130
log file, 109
and PHP, 411–420
root user, 110
SELECT command in, 115–117
SHOW DATABASES command in, 111
SHOW TABLE command in, 112
table in, 227
table joins in, 127–129
tutorial, 109–122
UPDATE command in, 117–118
USE command in, 111
mysqladmin command, 120
mysql_affected_rows() function, 416
mysql_change_user() function, 419
mysql_close() function, 412, 413
MySQL commands, 110
mysql_connect() function, 411, 413
mysql_create_db() function, 419
mysql database, 119, 120
MySQL database, persistent connections
    to, 328
mysql_data_seek() function, 419
mysql_db_query() function, 412, 413
mysql_drop_db() function, 419
mysql_error() function, 412, 413
mysql_fetch_array() function, 416
mysql_fetch_field() function, 419
mysql_fetch_row() function, 412, 413
mysql_field_name() function, 419
mysql_field_table() function, 419
mysql_field_type() function, 419
mysql_free_result() function, 417
MySQL functions, Part 2, 416–418
mysql_list_dbs() function, 419
mysql_list_fields() function, 420
mysql_list_tables() function, 420
mysql_num_rows() function, 412, 413
mysql1.php, 413
mysql_query() function, 416
mysql_select_db() function, 416
MySQL server, 110, 258
    closing connection to, 412

MySQL server (*Continued*)
    connecting to, 411
    disconnecting from, 126
MySQL user, Linux user differentiated
        from, 120
my variables, arguments copied into, 91

N
$name, 326
name, in navigation bar definition, 153
nameage.cgi, contents of, 208–209
Named anchors, 149, 150
Named parameters, *versus* ordered
        arguments, 202
name field, 304
Namespace, 244
Name/value pairs, in Mason
        components, 351
National Center for Supercomputing
        Applications (NCSA), 33
navbar definition, 152–153
<navbar:epilog> tag, 153
navbar:jsfuncs, 154
<navbar:prolog> tag, 153
<navbar:render> tag, 154
navbar.wml, 154
Navigation bars, 151
    designing, 152
    rendering in WML, 154
neat program, 30
nessus program, 30
Nested if statements, 77
Netscape, 33n
Netscape/Mozilla, 3
Network connection, 3
Newline character ("\n"), 60, 192
    removing, 94, 95, 104
    and standard input in Perl, 93
new method, in Perl, 105
new() method, of Apache:: Request
        class, 261
newtitle.html, 318
    using title redefined in, *319*
*nix systems, xxxii, xxxiii
no_default_args function, 402, 404
Nondestructive functions, 67
Nondigit character (\D), 83
Nonspace character (\S), 83
Nonword character (\W), 83

<nostrip> tags, 138
now() function, 421
NTFS filesystem, 16
ntop program, 30
$NUM_BOOKS variable, 261
NUMERIC, in MySQL, 113
Numerical comparison, in Perl, 73–74
Numeric literals, 63

O
Object-oriented programming (OOP),
        introduction to, 104–106
Object-oriented techniques with Mason, 331
-o example.html option, 136
offline mode prompt, 199
-oi, sendmail invoked with, 271
OmniWeb, 3
<%once> block, in Mason project, 358
<%once ... %once> tag, in Mason, 354
Online manuals, removing
        in Apache, 41–42
open() function, 95, 96, 98, 258
Open Office, xxix
Open Source, 11, 377
    model, drawbacks with, xxx–xxxii
    software, description and philosophy of,
        xxviii–xxx
    web development, 9
Open Source Standard Query Language, 109
Open systems, xxix
Opera, 3, 50
Operators
    Perl, 71–77
    PHP, 390–391
/opt directory, 28
Options directive, disallowing Indexes
        in, 44
Oracle, 109
Ordered arguments, *versus* named
        parameters, 202
or die() code, in DBI, 125
or operator, 96, 391
oswb.wml, 170, 179
OS X, xxxii
OUT, in Embperl, 329
Outer HTML, and templates, 163
output.txt, 98
Owner, 22
Ownership, of file, 23

P

p(), in CGI.pm, 200
Packages, in HelloWorld, 244
PAGE_BODY, 182
<page> tag
  for WML file, 148
  with wml::std::toc, 150
$(page) variable, 176, 178, 180
Paragraph breaks, in CGI.pm, 200
Parallel printer port, 3
Parameters
  in Mason, 331
  passing to WML files, 140
param() function, 213, 299
param() method, 209
%params hash, posted data in, 247, 248
Params::Validate, installing, 333
Parentheses
  with wml::fmt::xtable, 158
  in WML template files, 140
Partition Magic, 16
Partition sizes, Linux, 16, *17*, 18
password_field(), for form widget
        creation, 218
Password files, creating, 51–52
Passwords, 9
  choosing, 120
  combining with IP verification, 55
  MySQL root, 119
  sniffing, 53
Patches, xxxi
PATH, 24
path_info() method, 203, 251
PathInfo.pm, 251
Path information
  and mod_perl programming, 243
  obtaining in mod_perl, 251–253
  received by CGI program, 202, 205–206
Pathnames, with system() and
        backquotes, 104
PATH variable, 104
Patterns, rules for in Perl, 82
PDFs, PHP and creation of, 377
people database
  DBI module connected to, 123
  in MySQL, 110
  mysqldump command with, 130
  and privileges, 120, 121
  and table joins, 128–129

Percent character, in format of query
        string, 208
<%perl ... %perl> tag, in Mason, 342–343
Perl, xxix, xxviii, 10, 57–108, 130, 188, 377,
        382, 391
  arithmetic operators in, 71–72
  benefits with, 187
  and CGI.pm, 197
  and CGI use, 191
  documentation, 58
  Embperl based on, 329
  expression modifiers in, 100
  file I/O with, 93–98
  flow-control constructs in, 77–81
  increment and decrement operators
        in, 75–76
  local variables in, 89–90
  logical operators in, 76–77
  and memory, 85–87
  mod_Perl based on, 231
  numerical comparison in, 73–74
  operating system calls made in, 103–104
  quantifiers in, 83–85
  reading from file in, 95–98
  reformatting/transferring data with, 256
  regular expressions in, 81–87
  return values in, 88–89
  scripts in, 191
  short-circuited logic operators in, 101–103
  string comparison in, 74–75
  string operators in, 72–73
  usefulness of, 107
  WML and power of, 184
  writing to files in, 98
perlcc, 60
Perl code, embedding into Mason pages,
        336–338
[! Perl Code !] Embperl command,
        294–295
[+ Perl Code +] Embperl command,
        292–294
[- Perl Code -] Embperl command, 294
Perl.com, 59
Perl constructs, embedding in Mason
        HTML files, 338–341
Perl DBI, 109, 122–127
perldoc, 59, 328
perldoc CPAN, 106
PerlLogHandler, 272

Perl pragma, 105
perl process, 232
Perl scripts, 93, 106
PerlSendHeader, 236
Perl Server Side Includes, 272
Perl syntax rules, 59–104
  backquotes, 104
  control flow constructs, 77–81
  declaring variables with use strict, 61–63
  expression modifiers, 100–101
  file I/O, 93–98
  functions, 87–93
  hello, world program, 59–60
  and making operating system calls,
    103–104
  for Mason, 331
  operators, 71–77
  regular expressions, 81–87
  short-circuited logic operators, 101–103
  unless statement, 99
  until loop, 99–100
  variables, 63–71
Permissions, 48, 218
  for peoples database, 121
  and server errors, 197
  UNIX, 23
Persistent database connections,
    with Embperl, 328
Personal computers, economics and, xxvii
Personal digital assistants, 11
Personal digital video recorders, 11
PHP, xxviii, 7, 8, 57, 122, 286, 377–432
  arrays in, 384–386
  built-in functions, 405–411
  configuration of, 379
  data types in, 383–384
  embedding into HTML, 378–379
  examples, 379–380
  flow-control constructs in, 391–398
  form 1, *387*, *389*
  functions in, 399–404, *405*
  if example, *393*
  information with phpinfo(), *381*
  introduction to, 377–378
  language syntax, 381–404
  loops example, *398*
  and MySQL, 411–420
  mysql examples, *414*, *415*, 417–418, *419*

  and MySQL functions, 411–418
  operators in, 390
  project, 420–431
  variables in, 382
  Web variables in, 386–387
PHP: Hypertext Preprocessor, 377
.php extension, PHP files named with, 379
PHP functions
  arguments passed to, 401–404
  example, 403–404
  writing, 399
phpinfo() function, 380, *381*
PHP project, 420–431
  add page, *423*
  journal MySQL database, 420–421
  launch page, *422*
  pages in, 422–431
  view entry page, *430*
  view page, *426*
PHP Version 4.1.0, 388–390
PID. *See* Process ID
Pipe, 271
Pipe character (|), 27
Placeholders, 126
Plain text, 4, 192
Plus sign (+), in format of query string, 208
.pm files, readability of, 245
popd command, 26
pop() function, 66
popup_menu, for widget creation, 216
Pop-up windows, 6
Portability
  design for, 123
  with Perl, 187
Ports, 3
POST, 247
$posted_city, 321
Posted data
  and %fdat, 299–301
  handling with %ARGS and %args, 343–348
  handling with mod_perl, 241
  and PHP, 378, 388
Posted form data
  handling with mod_perl, 246–249
  and mod_perl programming, 243
  name and age results, *210*
  processing, 206–216
  received by CGI program, 202, 206–216

PostgreSQL, 109
Postincrement, 75, 76
$_POST variable, 390
Pound sign (#), comments begun with, 144
Pragma, Perl, 105
Precedence
    differences with logic operators, 103
    of PHP operators, 390
Preincrement, 75
prepare() method, in DBI, 125
preserve href, 172
preserve text, 172
Preshipped CGIs, avoiding, 218–219
Previewing, with Mason, 331
price field, in products table, 304
Primitive data types, in PHP, 384
printenv command, 24
print() function, 60, 93, 98, 188, 191, 192, 199
    content type sent with, 195
    in PHP, 405, 406, 410
print() method, HTML content generated
        with, 244–245
printtool program, 31
Priroxy program, 30
Privileges, 120, 121
/proc directory, 29
Processes, 23–24
process_form_data(), 226
process_form_data subroutine, 225
Process ID, 23
Processing instruction, in XML, 378
_prod_form_, in Mason, 368
prod_id field, in products table, 304
$prodid, 366
Product detail, in Embperl project,
        324–325, *327*
Product filter, in Embperl project, 319–327
Product filtering system project, in Embperl,
        304–327
Product ID, in Embperl project, 325–326, 327
Product page, in Mason project, *368*
Products in Embperl project, fields in, 304
Program execution, and SSI, 277
Programmers
    hacking done by, xxx
    and Mason, 332, 333
Programming construct expansion (Pass 3),
        in WML, 136–137

Programs
    CGI, 191–196
    with DBI, 122
    with two functions, 91–93
    WML, 134–135
Projects
    CGI/MySQL/DBI, 223–229
    Embperl, 304–327
    MySQL, DBI and mod_perl, 253–272
    template for www.opensourcewebbook.com,
        179–183
<protect> tag, 138, 306
Proxy servers, warning about with Apache,
        44–45
ps command, 24, 37
ps2pdf, xxxii
-p switch, and MySQL root password,
        119, 120
Public_html web sites, disallowing
        in Apache, 42
Pure mod_perl programming, 243–253
    and Apache::Request, 249–251
    getting path information with, 251–253
    note about mod_perl and, 246
    posted form data handled with mod_perl,
        246–249
Pure mod_perl programs, 231
pushd command, 26
push() function, 66
pwd command, 26
Python, 57

Q
Quantifiers, in Perl, 83–85
Queries, executing, 412
Query string, 206, 208
query_string(), 203, 208, 270
QUERY_STRING_UNESCAPED variable,
        and echo directive, 279
Question mark (?), 205
    as placeholder, 126
    and posted data, 207

R
$r, 244, 259
Radio button group, in posted form
        data, 211
Radio buttons, 360

radio_group(), for widget creation, 216
rc file, with WML, 167
Readability
  and background color, 264, 323
  whitespace characters for, 126
Read mode, 96
REAL, in MySQL, 113
Reboots, xxxii
Records
  in age_information table, 124
  and auto_increment integer, 420
  and DELETE command, 118–119
  entering of into tables, 125
  in MySQL, 111
  and SELECT command, 115
Red Hat, xxxiii, 12, 13, 14, 17, 288, 333, 377, 388
  installer, 16
  Linux programs with, 30
  and security, 20
Red Hat Package Manager, 12
Red Hat up2date mechanism, 12
red tag, defining for www.opensourcewebbook.com, 179
References, 107
Referer
  and Apache log, 40
  and session information received by CGI program, 203
Referer information, distrust of, 221
Regular expressions, in Perl, 81–87, 86
Relational databases, 127
remote_host(), and session information received by CGI program, 202
REPLACE command, 371
$report_contents, in Mason, 374
$req, request object assigned to, 320
$_REQUEST, 390
Request API, in Mason, 373
Requested file, 311
Reset button, in posted form data, 212
restore href, 172
restore text, 172
$result, 367
Result identifier, 412
return operator, 89

return statement, in PHP, 399
Return values, in Perl, 88–89
reverse() function, 67
REXX, 57
Richter, Gerald, 287
Right rail, WML with, 181–183
$(rightrail), 181
RIGHTRAIL section, in www.opensourcewebbookpage.com, 183
rm command, 26
$(ROOT), 169, 176, 181
root access, 23
root account, 18–19
/root directory, 28
Rooting your box, 41
root ownership, 23
Root user, 110
$(ROOT) variable, link hrefs based on, 179
$row, and dynamic table generation, 301, *303*
Rows, 111, 159
rpmfind.net, 30
rset(), for widget creation, 216
rsort() function, in PHP, 407
RTFM Web site, xxxi*n*

S
SAINT, 30
Samba, 18
Sanity checks, 321, 369, 425
SARA, 30
/sbin directory, 28
Scalar variables, 61, 63–64, 93
Scams, and hidden fields, 220
Scientific float, 63
ScriptAlias directive, 190
script_name(), and CGI program, 203
Scripts, 122
  CGI, 187
  Perl, 93, 106, 122, 191
  security warning about running of, 107
  unexpected fields passed to, 219
<SCRIPT> tag, 378
scrolling_list(), for widget creation, 216
Scrolling list box, 248–249

Scrolling list box widget, 212
$search, 427
Search engines, 187
Secure shell, xxxiii, 3, 20
Security, 9, 225, 307. *See also* Apache security
  and books listing database, 270
  CGI, 218–222
  Embperl project, 325
  and Linux, 20
  and MySQL root password, 119
  with PHP, 387–388
  with Server Side Includes, 286
Security bugs, xxxi
sed, 28, 57, 87
Select buttons, 360
SELECT command
  in MySQL, 115–117, 122
  and table joins, 128
_select_form component, in Mason, 359,
    361, 371
SELECT * FROM age_information
    SQL query, 124
SELECT query, 122, 227, 371
<select> tag, 211
Semicolon (;), PHP statements terminated
    by, 382
send_http_header(), 244
sendmail, xxx, 271
Server errors, 190, 192, *196*
server-info, removing in Apache, 43
Server misconfigurations, 51
server_name() method, 201, 203
server_port, and CGI program, 203
Servers, 4
  information received by CGI program
    from, 202–216
  status of in MySQL, 110
Server Side Includes, 7, 277–286, *278*
  config directive, 284–285
  configuration, 278–279
  echo directive, 279–280
  exec directive, 283–284
  flastmod directive, 282–283
  fsize directive, 281
  if directive, 285
  include directive, 280–281
  introduction to, 277–278
  security considerations with, 286

  set directive, 285
  tutorial, 279
Server-side processing, 133
Server-side programming, 6
server_software(), and CGI program, 203
server-status, removing in Apache, 43
$_SERVER variable, 390
Session handling
  in Mason, 373
  with %udat and %mdat, 328
Session information, received by
    CGI program, 202–204
$_SESSION variable, 390
set directive, 285
SetEnv directive, 290
<%shared> tag, 373
Shell programming, 61
Shells, 22, 35
Shell scripts, 138, 382
shift() function, 66
Short-circuited evaluation, 96
Short-circuited logic operators, in Perl,
    101–103
SHOW COLUMNS FROM age_information,
    in MySQL, 114
SHOW DATABASES command, in MySQL,
    111, 121
SHOW TABLES command, in MySQL,
    112, 122
.shtml extension, 278, 279
Single disk, dual and Linux boot installation
    options, 16
Single quotes
  in PHP, 383, 425
  string literals created with, 63
  and WML, 138
Slackware, 12
Slashdot, xxxi
Slices, 107
Slurp, 94, 95, 97
SMALLINT, in MySQL, 113
SMC Barricade, 20
sndconfig program, 30
Sniffing, 53
Socket connection, 3
Solaris, xxxii
[# Some Text #] Embperl command, 295
sort() function, 67, 70, 407

SORT_NUMERIC, 407
SORT_REGULAR, 407
SORT_STRING, 407
Source reading and include file expansion
    WML phase (Pass 1), 136
\space character, 83
Special characters, 137
Special variables, 106
Speed, with mod_perl, 231, 232–233, 241
sprintf() function, in PHP, 410
$sql_cond string, 322
SQL databases, and DBI, 122
SQL query, for inserting data into
    manufacturer's table, 370
Square brackets ([]), in character class, 82
SSH. *See* Secure shell
SSI. *See* Server Side Includes
Staging/production modes, with Mason, 331
Standard float, 63
Standard input, and Perl, 93
Standard mode, CGI.pm module used in, 212
Standard output, and Perl, 93
Standard Query Language (SQL), 109, 126
Standard style, of programming, 197
Star character (*), and navigation
    bar definition, 153
start_form(), for widget creation, 216
start_html() method, 199, 229
start_form() method, for form widget
    creation, 218
startup.pl file, 234
state field, in manufacturers table, 304
Statement handle object, 125
Static content, 4, 5
Static data, serving up, 5
Static web pages, 184, 187
Static web sites
    and structural portion of LAMP, 130
    and Website META language, 133
STDIN slurp, 94
$sth value, 224, 259
strict, use of in modules, 244
String comparison, in Perl, 74–75
String functions, 107
    in PHP, 410–411
String literals, 63–64
Strings
    concatenation of, 72

in Perl, 72–73
in PHP, 383
replication of, 72
Subdirectories, in EmbperlObject, 313, 314
submit(), for widget creation, 216
Submit button, in posted form data, 212
Subroutines
    defining with Embperl, 295
    in Perl, 87
    for processing form data, 224–225
substr() function, 410
summary attribute, 158
Superuser, 18
SuSE, 12
swatch, 30, 50
switch statement, in PHP, 392–394
Sybase, 109
Symbolic links, disallowing in Apache, 44
Syntax
    for calling and declaring PHP
        function, 399
    for diversion, 162, 163
    for echo directive, 279
    in eperl, 175
    for for loop, 340
    for foreach loop, 341
    for foreach metacommand in Embperl, 297
    for fsize directive, 281
    for header and footer HTML, 165
    for here document, 195
    for if command in Embperl, 295
    for if directive, 285
    for if statement, 339
    for indexing PHP array, 384
    in PHP, 377, 378
    for PHP flow-control constructs, 391
    for PHP foreach, 395–396
    for PHP for loop, 395
    for PHP switch statement, 392–394
    for PHP while loop, 394–395
    for set directive, 285
    for unless statement, 339
    for while loop, 340
    for while metacommand in Embperl, 296
Syntax errors, in Mason, 336
system() function, 103–104
System information, and mod_perl
    programming, 243

T

-t, sendmail invoked with, 271
Table cells, defining, 158
Table joins, 127–129
Table of contents, indentation of with
    wml::std::toc, 149
Tables
    and DELETE command, 118–119
    and DESCRIBE COMMAND, 114
    dynamic generation of with Embperl,
        301–303
    in Embperl project, 304–305
    Embperl variables for, 328
    and INSERT command, 114–115
    in MySQL, 111
    and SELECT command, 116
    with three rows and two columns, 159
<table> tag, 156, 158
$tabmode variable, in Embperl, 328
Tag attributes, in WML, 172
Tags
    <%...%>, in Perl, 337
    <?...?>, in PHP, 378, 380
    <-...->, in Embperl, 321
    <!...!>, in Embperl, 319
    <&...&>, in Mason, 349
    defining, 174, 179
    in HTML, 170
Tarbals, downloading, 105
TCP/IP, xxx, 36
tcsh, 22
Telnet, 3
Template creation in WML, 138–146
    comments, 144–146
    file information, 143–144
    standard includes, 143
    use statement, 143
    varying template files, 140–142
Templates, 318
    and bread crumb trails, 176
    with Mason, 331
    for subdirectories, 314
    in WML, 184
test.cgi program, 189–190
test1() and test2() functions, 88
test.txt, 96
TEXT, 114, 225
textarea(), for widget creation, 216

Text areas, in posted form data, 211
Text diversion filter, with WML, 162–164
text field, in journal MySQL database, 420
textfield(), for widget creation, 216
Text-formatting commands, in CGI.pm, 200
Text processing, Perl used for, 187
Ticks, 64
Time
    and CGI.pm program, 201
    display in CGI program, 194
timefmt directive, 285
time() function, 238
TIMESTAMP, in MySQL, 113
timethese() method, 239, 240
TINYBLOB, in MySQL, 114
TINYINT, in MySQL, 113
TINYTEXT, in MySQL, 114
title field, in journal MySQL database, 420
title() function, 318
Titles
    default in embperl project, 318
    dynamic changes for in EmbperlObject, 316
    in Mason project, 358
<title> tag, 317
    defining for www.opensourcewebbook.
        com, 180
    in WML template files, 140, 142
/tmp directory, 28
<toc> tag, with wml::std::toc, 149, 150
-top, in Mason, 357, 371
top command, 24
.top component, in Mason project, 359,
    361, 363
top() function, 308, 309
top_html() function, 223, 260, 262, 266
Top-level components, in Mason, 374–375
Tried-and-true CGI, 6
trim() function, 411
Tripwire, 20, 30
true value, 73, 308
Tutorial, MySQL, 109–122
.txt extension, 291

U

%udat, session handling with, 328
UI()
    in CGI.pm, 200
    for generating HTML lists, 204

uname command, 27
Unclosed tags, ways for using, 171–172
Underscore character (_)
  in files in Mason directory, 355
  in integers, 63
  in Mason component files, 349
  in variable names in PHP, 382
University of Illinois Urbana-Champaign, 33
Unix, 11
  basic, 20–29
  commands, 25–28
  filesystem essentials, 28–29
  owner, groups, permissions, ownership,
    22–23
  PATH and Environment, 24
  processes, 23–24
  shell, 22
Unix variants, xxxii
"Unknown unknowns (unk-unk)," xxix*n*
unless statement, 99, 102, 103, 339
unshift() function, 66
until loop, 99, 101
UPDATE command, in MySQL, 117–118, 122
UPDATE MySQL query, 416
Uppercase letters, filehandles named with, 96
UPT, 25
uri(), 270
URI requests, and Apache log, 40
urlbase, in navigation bar definition, 153
URL encoded data, 208
URLs, 3, 149
$url variable, 293
USAH, 25
USB, 3
usbview, 31
Use, 144
USE command, in MySQL, 111, 121
#use directive, 143
use lib statement, 234
use pragma, 105, 197, 198, 234, 259
User, setting in Apache, 41
useradd, 41
User agent, and Apache log, 40
User_agent(), and session information
    received by CGI program, 203
User-defined functions, 87
user_name(), and session information received
    by CGI program, 202

use statements, 143, 178
use strict;, 61–63, 69
/usr/bin directory, 28
/usr/lib directory, 28
/usr/local directory, 28
USR1 signal, 38
/usr/sbin directory, 28
/usr/src directory, 28
/usr/X11R6 directory, 28

V

Values, 145
  PHP functions and return of, 399–401
values() function, in PHP, 409
VALUES qualifier, in MySQL, 115
$value variable, and PHP foreach, 396
VARCHAR, in MySQL, 114
/var directory, 29
$(VARIABLE), 168
Variable names, in PHP, 381, 382
Variables, 60, 63–66
  array, 64–66
  declaring with use strict, 61–63
  defining in .wmlrc, 168–169
  hash, 67–69
  initializing with Embperl, 295
  locally scoped in PHP, 401
  in PHP, 387
  scalar, 61, 63–64
  special, 106
  SSI and display/creation of, 277
  in WML, 184
/var/log directory, 29
/var/spool directory, 29
/var/tmp directory, 29
/var/www directory, 29
vi, xxxii, xxxiii, 379
virtual_host, and CGI program, 203

W

Web. *See* World Wide Web
Web design category includes,
    in wml::des::all, 161
Web designers, 7, 332
webmin program, 30
Web pages
  Apache webserver and user requests
    for, 34–35

brackets put on, 292
dynamic, 7, 187, 231, 377
SSI and embedding executable code
    into, 277
static, 184, 187
and traffic, note about e-mails and, 272
Webserver market, Apache's place in, 33
Webservers, 18
Website META language, 5, 133–184
    basics about, 135–138
    better template with, 165–167
    and eperl, 174–179
    helpful include files with, 147–162
    for HTML file creation, 306
    installation of, 135
    introduction to, 133–135
    macros and custom tag creation
        with, 170–174
    phases, 136–138
    programs, 134–135
    project with, 179–183
    template creation with, 138–147
    text diversion filter with, 162–164
    .wmlrc configured with, 167–170
Web sites
    consistent look and feel for, 305–306
    and Mason components, 348
    and structural portion of LAMP, 130
Web variables, in PHP, 386–387
WHERE clause, and UPDATE
        command, 117
where command, 27
which command, 27
[$ while...$] command, in Embperl, 299
while loop, 57, 77–79, 99, 101
    in Mason, 340
    in PHP, 394–395
    and SELECT query, 125
While metacommand, in Embperl, 295, *298*
Whitespace, 83
    in diversions, 164
    and Perl, 60
    pound sign after, 144
Whitespace characters, 126, 137, 171
    WML and removal of, 140, 142, 172
Whitespace-insensitivity, with PHP, 381
whitespace=tag, 171
who command, 27

Widget example result, *214*
widgets.cgi, 211, 213
widgets.html, 213, 215
widgets2.cgi
    else part of, 215
    if portion of, 214, 217
WiFi, xxvii
Wildcards, 26, 159
wmb: Website META Language Bug
        Reporting Tool, 135
wmd: Website META Language
        Documentation Browser, 134
wmk: Website META Language Make
        program, 134, 135
wmk command, 139
WML. *See* Website META Language
wml:des::all, 161–162
wml::des::gfont, 161
wml::des::imgbg, 161
wml::des::imgdot, 162
wml::des::lowsrc, 162
wml::des::navbar, 151–156, *156*, 162
wml::des::preload, 162
wml::des::rollover, 162
wml::des::space, 162
wml::des::typography, 162
.wml extension, 134, 135
.wml files, 133, 146
wml::fmt::xtable, 156–161
WML macro processor, 170
.wmlrc, 176
    -I option set in, 136
    variables defined in, 168–169
    WML configured with, 167–170
wml::std::info, 179
wml::std::page, 147–149
wml::std::tags, 162
wml::std::toc, 149–150, *151*
wmu: Website META Language Upgrade
        Utility, 134
Word character (\w), 83
World Wide Web, xxx, 3
    invention of, 33*n*
    pictorial overview of, *4*
Write mode, opening files in, 98
-w switch, 59
w3g, 3
www.example.com, 3, 5

www.opensourcewebbook.com project,
46, *47*, 48, 49, 179–183
bread crumb trail in, 181
errata, 182, *183*
left rail for, 181
new tags defined for, 179–180
PAGE_BODY included, 182
page without right rail, 182
page with right rail, 182–183, *184*
RIGHTRAIL section, 183
right rail–yes or no?, 181–182
title varied for, 180

X
Xconfigurator program, 31
xdvi, xxxii
x86 processor (Intel), 11
XML. *See* Extensible Markup Language

xpdf, xxxii
XSLT, Embperl integration with, 329
<xtable> definition, 159
<xtable> tag, 158

Y
Yahoo, 33
YAPL, and PHP, 378
YaST, 12
YDL, xxxii
YEAR, in MySQL, 113
$year, 374

Z
Zero-based arrays, in PHP, 385
Zero pairs, 68
zip field, in manufacturers table, 304
zsh, 22